EDITORS ON EDITING

EDITORS
ON
EDITING

Gerald Gross

Revised Edition

1817

HARPER & ROW, PUBLISHERS, New York
Cambridge, Philadelphia, San Francisco, London
Mexico City, São Paulo, Singapore, Sydney

Copyright acknowledgments appear on page 375

Designer: C. Linda Dingler

Library of Congress Cataloging in Publication Data
Main entry under title:

Editors on editing.

   1. Editing—Addresses, essays, lectures. 2. Editors—
Correspondence. I. Gross, Gerald.
PN162.E35   1985   070.4'1   84-48163
ISBN 0-06-015381-4   85 86 87 88 89 10 9 8 7 6 5 4 3 2 1
ISBN 0-06-091120-4 (pbk.)   87 88 89 10 9 8 7 6 5 4 3 2

FOR MY CHILDREN

Alison, Adam, and Seth
in appreciation for all
the joy and love they have given me

AND FOR ARLENE

my wife, my beloved,
my best friend

ACKNOWLEDGMENTS

Thanks to all the contributors of original essays to this book for being so generous with their patience, time, and talent.

Thanks to my editors at Harper & Row. To Carol Cohen, who honored me by asking me to revise *Editors on Editing,* I owe a great debt for these years in which you gave so unstintingly of your dedication, ideas, taste, and commitment. To Lucy Adelman O'Brien, my appreciation for the grace, tact, and discretion you employed, and the valuable suggestions you made.

CONTENTS

Preface   xiii

THE THEORY AND PRACTICE OF EDITING

Theory

WILLIAM TARG
What Is an Editor?   3

M. LINCOLN SCHUSTER
An Open Letter to a Would-be Editor   33

SAMUEL S. VAUGHAN
Letter from the Editor   39

SOL STEIN
The Author as Editor   54

BURROUGHS MITCHELL
The Manuscript   63

Practice

WILLIAM BRIDGWATER
Copyediting   69

BOB OSKAM
Negotiating a Publishing Contract   90

NANCY EVANS
Line Editors: The Rigorous Pursuit of Perfection (Anne
Freedgood, James D. Landis, Jeannette Hopkins, Marian S.
Wood, Pat Strachan)   102

RAYANNA SIMONS
Slush   117

CHARLES SANTINO
The Editorial Assistant   123

PAT GOLBITZ
On Being a Senior Acquisitions Editor   129

BETTY A. PRASHKER
A Life in the Day of an Editor in Chief   144

PAUL FARGIS
The Editors Who Produce   156

JOHN THORNTON
The Truth About Trade Paperbacks   164

MEL PARKER
Born to Be a Paperback   177

FAITH SALE
Editing Fiction   187

JAMES WADE AND RICHARD MAREK
Editing Nonfiction: In the Service of One Book and Many
Readers   202

HOPE DELLON
Editing the Mystery Novel   214

DAVID G. HARTWELL
Editing the Science Fiction Novel   222

PAUL ANBINDER
Editing the Illustrated Book   233

JANE ISAY
Editing Scholars and Scholarship   240

JONATHAN GALASSI
Double Agent: The Role of the Literary Editor in the
Commercial Publishing House   248

ANN BENEDUCE
Planting Inflammatory Ideas in the Garden of Delight:
Reflections on Editing Children's Books   258

EDITOR-AUTHOR CORRESPONDENCE

JENNIFER CRICHTON
Dear Editor . . . Dear Author . . .   268

MAXWELL E. PERKINS
Selected Correspondence   278

HAROLD STRAUSS
Selected Correspondence   308

JOHN FARRAR
Selected Correspondence   320

SAXE COMMINS
Selected Correspondence   340

THOMAS C. FENSCH
Between Author and Editor: Selected Correspondence Between Pascal Covici and John Steinbeck   356

PREFACE

It has been twenty-three years since *Editors on Editing* first was published. A whole generation has passed! Young men and women who were not yet born when the first edition appeared are beginning careers in publishing. So much has changed since 1962, and yet so much has remained the same.

I hope now, as I hoped then, that this anthology provides today's aspirants to a career in editing with an introduction to and insight into the multifaceted responsibilities of the working editor.

Also, I believe now, as then, that two other audiences will find the book of value: the many young authors, as yet unpublished, who will one day work with editors (even some published authors are not always aware of the many skills an editor must have in order to function effectively); and the general reader who would like to know something about how books come into being, and what can be expected from the editor-author relationship.

Editors on Editing attempts to give a rounded, clear-cut portrait of the editor as an individual and as a skilled professional. I have tried to reveal editors' various personalities and temperaments, their wide-ranging attitudes toward literature, their differing educational backgrounds, their involvement with or detachment from their authors. In addition, I have tried to show many of the areas in which an editor functions: how manuscripts are obtained and selected, the criteria used in evaluating the quality of a manuscript, the variety of editorial approaches possible in the line editing of a manuscript, the revising and rewriting of the manuscript, how projects are "packaged," the intricacies of dealing with authors and agents, etc.

Again, as I did in compiling the first edition of *Editors on Editing,* I went directly to the men and women who know their craft best—the editors themselves. The top professionals who have contributed to this collection write knowingly and frankly on the special demands and skills necessary to their specific field of editorial expertise. Their comments and experiences should provide valuable background, insight, and firsthand information for the would-be editor planning a career either as a generalist or in a specialty field such as mystery, science fiction, mass-market paperbacks, the illustrated book, or any one of several other editorial disciplines discussed herein.

In my Introduction to the first edition of *Editors on Editing,* I wrote: "I would suggest that in the next ten years there will be many additions to the literature of editing written by editors." Well, I was wrong. Editors continue to be, as I expressed it back then, "comparatively inarticulate in print, content to remain behind the scenes." Surprisingly little has been written by editors on the art and craft of editing.

Many editors I invited to contribute to the revised anthology backed off because of the heaviness of their work load. But just as many declined to contribute because they could not or would not delineate how they go about their craft and art. It was almost as if, consciously or unconsciously, they preferred to maintain a mystique about editing, as a mysterious and arcane process practiced by an almost anonymous society of sorceror-initiates.

Yet while some editors share this attitude, many others graciously lavished their time and talent on essays that clarify what they do for a living and how they do it. The result is, I believe, a volume that represents the very best of what editors have said about themselves and their profession.

A small portion of this new *Editors on Editing* has first been published elsewhere, and a small portion comprises pieces from the first edition. But most of the material has been written especially for this edition.

All in all, the cast of contributors to the anthology is a stellar one. Included are some of the most distinguished names in American editing.

The anthology is divided into two parts. "The Theory and Practice of Editing" forms the bulk of the book. Under "Theory," the well-known editors William Targ, M. Lincoln Schuster, Samuel S. Vaughan, Sol Stein, and Burroughs Mitchell offer informed opinions on and insights into various aspects of the philosophy of editing. The "Practice" subdivision presents an impressive array of editorial talents discussing the specific skills involved in being a science-fiction editor, a mystery editor, a scholarly editor, a literary editor, a mass-market-paperback editor, etc. And in the second part, "Editor-Author Correspondence," the almost lost art of editorial letter writing is displayed in all its glory by some of its greatest classic practitioners, among them Maxwell Perkins, John Farrar, and Pascal Covici, together with an illuminating article by Jennifer Crichton on the decline and change in editor-author correspondence.

As I said earlier, much has changed and much remained the same since the 1962 edition of *Editors on Editing*.

Salaries are still low. Editing is not a career to pursue if one has hopes for great riches. Other publishing skills, such as marketing, sales, and subsidiary rights, command more money and perks. I find this ironic because it all begins with the editor and the book; without those two components, marketing and sales and subsidiary rights wouldn't exist.

Bright young college graduates are still eager to enter publishing, particularly the editorial departments, seeing it as a glamorous, artistic way to use their taste and intellect. Today, though, what more and more of these bright young people are given in the publisher's office is an education in the business and economic factors involved in an editor's decision to take on a book. Profit-and-loss statements are worked up, marketing assessments are made, and there is an increasing awareness of the new technology's impact on production and editing. The younger editor is trained early on to be a publisher-editor, and that is all to the good. The more information and knowledge an editor has at his or her command, the more effective that editor can be. And perhaps one day the myth of "ivory tower editors," ignorant of the demands of selling and business, will fade away finally and forever.

In reviewing the table of contents for this edition of *Editors on Editing*, I note that there are articles on aspects of editing that did not appear in the first edition: themes such as trade paperbacks, line editing, book producers (otherwise known as book packagers), literary editing, scholarly editing, and editing the illustrated book. These are issues and skills that did not seem to be—or were not—important enough to include twenty-three years ago.

Since 1962, the increasing conglomeratization of publishing has had some interesting, often contradictory, effects on editors. While it is true that many houses are run by committees, with the market-

ing director often assuming greater decision-making powers than
the editor in chief, other houses have developed personal imprints,
such as Richard Marek, Seymour Lawrence, and John Kahn
books, which hark back to the publisher-editor as decision-maker
that dominated nineteenth-century American publishing and editing.

Since 1962, as well, there has been a proliferation of small
publishing houses, often run by one owner-editor-publisher, completely independent of the big publishers and not a user of the
corporate facilities and machinery available to the personal-
imprint editor. Many of these smaller houses have been successful,
carving out for themselves a small, specialized audience to publish
for. They have no goals to become as big as McGraw-Hill or
Macmillan or Doubleday. Small may not necessarily be beautiful,
but it is right (and often profitable) for them, and it permits them
to exercise all the skills that an editor must call into practice.

It is my hope that this book will attract many more bright,
creative men and women to the profession of editing. It is not a
career for everyone. "Of that," to quote Mr. W. S. Gilbert, "there
is no possible shadow of doubt whatever." For the frustrated
writer, editing other writers could prove to be excruciating torture
and put a damper on one's own creative efforts. For the dilettante
"who just loves good books" but who has little knowledge of or
concern for the reading trends and tastes of readers, editing can
prove to be a most traumatically disillusioning experience. For the
young man or woman who believes editing means endless rounds
of glamorous cocktail parties with literary lions, and access to
unlimited expense accounts, a few months in an entry-level job will
disabuse him or her very, very quickly.

So much for what editing is not. It is, for one attuned to its
demands and responsibilities and often tedious tasks, a most rewarding career—fully as creative, imaginative, and satisfying as
being a writer. And some editors might even go so far as to say,
"More so."

In my long career as an editor, I have been always fascinated,
sometimes inspired and exhilarated, occasionally frustrated and
disappointed, but never, never bored. I have looked upon my years
as an editor as analogous to being a perpetually stimulated student
who is attending a nonstop, incredibly diverse series of courses at

the world's largest, and always expanding, university. I learn from editing each author more about the subject of his or her book than I had ever known before. Publishing has permitted me to meet unusual, even spellbinding and truly unforgettable people, some of whom are professional colleagues and some among my roster of authors. My need for creative self-expression has been more than amply satisfied by the editing I have done on many, many books and by the pleasure I have always experienced from getting a good and valuable book from a fine author. I still get a charge of exhilaration when I receive the advance copies of a book I have worked on for a year (and sometimes two). I look at that book and remember, perhaps, that it all began as an idea over lunch, or an outline and a chapter or two. I am proud of the contribution I have made to helping that idea come to fruition, to helping that outline and chapter grow into an important or entertaining book, one that the author and I believe will be in print for many, many years. I have never lost this involvement and commitment and pride in being an editor and I hope I never shall.

This book was compiled with a devotion and care that I hope express my deepest feelings about the profession of editing. I have loved it from the beginning and I love it even more now, after thirty-two years of joy, fulfillment, grief, and frustration. I still am eager and excited as I begin to read yet another proposal, dip into yet another novel, hear about a fresh and innovative writer. May this new edition inspire would-be (and currently practicing) editors to similar heights of dedication and delight. May authors who read this book discover that the editor-author relationship need not be or should not be an adversarial one. At its best, it can be an unforgettably rewarding collaboration. Finally, I hope that the general reader will discover the subtle, complex, and often ineffable factors that inspire both editor and author to give unstintingly of their time and their talents to that singular act of creation—the book.

Croton-on-Hudson, New York
July 1984

THE THEORY
AND
PRACTICE OF EDITING

Theory

WILLIAM TARG

William Targ began his career as an office boy with The Macmillan Company in 1925, at the age of eighteen. He also ran an antiquarian bookshop in Chicago. Later, Mr. Targ became editor in chief of The World Publishing Company and G. P. Putnam's Sons. He has written and edited numerous books about books, and from his autobiographical work, *Indecent Pleasures* (Macmillan, 1975), I have excerpted the following comments on the role of the editor. From the American Writers Congress report of October 1981, I include some of Mr. Targ's comments on publishing and bookmanship, comments made when he was asked for his views on computer decisions in publishing houses, the character of literary agents, and similar matters.

Since leaving the world of commercial publishing, Mr. Targ has been engaged in the publishing of signed limited editions for collectors—small printings of hand-set and hand-printed books by distinguished authors. It is a one-man operation, a reaction, he says, to the vitiating climate of conglomerate corporations from which he escaped. He is interested in adhering to the great printing and bookmaking standards of the past. "Some call it neanderthalic," he says, and adds, "So be it, but I hope I can encourage a few young would-be publishers to remember the qualities of good bookmaking of the past."

•   •   •

The answers to the question "What is an editor?" are many, and Mr. Targ, one of America's most distinguished editors, provides just about all of them. Opinionated, idiosyncratic, idealistic, eminently practical, an aesthete, and the editor of some of America's most commercial successes (including *The Godfather*), Mr. Targ offers no easy answers, but he does offer provocative ones. He guides you into the mysteries of the publishing lunch, offers ideas on how to get good books sent to you, suggests the right way to get on an agent's good side (be prompt in reading manuscripts), cites the psychological and the counseling skills an editor needs to deal with an author, and . . . But why not let Mr. Targ reveal the lore and lure of the editor's life in his own pungent and memorable words.

WHAT IS AN EDITOR?

I'm often asked, "What does an editor do?" The questioner could be someone from the shoe manufacturing business, the mortuary profession, the sports world. Or a nosy IRS investigator.

What is an editor? Can the profession/*calling* be defined?

No matter what the dictionary tells you, it isn't possible to nail down the precise role of the editor. In a sense he is a publisher. An entrepreneur. It's a cliché to remark that editing is neither an exact science nor a skilled profession. Some opprobrious epithets are used in describing editors, especially when it's realized that one of the major qualifications of an editor is the ability to *procure*.

In the following pages you'll get a composite picture of the book editor: at worst, a caricature and slavey, a working fool; at best, a saint or lucky devil, a home-run hitter. Some editors are happy, carefree; some, disgruntled. Speaking for myself, I think I'm all of the above at various times, with luck and good reflexes close to the top of my qualifications level.

So what does an editor do?

The best way to answer this question may be to describe my own activities. Let's take a typical year, as an example when I produced (processed) thirty new titles for Putnam's. These books had been negotiated and contracted for by me through solicitation, submission, old-fashioned negotiation with agents, authors, and European publishers. None of these came to me "over the transom." Each book had been presented and discussed at editorial meetings. Each had been given a sales and subsidiary income examination before a contract was issued, a house (collaborative) enterprise.

These thirty books were handled (edited, processed, published) by me with the aid of one secretary-assistant within twelve months. Of course, there were many other hands involved in the overall operation, including the accounting department.

To produce and publish a book means that one has read the

manuscript, worked with the author (discussions relating to textual changes and other pertinent matters), turned the manuscript over to a copy editor to check for errors, grammar, inconsistencies, repetitions, and the like. The book must be estimated for cost and approximate retail price, based on a minimum sales expectancy. The rights department comes up with an evaluation of income. Then the manufacturing department gets the manuscript. The book is placed on a production and publication schedule, involving about six to eight months from start to publication date. And the editor is involved in each of these steps; the book is his baby all the way.

The physical book, the jacket, the typographical treatment (sometimes), jacket blurbs, and the author's photo and biography are also the editor's concern. He must look after each of these details. He must prepare an "editorial presentation"—a description of the book for use by everyone: the publicity, sales, rights, promotion, and library departments. The editor also "presents" his book at the company's sales conferences—*sells* it to them, verbally.

The editor must hold the author's hand when the going gets bumpy. He must keep author and agent apprised of all matters of concern, including sales, publicity, and income from rights. Discretion is sometimes essential; certain information such as a bad advance review might be withheld temporarily. Certain sales information might also be held up when it could be erroneous, premature. Intelligent censorship is advised. The author's spouse is also someone to consider when tension builds.

The editor must try to wheedle advance comments from VIPs. A statement by Saul Bellow, for example, proclaiming your novel almost as good as *War and Peace,* will do the book a lot of good. A limited number of reading copies, sent in advance to key booksellers, will help, too.

While the editor is working on his various manuscripts for publication, he is also reading—searching for *new* material—and considering manuscripts and proposals submitted all during the year. (In one year I might receive and examine over 250 manuscripts and about the same number of outline proposals. I may contract for eighteen titles from these submissions, the books, with luck, to materialize in the next year or later.)

The editor usually reads manuscripts "on his own time," which means away from his office. He reads nightly, weekends, holidays. If this sounds like medievalism, or cottage industry, it may very well be; but that's what editing is—a full-time job with an occasional break for relaxation. Somehow, too, an editor manages to read books published by other houses.

An editor travels as part of his job, and obviously it isn't all unpleasant work, especially if one's author lives in London, Malibu, the south of France, or Paris. But long, hard, grim hours of reading manuscripts and proofs are the editor's destiny, and there's no substitute yet known for reading a book. Getting someone else to read for you is not the answer because, in the end, your decision to publish is based on your firsthand knowledge of the book under consideration. A rave report from a "first reader" is not enough on which to make a publishing judgment.

Manuscript reading is rarely done in one's office except in emergency situations. I usually sample a manuscript from an unknown before taking it home, to make certain the book is not illiterate, hopeless, or out of my range of interest. But I repeat, manuscript reading by an editor is *homework,* in the old-fashioned sense.

What else must an editor do in his job?

He must think up ideas for books. Then he must find authors to match the ideas. This subject is discussed elsewhere in this section.

The editor must present and convince his firm's editorial board of the merits of his book, the book under submission. He may be wildly enthusiastic about the work and eager to sign a contract. But after discussion with his associates, he might discover a number of things: the author's reputation is that of a loser; the book is similar to one recently published or about to be published; the asking price (dollar advance requested by the agent) is risky, too high for the particular book. Finally, the sales and rights departments may express negative views on the project—which means, in basic English, no support. To buy a book in which very few of one's colleagues has any faith is hazardous. It is possible to be a minority of one and come up smelling like the proverbial roses; but it takes nerve, experience—and luck.

An editor often writes some of his own letters because no single secretary-assistant can handle all of the correspondence.

Handling galley proofs (for authors, agents, and others) is important, calling for "good housekeeping." Likewise the physical movement of manuscripts to and from the author, printer, and copy editor requires maximum security-type care. An original manuscript that is lost is a disaster situation, especially when no carbon or Xerox copy exists. Scrupulous care and vigilance are called for. A sloppy editor gets into trouble sooner or later.

THE RHYTHM

By 9:00 A.M. (I get to work at eight-thirty) I've finished with the morning's mail—opened it, noted brief replies for my secretary on some letters; typed a few informal answers without carbons; begun reading two book proposals sent by agents. Neither is of interest; one deals with cancer, the other with some insurance scandal. An invitation to a Columbia film screening; two authors seeking contracts on the basis of brief (three- and four-page) outlines, both first books. My secretary will know how to handle these, based on a few sentences I scrawl on the accompanying letters.

The upcoming Sunday *New York Times Book Review* reaches my desk; I check it for reviews of our books and find one, about a column and a half in length. Of no use to anyone since it doesn't review the book but rather tells us what the reviewer knows about the subject. The front page offers a familiar "kiss of death" essay-review, elegant literary formaldehyde.

Now to make some notes preparatory to a meeting in my office with a first novelist. The manuscript has been read by me; a contract has been signed ($4,000 advance) and a bit more work is called for by its author. She is skittish, reluctant to make further changes or additions—or so it seemed on the telephone. I don't want to ruffle her feathers, make a fuss, but . . .

I decide to be persuasive. The first eight pages of her novel introduce nine characters, mostly by name. They're faceless. Hard to assimilate. They must be established. If one of them were called, say, Popeye . . . well, *that one* would stand out. But Allen, Mary, Alexander, Harriet, Lawrence, Fred, et al.—they simply must be visible, sketched in somehow.

Chapter Three must be cut; it drags. There's too much school minutiae, not enough interesting dialogue. Something spiky needed here. The secondary lesbian character is shadowy—all we know is that she has a letch for the heroine. But what is she *like?*

The psychological damage the author is concerned with in the motivating of a strange young boy is not clear at all; calls for something less oblique. Clear the air!

And so on. I make my notes, and at nine-forty-five, in comes the author. A lovely young woman. She is surprisingly amenable, amiable, willing to do more work—in full agreement. No contest! She promises to return the manuscript in four days. I promise her lunch if she keeps her word.

A rush call from the production department for jacket flap copy. A book of mine on primates, on which I've worked for six months, is coming off press in a few days. I pull out my file on the book and make notes, then proceed to dictate the blurb, biography, and so on. I rather dislike this part of the job, but we have no system that accommodates blurb writing. It's the editor's responsibility. It gets done in a half hour. I really don't mind—I have a special warmth for the book and its author, and I'm hoping for some decent sales, a paperback deal.

At 11:00 A.M. two manuscripts reach my desk, sent by messenger from two agents. Both look promising, but after sampling the opening pages of each, I decide to take only one home for reading. A Western novel, not quite an "oater," apparently well written. The author gives us two opening pages of sheer Western poetry: a magnificent sunset scene, with a giant oak silhouetted against a blood-red sky, ragged rocks—the works!—bringing echoes of Walter van Tilburg Clark's *The Ox-Bow Incident.* (That novel and its film were first-rate; set in Nevada in the late 1800s, the story of the lynching of three innocent men accused of cattle rustling is now enshrined as a Western classic.) I fantasy finding something of that quality—or perhaps a Western Faulkner.

At noon I head for a luncheon meeting with a literary agent. He's one of the old Establishment, a horse thief at heart, but venerable. His list of authors is formidable, mouth-watering. We've been negotiating for a week on the terms for a first novel by a Southern woman of considerable talent. My plea for a modest advance cuts no ice with this pirate in navy blue flannels. He finally makes a minuscule concession, a compromise; and it's a deal. A bottle of wine is called for, to celebrate—but whose victory? As we leave the restaurant he hands me a manila envelope, an outline for a biographical-cum-legal work by a well-known jurist. I promise him an answer in a few days. I never keep this particular agent waiting.

Back at my office—a pleasant ten blocks' walk—and some phone messages await me, one from my wife. I call her back and learn that we will be entertaining a Brazilian publisher for dinner that evening. (There goes my manuscript reading.)

An author phones to inquire: "How come my book can't be found in the Eighth Street Bookshop?" Another author wants to know if we can persuade Scribner's to give his new book a full window display if he "pays the *rental charge*"! (Now there's a notion.) Another call from a friendly publisher whose ploy is usually to pass on a bit of juicy gossip and then cadge a book— this time he wanted Edward Gorey's *Amphigorey.*

The next call is a messy one: how come his royalty statement shows 20 percent fewer sales than I reported a year ago, on publication date? I point out that the figure I quoted was for "copies shipped"; that a returns policy exists and a vast number of books were returned by the booksellers and wholesalers. He's outraged, calls the net figure a lie, and threatens to get his lawyer and accountant to look into the matter. I beg him to think twice; the expense will be great and the result, zero. Our figures are accurate.

A call asking if I will appear on a panel to discuss censorship. I decline.

An author rings to ask when an ad will be run on his new book. I point out that we ran one two weeks ago. "Yeah, but for chrissakes, that was a chintzy one. I mean a man-sized ad." I ask him for patience; let's wait a bit until we see if there are reorders in the next ten days or so. He mutters something and hangs up.

Am called into an emergency meeting to discuss an offer made to us through one of our editors—a multiple submission (auction) —a six-page proposal by a VIP from Washington. The agent asks for a $50,000 "basement" and a ten-day deadline. We spend over an hour on this discussion, then decide not to participate.

Four-thirty; mopping up, last-minute paperwork, signing some letters. Gossiping with the rights director, hoping for a piece of good news. A first novel of ours is being "auctioned." (The figure stands at $7,000—nothing dramatic, but considering everything, acceptable. It's a tough season for reprints.) The author will be told of the deal when we speak to the agent. I decide to take him to lunch to pass on the news—after the sale is officially closed. (It closes at $15,000.)

Homeward-bound at five-thirty. A taxi to the Village. Our

friend from Rio will meet us at seven for a drink, and I phone Casey's for a table at eight.

We part company at around eleven. I manage to read some of the manuscript, after all—some fifty pages. I find it less than enchanting. The opening pages deceived me; a few pages had been gussied up to catch the eye. The story was pretty banal (big-mortgage-foreclosing yarn) and the author had imposed some literary icing on a cliché story. His limitations will confine him to the old level of horse operas, despite his try for effects. Too bad. Well, at least the agent will get a prompt report (alas, negative) in the morning.

And so to bed. Lying there and reviewing the day before slipping off to sleep. My mind shifts to the editorial meeting we'll be holding the following morning. I begin to analyze the several projects I will present to my associates—and I fall into a dream: a ballet of sandpipers on a sugar-white beach in Antigua.

Ken McCormick,* grand old-young man of Doubleday,* once said, "The most important change in an editor's job today is that he has slowly acquired the publisher's responsibility."

Of the thirty books handled and published by me in our typical year, ten were novels. Thirteen were by authors I had published before, such as Simone de Beauvoir, Art Buchwald, Harry Golden, Ashley Montagu. Fourteen of these authors appeared on my personal list for the first time at Putnam's.

The thirty books included memoirs, anthropology, science fiction, history, humor, fiction, medicine, occultism, psychology, and so on.

A few were taken by book clubs; about 30 percent were contracted for by paperback houses. There were no art books or technical works among them.

We may have lost money on seven or eight of these thirty books. We made a good profit from subsidiary income: one title alone brought in a gross of $300,000 for reprint rights, plus a good five-figure advance from a club. Others went to reprinters for figures ranging from $50,000 to $35,000, $25,000 and less. One book went for a modest $3,500. Because of a depressed (cyclical) paperback inventory situation, we were unable to place every title

*Mr. McCormick was the editor in chief of Doubleday for many years, then a consultant to the firm. —ED.

with a reprinter, but this doesn't preclude a sale at a later date. There's always a reason for a delayed subsidiary response. Sometimes, however, a book simply isn't wanted, has too little appeal, or is not the best of its kind. In a few cases, we earned income from foreign rights—where there was no agent involved.

Some editors can produce more than thirty titles in one year, while some veterans handle less. Years of involvement in publishing are needed in order to develop a "stable" or acquisition rhythm. I know some young editors, gifted men and women, who can't come up with more than eight or ten books a year. But they will increase their productivity in time.

ADVICE

Giving advice to newcomers to the publishing business reminds me of what Flannery O'Connor once said to a class in writing where each week a new writer-instructor would hand out advice: "What you hear one week from a giraffe is contradicted next week by a baboon."

The long and short of advice-giving is: Try to be practical and understated; follow instincts, not textbooks.

An editor should sleep on it, that is to say, let a few days or a week pass after reading a manuscript. It may provide a better perspective. In the end, the editor's decision to accept or reject is as lonely a role as the writer's. It's got to be his decision, and he's got to stand on it. If it turns out to be a mistake, admit it and write it off.

THE EDUCATION OF AN EDITOR, PART 1

The need to reject manuscripts turns an editor into a judge-executioner, an uncomfortable role for any sensitive person.

With the knowledge that an author will suffer from rejection, knowing that some writers will be devastated by a cold and impersonal letter, the editor has no choice but to say no in cliché terms: "Sorry, not suited to our present needs." This is the message that will protect the editor though it is a coward's way.

I recall a letter from Ezra Pound to an aspirant. Pound, who was anything but shy, opened up by saying, "Come now, you can do better than that!" I cherish that sentence as a perfect opening for a rejection letter, but am reluctant to use it.

Don't get involved editorially or show paternal anxiety unless you intend publishing the author's work: that's the best advice I can give to an editor. Offering gratuitous editorial advice usually leads to heavy breathing on the part of the author—and in the end, hostility.

A British publisher sends the following rejection slip, which, on unsolicited manuscripts, seems to me humane:

"We regret having to say 'no' to your manuscript. The fact that it proved not to our taste does not necessarily mean your work is unpublishable, but all we can do, under the pressure of submitted books, is to wish you better luck elsewhere."

I don't think a publisher has any further obligation to the author of an unsolicited and unwanted manuscript. In fact, he can't afford to indulge in correspondence. Ask an accountant what it costs to write a critical letter, stamp and mail it, and file the carbon. Of course, cost is not the only factor. Getting involved with a writer on a work of no interest to you can have no small effect on the nervous system.

Many good talkers are lousy writers; never judge a prospective author's work by charm, vocabulary, diction, or "verbal music." I've found that most good writers are mumblers, deficient as speakers, and seldom witty in person. Insist on *reading* something by the author before a meeting. Don't let an author con you into a conference or serious discussion of his work (there are exceptions, of course) before seeing something on paper. When an author has to *explain* his work, caveat emptor. Needless to say, the above does not apply to a writer with a publishing history.

To Be or Not to Be

The nightmares and indecisions that plagued Hamlet are nothing compared to what an editor suffers when trying to make a judgment about a troublesome manuscript.

He found that he enjoyed reading it but his conscience told him it had no future.

"It's a loser," says one part of his brain.

"But what about the wit and elegant style?" says another part.

"Yeah, but there's no story."

And so on. I've often awakened during the night, wondering what decision I would render the next day. Sometimes one is deliberately imprudent. Or else too logical. Very often the illogical prevails—and succeeds.

If you toe the party line and lean hard on the track records of "similar" books, you're lost. The rip-off book, the careful imitation, riding the coattails of a successful genre book, can lead nowhere. The intuitive editor can go farther than the cerebral slide-rule editor. In the end, the big successes are surprises to everyone. For example, there's the story about a little book dealing with a seagull that most of the publishers in New York turned down and which Macmillan signed up for a $2,000 advance. . . .

Get Carried Away

An editor *must* do something reckless at least once a year: outbid everyone for a book; overadvertise; fire an employee for purely personal reasons; take a lover/mistress; demand a raise out of hand; print a book in white ink on black paper (figuratively) in order to shake up the scene. Life is short, and an editor takes too much abuse not to deserve some indulgence.

Occupational Hazard

Most editors drink too much. Liberal expense accounts are responsible in part. And tension. Alcoholism sneaks up on the unwary drinker and by post–middle age the effects are visible—and a problem. *Show some character!*

Advice: Lay off all drugs; they can give only temporary relief, and the dependency grows.

To cure a headache or ease tension, I've found a simple remedy: a glass of chilled Pouilly-Fuissé taken with two aspirins.

As for hard liquor: take only *one* drink at lunch and *one* before dinner. Don't wind up a sot, with cirrhosis of the liver or worse. And a reputation to match.

THE EDUCATION OF AN EDITOR, PART 2

A working, qualified editor of books must read. He must have read from the earliest days of his childhood. His reading must be unceasing. The *lust* for printed matter is a biological thing, a visceral and intellectual necessity; the urge must be in the genes.

An editor must read everything—newspapers, magazines, advertisements, labels, encyclopedias, novels, history, short stories, poetry, lectures, essays, editorials, speeches, political oratory, plays, and all other written matter. Even the *Congressional Record*.

As a rule, schools don't provide the incentive to read. An antiquarian bookshop or a library can be the basis of an editor's education. You'll find books, old and new, including forgotten masterpieces of literature that are not as yet available in paperbacks.

I was delighted not too long ago to find Erica Jong saying: "When I was a ten-year-old bookworm and used to kiss the dust-jacket pictures of authors as if they were icons, it used to amaze me that these remote people could provoke me to love. Once I discovered that some author I loved had been dead for *years,* and my response was astonishment. Love beyond the grave! Love from people you will never meet! Love seeping through paper and parchment and ink!" Jong goes on to say: "Here was the solution to loneliness. A piece of paper would be the magic mirror through which I stepped to join the imaginary friends who really loved me. Through the looking glass. Narcissus finds her one true love. Papagena finds Papageno."

As I began by saying, an editor must read all his life, and start early. Read Jean-Paul Sartre's *Words.* He said, in speaking of writing, "It's a habit, and besides, it's my profession." This is how I view reading. Sartre's book, by the way, is one of the really tolerable memoirs of a young writer; most preadolescent confessionals are boring.

Sell: The Editor Gets Out of the Ivory Tower

What I'm about to say here is fairly basic, perhaps overfamiliar. It may be that you are a veteran for whom this is elementary stuff and therefore boring. In which case, feel free to skip.

Until an editor gets out of the ivory tower and into the selling arena, he's only *half* a publisher. He must understand, through personal experience, how a book is exploited, sold, "noised around."

Signing up the author's book is Step Number One, and in itself is as important as the creative act from the publisher's standpoint.

Once the contract is signed, the book written, and the manuscript is about to emerge as a Book, the editor's selling job begins —long before the salesmen get to work on it. At this point the editor's worth begins to become apparent; it is here where we see how much he really cares about the welfare of his book.

Step One: *Start by being shameless.* Try anything within reason to get your book noticed. Galley proofs should go off to key salesmen. (Some salesmen can do better by *not* reading a book.) Copies should go to a select group of booksellers (over the sales director's signature), to certain writers, and to those persons with access to the press or the air—persons likely to respond favorably to the book. *Publishers Weekly* should be given brief running stories about the book or its author.

The foregoing may seem like the publicity department's job, and in the final and larger sense, it is. But first the editor must start sending up flares, writing letters and memos to all concerned, and *talking,* so that the baby about to be born gets enough oxygen, *attention.* Advance comments from readers who are influential in the trade or in the press are the lifeblood of the book. Stories in the press about a book can often produce wonders. Word-of-mouth press agentry is important, much more so than paid space advertising. Please write across your memo pad: *Word-of-Mouth Sells More Books than Printed Advertisements.* (Your author won't believe this, of course, but it is the truth.)

To put it in the crudest of terms, an editor who wants to make it must get off his ass and *do* many things *himself,* and that includes delivering proofs, advance copies, urgent and personal messages to the VIP contacts who will help get that book on the escalator. Taking a book buyer to lunch sometimes helps, but please—no hammer-swinging, no ear-bending. Easy does it. Book buyers are intelligent as well as sensitive.

Selling is a creative business if you take the job seriously. One of the first commandments in selling is: Never lie. Liars get found out, and to be known as a liar in the book trade is suicidal. Honest enthusiasm is enough.

Keep an eye on all publicity releases, the review- and gift-copy lists, copy and layouts of the ads, and the mailing pieces sent to the trade. Check out jacket and biographical blurb copy with your author.

There's nothing easier than printing a book. Next to writing a book, there's nothing tougher than selling it. If you're inclined to believe in miracles, then consider every best-seller a miracle. Think of the odds and you'll see why.

An editor can help along the realization of a miraculous act, but it's a sixteen-hours-a-day job. Is it worth it? It's almost as good as sex when it works!

One of the essentials in an editor's training is learning what the customer wants. Taking money in exchange for a book. This is why it's important to work in a bookshop for at least six months.

Any editor can do a bit of moonlighting to get the experience by working, say, as an extra on Saturdays or evenings. The pay is far from princely, but consider the job educational. Observing a customer making up his or her mind about a book is an experience.

Persuading a customer to part with $7.95, $10.00, or $15.00 for a new book* is an act of magic, in my opinion, and any bookshop salesperson who understands the art of prying money out of a reader is beyond price (and is probably underpaid). Intelligence, taste, and salesmanship—that's a combination to cherish.

Selective Morality, or Old Whores Never Die:
A Few Basic Facts for Junior Editors Only

One must begin with the premise that book publishing is a business.

Back of every business is the profit motive.

Cash flow plus profit makes the business world go round.

Regardless of one's passionate zeal for beautiful letters and the dissemination of learning, business principles must prevail. (Obviously, it is recognized that no one takes a job in publishing if one is devoid of some interest in, or love of, books. Some aspect of publishing, one or many of the publishing processes, must interest one.)

Young editors and also so-called mature adults are sometimes unable to make publishing judgments because of certain emotional

*These were typical book prices for 1975, when Mr. Targ's book was published. Today, of course, $15.00 is an average price for a hardcover book. It certainly is not the high end of the price scale, as it was in 1975. —ED.

or mental blocks. The question of values arises. Integrity. Morality. Taste. Aesthetics. Standards. These virtues are sometimes obstacles to an editor's business judgment.

Let me give an example. A "Gothic novel" comes across one's desk.* It is a formula piece of fiction, with the usual trappings. The editor is bored with such material, doesn't consider it serious writing. Recalls du Maurier's *Rebecca,* Brontë's *Wuthering Heights,* and sighs. This manuscript on his desk, awaiting his decision, is an offense. He declines it. What he did was turn down a book that probably would have sold at least 7,500 copies and produced a paperback contract of anywhere from $3,500 to $25,000 or more. Because of any one of the editorial reasons cited above, the editor's judgment was out of order. He failed to recognize the simple business responsibility placed before him. He was bored with, or contemptuous of, the book, its author, the genre.

Young editors are sometimes inclined to forget the name of the game. It's easy to sneer at second-class goods. Standards and pride will often force an editor into an eventual dead end; he will become one of the nonproductive ones. He will bring in books, books which *he likes* but which have no basis for existence in a commercial publishing world. I knew one editor who spent a lifetime losing money for his publisher employers because of his "standards."

An editor can be an angel soaring in the stratosphere of Literature; he can also be lower than a pimp in hell, a procurer. He can be a "moral fool"; he can echo Cicero's *"O tempora! O mores!"* as he struggles with his conscience in the abattoir of publishing each day, compromising for the sake of sweet commerce. His dilemma is that he *must* make decisions that violate his personal, sacred ethos and his sensibilities.

The editor must cajole, flatter, kiss hands and cheeks, praise extravagantly, even when it hurts. What is sad is that he does all this while often involved with hacks and *dreck* writing. If he's lucky, 5 percent of the books he publishes (and their authors) will give him pleasure; if he's *very* lucky, 50 percent of the books will make money. If he's one of the anointed, he will get one of his books on the best-seller lists once a year. (I know editors who have

---

*Today Gothic novels are almost entirely published by paperback publishers as original novels. Few hardcover houses publish them, and then only by "name" authors. The numbers Mr. Targ mentions would not be realistic in today's marketplace. —ED.

never had a book on the best-seller list after more than fifteen years in publishing.)

Does morality enter into all of this? Is there a moral issue, a moral attitude we must adopt in this profession? When a first-rate author with a first-rate book comes along, life becomes beautiful; then the editor contemplates his mirrored visage and his soul with a smile and equanimity. So we must ask: What manner of man is he?

It's all very simple. An editor must be a realist, must be able to avoid taking himself seriously, must be able to laugh often. If not, then alcohol, pills, and the other assists become his lifestyle. If the dual role, the selective morality, becomes an issue, a problem of functioning or "living with oneself," then one must get out of this particular arena and look elsewhere for a way of life and a livelihood.

Having made numerous flights abroad, visiting publishers, editors, authors, and agents in quest of manuscripts and co-publishing deals, I must report that most of the books I've secured and published are not, could not, be labeled prime goods. (I'm not apologizing.) And lest I be misunderstood, the same holds true of the books I've signed up on American terrain. A lot of these books could be called anything from wretched to publishable; some are pride-filling books, books I'd want to remember and perhaps fondle in my years of inactivity. I refer to books that could be said to justify my existence by association. But I have no illusions and I'm trying here to differentiate, for the young editor, between commerce and the occasional lucky strike.

Many of the books I've contracted for over the years resulted in handsome profits for my publishers, and a respectable income for myself. I prefer not to mention titles or authors here. I'm not anxious to play a look-how-good-I-am role. I enjoyed my work most of the time, ate in fine restaurants, slept in good beds, had my cake, enjoyed the publishing fellowship in Europe and America. Many of the European publishers and agents were amiable, interesting, fun to be with. A few were bores, sticks. A few others were alcoholics; two notable agents were outrageous liars. Some were merely stupid. Ditto a few American agents.

I contracted some books in London that made their authors rich, mainly by virtue of six-figure paperback sales here. In most cases the books were nonsense, fake passementeries, embarrassments. I suppose one will wonder how a devotee of good books and decent writing can play this dual role, how endure working year after year with so much second-class goods. The answer is this: There are not enough good books coming our way. The noble book, that gleaming chimera in every editor's fantasy, is not something one sits around and waits for. It does happen to some editors named Alfred A. Knopf, but not too frequently of late. (*That* golden epoch has ended.)

The toughest part of the editor's job is playing psychiatrist to a third-rate writer: that's "overtime" work. Trying to provide comforting words to an otiose novelist whose latest book has been destroyed by a reviewer—that's no fun. Taking an ego-tripping author's tantrum (or his agent's) in stride should justify time-and-a-half pay.

I repeat my question: Is morality an issue here? Does the editor, in compromising his values and his self-esteem, do himself injury? Is there scar tissue to show for the violence to one's psyche? I don't think so, not if you laugh enough. When you begin to wonder and brood, then it's time to look at your assets, your bank balance, your lifestyle, your wine cellar, and your working conditions. If you aren't getting your just compensation, then you are a fool. But if you are getting yours, including some of the kudos properly due you, then grin and bear it, and order another very dry martini. (My physician once told me to take a very dry martini and two aspirins for my aching, arthritic shoulder. If that didn't help, he said, take another. "But," added this sage old man, "don't do anything drastic.")

My advice is the same to all editors whose authors and books are giving them a pain in the neck: be sure the martinis are extra dry.

Robert T. Wood, who worked for the CIA for some seventeen years, speaks of the term "old whore" in referring to a worker in the Central Intelligence Agency. He says "old whore" is a term to describe an officer "so experienced, so devoted to his trade, so loyal to his organization, and so accustomed to following orders that he will accept and do a creditable job on any assignment without regard for moral, ethical, or possibly even legal considerations. Within the Agency it is a high compliment to professionalism."

One final word (and you might stick this up on your wall over your desk): *Publishing Is a Business, for Gosh Sakes!*

THE EDUCATION OF AN EDITOR, PART 3

Becoming a book editor, a publishing executive, or head of a publishing house is a good fate for any man or woman of intelligence and taste. It is fulfilling in the extreme, it provides (forgive the word) status and opportunities for a very interesting life. There are worse fates. But one of the penalties of the good life in books is the necessity of dealing with neurotic and anal-erotic men and women—people with talent but insufferable behavior patterns and hangups. This group, by the way, includes editors and agents as well as writers.

It must also be said for the record that a great many editors are worse than their so-called difficult authors. A problem of vanity and identity crisis. Many of the new breed of editor confuse their role with that of their authors. They often take on the coloration of their famous writers, going so far as to wear the same kind of clothes and to adopt their eating and other habits. The new breed is a boastful peacock, letting the world at large know how he/she single-handedly "saved" a manuscript from disaster by putting some "creative pencil work" into the project. "I spent a month rewriting Joe's book," says the editor, sighing in martyrlike fashion, "but it was worth it. Look at the paperback sale we got." And so on.

The simple truth is this: no matter how skilled an editor may be, he can't write a first-rate book. If by chance he can, he leaves his job and writes. He can't do both. There are, of course, a few exceptions.

But to the young editors who are in the majority, I say: Don't turn into a frustrated writer and start competing with your authors. You can't win. Unless you have unmistakable talents, don't try to write. Edit and enjoy!

Etiquette for the Publisher

It is essential that an editor and publishing executive remember his *humanness.* Here are some rules of etiquette to enable one to survive and function decently, a few *reminders* relating to values and good business practice:

1. The author and his manuscript are the most important elements in your professional life. Let the author know this. Everything you do, every action you undertake, should be with this in mind. Carl Van Doren once said to me when I was getting sticky about some publishing detail, "Everything other than the manuscript is *bubbles on the horse piss.*"
2. Treat the author with every possible courtesy; remember, he's palpitating from blood-drain, from the efforts expended on his book, and needs encouragement and friendship.
3. Answer all authors' letters and calls promptly. Be available.
4. Never keep your author waiting beyond reason for a report on his new manuscript; you are probably the first reader of the work and your response to it is vital.
5. Keep your author informed regularly as to sales and any interesting news, especially good news.
6. Return the original manuscript to the author promptly after publication. It has sentimental and archival value to him, and it is his property. Likewise original art.
7. Most royalty statements are hard to read; help the author out by clarifying some of its mysteries. It is his "bank statement" and pretty important to him.
8. Be sure the author gets press clippings promptly.
9. Take your author to lunch or dinner at least once a year.
10. Your author must know in his heart that you are always leveling with him. If you don't like something, tell him/her; if you are pleased, speak up. Your author must trust you, and must know when you are bullshitting.
11. Don't promise your author anything you can't deliver.
12. Speak respectfully of your author's agent.

Echelon

The editor in chief is "responsible" in most trade houses for the entire list. He not only acquires books and processes them, but he also presides over editorial sessions, confers with editors, reads or examines submissions to various editors. The lists—and the bottom-line results—reflect in a large measure the talents of the editor in chief. It is to him the head of the house goes for an overview of the "shape of things to come," including an estimate of the big books' potentials in the market and their subsidiary income. The editor in chief keeps in close touch with the sales, promotion, publicity, and rights departments.

If an editor in chief vetoes the wrong books enough times, his head rolls. If he allows too many marginal books to appear on his lists, eyebrows will be raised. If he permits unjustified extravagant advances to be paid too often, he will put his company and himself in jeopardy. The editor in chief must develop the best possible public relations; agents and authors must respect him, trust his judgment. He should represent the house everywhere in the world of books and should be visible at all important literary functions. A once-a-year trip to Europe is mandatory for the maintenance of contacts. He must be a reader, a bookman in every sense. His judgment should be reflected in the jackets and physical books, and in the company's advertising.

Next to the head of the house, the editor in chief ranks highest insofar as the outside world is concerned.

The senior editor is primarily concerned with his own books and authors, his personal stable. He is available for consultation with editors and should appear at all editorial meetings. A senior editor is a responsible executive who, through years of experience and maturity, is useful as a sounding board to the staff. But he must first and foremost pull his own weight by bringing good and profitable books to his house.

The above two editorial executives, plus a staff of alert and informed editors, make up the editorial department. The copyediting department is an adjunct, and makes no editorial acquisition determination.

Bringing Home the Bacon

The game is *acquisition.*

Acquiring a publishable, salable manuscript is what publishing is all about.

Cocktail parties, literary luncheons, junkets, film screenings, socializing on behalf of your company—a lot of it can be fun. But unless a contract for a book results, it is a sleeveless errand you are on, and the name of your game is *Kinderspiel.*

Acquisition of a manuscript is the first order of business. Nothing else deserves priority. Turning a manuscript into a publishable book is the next step. What follows is publicity, sales, and getting the author to produce another book. (Keep him occupied with the *next* book and he'll understand why he should "leave the driving to us.") A lot of executives in publishing houses (and especially in the offices of owner-conglomerates) often forget that the author sweating out a manuscript in the loneliness of his home or office or penthouse is the heart of the matter. The book is all, the whole game. In the beginning was the manuscript. . . . Try not to forget it.

An acquisition editor is at least as valuable as a home-run hitter on a baseball team. If his percentage of home runs is decent, then he is a major factor in the welfare of the company. He should be spared the stresses and tensions of corporate problems; he should not be checked out and scrutinized in matters of hours spent in the office, on his expense reports, or on his numerical contribution to the manuscript stockpile.

The pretentious, "literary" editor who talks unrealistically about "better books" should be forced to prove his worth in dollars and cents. I don't hold with the principle of auditing an editor; his efforts, if meaningful, are evident to all. But the blowhard who scorns the commercial book and makes light of the popular bestseller must be put into focus. Editors with taste and high standards should be supported and encouraged, obviously; otherwise the publisher's lists would be embarrassing, and get damned little respect in the book trade. Booksellers must take a publisher seriously, and if one issues only shoddy goods, he will waste away. Possibly go broke.

In short, the acquisition editor who takes his job seriously should go after the big popular book as well as the book of quality. He should seek out fresh talent, first novelists, poets who show genuine talent. And authors who sell! So bringing in the bacon means publishing money books *and* books of distinction. The good acquisition editor will try to avoid the stereotype book; the tired, overfamiliar theme; the marginal book that is at once publishable but unsalable. Originality often pays off. Admittedly, luck is a factor in bringing in the successes. Luck, interestingly, follows the avid and eager worker.

How to Get a Book

Being seen in the Russian Tea Room or the Four Seasons, the Algonquin, "21," or Lutèce will not, *per se,* bring you manuscripts. How, then, does one get a manuscript?

Keep a file or card index of book ideas. When talking to agents, find out which of their authors are looking for assignments. Matching a good idea with the right author is a reasonably safe procedure. My colleagues and I have processed dozens of good, salable books by studying the works of authors who could be approached with the "irresistible book idea." One example that comes to mind is the biography of Al Capone, which I had for years believed worth nailing down. One day I was told by the William Morris Agency that John Kobler, a veteran *Saturday Evening Post* and *New Yorker* writer, and the author of several books, was eager for a book assignment. I discovered through scanning a few dozen of his articles that true crime interested him. I proposed a definitive life of Capone. Kobler accepted the proposal with high enthusiasm and produced a first-class book. The book was on the *TBR* best-seller list for a number of weeks. It was also a best-seller in France and in Germany.

Another case history: In the spring of 1956 I approached Marchette Chute to ask if she'd write a book in which the plays of Shakespeare would be retold for today's readers. I had read her books on Chaucer, Ben Jonson, and Shakespeare and had responded to her scholarship, style, and feeling for the Elizabethan world.

Serendipity helped. I had met Miss Chute by accident at a P.E.N. dinner; luck got me seated next to her and I fell in love with her instantly. The opportunist-editor within me also responded, and editorial brain cells began to click. The next morning I phoned her, reminded her that we had met the night before, and said I had an inspired book idea for her.

"I never accept book assignments," she replied.

Silence. Then I asked if she'd care to hear what my proposal was, anyway. She consented to listen. When I finished, there was a pause. Then she said that I did indeed have an interesting idea, but that she would have to think about it and discuss it with her mother and sister, and her publisher, Elliott Macrae, of Dutton.

The next morning she called to say she would take on the job. She agreed that Charles Lamb's *Tales from Shakespeare* was a bit creaky for the readers of our time. I know that Macrae hated me ever after for having presented a book idea to his star author.

The point of this story is, by "exposing myself" to a P.E.N. dinner, and acting on a social encounter, I secured a book that is now a minor modern classic. It has sold well over 100,000 copies in its trade edition, many more in the Book-of-the-Month Club edition, and countless thousands in the NAL paperback edition. It is also published elsewhere in the world.

There are many good, professional writers who are "between books," and looking for projects. Seek them out, but first do a bit of "creative" homework.

Public exposure is essential for an editor. Parties may bore or tire you, but inevitably you will meet someone who will lead you to a manuscript or to an author. The more time you spend among people, the better your chances.

Read the newspapers and magazines; watch TV and listen to radio. When you encounter an interesting personality or a story that might be built up and shaped into a book, pursue it. Keep alert, on top of public events. Waiting for a good manuscript to fall off a tree is not the way to acquisition. Acquisition is the heart of publishing life, and all it takes is energy and imagination.

Book Ideas: Creativity-Can-Be-Fun Kit

Let's begin by admitting a fact: there are no *new* book ideas. Taking the name of Creativity in vain is sacrilegious. But there's always room for a *good* new book on a basic subject.

Actually the key word should not be "good" but "better." The new one should supplant the previous work on the same subject and have a real justification for existence. In my opinion, a new book on a familiar subject that doesn't add anything to the category, or to the enhancement of human knowledge, is a *glut book* —a who-needs-it book.

The object is to find the *right* author for the *particular* book idea. There are writers who can write good books on given subjects, but you've got to be sure they understand the specifications of the job. Each book must have a fresh slant, an honest-to-God purpose.

I'm thinking here of several book ideas that call for good writers who are expert in the areas indicated and who are also able to write in a certain vein, *sans pedantry,* for the broadest audience or for the audience for whom the subject is important.

Happy Hunches

The acquiring editor must be as nimble-footed as a gazelle. As I've already said, he must be the ubiquitous traveler, attending parties, meetings, public-affairs sessions, symposia, and the like. He must be available and approachable. He must be a well-mannered eager beaver, and he must never show impatience.

Be gregarious and be available to potential new writers. But don't expect lifelong devotion from young novelists. Consider the relationship as one might a marriage—and then think of the divorce rate.

There are too many examples of serendipity in publishing to make a case for the importance of being available.

Small risks are worth considering, and if one encounters a fine book of poems or essays by an unknown, it is not a bad thing to gamble on occasion. Although the chances are slim, a great literary career is sometimes preceded by a modest book of poems.

Special Dividends

One of the special bonuses in this editing profession is the unexpected chance to work with an author one has admired over the years. Writers often change publishers for one reason or another (money, paranoia, insufficient promotion and advertising, and so on), and when a major writer switches allegiance, it's a happy day for the lucky editor who inherits him.

I'm not referring to authors secured by direct solicitation; no self-respecting editor will make a direct overture to any author who is presumably happy and established with a publisher. Editors know directly or instinctively when an author is unhappy and ready to make a change. The word gets around or the author himself speaks up.

Moral Courage Required

Madeleine B. Stern, bibliophile and scholar, brings our attention to a book on phrenology (!) published in 1874, *What to Do, and Why,* by Nelson Sizer, from which we offer you an excerpt—a bit of philosophy and also some guidance for editors:

An editor should also have courage—no position needs greater; having a selfish world to deal with, he should be willing to utter the truth when justice demands that an unpleasant truth be spoken, and then to back it up. *A want of courage in an editor is as bad as a lack of courage in a soldier* [italics mine]; for while cowardice or treason in a soldier may cause the loss of a battle, a lack of courage or conscience in an editor may poison the public morals, and, perhaps, contribute to the loss of a battle as well. ... We would not give him excessive Benevolence and Ideality; while lack of Combativeness, Firmness, and Self-Esteem renders the editor pusillanimous, and leads him to soften the truth until its very back-bone is withdrawn; but there is such a thing as manly courage, unyielding determination, serene dignity, and unflinching justice, combined with kindness, affection, and proper consideration for the rights, prejudices, and even the ignorance of others.

Phrenologist Sizer's observations and values seem to hold up after over a hundred years, but who's listening!

Alacrity

Every literary agent respects, and shows partiality toward, the editor who turns in an early decision on a manuscript.

Get a reputation for alacrity. Don't keep an author waiting. If a delay is unavoidable, send in an interim report or indicate in some manner that you are not simply *sitting* on the manuscript.

Good manners require promptness. I know some agents who have blackballed, and properly, certain editors because they were notorious for sitting on manuscripts for three, four, or more months, and for being inaccessible. A reputable agent is entitled to prompt attention. And an editor must never forget where his bread and butter (or cake) comes from.

There are many editors who have almost no stock-in-trade, and without alacrity they are damned close to bankruptcy as acquisition editors.

The Payoff

Many editors must wait until they get to heaven for their reward. Some never get there! Most employees of publishing houses are underpaid, certainly underpaid by living-wage standards and by special qualifications, such as education and creative potential.

The turnover rate among editors is scandalous, and the reason is apparent: not enough pay. Editors with decent credentials can be easily wooed and won by competing firms which offer more money.

Publishers should take a hard look at reality, which includes the cost of training a new employee, getting him settled into his job and becoming a meshing member of the organization. At least three months is the minimum for orientation. Publishers should offer a bonus incentive to every contributing and creative employee —that is, a percentage of the profits on books acquired. A best-seller should certainly provide a payoff for the procuring editor. Any employee who shows loyalty, diligence in his work, and a lively intelligence that results in moneymaking books or books of distinction deserves careful money consideration.

So, publishers: If an editor is a credit to your firm, pay off! Cherish your worthy employees in a tangible, palpable way by surprising them occasionally with unrequested increments.

There are always a few goldbricking editors who earn more than they are worth, riders of coattails who sweet-talk their way through their jobs; phony intellectuals with a certain cultivated style who deceive their bosses—for a while. In the end, of course, their lack of real production (*production* is the operative word) catches up with them.

In a publishing house, a woman can do anything a man can do —even selling on the road. To suggest that a woman be given equal pay is not enough. Discrimination because of sex is immoral, unethical, and possibly a misdemeanor.

Publishing heads: If you get the urge to sell your company to a conglomerate or some other organization, take care of the loyal employees who helped build your business. Don't let them drift for themselves. Consider the possibility of selling the business to *them* first. Publishing houses are simple entries on the balance sheets of conglomerates. The employee's name is less than a cipher. Take note!

They Want to Be Alone

One or two successes often can transform an editor from an eager and avid pursuer to a character who "wants to be alone."

From a private study, I've learned of more than a dozen top editors who won't take phone calls or manuscript submissions seriously except from a few very select agents and friends. "The arrogant ones," we might term them. I know heads of houses who answer their own telephones; but not many top editors can be reached even through secretaries and assistants.

The legitimate business of the editor involves communication, and while the telephone is often a menace and a burden, it is the instrument by which a vast amount of our business is done. (I must confess that I have a Pavlovian reaction—negative, that is—to answering the phone at home. Nevertheless, I take calls and return calls quickly.)

The First Novel

All editors want to discover a Thomas Pynchon, a Thomas Wolfe. Some publishers encourage their editors to publish first novels.

Editors seek out the first novels with the seductiveness of Don Juans; the pleasure of discovery is one of the obvious reasons. I've always been a sucker for a first novel, although I must admit that very few of those I've taken on—very few—have made any profit for us, and only a handful of the writers have gone on to writing careers. There are countless first novelists who never turned in a second work; most are not hardy; they dry up and blow away.

First novels are challenges to the sales and publicity departments. How do you get the TV and press to rouse themselves over first novels, novels that have excellence but are not sensational? The editor beats his small drum, bores his friends, begs for advertising money, clutches lapels of famous writers, pleads for advance comments. He scrutinizes each bit of publicity in the hope that a fire will ignite. Meanwhile, the new author is on the verge of hysteria or suicide. Of course, the editor and his publisher shoulder the blame when failure is the end result. Often, if the first book fails, a novelist will turn to another publisher with his second one. (First-novel paranoia: we're out to destroy the new writer; we hate first novelists, etc.)

When a first novel hits the jackpot—clubs, big paperback sales, and the best-seller lists—then life can be beautiful. It can also be a time of trial for the publisher because other publishers begin to seek out and woo the lucky newcomer.

Without a true zeal for first novels, American fiction can't thrive. It's the obligation of every publisher to issue as many publishable first novels as he can. In the end, the payoff will come in one way or another.

Zeal is the operative word for the editor. A lazy editor, an editor who is casual in his attention to detail and to the welfare of his authors and their manuscripts, should take a hard look at his orientation. Being an editor means a seven-day-week commitment to the profession. Editing and publishing books is one of the most gratifying professions imaginable, but one must prove worthy of the label Editor. One should take a look at the points of the compass and decide whether one has the calling.

Remarks made by William Targ at a meeting of the American Writers Congress, October 9–12, 1981:

I don't think that decisions are being made by computers—not publishing decisions. But they are being made by blockhead (blockbuster-obsessed) business school graduates who don't know which side of a book is up. Marketing directors are deciding what is good to publish. The old-fashioned editor—who read manuscripts and worked closely with an author—is becoming obsolete. Some executives who call themselves editors don't know much about literature—except the best-selling titles and authors—and each one of them should be sentenced to a two-year apprenticeship in an antiquarian bookshop.

The lack of bookmanship and sensitivity to the book (the physical book, too) is a national disgrace. Amateurs are designing trade books today. The great traditions of book design and printing and binding are gone; most trade books today—despite high prices—

are trash insofar as physical qualities are concerned. Knopf and Random House are among the half-dozen exceptions. Atheneum is another maverick, doing well what most ignore: making good-looking and enduring books.

Countless good books are never stocked because they are not "merchandisable." When a chain store buyer says no to a particular title, that means it may not appear in any of several hundred or more stores throughout the country. Censorship? Yes.

Many agents and editors are getting lazy, uppity, and more and more it is not possible to reach them by phone or get replies to letters. "In conference—will call you back" is what secretaries tell authors. But the call rarely comes back. Editors read less and less, and they make decisions on the reports of their assistants or junior editors. I know of cases where a major book was declined because a "reader didn't like it." The editor didn't bother to read it.

I think a writers' union is a constructive idea, although the agents do try to help the authors with closer scrutiny to certain elements in contracts. I think an advertising budget should be included in all book contracts: space advertising with the author's photo included! Knopf is outstanding in this respect.

M. LINCOLN SCHUSTER

M. Lincoln Schuster, along with Richard L. Simon, founded Simon and Schuster in 1924. They gambled everything on their first book—Margaret Petherbridge's first compilation of crossword puzzles—and won! That kind of imagination and innovation was typical of Mr. Schuster during his long reign at Simon and Schuster (1924–1966).

• • •

"An Open Letter to a Would-be Editor" was written for the first edition of this anthology, in 1962. It is really a collection of *pensées,* their sum total being a distillation of Mr. Schuster's many years as one of trade publishing's most creative and unconventional editors. In just twenty-four trenchant comments, he offers a lifetime of advice to any young editor ready to read them, remember them, and, when possible, act upon them.

Since their first appearance over twenty years ago, I have heard many of these comments quoted at publishing seminars, sales meetings, editors' symposia, and wherever publishing people meet to discuss the latest metamorphosis of the publishing industry. Except for a reference to "the moment of truth . . . when you ask yourself the $64 question,"* they have not dated; they could have been written this year, this month, or this week. Perhaps even in our current age of bigness and emphasis on the bottom line and personal imprints and conglomerates, some things in publishing just don't change—things like editorial integrity, taste, and dedication.

*A reference to a popular 1940s radio quiz show, upon which *The $64,000 Question* television show of the 1950s was based. —ED.

AN OPEN LETTER TO A WOULD-BE EDITOR

I

The great danger in applying for a job is that you might get it. If you are willing to take that as a calculated risk, I will set down some possibly helpful suggestions in the form of a few *short sentences* based on *long experience.*

II

You ask for the distinction between the terms "Editor" and "Publisher": An editor selects manuscripts; a publisher selects editors.

III

An editor's function doesn't begin with a *complete* manuscript formally submitted to him, all neatly packaged and ready to go to press. Almost the first lesson you must learn is that authors (or their agents) frequently submit not manuscripts, but ideas for manuscripts, and give you the privilege of "bidding blind." You are lucky if you can see an outline and a sample chapter first. Sometimes you *don't even see a single word.*

IV

A good editor must think and plan and decide as if he were a publisher, and conversely a good publisher must function as if he were an editor; to his "sense of literature" he must add a sense of arithmetic. He cannot afford the luxury of being color-blind. He must be able to distinguish between black ink and red.

V

It is not enough to "like" or "dislike" a manuscript, or an idea or a blueprint for a book. You must know and be able to tell convincingly and persuasively *why* you feel as you do about a submission.

VI

Don't pass judgment on a manuscript *as it is,* but *as it can be made to be.*

VII

Forget all clichés and myths about a "balanced list." If you think in such terms you will soon be stricken with *hardening of the categories.*

VIII

The greatest joy and the highest privilege of a creative editor is to touch life at all points and discover needs *still unmet*—and find the best authors to meet them.

IX

There are times when you must finally say: "Although this is a bad idea, it is also badly written."

X

Learn patience—sympathetic patience, creative patience—so that you will not be dismayed when you ask an author how his new book is coming along, and he tells you: "It's finished—all I have to do now is write it."

XI

Master the art of skimming, skipping, scanning, and sampling —the technique of reading part of a manuscript all the way through. You will have to learn when you can safely use this technique, and when you *must* read every single line, every single word.

XII

Learn to read with a pencil—not simply to note possible revisions and corrections, but to indicate both to yourself and to your colleagues ideas for promotion and advertising which may be activated many months later. Such ideas will be infinitely better if you spell them out while you are excited and inspired with the thrill of discovering the author or the book.

XIII

Deliberately practice the art of reducing to a short sentence or two the basic theme or impact of a book. You will have to learn to put the quintessence of the book on the back of a visiting card. This will later give you the nucleus for your editorial report, your jacket copy, your publisher's preview, your letters to reviewers, opinion-makers, salesmen, and booksellers.

XIV

Don't worry too much about mistakes you make deliberately; that is, disappointments and failures that may come from taking a calculated risk. Editing and publishing are risk-taking professions—sometimes they are wild gambles.

XV

Don't follow current vogues and fads, and never think of doing "another" book imitating the best-seller of the moment. Start trends, don't follow them.

XVI

Give great weight to an author's potential for growth—and to the long-life "survival value" of a given book for your back list— a criterion far more crucial than immediate sales appeal.

XVII

If you are prepared to cast your affirmative vote for a book because of its prestige value—treating it realistically as a *succès de fiasco* or a *flop d'estime*—spell out the *reasons* for your enthusiasm, and calculate the fiscal arithmetic, so that you know just how much you are willing or prepared to lose.

XVIII

If you feel you must enlist the aid and advice of a recognized authority or specialist on a given subject, remember that an expert frequently avoids all the small errors as he sweeps on to the grand fallacy. A truly creative editor must become an expert on experts.

XIX

Don't be dismayed or disheartened if you learn that another publisher is getting out another book on the same subject. Far more important than being the first, be willing to settle for the best.

XX

Welcome suggestions and recommendations from your sales staff and your promotion and advertising colleagues, but resist any pressures that will be exerted by them for "sure things" and easy compromises.

XXI

Forget or disregard any glib oversimplifications about "the reading public." There is no such thing as one reading public.

XXII

Learn to win the confidence of your authors *before* the book is published, *during* the publication process, and *after* the book is released. Unless you inspire and enlist such confidence and cooperation, you will find yourself going back to the early days when the booksellers were also publishers, and the relationship between an author and a publisher was a relationship between a knife and a throat.

XXIII

For an editor the moment of truth comes when you ask yourself the $64 question: Would you buy this book if it were published by some other firm? This challenge, this test, can be expressed in many rule-of-thumb formulas, such as these: Stab any page and see if it bleeds. Do you feel that if you skip a paragraph you will miss an experience? Does it make the hair on the back of your neck stand on end (this test was suggested by A. E. Housman). But all these criteria come back to the two basic questions: Would you put your own money on the line to buy the book you are considering and, even more important, would you want to keep it in your own library—so much so that you will be happy to find it there years later, and look forward to the joy not only of reading it but of rereading it?

Always remember that you are being watched and judged by your colleagues and by your publisher, by authors, agents, booksellers, critics, and reviewers. They will rate you not on any single success or failure, but on your overall batting average. Babe Ruth, Ty Cobb, Mickey Mantle, and Roger Maris became world-famous champions by batting between .300 and .400—or somewhere between three and four hits for every ten times at bat. Therefore, within reasonable limits, you can luxuriate in integrity by acting with courage, with imagination, and above all, with the creative motivation that means fulfillment.

XXIV

Editing can, and should be, not only a life-enhancing profession but also a liberal education in itself, for it gives you the privilege of working with the most creative people of your time: authors and educators, world-movers and world-shakers. For taking a lifetime course for which you would be willing to pay tuition, you are paid, not merely with dollars, but with intellectual and spiritual satisfactions immeasurable.

SAMUEL S. VAUGHAN

Samuel S. Vaughan is the vice-president and editor in chief of Doubleday & Co., where he has worked since 1952. He is a well-known and much sought after lecturer and writer on all aspects of publishing. He serves on the advisory boards of several distinguished organizations dedicated to publishing practices and education. Among the authors with whom he has worked are William F. Buckley, Jr., Stephen King, Leon Uris, Arthur Hailey, Irving Stone, Gay Talese, Shana Alexander, Hortense Calisher, and Bruce Catton.

●   ●   ●

In this wise and witty philosophical "letter" on the many roles an editor plays in the author's life and the life of the book, Sam Vaughan offers some expert advice on the conduct and realities of the editor-author relationship. Disarmingly frank, it is a professionally intimate discussion of the editor's diverse efforts to get the best possible book from the author, and the many ways the editor employs to see to the book's publication in the most successful way possible. Mr. Vaughan illustrates the dynamics of the editor-author relationship, demolishes some myths about that relationship, offers some hardheaded views of what the editor and author need from each other to make the book work. As Mr. Vaughan so ably puts it: "This is a letter *from* an editor, to suggest a number of things you have a right to expect from your editor; a few things which, perhaps, you do not; and to tell you about the editorial life."

Mr. Vaughan neither unrealistically elevates nor diminishes the importance of the editor, concluding that "We have our uses and our laughter and problems and rewards."

Invaluable as a guide to the practice and etiquette of good editor-author relations, "Letter from the Editor" may best be described as a reasoned and cordial entreaty for a working relationship of peaceful and necessary coexistence.

Parts of this piece appeared in a different form in *The Writer* magazine, November 1969.

LETTER FROM THE EDITOR

DEAR AUTHOR:

For years now, there have been steady suggestions that the art of letter writing is dead. Like other announcements of the end of literary forms (and everything else), the obituary is early. As you know, many people write letters to editors. Letters to the editors of newspapers, for example, can be crank notes or valuable contributions to the paper. In England, they are a form of folk art. Many letters are written, too, to those of us who edit books. Some of the best moments in my life arrive in the mail.

Most authors' letters are entertaining and illuminating and well written. Most set forth the authors' intentions and, between the lines, expectations. This is a letter *from* an editor, to suggest a number of things you have a right to expect from your editor; a few things that, perhaps, you do not; and to tell you about the editorial life.

The object? First, to help you realize your ambitions. Second, to help you avoid disappointment because of unreasonable demands or expectations. Or an insufficient understanding of the editorial process—or insufficient explanations by those of us who edit. The letter, then, is in the interest of what diplomats once described as peaceful coexistence.

Forgive its faults. My "writing" proves only that everybody needs an editor, perhaps especially editors.

And if I tend to slip into linguistic sexism, please excuse the "he" where "she" would do as well. I haven't mastered androgynous prose and find some attempts to do so unnatural and ungraceful. More women are at work in general book editing today than men, and the leading women are among the best in the business. So there.

In fact, "I" might be better, if it weren't for this editor's aversion to the first person singular. I cannot speak for all editors, only for some of us, which is one reason for choosing the informal letter rather than attempting an essay.

If you write at book length, you could find yourself facing a person across a desk one day who is called your editor. Confusion arises at times about what an editor is supposed to do for the author or do to the written work. When an author and an editor proceed toward the climax called the contract, both tend to hear what they want to hear. The author envisions an inspired publishing performance; the editor envisions a golden book.

If we confuse authors (and not infrequently our employers) about what it is we really do for a living, perhaps it is because your editor can turn out to be a slightly helpful, businesslike acquaintance or a valuable friend or, on rare occasions, a deeply involved collaborator.

The thoroughly professional author, or the singular and striking one whose book is a work of art, may require little or no editing —that is, little application of pencil to paper. The beginner, or the writer with ideas but stylistic problems, or the stylist who lacks ideas or a sense of structure, needs more help. In every case, each book requires "handling" in the publishing process.

One of the shocks that lie ahead is that you might overhear your editor referring to what you have written as "my" book, as if it were the editor's.

Whose book? Good question.

If an editor recommends your manuscript for publication, it becomes—in the house—the editor's book. But one of the pleasures and genuine rewards of being an author is that a book, unlike a magazine article or a play or a motion picture, is first and last the author's. It belongs to you: it is yours, an individual creation, unique in an age of committees and collaborations. As an author, you might feel powerless at times. The designer of an automobile has little to say about how it will be manufactured or marketed. The musician may exert influence on his recording company, but by and large what happens to that recording is largely the company's decision. The playwright or screenwriter is one important element in the creation of the play or the motion picture, but does not determine the end "product," its shape, length, or final presentation. By comparison, even when feeling neglected or ignored, the author is God.

Still, the editor's proprietary interest, that feeling that it is "his" or "her" book too, works in your best interest.

It is the editor's judgment that is on the line, the editor's recommendation that the house take the risk of publishing the book. This means that your editor identifies himself with your work and will be identified with it.

In practice, this attitude is more beneficent and less heavy-handed than it appears. On a magazine, the editor seldom thinks of an article or a story as his own—or, for that matter, as the writer's. Instead, he thinks of it as the magazine's. Magazine editing can be much tougher and more arbitrary (and sometimes better) than book editing. Still, it is frequently done with little or no consultation with the writer. Even where there are sensitivities, a piece for *Time* becomes *Time*'s. A story for *The New Yorker* or *Commentary,* especially after their skillful checking, editing, and sometimes cutting and rewriting, takes on the tone and feel of a *New Yorker* or a *Commentary* piece, if that tone was not there before.

But the book, slightly edited, extensively edited, or unedited, remains yours. The only tone and content it can have ultimately are whatever *you* finally agree to. Your editor is for a brief time central, trying to bring your work together with your readers, first in the house and then *out there* somewhere, and for a time the editor will tend to think of what you have written as, at least in part, his book.

What can you expect from the person across the desk? Well, if authors take a great deal of understanding, so do editors. The more you understand your editor and the nature of publishers, the more likely you are to make a good team.

Your editor is usually an anonymous figure, a curious combination of ego and self-effacement. The job is somewhat akin to that of a director in the theater or in motion pictures. It is to help give direction, if needed, and assist with shape, clarity, and pacing, to point up climax and conclusion. The editor's hand should remain invisible and the editor tends to be, and should be, much less well known than the director. Further, there is no *auteur* theory of the book: the editor-"director" is not the major creative figure. You are.

The editor as representative has three roles. One is to represent you in the publishing house; the second is to represent that house to you; and the third is to represent the unseen, unknown reader. In representing the house, the editor should help you to see that any book has a great many people working for it, most out of sight of the author. Even the quietest publishing job is the sum of a thousand separate efforts and actions.

It is reasonable to suppose that the book editor's job is to edit books. Most of us understand, too, that the editor must also seek out people with talent or intelligence or information, with special experience or celebrity or, now and then, genius, who want or can be persuaded to write at book length. If we can agree on such sensible, common assumptions, we can give up common sense for the next couple of pages. For obviously, then, one would expect the editor to spend his day looking for writers, as well as reading and editing their work.

He does not. He spends some of his time in editorial meetings, discussing what was in the *Times;* or in meetings on the budget, explaining why the data that were in the budget when it was originally made up are no longer pertinent. (Not all fiction in publishing houses comes in the form of manuscripts.) The editor spends part of the day filling out forms to accompany the transmission of manuscripts to production managers. Or badgering his colleagues in sales and advertising and publicity and art departments. The editor often spends his morning drinking coffee, his lunchtime drinking white wine, and his afternoon repenting the lunch. (Though it must be said that editorial drinking has diminished greatly. In my first years in editing, the paths of publishing were littered with the bleached bones of editors—and authors—who had succumbed to a diet of too many gins.) On becoming an editor, he assumes that his days will be taken up with writers, people with patches on their elbows who write dazzling books. Instead, he finds his days given over to agents, lawyers, PR men, MBAs, or persons with patches over their eyes who like to negotiate killer contracts. Once in a while, a fine writer makes his way through the lines, past the sandbags and shell holes, and the editor is usually so glad to see this rare creature that the writer instantly mistakes editorial enthusiasm for blanket approval of the manuscript and a guarantee to sell 100,000 copies.

Manuscript? The editor does work on manuscripts but spends

a good deal of time trying to have manuscripts delivered that were contracted for years earlier. Recalling a well-turned book title, a "fine madness" pervades the business.

Why isn't the manuscript ready? Because every book is more work than anyone intended. If authors and editors knew, or acknowledged, how much work was ahead, fewer contracts would be signed. Each book, before the contract, is beautiful to contemplate. By the middle of the writing, the book has become, for the author, a hate object. For the editor, in the middle of editing, it has become a two-ton concrete necklace. However, both author and editor will recover the gleam in their eyes when the work is completed, and see the book as the masterwork it really is.

Nonetheless, this does not exhaust the question, however exhausting it is to think about, of what else the editor does with a day. He also contends with something called the List. Publishing people spend countless hours worrying about not each book but the group of books they plan to release to a suspicious, distracted, and apathetic world. Endlessly, we discuss the spring list, the fall list, the winter list. Authors play the game too, because everyone, especially your mother, your agent, and your typist, knows that autumn is the best time for the publication of your book. After all, nobody reads in the summer. Release it in time for Christmas, we are urged: Almost everybody believes that most original clothbound books are bought for gifts, despite the scarcity of solid facts on the subject, and the fact that reliable information shows such months as January and June to be excellent months for retail book sales or that August is a good time to launch a best-seller.

There are also the bothersome details of practicality. Set aside the details—that you delivered your manuscript in April, "almost complete"; that your editor could not begin the editing for six weeks and then spent most of the month doing so; that you got the balance of the book in five weeks later, with a few revisions yet to come; leaving about two-and-a-half months to make the fall (most books require about nine months from finished manuscript to publication). No matter, because you and your editor are not likely to make the final decision about the publishing date anyhow. Other sensitive minds are at work on the problem.

They will agree, in tones of sweet reason, that fall is the best time to issue your book. ("*Fall?* You'd have to be out of your mind to release her book any later than September!") I mean spring. ("You some kind of addict, you want to do that kid's little novel in May? Who reads in May?") Or do I mean winter? ("Come *on,* Sam— you can't do a political book in February. Everybody's in the Bahamas in February.") Okay, it just occurred to me—how about just before Christmas? ("Now you're talking. Put that book on the list for Christmas, make a nice fat package out of it, and it'll walk out of the stores.")

It is necessary to understand that a publisher's "Christmas" begins around Labor Day. His notion of Christmas Eve is, say, August 15. Any expensive or illustrated volume must be published in time for Christmas, everyone says, or it will die. This is one of publishing's ironclad truths. Except, of course, for the expensive illustrated volumes that are, for reasons beyond anyone's control, published in other seasons and sell nicely—while, silently, all those unsold expensive volumes from the previous Christmas are returning to the warehouse.

At any rate, the purpose of offering you these glimpses into the philosophical life of your publishers is to show a little of what your editor is doing when not actually editing.

In short, the editor's days are taken up with publishing; his nights and weekends with editing.

What's happening to you while the editor is busy with all that daily publishing detail? The expression "suffer in silence" was coined for authors. Among the formidable problems an author faces are the silences: first your own, in the long process of writing the book; second, the silence that follows the first submission of the manuscript; then that between the occasional communiqués from the editor. Why is your editor so silent—or so bafflingly slow?

Because there is a small mountain of manuscripts to deal with that arrived before yours did. Because other editors will ask him to read manuscripts and to write reports. Because he conducts an elaborate correspondence, his list of unanswered phone calls has twenty-eight names and numbers on it at the moment, and on his desk an English publisher's cable is fighting it out with a California agent's telegram, atop a six-foot stack of memoranda headed "Urgent."

The problem is not the time spent reading your manuscript; it is finding the time to *begin* reading it.

Your editor is slow, too, because he cannot always know with certainty things he asserts positively. ("Young Bill Breadloaf is brilliant, a total *original*. He'll go on to become one of the titans.") The editor needs time to know what to make of a book. A novel that might have taken you years to create is an artifact to which the editor is supposed to react in days. He must think also about the most effective way for your work to be published. How can he get the house "turned on"? How should the book be "positioned"? These are phrases of the moment, but they indicate that the editor needs *(a)* as full an understanding of your book as possible and *(b)* time to think how best to get it in print and in public.

Unless he has a streak of sadism, of the sort attributed to some surgeons, the editor will be reluctant to put pencil to paper unless he can see clearly how the manuscript can be, and how much it should be, improved. He may know that something is wrong with the manuscript but is not sure yet where the problem lies; he may know what is wrong but not quite how to tell you. He may want to fix it himself but be unable to do so; some editors can write, others cannot. (Both, oddly, can be excellent editors.)

Editing takes time because thinking and feeling take time. As editor-publisher Robert Giroux puts it, "There are three qualities that cannot be taught, and without which a good editor cannot function—judgment, taste, and empathy." And though these qualities may help to nurture an author, they are not fast foods. They require hours, days, weeks.

The editor is often tempted to take more time with a manuscript than it is likely to be worth—in commercial terms. He is pressed not to take a great deal of time with some manuscripts. Yet the least likely books are among the ones that intrigue him most. And the danger of underediting is sloppy editing. Not, in short, doing one's duty. The manuscript you can't take the time to edit is one you shouldn't take time to publish.

Then there is always danger lurking off there in the dark. An alert reviewer can lay into a book when it is published, attacking author, editor, publisher, printer, proofreader, and their antecedents. Once, when I was twenty-eight, I leaned into the office of my boss, the legendary Ken McCormick, then Doubleday's editor in chief. He was working at his stand-up desk. A book he had handled, on its way to soaring best-sellerdom, was being greeted in certain quarters by questions rich in human charity. ("Why wasn't this miserable mess edited?" "Whatever happened to

American editorial standards?" "There are no editors left," etc.)

"Ken," I said, a cub seeking light from a lion, "how do you feel when a book you've handled is one that a reviewer says needs editing?"

"I say to myself," Ken remarked, without looking up, "that he should have seen the book *before* I got it."

Your editor travels, as well. If his traveling leaves you somewhat out of touch, take heart. At least some of that motion is on your behalf. He could be off to a sales conference, selling your book, or talking with friends who are reviewers, magazine editors, or publishers from abroad; or in other ways trying to advance your reputation.

When does your editor edit? On the road, at times. Long plane trips are perfect. And, as suggested, on weekends and at night, when he would rather be buying dinner for a friend. ("What a day I've had! Postponed half my list from spring to fall.") Or helping the kids with their homework. ("Where do you go to school—at IBM?")

To be sure, a number of editors read and edit in the office. But the busier an editor is—and most editors are purely and not so simply overloaded—the less likely he is to do so.

Do editors edit? Yes. Some overedit, some are lazy. The rare experience is a manuscript that can be read without a pencil in hand. At the other end of extremity, now and then one of us has to sit down and run the manuscript through the typewriter. (Going to such an extreme is considered for both author and editor a failure of promise—though, in the editor's case, not a failure of nerve.)

So what is editing? What should you expect this peculiar person to do? The editor is, to start with, your first reader, a privileged, sympathetic, but ideally objective one. You can risk making mistakes in front of this reader; you'll be making them in confidence and in private, not in public.

The editor should offer you comment, general and detailed, on style, structure, substance, story; offer suggestions for improvement where appropriate; and, as the expression goes, resist the impulse to fix it if it isn't broken.

In fiction, the editor ought to respond to the four *s*'s above, including characterization, plotting, plausibility, length, pace, the title, and—if he understands it—your theme. For a work of what is called (unfortunately) nonfiction, many of the same comments apply, including such matters as characterization, oddly enough. People in books, nearly all books, are important.

One type of editing, as expressed by Betty Prashker, editor in chief of Crown Publishers, is "editing the author's head." By which she means that it is important to talk with the author, determine his or her intentions, offer comments, written or unwritten, on the book, and stand ready to help the author over the inevitable hurdles. For instance, Betty suggested to Lucian Truscott III that he convert a work he began as nonfiction into a novel about West Point. *Dress Gray* became a considerable best-seller. Betty proposed to Tommy Thompson, who was having problems with his first novel, that he write it as if it were one of his nonfiction works, a little suggestion that helped result in the best-selling novel *Celebrity.*

Each editor does the job in an individual manner. Editing involves working with words and with lines, and it also involves something larger. As Giroux, one of the best of contemporary editors, says: "The truth is that editing lines is not necessarily the same as editing a book. A book is a much more complicated entity and totality than the sum of its lines alone. Its structural integrity, the relation and proportions of its parts, and its total impact could escape even a conscientious editor exclusively intent on vetting the book line by line."

Behind every author and editor is the silent hero or heroine, the copy editor. First-rate copy editors are a Godsend, helpmates to the author, people who make an honest man of the editor. Basically, the copy editor is responsible for spelling, punctuation, grammar, and—you should discuss this in advance—"house style." This includes such matters as the rules for capitalization, the use of commas in series, the dictionary that will be relied upon as final authority, etc. The copy editor will be on the lookout for inconsistencies, repetitions, and may do a certain amount of fact-checking.

But in general or "trade" publishing, neither the editor nor the copy editor should be expected to serve as researcher or coauthor. *You* are the authority. If you have written about the Battle of Britain or, as we say in flap copy, a notable battle of the bedroom or boardroom, don't expect your editors to check every fact, as they would in a news magazine. If required, you or your editor should arrange for outside readings by experts (sometimes called "vettings," although this word also applies to legal check readings).

What about the relationship between you and the man or woman across the desk? Is the editor required to be your friend?

No. Forced friendships work no better in publishing than anywhere else. An editor and an author can work together smoothly if they remain a little distant. A touch of distance may be an asset. Relationships have broken down when an author and an editor became too intimate. When genuine friendship occurs, and it does, of course, it can be wonderful. It had better be genuine; it is certain to be tested.

Editors have the privilege of serving as the writer's reader, adviser, devil's advocate, sponsor, censor, sensor, financial and legal consultant, and lay analyst. The editorial job has been made more complex since the era when an editor judged what he *read*. Increasingly, we are asked to counsel the author on—and to recommend investment in—words the author wishes to put on paper but has not. We make many of our judgments based on brief descriptions, ideas, reputations, previous books, outlines, scenarios, "treatments," talk, and evidence of promise.

For every promising first novelist, there is an editor who has made fifty promises—about the future of fifty writers.

We must also try to appraise not only the proposed book but what books might lie ahead. Serious publishers undertake to publish an author, not only a book. We're looking for writers who will go on writing and, ideally, grow and develop, not just for a person who is momentarily with book.

So think on these things too. The relationship between you and your editor can be enhanced by understanding or exacerbated by one-sided displays of ego, anger, or impatience.

Your editor has to suppress not only his ego and anger but also his reading. Is your editor well read? Once he was. He used to read a great deal, the good stuff. That was one of the things that drew him to the occupation. Now he doesn't read a lot, he reads all the time, although not every manuscript is a modern classic. Meanwhile, his spontaneous or voluntary reading is drastically curtailed and he secretly suspects that functional illiteracy is creeping up on him.

One happy result is that the reading done for duty is reading we hope to enjoy as readers. Thus, the editor reads with high hopes. He wants to respond to, enjoy, admire what is to be found in the manuscript. When the going gets rough, or while you are waiting through the silences, remember: *The editor wants to like your book.* And if the editor has gotten you a contract for it, the editor does like your book, probably likes you, and has acted on those opinions.

Now for the next and somewhat less cheerful point. *Maxim:* However much he may like it, no one on earth cares as much about your book as you do. Not your editor, your spouse, your lover or child; not the reviewer who pronounces it a "masterwork," not the book club member who said it changed her life. Any of them, all of them, probably like the book a great deal. Still, no one will like it as much as you do or can care about it quite as much as you do.

But the moral behind the maxim is implicit: After you, then, who cares most about your book—and who is most likely to do something about it?

Right. That is why the good opinion of your editor, however imperfectly expressed, should weigh more heavily with you than other opinions. Let's be realistic. The admiring opinion of almost everybody else, prepublication, counts for nothing besides the opinion of the editor, who is willing to take risks (money, standing, embarrassment) to bring your work to others. Your success is, to a considerable extent, your editor's success. It is a shared happiness—with you as the major partner.

Even at that, your editor in some ways will disappoint you. Editors deal with glimmers of talent and flashes of hope; with changing, fickle fashion; and with the simultaneous search for the durable goods called literature. Your editor is up against numerous short-term deadlines and the always elusive future. What you would like is the immediate and the concrete—readers and dollars and advertisements filled with praise for your name. That's understandable.

Understand, too, that the powers of most editors are limited and are easily diffused or defused. Our authority is arbitrary and usually informal. We cannot *command* colleagues or reviewers or booksellers or readers to react as we want them to. We can only try to present your work with intelligence, force, flair, and conviction; to be reasonably persistent in your behalf; to temper your expectations with realism; and yet never to give up hope. To endure frequent frustration and disappointment, the editor must rely on a deep well of optimism that springs eternal, despite the fact that rain often falls on his parade.

Daily, your editor, all previous small jokes aside, faces fear and failure. In a job demanding concentration, the editor works by fragmentation. The work is one of visions, some grand, some strange; of ideals, frequently compromised; of high standards, seldom met (by authors, by publishing, by himself). The editor has a chance to do a bit of good in this world and an almost equal opportunity to add to the tide of meretricious, indifferent, or redundant books that threaten at times to swamp the continent.

Still, this is no plea for sympathy. If all this is such a struggle, why are editors apt to be fairly cheerful people, worn but younger than their years? Because the job allows the editor—in fact, requires the editor—to indulge his taste. To not only have opinions but live by them. The work permits grown men and women to tell other men and women that their work is appreciated, that *they* are appreciated. In a society where people are often too embarrassed or inhibited or "sophisticated" to openly and genuinely admire someone else, where almost everyone seems bent on being a critic or an adversary, the editor's job is to be positive, to admire, to advocate, and to pass on the praise of others.

For your editor doesn't have just a job. What he has is a vocation: a commanding, compelling kind of duty, full of intangibles and excitement and gambles. Editing can be plain hard work—detailed, intense, calling for craft, skill, diplomacy, and ingenuity (not the least of which is, as suggested, finding the time and residual energy to edit).

Another reason for the editor's spirit is that the work is, much of the time, fun. Although it's impossible to do all that can be done for a book, and certainly for a long list of books, doing what you can calls for a certain lift—and gives you one in return.

The continuing education of the editor is part of the reward. I was deep in a pile of manuscript one evening, when my oldest son stopped at the desk, looked at me for a moment, and said, "What are you doing?"

Fair question. I'd asked Jeff the same one at least ten or twenty thousand times. In fact, I was pleased to be asked.

"I'm working on a translation, terrific book, a biography of

Tolstoy." Then I told him a little of the riches of Leo Tolstoy's life and of the riches of Henri Troyat's book, and explained a few of the niceties of translation along the way.

After our brief talk, Jeff turned to go, to return to his own homework. But before he went, he said straightforwardly, as is his style, "You must learn a lot."

He was right. And I was grateful to him for saying so, for teaching me that fact again. For a parade of people come into the editor's life and each one has something in mind, something to say. If everything goes right, for a year or two we have the privilege of learning what the author is so excited about and staying with the subject. And a chance, along with helping the author to get it said, the story told, to become a temporary semi-expert in the field. As anyone buying a house becomes for a time a real estate specialist, I have been, briefly, an explorer with Heyerdahl and Hillary, a historian with Catton, an actor with Kanin and Gordon, a musician with Ellington, a President with Eisenhower, and a story-teller with Behan and Hailey and Garrett and Goyen, those magicians who can make people laugh, or move them to anger or tears or curiosity or comfort. And all by an arrangement of words, little symbols of this or that, on paper.

That is why, when you come face-to-face with the person across the desk, the editor is apt to be very pleased to see you sitting on the other side. For even if the morning was spent arguing about ad budgets, the diminishing market in paperback reprint rights, or the high price of printing and everything else, you are apt to see a genuine smile. For the author who can transform a box of blank typing paper into a living document is the most valuable visitor to the person who will help transform that manuscript into a book.

There is no automatic virtue in being an editor (and, if you believe what you read, none whatever in being a publisher), as there is none automatically in being a writer. But for each, from the start, the possibilities are splendid.

The editor, with work, the right authors, and what was once called luck and pluck, may have found a vocation. And the writer, with work and the right editor and luck, etc., may become an artist, an established authority—and/or rich.

It's easy for editors, especially when we get together (in assemblies such as this book or at parties or at the inevitable lunches), to overemphasize our importance. We should guard also against mock-modesty. We have a special task, a distinct utility, and a particular privilege. We should never confuse the midwife's role with that of the mother or the father. We have our uses and our laughter and problems and rewards. But the magic, the art, that's yours.

Best,

Sam Vaughan

SOL STEIN

Sol Stein is the author of seven novels, one of which, *The Magician,* has sold one million copies and is widely studied in American schools. His novel *Other People* has been held up as a model for writers. His plays have been produced both on and off Broadway and have won several awards.

Mr. Stein has also published poetry, articles, and reviews. With Jacques Barzun and the late Lionel Trilling and W. H. Auden, he founded the Mid-Century Book Society. He has lectured on the craft of writing at many American universities.

Mr. Stein and his wife, Patricia Day, head the publishing firm of Stein & Day.

• • •

In this lively and provocative essay, written especially for *Editors on Editing,* Mr. Stein discusses the editor-author relationship from a special vantage point—that of the editor who is also an author—and offers many insights into the situation wherein an editor has a special affinity with the author's creative processes, problems, and professional aspirations. Of particular interest is the editor's exercise of his skills to ensure that the author reaches and holds the audience for which he writes by developing his craft to its most expert expression, so that the editor becomes "the now silent partner whose previous advice informs the writer's present work."

THE AUTHOR AS EDITOR

All editors are authors—of postcards to friends, memoranda to ex-spouses, reminders to themselves. Some editors write for publication. A very few have as intense a commitment to their writing as to their work as editors. Still fewer work both sides of the desk, so to speak, every day. It has been my habit for many years to write the first thing every day for several hours, and at about nine in the morning to turn my attention to editing the work of others. Moreover, since I am also the publisher of the writing I edit (others publish my work), I take the financial risk of putting the results of my editorial work out into the market place. The author and I will both live on and by the results of our work. What I have to say about the editor-author relationship stems, in part, from having daily to practice what I preach, and to benefit or suffer from the results. What have I learned from this two-headed role that might be useful to other editors?

If what the author and I are working on is entertainment fiction —at times priggishly referred to as commercial fiction—the result is measurable most often in dollars. If what we are working on is literary fiction, the result is measurable by the author's satisfaction with the relationship, my satisfaction with the relationship, the critical response from outsiders who know nothing of the intimate process in which the author and I have been involved, the vitality of the work a year and ten years later—and sometimes it is measurable in dollars too. In either case, most authors will admit that it is the ultimate success of the book that is the glue of the relationship; the others are liars.

To achieve that success, it is commonly said that the editor's job is to assist the author in realizing the author's intentions. That is both right and wrong. Wrong, when the author, however talented, has not understood the nature of the craft or art he is engaged in. Fiction writing, which can have a cathartic effect, cannot be *under-*

taken as catharsis or as a means of conveying to others one's experiences, insights, and wisdom. Those enter into it, and the greatest of editors, like good tutors, can often help a novelist cut through the superficialities we all drown in and reach into his throat for the gut of an experience (one well-known novelist once told me I knew more about him than his psychoanalyst of seven years did) or into his soul for whatever convolutions there individuate that particular writer from his brethren. That happens seldom. What is usual is that the editor—before he can deal with the craft of achieving ends—helps the writer understand that the proper intention of his work is to create something that will move an audience of readers most of whom he will never meet or see, and some of whom live in Japan.

This great hurdle comes first. It is a process of consciousness-raising. Perhaps I am especially aware of audiences because I was a playwright before I was a novelist. A playwright sees his audience, hears their coughs as well as their applause, the rustle of their fidgeting as well as their bravos if earned, and cannot blink the fact that he is creating something to move an audience. Novelists sometimes think of their audiences as subordinates being exposed to what is good for them. My role as editor is to disabuse them.

I deal with this by sitting down with the novelist with a table or hassock between us, as if we are about to embark on a game of chess. I put down three objects between us: let us say, impedimenta as common with me as a book of matches, a pipe, and a key case. The three objects can be anything. I am about to describe a triadic experience, and ask the author to indulge me by imagining that the book of matches is himself, the pipe is his novel, and the key case is the audience. It is the function of the book of matches to create a work (the pipe) that will affect the key case (the audience). When the work is complete, should the book of matches vanish (or the author get hit by a truck), that should not stop the work from continuing to affect the audience in the same way. In other words, the author is creating an object (the work) that has to affect the audience without the presence of the author. This is sad for the author to contemplate, not only because of the human temptation to think of ourselves wrongly as immortal, but because the process says *This work is finite.* It has to be complete and do its work reliably with or without explication from reviewers, critics, or the novelist. The work must stand, as it were, on its own feet, not on the novelist's, and must affect an audience as much as a musical composition must. Moreover, the author is composer and conductor both. He will get better and worse interpretations from readers, but the work, unlike a work requiring interpretation by performers, is indelible.

If one raises an author's consciousness of the process, what does that mean in practical terms? It leads a novelist to be able to view the constituent elements of his work. The novel, since its beginnings three centuries ago, has consisted of three elements. For convenience, I will term the first "immediate scene," meaning scenes that one can see before the eye, that might, indeed, be filmable. The second element is narrative summary, or what happens offstage. The third element is description—of an environment, a particular place, a climate of opinion, a setting for the narrative summary or immediate scene to follow.

Now comes what is sometimes a shock to the innocent. Because I am an editor who is also a publisher, I am acutely aware of the fact that one's first audiences matter, that the snorts, laughs, and attentive silences of Shakespeare's standees not only encouraged him in his craft but made it possible for students of later generations to be included in his audiences. A novelist writes first for his time. If his observations of human nature are correct, his time may exceed his life. But first audiences first, and the readers of novels today have for more than half a century been influenced by motion pictures and then television to expect visual scenes. This has influenced the novel to use less description and narrative summary and to focus on the immediate scene. Moreover, certain techniques essential to the cinema arts have helped to shape the novel's audience. The reader has been exposed to montage and has come to accept jump cutting, the elimination of interstices or linear connections between scenes. It is an impatient audience, which wants to see the next event happen.

I once sat with a distinguished writer, a critic who also wrote fiction, over a scene that didn't work because it took place in a matter of seconds and the crucial ending of the scene was a dreaded but easily recognizable sound. We talked about how this scene might be filmed, what the scenes would be like from the camera's point of view. What are we looking at, at this moment, what concrete detail, and then what do we see, and finally what are we looking at when we hear the offstage sound? The result was a perfect reordering of the ingredients of the scene into something very moving.

One hears often the nonsense that one can teach physics or sociology but not how to write fiction. One cannot give the fiction writer—any more than a composer—an ear. But craft can be learned, and, surprising to some, even observation can be trained to be more acute, precise, particular. I recall attending a party with a novelist who, observing someone across the room, nudged me in the ribs and said, "Gatick," his invented word for the sound of a focal plane camera. In other words, *catch that, notice, remember, keep for future use.*

I once heard it said at a seminar for professional writers that pace could not be learned. Of course it can, but beforehand it must be understood. We tend, glibly, to associate pace with thrillers and the like. Pace is actually at the heart of "line editing," the term we use for the word-by-word examination of what has been written to see what is imprecise or irrelevant or unneeded. In my editorial shorthand, I have a rule: "One plus one equals one-half." It means that if two adjectives are used, either one will probably produce a stronger effect than the two together; if two phrases say the same thing in different ways, the effect will be strengthened by choosing the better of the two and dropping the other. This process removes the flabbiness, the least good in favor of the best. The same principle applies to works as a whole: ten strong scenes are better than ten strong scenes plus two weaker scenes.

My minimal contribution to one of the first books I edited a long time ago, James Baldwin's *Notes of a Native Son,* was to suggest the elimination of the weaker essays because they diminished the level of the whole. Baldwin, received as one of the best American essayists since Emerson, allowed me, after argument, to interfere with his natural instinct to preserve rather than let go of essays that would devalue the book as a whole.

In fiction it is the elimination of the interstices between the scenes—as in jump cutting in film—that can most improve pace. If a woman is leaving the premises, we do not need to see her go down the stairs and out into the street. We want to see her at her next destination where something will happen. We want to hear her thoughts when we are also seeing something. Preferably not the lighting of a cigarette, or the sip of a drink, which are the cliché reflexes of the lazy writer who does not take the time to individuate his concrete images and give us something memorable, poignant, or particular.

It is sometimes argued that while structure in fiction can be taught, the higher the author's ambition, the less can be said about structure. I learned the falsehood of this when, in the early 1950s, I had the advantage for several seasons of the MacDowell Colony, where I had ample opportunity in the evenings to eavesdrop on composers discussing their music-in-progress with each other. Discussing music? Yes, and I was impressed by the general acceptance of the idea of *line,* as in a clothesline, something that stretches from beginning to end, from which other things hang—the necessity of the line, the connection, Aaron's-rod-into-a-snake, the magic of the changing of shape, which would not enthrall us if we did not know the shape from which it changed.

The line in a novel is the desire of its protagonist. Ahab wants that white whale. Is the great chapter on the whiteness of the whale then a digression? Not really, because it describes in the fullness of the author's imagination the object of the protagonist's desire. But digressions that do not enhance the desire, or characterize it, or thwart it, are off the line. I remember the momentary pain in a well-known author's face when, though he was a guest in my home, I faced him with an editor's inevitable rudeness and said I thought his novel started on page 159. After two hours alone, he emerged from the library now happy with the bad news, because in rereading he saw what he would have seen without aid a year later, that on page 159 the line of his tale began.

"Drama," Elia Kazan once said, "is two dogs fighting over a bone." Yet even novelists educated in the classic theater sometimes write without an antagonist or without a bone in mind. It is the editor's function to remind the novelist of what he knows but does not always use: unimpeded desire does not a story make. An antagonist must be worthy of the hero. Their combat must be seen.

During the decades when Freud's perceptions were infusing themselves into popular dogma, some novelists were misled into thinking that it was enough for the combatants to be within the same person. The flaw this leads to is the misperception of previous fiction, which often had internal duels. In a skilled author's hands, the combat takes place within the antagonist as well as the protagonist, and within their friends and family and chiefs of state. For it has always been the storyteller's function not to merely describe events, whether over a fire or in a book, but to particularize human nature, which is often an internal battlefield. The mind that stays the daggered hand can be beset not only by self-doubt and conscience, but by the possible outcome of getting caught. While two dogs fight over a bone, society watches.

Society, in the form of an audience, likes to watch with bated breath. It derives pleasure from suspense. It doesn't demand that outcomes be deserved or undeserved, only that each outcome be plausibly—even if surprisingly—connected to what has come before. The audience wants from a duel what the duelist wants—satisfaction.

An editor working with writers who differ greatly from one another learns that there are many audiences. Some want only verisimilitude. Some dote on the fantasy of *Watership Down*. An audience will accept anything the author expertly prepares them for. But an editor sometimes has to point out that rabbits don't talk in thrillers.

Once, in the early 1950s, in a meeting of a small group of playwrights, Lillian Hellman said, "Anything can be put on a stage." The editor within me couldn't help blurting out, "What about cossacks on horseback?" Miss Hellman calmly answered, "Anything but cossacks on horseback." Some things do not lend themselves to fiction, either. Arias—very long and uninterrupted speeches—are difficult for the reader who is used to verbal exchange when he reads. I know a gifted novelist who did not quite realize this until his own words were laid out anew on a fresh page that was actually longer than the original but seemed to move much faster because of the interchange.

Some subjects pose nearly insurmountable difficulties; even the grand master of fiction in our century, Joyce, in *Ulysses* wrote a less good chapter on ennui than he did on other things.

One might say that ennui in extremis—boredom—is the writer's worst enemy because audiences that will tolerate almost anything refuse to be bored. They will skip paragraphs and pages, or close the book. It is the editor who, in the absence of a restless audience, must point to the dangerous misadventure that will cause a writer to lose the war—the reader fled, uncaptured by his storytelling.

And that is by no means all. An editor of novels who is also a writer of novels knows three secrets. First, while the Greeks killed messengers who brought bad news and the editor must risk the same, he knows that if as a result of the information gained the author will win his war, the editor must constantly put tranquillity at risk. I'll never forget that when I thought I had finished my subsequently best-received work, my editor said to me, "Yes, all right, the story's good but the central character is so ordinary." I had to steel myself from instant murder, then went back to the drawing board to rewrite *The Magician.* I value most the editors who have seemed harshest to me at the time. Writer and editor must both know they are at war in the same cause.

Second, I know that writers write *against* other writers, that they are at least as competitive as businessmen are reputed to be. They secretly write to prove that they do it better than So-and-so. I have given some writers small comfort in passing on the word that other writers, even as they are publicly tactful, feel as they do. It is a writer's job not to lie to himself, and it is sometimes the editor's horrendous task to call, with trepidation, a spade a spade.

I know, too, the guilty secret that corrupts and motivates every author who has a sense of himself as well as his work. Where does he stand in the pantheon of writers? The commercial writer itches with a variant: Where does he stand in the earnings pantheon or the clout pantheon or the bookstore ratings? And the truth is that even the finest writers with the highest hopes often lack immunity to the variant; they want a little bit of posterity now. Can an editor help?

If there is a bond, a rapport, he can—with tact, knowing the pain involved for the recipient—interpret messages from the field. *This is where this story may move your career.*

In conclusion, I would say that an editor's primary function is to help the writer realize that he must keep his audience in mind while writing: in fiction, with a view toward moving that audience as often as possible; in nonfiction, toward getting that audience to accept what the writer has written as accurate, true, and, if possible, wise. This is often done by encouraging the writer to marshal his evidence so that the reader will be ready to accept the author's conclusion or thesis when it is finally presented. Writing is not thinking out loud. It is presenting the results of silent thought in a manner that will lead the reader to the same conclusions.

But just as the writer must keep his audience in mind while he writes, the editor must help the writer to resist actual audiences after each draft. The writer needs time away from each draft to see it in perspective. If he does not have the luxury of such time (few writers are that patient), the editor sees the draft with the objectivity the writer cannot yet muster. If the editor and the writer develop a trusting rapport, the writer will be able to come back to each new draft refreshed, with the ability to see the virtues and faults that the aura of first love kept him from seeing. As the author learns to revise and revise again, he will need an editor less and less. It is the editor's ultimate task to make himself dispensable, to function as part of the writer's knowledge of craft and awareness of audience, to become the now silent partner whose previous advice informs the writer's present work.

BURROUGHS MITCHELL

For thirty years, until his death in 1979, Burroughs Mitchell edited the work of some of America's most celebrated writers at Charles Scribner's Sons, where he worked with perhaps the greatest of all modern-day American editors, Maxwell Perkins. Among Mr. Mitchell's authors were James Jones, W. A. Swanberg, C. P. Snow, and Marguerite Young.

•   •   •

". . . I cannot see how the foremost editorial responsibility can diminish—that is, the hopeful, understanding reading of a manuscript. Here is where an editor's education begins, and it is an education that never ends."

These lines from Mr. Mitchell's brief reminiscence, *The Education of an Editor,* published in 1980 and excerpted here, exemplify his sensitivity and dedication to the editor's role as the author's inspirer and guide. Mitchell learned from Maxwell Perkins an invaluable skill: how to enter the writer's solitary enterprise without ever intruding. And it all begins with the editor's first reaction to the manuscript itself: ". . . a book becomes a public matter. But the manuscript just discovered may be undergoing its first exposure when you, the editor, read it. You have joined the author in an odd, intimate association between two strangers." Reaction to that manuscript is essential and it cannot be uncritical, for unlike what an author seeks from a friend or a loved one, "In the support from an editor, a writer demands hard, critical honesty." Mr. Mitchell's comments on the editor, the author, and the manuscript that links them illuminate the best that can be in the creative relationship between these two creative partners.

THE MANUSCRIPT

Every book editor has started out by reading manuscripts. As he advances in his education and in his responsibilities, he must puzzle his way through a variety of duties, which have been unfavorably compared with the functions of a psychiatrist, and an errand boy, and a plantation overseer. In all this, an editor may lose sight of a simple fact, that the manuscript remains immovably central.

I think there are three signal movements in an editor's working life compared with which the many dreary jobs and frustrations seem trivial. The first of these moments comes with finding a manuscript that is animated with a life particularly its own. Only someone who has worked in a publishing house can have a sense of how inexorably the manuscripts flood in, from everywhere, as if every household in the world had a typewriter. And so, if he is to survive, an editor, it seems to me, must have one deeply rooted trait—the ability to pick up each new manuscript with curiosity and hope. If he has that, his day will come, sooner or later.

Much later, it often seems. The flow of manuscripts brings so much failed work—so many earnest, ponderous efforts, and smart posturings, and little flashes of talent that die out before the book ends. It is easy for the manuscript reader to become depressed, especially because he can recognize that many of these failures represent high purpose and hard work. But then the unexpected, hoped-for moment comes—the manuscript with the indescribable and yet immediately evident property of life that signifies a real writer. Can the writer sustain the vivifying quality of the first pages? I clearly recall my increasing pleasure and confidence when, twenty years ago, I read into the manuscript of Sue Kaufman's first novel, *The Happy Summer Days,* which Carol Brandt, the agent, had sent me. Just as firm in my memory is my bewildered curiosity as to what Thomas Berger would do on the next page, and then the next, of *Crazy in Berlin.*

Reading a manuscript draws an editor into a contract with the author quite different from a reader's relationship with a published book. When a piece of writing goes into type, a change results. Jim Jones told me that this was a lot of mystical nonsense, but he was wrong. The printing process does make its effect; good or bad, the piece of writing now assumes an air of permanence. And moreover, on publication, a book becomes a public matter. But the manuscript just discovered may be undergoing its first exposure when you, the editor, read it. You have joined the author in an odd, intimate association between two strangers.

Once having encountered the writer in his work, you are inevitably curious about the shape of the actual person. The meeting between editor and writer becomes the second of the three moments I have spoken of. And it may be a meeting filled with unexpressed complications. Perhaps the author of a first book has heard some of the prevalent tales of horror about publishers; he will then arrive encased in suspicion and determined to protect his work from corruption. On the extreme other hand, the author may be in an incoherent state, stunned by the fact that some unknown person—and a publisher!—claims to like his book. He may sit in virtual silence at the meeting, smiling a little foolishly. In either condition, with guard up or struck silent, the writer, in his real self, will remain out of reach.

To be sure, I have offered two extreme situations, neither one common. But variations between these extremes are common enough. What is apt to happen is that the author will arrive with conflicting feelings of worry and hope—the dark suspicion that he must keep his wits about him and the readiness to be joyful. If the editor manages to allay worry (at least temporarily) and to transmute the author's hopefulness into the beginning of trust, he will have done his best. It may be that the biggest accomplishment he can expect will consist in persuading the writer that here is somebody who actually appears to understand what his book is about.

Max Perkins spoke in his letters of "the motive for fiction" and of how it was often misunderstood in its seriousness of intention. While a writer and an editor sit, perhaps uneasily, in their first meeting, the editor will be attempting to get at the motive, the impelling force, in this stranger. He will gain no more than a sense of it. In fact, if the writer should announce a portentous statement of purpose, that will be cause for doubts. But an editor has got to look for reassuring indications that, having found a book, he has also found a writer—a writer with the indispensable supply of energy and bullheadedness. In the end, that first meeting between editor and writer may not come to much, but it will have been invested with an excitement that neither is likely to forget. I can remember nothing of what was said the first time James Jones came to see me at Scribner's. But I do still have an impression of his general look—friendly, uneasy, but determined.

The third occasion I think of as a high moment is the publication of the book. It is a time of great strain, the approach of publication day; the author jitters, or drinks too much, or pretends he doesn't care, fooling no one. As for the editor, I am sure that many of them have had my persistent experience, the total loss of objectivity. While the book exists only in manuscript, it remains open to revision and the editor therefore maintains a degree of critical detachment. But that stops on publication day, and the editor becomes as violently partisan as his nature permits. His job is to calm the author, but, just the same, the first unkind word from a reviewer may cause him to react with unreasonable heat.

Once in a while, the great thing happens. The reviewers, one after another, discover the book and hail the author. The book becomes visible everywhere, in bookstore windows and even in the hands of subway riders. It is discussed knowledgeably by people who haven't read it. All the little explosions of publicity go off. And the publisher rejoices over the dilemma of how large to make the second printing. Through these bewildering days and weeks, the writer, if the book is his first, has been going through a change within himself—from amateur to professional. The editor has had his judgment confirmed and his secret doubts silenced for good, and momentarily his ego luxuriates. But perhaps, in all his ebullience, he will be able to remember those admirable books that died very quiet deaths. They should be remembered, and with respect.

Many events in publishing may turn out to be more important than the three I have singled out, but I suspect that none will have an equal excitement. These are the three chief steps of entry into association with a writer and his career.

Having entered this far, an editor stands in danger of overestimating himself. The invigorating lift of a publishing success may very well lead the editor to feel possessive toward the writer.

Fortunately for everyone, the possessiveness will not work. No editor tried harder to avoid it than Max Perkins, and yet Thomas Wolfe thought he felt it and went thundering off, having exhausted Max with his torrent of explanations. Possessiveness will not work because it implies a transcendent importance in the editorial function that simply is not true. The editor did not write the book; the author did, and what is more, he knows it. We now hear the phrase "creative editing" a good deal. Some years ago, Herbert Read wrote that "creative" was "a word to be used with discretion," and his good advice has been conspicuously unheeded. I don't believe that an editor's part in a book is a creative act. The writer performs that act.

That is not to say that an editor limits himself to correcting the spelling. Editorial work does require imagination—the imagination to see the contours of a book with something close to the author's vision. The capacity to do that makes the editor a valuable ally for any writer.

Early in this book I said that the act of writing is a lonely one. In fact, a writer lives in a peculiar and contradictory condition. He treasures his independence (sometimes to the point of egomania); he values the times of solitude necessary for his work. And yet it is often a troubled solitude, and it can grow so painful that there must be relief. That is what the editor can provide more satisfactorily, perhaps, than anyone else. Assurances of confidence from family and friends cannot wholly sustain the writer, for the simple reason that he takes for granted their uncritical, unquestioning support. In the support from an editor, a writer demands hard, critical honesty.

I suppose that as the publishing business grows in complexity, reverberating with million-dollar deals, an editor's duties will become even more multifarious and bizarre. But I cannot see how the foremost editorial responsibility can diminish—that is, the hopeful, understanding reading of a manuscript. Here is where an editor's education begins, and it is an education that never ends.

It is an odd sort of occupation to take up—reading manuscripts. The truth is that the occupation lays a claim on one's life. It might seem, then, not to be very much of a life; but since I began to read manuscripts professionally, more than forty years ago, I have not ever wanted different work, nor have I felt that work of any other

kind could give me so strong a sense of purpose. When I ceased
my editorial job at Scribner's, I could have taken it as a release
from drudgery. But instead what I did was to start at once to look
around here and there for manuscripts. And quite soon they began
to appear.

Practice

WILLIAM BRIDGWATER

William Bridgwater was the editor in chief of Columbia University Press and an advisory editor of The Dryden Press. He died in 1966.

●   ●   ●

Since 1962, when Mr. Bridgwater wrote this article for the original edition of *Editors on Editing,* technology has changed the way the copy editor works. Yet although these changes continue, the copy editor's responsibilities to the book remain fundamentally the same. The copy editor does far, far more than just make sure that everything in a manuscript is spelled, parsed, and punctuated correctly. Mr. Bridgwater's comprehensive discussion of the wide range and high importance of the copy editor's craft concludes with these solemn yet glorifying words: ". . . upon his shoulders lies the weight of centuries of learning. . . . The little marks he puts on paper are for the betterment of mankind."

The young, apprentice editor who feels burdened with the necessity of learning copyediting would do well to commit those lines to memory and believe in them. They very well can transmute his "drudgery" into a noble "calling."

COPYEDITING

Take the manuscript of a book. Set it firmly upon a desk or a table so that it cannot slip or slide. Pick up a pencil. Start reading through the manuscript, and as you read correct typographical errors and note passages that may confuse a reader and usages that may cause trouble for a printer. You are doing copyediting.

THE SCOPE OF THE JOB

If the task sounds easy, you do not understand it. There are many complications, not the least of them being that it is a task without thoroughly set limits. What is called copyediting in one publishing house is almost never identical with what is called copyediting in another. Thus it is in book publishing, which exists solely to provide human communication through the printed word, yet violates principles of communication by using terms vague and multiple in meaning, but triumphantly workable. Everyone in publishing knows what copyediting is, so why define it precisely? It is not editing as such—or general editing, as it is called here—for that, as has already been shown in this book, is a supernal occupation concerned with telling an author Yes or No as to whether his book will be published, with admonishing him to alter whole chapters, and with other such high affairs. It is not production work, for that involves familiarity with type, sinkage, the moving of space from one place to another, and other matters shared only with printers. Yet in the spectrum of publishing, copyediting lies between general editing and production. Copyediting is basically the mechanical marking of a manuscript so that it is in literal and literary form ready to go to a printer.

In publishing, the edges within the spectrum are blurred. The general editor may do the copyediting himself. Even the publisher may deign to make all necessary changes on a manuscript (usually in a hand totally illegible to the printer). Sometimes the copy editor is called upon to rise above mere marking and rewrite large portions of a book. Occasionally the bearer of the title "copy editor" has as his only duty the marking of a manuscript with direct instructions to the printer as to matters of typographical style and manufacture, but such workers are more properly called production editors. They are concerned with the manuscript but not with copy.

The fundamental, unavoidable, and not infrequently boring part of copyediting is the discovery in a manuscript of all usages that may hinder the reader or may stop him short and make him leave the book altogether, like a man dragging his feet out of a swamp. And "usages" include not only misspelled words and missing or excessive punctuation, but also more important items, such as meaningless headings and references to nonexistent illustrations. These hindrances the copy editor must find and remove by exercise of his pencil, by suggestion to the author, or by referring the matter back to higher authority (usually the general editor or publisher; in short, the boss). If, for instance, an author persists in writing *quarternary,* the copy editor simply cuts out the offending extra *r* wherever it appears. If, in a numbered list, Item 3 and Item 5 are present, but Item 4 is absent, he writes a polite note to the author asking for Item 4. If he comes upon a chapter that he knows to be filled with error—in which, for instance, towns and cities of Australia are persistently misnamed and confused and there is a long description of a journey by boat from one place to another whereas in geographical fact neither place is remotely connected with a waterway—he usually takes the manuscript back to his superior. Such actions would at least qualify as normal copyediting procedure, though other answers might be found. Copyediting will vary with the practice of the house, the nature of the boss, the character of the book, the attitude of the author, the amiability of the copy editor, and sometimes with the weather. Yet if no action at all is taken in such circumstances, the worker is no copy editor.

Of these forces that control the scope and variation of copyediting, by far the most determinative is the character of the book itself. The more creative the writing, the less the copy editor can or should do.

In books of poetry the author is almost entirely responsible for the whole, including the spelling and the physical appearance of the pages; the responsibility of the publisher is purely to translate the author's intention into terms of type on paper, and this responsibility lies almost exclusively in the hands of the general editor and the typographic designer. The function of the copy editor shrinks to measuring and proofreading, and even the measuring is strictly under orders of the designer and the proofreading under orders of the author (who may, if he pleases, scorn all dictionaries). It is true that in anthologies, texts, or quotations of poetry the copy editor has somewhat larger duties, but these are still strictly mechanical: determining whether indentions must be kept as in the original publication, whether Elizabethan spelling may or may not be modernized, and deciding like issues, all of them involving meaning and therefore involving the copy editor, but all of them verging upon the prerogatives of the general editor or the designer or both. For the copy editor the requirement for editing poetry is plain: HANDS OFF!

The requirement for editing plays is a bit less stringent: Hands off the text! The actual words written to be spoken—or, in the case of "literary" plays, written as *if* to be spoken—should normally be regarded as sacred, subject only to proofreading. The acting and stage directions must, however, be tested in detail by the copy editor to be certain that a sane and reasonably intelligent person can follow them. Even this limited function disappears when the author has melded everything into a conglomerate and sometimes deliberately obscure whole. Designer, general editor, and author usually determine what typographical mechanics should be employed, as, for example, whether names of characters speaking are to be in small capitals, in italics, in boldface (rare in these days), or in plain roman. The copy editor gleans the wheatfield after them; he questions inconsistencies, unintelligible abbreviations, and other usages that might trap the reader. Again, as in poetry, he has a greater responsibility in new editions or reproductions of old works. It may fall to his lot, for example, to point out to the author or the general editor that the manuscript contains detailed attempts to "picture" the original in ways that, except in a facsimile edition, are foolish, delusory, or even downright dishonest.

In ordinary prose fiction the scope of the copy editor is less, but not much less, limited. The job of "creative" editing, if it is to be done at all, is within the province of the general editor. Some fiction, such as stream-of-consciousness novels and short stories, even defies the crudest type of proofreading, and here the copy editor's job is almost nil. But the pendulum swings in a wide arc. In most romantic and mystery fiction, the dispassionate eye of a copy editor is of value in checking expression and fact. In one quite distinguished novel, when the author asked that no copyediting be done, none was, and to the disturbance of readers one of the minor characters quite inexplicably changed his name from Bob to Bill in the middle of the book. It is this sort of thing, and not cadence or charm, that is supposed to occupy the time of the copy editor of fiction. Occasionally the copy editor is also asked to cut the copy of a story to a predetermined length. He should have sufficient skill at abstracting to perform such a task without doing violence to what the author has created. No matter what the circumstances, the copy editor never has the slightest excuse for trying to preempt even the smallest section of the author's creative job.

It is in works of nonfiction that the copy editor is called upon to do his broadest and most useful work. The classification nonfiction covers all sorts of books, good, bad, and indifferent; cheap in idea and approach or elevated to the point where only the most highly trained can follow what is said; intended to be read to children of two or three years or to be read by graybeards in libraries. Each book varies in its audience and in its demands on the copy editor. Art books, for example, require that copy editors know enough about printing reproduction to be sure that the meaning of the text and captions meshes with the illustrations. Juvenile "fact books" should have copy editors as alert as general editors to the demands of word levels and to the responses of children. Copy editors of textbooks must support the efforts of the publisher to produce books that meet the needs of large groups of students of a particular subject at a stated level; in such books, meaning and approach become one with expression and form. The range in nonfiction and in the resultant demands upon copy editors is infinite. Yet in the copyediting of works of nonfiction of all types there are basic procedures and techniques, which must be adapted to the purpose of the publishing house and to the book itself. These principles may be extended to all sorts of copyediting.

FIRST VIEW OF THE MANUSCRIPT

The process usually starts as this chapter does, with a manuscript spread out on a desk. In former days, when printing costs were lower, copyediting was by some publishers permitted to wait until the book was in galley proofs, and in exceptional cases this practice still holds. But the risks of expense for the publisher, exasperation for the author, and frustration for the editor and the printer are great indeed, and copyediting in proofs is inadvisable and rare. Usually the copyeditor is handed a manuscript. It is given to him by the publisher, the general editor, the author, or some other agent, with the assurance that there are practically no flaws in it (even if the author is an Eskimo who has just learned to read and write) and almost always with the admonition that it must be edited immediately and in great haste because of the publication schedule.

A good copy editor listens and heeds these words, even if he has heard them in variant form a thousand times. They are a reminder that in a job largely concerned with discovering faults, the temptation is always to find too many and not too few; in a job that must be meticulous if it is to be good, attention to detail can easily absorb too much time and painful effort.

With such sobering considerations in mind, he begins a quick inspection of the manuscript as a whole—or at least the whole of what has been given to him. Not all copy editors make this preliminary run-through, but most good ones do. The purpose is twofold: to get the shape and feel of the book, and to uncover major discrepancies in usage and serious copyediting problems. Such a full view gives the copy editor a better chance to unify his editing and generally improve the book. Therefore, in Utopia a copy editor would always receive the full manuscript at once, including the title page, preface, and other front matter, as well as bibliography and notes, if such there be. Yet in this workaday world, schedules frequently make necessary the submission of manuscript in driblets from the editor or the author, and the copy editor must work away on what he has, hoping fervently that there are no large bears behind the bushes in scenery not yet viewed. In some publishing houses the title page, preface, and the like never pass through the hands of the copy editor at all. This practice has the advantage of keeping the copy editor busy at the task in which he is most useful, minute examination of the text. It does, however, have the disadvantage of preventing the copy editor, who necessarily ends by having a more intimate knowledge of the book than anyone else in the publishing house, from detecting in front matter usages and even statements that flatly contradict those in the finished text.

GETTING DOWN TO DETAILS

After the first rapid and informative survey, the copy editor buckles down to his real work. He goes through the manuscript chapter by chapter, paragraph by paragraph, sentence by sentence, word by word. He always has in mind how the pages of the manuscript will be in detail translated into pages of type. He is trying at the same time to read the text in terms of the readers expected for that particular book. This judgment is not always arithmetical. Thus, if the book is intended for the wider general public, the copy editor must try to prevent it from containing words, allusions, or tone addressed exclusively to the literati or the cognoscenti. Such editing does not mean eliminating all difficult words, elegant figures, and serious information. Any reader is by definition literate. Most readers, even when they peruse a book for sheer entertainment, are happy to improve their stock of knowledge, for this is, after all, the essence of reading, and they may even from a hard-boiled detective story or a sex-charged historical novel garner an astonishing harvest of exotic and authentic information. In every instance the copy editor must keep in mind the virtues and possibilities of the manuscript in hand. To each book its own copyediting problems.

Copy Reading

Rudimentary but fundamental is direct proofreading of the manuscript itself. Many authors are proud of their inability to spell and leave such trivial matters as spelling to menials. Copy editors, as those menials, may quietly harbor contrary opinions about the value of spelling, but they must of necessity spend their time in quietly bringing the spelling into line with the pronouncements of the dictionary that the publishing house has chosen as authoritative. To do so is not a simple business of going from manuscript to dictionary and back again, pencil in hand. Always there is the problem of exceptions. The makers of dictionaries must choose among various spellings used and understood by educated English-speaking persons: there is no unanimity in English spelling, and the problem of preference often arises. An author has the right to cling to his idiosyncrasies. If he likes to write *meagre* instead of *meager,* his book should have *meagre,* even though the copy editor must take a note of the exception and watch carefully to change to *meagre* any occurrence of *meager*. Worse, dictionary makers cannot in the nature of things be up to the very last moment in decisions on innovations. New words and phrases are being added almost daily to the English language. They come not only down from science and technology, but also up from popular speech and across from foreign languages. Consider *spinors, rock 'n' roll* (or *rock and roll* or *rock n roll*), and *caudillismo*. An expression or a word that has become current with the author and his audience cannot be despised. Since dictionaries must follow usages and not create them, the copy editor must be familiar with new words before they enter dictionaries.

Among words, proper names occupy a special position. Many authors are just as careless with these as with common nouns, and proper names are harder for a copy editor to check. Most editors develop a certain wariness and caution toward names, both personal and place. Authors who spell by ear can easily create orthographic monstrosities; only too often Nietzsche becomes Nietsche and Khrushchev becomes Kruschev. For this sort of error the good copy editor is ready. He is even able to cope with the fact that the name of the sacred city of Xauen may also be spelled Xexauen, Chauen, Shishawen, Sheshawen, or Sheshauen; he merely finds the form most frequently used by the author and asks if that may not be used throughout the book. The author will usually consent, and that particular name problem is solved. If the author wants to follow the practice attributed to T. E. Lawrence of educating the reader by throwing at him all possible English forms of the name, it is legitimate for the editor to point out that the reader is more likely to be confused than educated. He may even go so far as to hint that an eccentricity which the public found enchanting in T. E. Lawrence may prove only annoying in the works of John J. Jones.

The checking of names is a delicate and many-sided operation. Offhand it would seem that an author using foreign names would be in a position to dictate what forms of names should appear. Generally this is true, but the exceptions cause trouble. An American book that has Roma and Firenze and Bruxelles instead of Rome and Florence and Brussels is pretentious and absurd; an American who tried to say Bruxelles in conversation would be laughed at—and justifiably. A book in English should be in English, proper names and all. A good copy editor tries to steer an author toward name forms that will be usable for American readers.

Even in the editing of an insipid novel, names can be an aggravating and complex problem. In considering them, the copy editor is always halted by the caution of time. He may look up every American and English personal name in the appropriate *Who's Who,* if the volumes are at his elbow. But he may not devote hours to such checking. A sampling is all that is required. If the samples turn out, on assay, to have small gold content, then the matter must be referred back to the author or the general editor. The copy editor has only a limited number of hours to devote to a particular book.

In the checking of names the copy editor also encounters danger; he may only too easily commit the cardinal sin of copyediting. He may change something that is right into something wrong.

Proofreading and Proper Names

Words, including names, are of prime importance to the copy editor. Facts, as such, are more important to author and general editor and less the concern of the copy editor. One function of the copy editor is, however, to act as watchdog. It is part of his job to be suspicious. The author is responsible for all misstatements, falsehoods, and misapprehensions. He makes the statements, and the copy editor has only a small chance to check them. Yet, so far as a copy editor can review the facts, he must. In every book he edits he brings to bear all his knowledge, derived from experience or from reading. When there is due reason for querying an author's assertion, the copy editor must query all that seems wrong or dubious. He must point out demonstrable errors, giving his reasons for querying. In many cases, disagreement with a reference book is not quite sufficient to justify more than a mild query, for usually the author should know as much as or more than the author of an article in a reference book. The copy editor is obliged to bring to bear all the knowledge that he has. As a native of Kansas City, he will not tolerate geographical misinformation about that metropolis. If he does, he is being a knave as well as a fool. He must, further, query facts if he has good reason for doubting their authenticity, even if he is not absolutely certain. Usually such queries are addressed to the author, who will take great satisfaction in declaring his statement right and the query useless, if such is the case. When a copy editor finds the queries growing to a bulk too large for comfort, it is usually time for him to ask the editor or the publisher to intervene and request that the author check and rewrite his material or hire someone else to do so; in rare instances only is it the copy editor's business to talk directly with the author on total revision.

The Phrase and the Meaning

Words, facts, and finally usage. The most troublesome part of an editor's job is the review of a manuscript in search of grammatical and rhetorical vagaries.

It is in making decisions on usage that the copy editor receives most guidance from the house stylebook, if there is one. Such stylebooks vary in an enormous range. They may be glossily written, expensively produced pamphlets intended primarily to impress authors; they may be stodgy collections of decisions about hyphenation (for example, Never hyphenate an adverb ending in -*ly* with a succeeding adjective), word choice (for example, Do not use *implement* as a verb), paragraphing, and chapter division. The prescriptions of stylebooks may be restricted to directions for the author in preparing a physical manuscript: typing in double space on standard-sized paper, with no short pages or random pieces of manuscript; no use of pins, stapling machines, or Scotch tape to fasten inserts to the pages; and reams of other practical advice. On the other hand, the stylebook may be a compilation of exceptions, additions, and expansions of dictionary rulings. If such rulings are prescribed, the copy editor who is trying to trim up the manuscript must hold to them and try to make the author hold to them.

The true danger for a copy editor who is undertaking revision of expression is a sort of overconfidence, especially marked in young editors. The neophyte is sometimes under the mistaken impression that he has been hired as a literary critic. Without long experience he finds it hard to read a typewritten script with the same respect that he gives to the printed word. In a course in copyediting I have made the experiment of giving students sentences written by masters of English prose. Always a large percentage of the students with earnest abandon will "correct" the phrasing of Walter Pater and Virginia Woolf. Perhaps their changes are improvements; I am no more in a position to judge their alterations than they are to judge the original. But clearly the alterations are unwarranted interference. The copy editor should do his rephrasing in material that has palpable errors—incomplete sentences, confusing use of "it" and "this," and other such dreary mistakes. If the author of a manuscript has recently come from some other language area into English, both general editor and copy editor must spend tedious hours testing the prose to be sure that foreignisms have not damaged the reading value of the English. In editing translations, the task is even more exacting because translators often have such reverence for the original that they leave bits and pieces of it lying about in the translation, like logs washed upon a beach in a storm. Cleaning up a manuscript is honest work for the copy editor, writing old sentences over again in form or in consonance with the book is invaluable, but useless "improvement" of an author's literary style is futile and wrong. The course that a copy editor should follow is easy to indicate: aid the author, do not judge him.

At the same time certain accepted usages of English writing must be maintained so that a publisher may hold up his head among his fellows and boast of the editing of his books. He employs copy editors to support that pride. Therefore every copy editor should come to his desk for the first time with those usages already firmly in mind. This does not mean that he must know all the rules that schoolteachers in the late nineteenth and early twentieth centuries attempted to foist upon the language of Shakespeare and Dryden. The most familiar examples of these mistaken ordinances are the prohibitions imposed on split infinitives and sentences ending in prepositions. The revolt against formulations of this sort was severe, but now it seems to have run its course. Today copy editors may edit on the sure principle that certain usages are accepted as standard in English without fear of being castigated as reactionaries because they hold to principles at all. Almost no copy editors today attempt to follow the rigid and now discarded rules of yesterday. But almost all of them do think in terms of standard and substandard English, standard English being the body of usages accepted by educated people today (but not necessarily tomorrow) and substandard English comprising all forms frowned upon by those same educated persons. The line between the two wavers, but any good copy editor knows that standard

English is the source of dictionary and stylebook formulations, not the product of them. He edits by knowledge of the language, not by rigid rules.

Punctuation

Considering the use of punctuation throughout a manuscript is only a part of the general editing of the text. The mechanical marks for guidance in reading are an intimate and inseparable part of an author's presentation of what he has to say. How intimate a part it can be is shown with blinding clarity in the poetical works of E. E. Cummings. Less astonishing to the ordinary reader than the profuse parentheses and missing periods of Cummings's poems but no less illustrative of the point are the methods of punctuation used by many modern novelists in English, from James Joyce to William Faulkner. Punctuation may be used to set the pace in narrative of the stress in exposition, to push phrases together or to thrust them apart, to slow or to hasten reading, to supply overtones absent from the words themselves. Literary archconservatives— among them a few copy editors—who decry such usages as twentieth-century innovations would do well to reread such masterpieces as the eighteenth-century novels of Laurence Sterne and the nineteenth-century works of Lewis Carroll. The employment of punctuation in wary and unusual fashion has a long and honorable tradition. Punctuation is part of the text, not a separate little engine throbbing away at a separate business.

True, for workaday nonfiction intended to inform or entertain the reader, full-blown theories are pretentious and even downright silly. Any copy editor of long experience has come upon authors who punctuate in bland carelessness or ignorance and then defensively claim that the periods, exclamation points, commas, and the rest are intricate parts of a well-laid plan and that it is not mere accident that an appositional phrase has a comma before it and none after it. A favorite explanation is that the punctuation is for the ear or for breathing. To this claim the copy editor is not allowed to answer *(a)* that if the author takes the book home and reads it aloud there will be in the annals of the book a total of oral readers amounting to one, or *(b)* that anyone trying to follow the punctuation marks in reading aloud will find himself panting like a dog on a hot day. In extreme cases he may, however, point out the same things in a polite way, saying *(a)* that since the book is of a type that would be read by most readers with silent attention, perhaps it would be better to punctuate for the eye rather than for the ear, or *(b)* that readers have the privilege of altering stress to suit their own speaking styles and might find marking according to the author's stress a hindrance rather than a help. In other words, one may question how an author's system of punctuation may work. One should not question his right to choose a system. If he elects close (or tight) punctuation—that is, inserting a comma, a semicolon, a colon, or some other mark at every conceivable pause—it is the copy editor's business to point out spots that have been neglected. If, instead, the author chooses open (or loose) punctuation—that is, having only the minimum of marks necessary to carry the meaning—then the copy editor may suggest removal of punctuation that exceeds that bare minimum. Every copy editor should know, however, that the present tendency is toward open punctuation and that in cases of doubt the simpler forms have more present-day virtue. Further, if the house stylebook was drawn up long ago or concocted by someone with ideas from the long ago, the copy editor must do his best to circumvent the house rules up to the point of actual defiance.

In all editing of punctuation it is well to keep in mind several indisputable facts.

One is that no rules for punctuation were handed down by a stern God from a cloudy heaven. Writing existed before punctuation, and can still serve to communicate ideas with no punctuation as such. Consider ancient Roman inscriptions and such modern signs as this:

DO NOT LITTER THE STREETS
PUT WASTEPAPER IN THE BASKETS PROVIDED
THIS IS YOUR CITY   KEEP IT CLEAN

Admittedly the line breaks and spaces in the sign operate like punctuation, but they are hardly punctuation marks. Those marks were invented only to aid more rapid and precise reading, and that is their major function now, though they may be quite legitimately used for other purposes.

A correlative—one might even say a consequent—fact is that punctuation varies from one language to another although they may all use the same alphabet. The Germans put commas before all dependent clauses. The French use *guillemets* to mark off quoted passages. The Spanish warn the reader that a question is coming by putting an upside-down question mark at the start. Though alien to usage in English, these practices have developed according to logic and seem to serve their purposes admirably. They are just as virtue-filled as English usage—but different.

A third fact is that in English punctuation there are fashions, just as there are in dress and in popular use of phrases. Certain punctuation practices seem to be fairly stable, for example, the use of capital letters to mark the beginnings of sentences. Some are almost universally accepted by English-speaking readers, for example, identifying a clause as nonrestrictive by introducing it with a comma; these are usually clearer when defined in texts of English composition than when met with in actual manuscripts, where a restrictive clause can approach easily the barrier that keeps it from being nonrestrictive. Some practices are demonstrably obsolete: not too long ago chapter numbers and chapter headings had periods after them; now those periods have the old-fashioned effect of Victorian lamps, beautiful in a proper setting, but ludicrous in a modern décor.

To all these facts a copy editor must be sensitive. The conclusions to be drawn are obvious, but it will do no harm to state them obviously. A copy editor should know that punctuation is inferior to the text in editing, and should avoid becoming a "comma chaser." He should try, within the limitations set by the author, to promote punctuation that will aid the reader today. Period, colon, semicolon, dash, parentheses and brackets, exclamation point, question mark, suspension points, and quotation marks—all are intended to illuminate the text. The copy editor should see that they do illuminate and not obscure.

Copy Editor and Author

Copyediting of a manuscript should fall into several patterns. There are changes that must be made. If an author violates house rules or standard usage—if, for example, he writes *phrase* when he means *aspect* or writes *specific* when he means *particular*—the copy editor must make the required alterations in a firm, clear hand. If difficulties arise not from such obvious faults but from ambiguity or possible error, the copy editor should not be so brash; he will note these in the margin of the manuscript or, if there is no room there, on slips of paper attached to the proper page of manuscript. Finally, mere suggestions that the editor thinks may be helpful to the author but in no way essential should certainly not be written on the manuscript itself but only on accompanying slips or sheets of paper, so that they may be removed when the author has settled the question. These distinctions turn out, in practice, to be only rough, but the principle is sound.

In making such changes, queries, and suggestions, the copy editor must keep firmly in mind the truth that he is not a teacher instructing an incompetent student. Any editor who persists in writing notes such as "Awkward" or "Meaning?" or just a contemptuous "?" beside a manuscript passage should be fired. An author, even an incompetent, semiliterate, and pigheaded author, is within his rights in resenting such unhelpful work.

It is in the realm of textual editing that battles between author and copy editor usually occur. Not infrequently copy editors call particular authors "uncooperative," "illiterate," and worse. An author may be plaintive ("My manuscript came back all bleeding") or belligerent ("That editor doesn't know good English when he sees it"). Usually, though not always, such contretemps are the fault of the copy editor. It is his business to see difficulties in advance and to make all adjustments possible, no matter how oversensitive, insensitive, or obtuse an author may be. It is his job, above all, to realize that the book belongs primarily to the author, secondarily to the publisher, and not at all to the copy editor. Even if the author is personally cut off, known only through his manuscript and through letters written to someone else, a copy editor must constantly be aware of him, his abilities and his faults, his crotchets and his genius.

In matters of "apparatus," on the other hand, the copy editor must be to a certain extent the authority above the author. If a copy editor does not know about the form of footnotes, bibliography, and appendixes, it is time for his education. Even if his work at the moment is entirely in juveniles or fiction or how-to-do-it books, in which footnotes are at a minimum, he cannot truly know his craft unless he can place a firm hand upon footnotes and beat them into submission. He may, if necessary, learn by consulting stylebooks, though indoctrination by a skilled copy editor is better. With their subject matter he cannot be concerned. Either the author has done his research properly and in good order, or he has not. If he has not, the copy editor may discover and sadly report that fact. In rare instances, he may be commissioned to check and reshape the notes. Any copy editor should know how to do so. He should at least know that the entries in the bibliography and the citations in footnotes should be coordinated and have some idea how the coordination should be accomplished. Amateur editors do not realize the unity of all the "apparatus"; professional editors should. To achieve the simplest and most workable form of notes, bibliography, appendixes, and subsidiary matter such as tables and charts is specifically the duty of the copy editor. In going through the manuscript he sees whether or not references to notes, tables, and charts match the corresponding notes, tables, and charts. If they do not, he must take measures to restore balance. This can be an onerous business. In one case in my experience the author decided to remove the first three of 159 tables, and all references to the tables had to be altered from beginning to end. The copy editor must in such circumstances plod along, looking at each table whenever a reference occurs. When that job is complete, he turns to editing the tables in series, to ensure that the reader is not misled by headings that seem to be similar but are, in fact, different. Notes, tables, charts, bibliography—all these challenge the best efforts of a copy editor, and as sure as there will be some rainy days in a northern autumn there will be some manuscripts with intractable notes, insoluble tables, and unreadable charts.

With illustrations a copy editor may or may not deal, depending upon the practice of the particular publishing house. A usual and wholesome practice makes him responsible for the suitability of the illustrations, responsible for fitting them into the total pattern of the book. Photographs and drawings that neither reflect the text nor supplement what it has to say may be and frequently are used to embellish a book. Yet they gain more value if they are closely related to what is said in words, and this correspondence is the business of the copy editor. In the best of all possible worlds, the copy editor knows enough about reproduction methods to warn the author that material he has submitted for illustrations—a tattered newspaper photograph, for example—will not yield satisfactory results; but his proper business is passing on content rather than form, unless he happens also to be involved in production, which is outside the normal copyediting scope.

When a book has been thoroughly surveyed, it should be ready to go to the production or manufacturing department and to the printer. In even the least troublesome manuscript, however, there are many problems that must, should, or might be referred to the author for decision. To take full advantage of the services of the copy editor, the publisher should submit the manuscript with all corrections, recommendations, and vagrant suggestions to the author before it is committed to type. To avoid trouble, it is normally wise to send sample editing—say of fifty pages—to the author for his approval before the entire manuscript has been canvassed. Then, further copyediting can be guided by the author's wishes. The author has at least as much proprietary interest as the publisher and will insist upon his rights. If he has at the beginning the opportunity to see some of the copyediting and express his tastes and his distastes, the publisher can gain more benefit from the copy editor's time; it can be an advantage, rather than an annoyance, to the author.

GALLEYS AND PAGE PROOFS

When the manuscript is completed and dispatched, the copy editor is not through with his duties. He must take care of the proofs, and in most houses not only the proofs of the books on which he has done the manuscript editing but also proofs of others. A copy editor must be a proofreader. He may at any moment be called upon to do the actual proofreading and do it professionally. In any case he is compelled to check all corrections made by the author in galley proofs. Such checking would be easy if all authors knew the limits of proof changes. The copy editor must be ready to see when an author's correction is about to create trouble for a compositor and suggest substitute changes that will not cause trouble. He must inspect all alterations that are made and adjust those that would not be clear to a typesetter, since all proof changes are intended as instructions to the typesetter. His function as intermediary between manuscript and type becomes clear at the proof stage.

On the proofs the copy editor must also usually give instructions for the beginning of new pages. He must issue instructions so that the page proofs, when they come, will properly reflect the meaning of the book. If he is charged with the "inventory" of the book, he must make sure by a rapid check of the records that everything the book is to include is accounted for, either at hand or expected at a set date—such things as dedication, preface by some eminent person, acknowledgments, and the like. The table of contents and the list of illustrations cannot be prepared finally until page proofs have arrived, but before galley proofs are returned provision must be made for them.

A few niggling tasks also fall to the lot of the copy editor before galley proofs are returned. Word divisions at line ends must normally be checked and made to agree with the dictionary or the style rule approved by the house. Violently uneven spacing must be noted and in extreme cases changed by transposition or rewriting of the text. All headings should be given special proofreading. And if running heads for the chapters have not been made up and listed previously, they must be written out and submitted with the galleys in usable form.

When page proofs are returned, the copy editor must check all the author's new corrections, repeating the procedure used in the galleys. Pages that for one reason or another have been left long or short by the printer must be examined. If facing pages do not match in length, slight changes must be made. The order of page numbers must be checked for that book, and once again headings must be considered. The running heads must be proofread. The copy editor must see that the tables and charts are placed as advantageously as possible in the text (since printers cannot always follow to the letter instructions issued with the galleys). When a book is "dummied up" to show layout of text, illustrations, and headings, the copy editor is usually, though not always, expected to aid the production department in making sure that the material in the dummy does not violate the meaning. When the pages go back to the printer, a good copy editor has already surveyed the whole and has filled out a form either for himself or for the production department, showing placement of all material. The copy editor must in some way assure himself that he has accounted for all content. If something is missing or wrongly placed, he is guilty, and, despite squirming, he must take the responsibility.

INDEXES

Indexes are a weight upon the spirit of the copy editor, though sometimes he is happily delivered of the responsibility when the general editor chooses to edit indexes himself. The copy editor is, however, best acquainted with the copy and normally best equipped, after the author, to perform a clinical inspection of the index manuscript. Some knowledge of indexes and indexing is of value, but if the copy editor does not have it to begin with he will probably gain it in the most laborious and unrewarding way, by experience.

Indexes, unfortunately, are not finished when they are sent out after editing. They return in proof, with author's corrections, and must be handled like regular page proof. In many houses and under many circumstances, all page proof is held until the proofs of the table of contents and of the index are ready to be released. It is a good idea, when possible, for the copy editor to see the whole of the page proofs at once and visualize the book as to entire content. Once this last glimpse is allowed, he has no further chance to change his mind or repent his sins. Even if folded and gathered sheets are sent to him later, he can on them do no more than try to discover catastrophes, for anything milder than catastrophic must be left. There comes a time when a book is finished.

TOOLS, TECHNIQUES, AND QUALITIES

The tools of copyediting are simple: a pencil (in some houses pens are prescribed, but since humans err, a pencil is better), an eraser, some bits of paper, some reference works, and a mind. These must suffice.

Chief among the techniques is the ability to mark clearly on copy. Even the beginner at copyediting should know proofreader's marks and especially know how not to use them. A copy editor who makes the mistake of writing corrections in the margin of manuscript rather than in the manuscript itself is being not only unprofessional but thoughtless, for he must know enough of printing to realize that a compositor goes through every word of manuscript and therefore is only impeded if he must look back and forth between copy and margin. He should be able to see also that the contrary holds true with galley and page proofs. In those the compositor is setting only the lines that are to be changed; therefore those lines should be indicated by signals in the margin. The ability to mark manuscript and proof simply, cleanly, and unmistakably is something learned only over the years—and sometimes never.

The duties of a good copy editor are exacting. What are the qualities and interests he should have?

First, I should say, he must love books. Books as such, not just their intellectual content. To say that a copy editor should like reading is supererogatory, since no one in his right mind would undertake the job of copy editing if he had no affection for reading. Only readers need apply. But more than this he should like the touch and the smell and the feel of books—possibly even the taste. He should be interested in how books are made, in general and in detail. It is well for him to know a bit of how they are advertised and sold in bookshops and in drugstores, by peddlers and by mail, if he is to take his proper place in the chain of publishing. It is imperative that he know the rudiments of printing processes.

Second, he must respect authors. Primarily he is the servant of the reader, but secondarily he is the servant of the author, and a servant should learn the methods, aims, and whims of even a secondary master. The worst disease that can attack a copy editor is arrogance toward authors.

Third, he must have an eye for detail and a passion for accuracy in dealing with detail: of this the fabric of his working life is made. Yet minute attention must operate within the frame of good judgment. Too much anxiety for detail will cost the publisher money, the author anguish, and perhaps the copy editor his job.

Fourth, he must be truly familiar, even intimate, with the English language and current English usage. Some publishers, many authors, and a majority of English professors would rank this requirement first. It is indeed of prime importance that the copy editor know whereof he speaks on words, grammar, and usage. He should know the old and outmoded usages as well as those that are current, for not all authors have current ideas—some, indeed, seem bent upon perpetuating the most unreasonable regulations that were obsolescent fifty years ago. Yet too great stress upon rules—upon "correctness"—is perilous. If the worst disease in copyediting is arrogance, the second worst is rigidity.

Fifth and finally, a copy editor must be curious, for it is curiosity that spurs him to awareness and to interest in even the dullest manuscript. If he learns a little from each book, he is a little more capable to edit the next. As his curiosity expands, so does his ability.

The ideal copy editor has these qualities and does these things. Could one ask for more? Yes. In special fields, such as science editing, juvenile editing, and reference-book editing, publishers ask for wider qualifications. Such employees are often called copy editors, but here I shall call them special editors and leave them out of account.

The professional copy editor, who sits at his desk with a manuscript planted squarely before him, is not superhuman. He is a humble man in a more or less humble job. Yet upon his shoulders lies the weight of centuries of learning. His calling is honorable, and he stands in line with the Scaligers and the Estiennes. The little marks he puts on paper are for the betterment of mankind.

BOB OSKAM

Bob Oskam is an author, free-lance editorial consultant, and literary agent. For several years he was an acquiring editor for Hawthorn Books and E. P. Dutton. Mr. Oskam is the coauthor (with Henry Calero) of *Negotiate the Deal You Want,* as well as coauthor-collaborator on several other published trade titles.

•   •   •

Sensible, practical, authoritative, Mr. Oskam's article, which originally appeared in *Winning Negotiations,* the newsletter of Advanced Management Reports, is a valuable, step-by-step delineation of the interaction between editor and author in the negotiation of a publishing contract. It follows a hypothetical project through the contract-negotiating stage and includes such vital areas of consideration and discussion as: laying the groundwork for the proposal in the publishing house, the personality factor between editor and author, sounding each other out on the expectations each has for the book, negotiating advance and royalty, negotiating the fine points of the "standard" contract, agreeing on advertising, publicity, promotion, and sales expectations. In short, it is a comprehensive review of the editor-author business relationship, a keystone in the *overall* relationship the editor and author will develop in the months and perhaps years ahead. The thrust of the article is direct negotiations between editor and author, though it does discuss how the process changes when the editor negotiates with an agent. This essay is a tool with which any editor can sharpen those all-important negotiating skills.

NEGOTIATING A PUBLISHING CONTRACT

THE PARTICIPANTS

The parties conducting a negotiation for a publishing contract are usually just two: the acquiring book editor and the author of the proposed book or his or her agent. From the editor's perspective, it makes a considerable difference which he's dealing with. Although there are any variety of personalities and levels of expertise to be found among agents, when dealing with an agent there is at least the expectation that the issues to be discussed will be clear to both parties. Each side will operate from a perspective that includes familiarity with industry convention; each side will have a sense of what the priority concerns are for the other side. It may well happen that both parties already have an established professional relationship. As often as not, they are on a first-name basis with each other. They will previously have discussed business in general terms; their relationship may be sufficiently long-established that they have previously negotiated contracts with each other.

If the acquiring editor negotiates directly with an author, the process can be quite different. Unless he's dealing with an author who has a background of experience in the industry or who's already been through several contract negotiations, there's a probable initial communications barrier of sorts. Before there can be an optimum discussion of issues between the two parties, the editor frequently has to explain what these issues are. A previously unpublished author is likely to have little sense of what the publishing process involves and consequently necessarily relies somewhat on information provided by the editor on how that process works. An intelligent author in this situation will make some effort to be independently informed. There are, after all, several references readily available detailing what publishing is generally all about and what the conventions and standard *caveats* are in negotiating a book contract. But surprisingly few unrepresented authors turn to these references. They more often just throw themselves upon the tender mercies of the spokesman with whom they are negotiating, trusting their own instincts to alert them to situations that might arise and work to compromise their interests. The disadvantages this can open an author to are self-evident.

For a sense of the negotiating process as it unfolds in relation to a contract for book publication, let's follow a hypothetical project through the contract negotiation stage. Let's assume author Julie Jordan has written a study of the interaction between alcohol and sex entitled *Love and Demon Rum.* Editor Ralph Jones has read the manuscript and decided he wants to acquire the book for his company, Better Books, Inc. Ms. Jordan, a first-time author, has no agent representing her. She managed to get her material to Mr. Jones via an acquaintance who works in the Better Books sales department.

LAYING THE GROUNDWORK

Before Mr. Jones can present Ms. Jordan with a proposed contract, he first has to win authorization from his superiors at Better Books to move to contract. In order to do that, he needs first to engage in something of a negotiation in-house. He has to sell the project to management's watchdogs in the editorial division. He has to describe the project in terms of content and packaging. He has to present convincing evidence of marketability. He has to project fairly accurately the cost factors involved. He has to answer satisfactorily whatever questions are raised on whether the book is worth taking on. In order to do so, Mr. Jones will almost certainly turn to Ms. Jordan for background and supporting material she is able to provide. In doing so he will play something of an ambiguous role. On the one hand he will be presenting himself as her confederate, acting in coordination with her as her representative before the company; on the other he will be sounding her out on her position as an opposite party in eventual bargaining sessions on contract terms. He needs to pin her down fairly nar-

rowly on financial expectations, because these affect his cost and
profit projections, which the company wants to evaluate before
giving the go-ahead for the contract to be negotiated. The effect
is that Mr. Jones is actually already negotiating with Ms. Jordan
before authorization to enter formally into contract negotiations
is granted. Were Ms. Jordan represented by an agent, the process
here would be virtually the same.

THE PERSONALITY FACTOR

Although Mr. Jones and Ms. Jordan are establishing a formally
defined professional relationship, a great deal hinges on the extent
to which they get along and like each other. Editor and author will
be working together over a period of several months, so it's to the
benefit of both that the relationship be pleasant. However, it's
important especially for Ms. Jordan that exchanges be friendly
from the very outset. She is, after all, dependent on Mr. Jones to
guide her through a negotiation situation that she is not familiar
with. Mr. Jones will, of course, have limits set on the extent to
which he can exercise discretion to influence circumstances in Ms.
Jordan's favor. Even so, he can work through areas of detail to win
or bar substantial advantages for her in the negotiation he conducts with her. He knows where loopholes or safeguards can be
inserted that can protect her interests. He knows where adjustments are possible that can affect her income opportunities one
way or the other.

Does this mean Ms. Jordan is best advised to assume a subservi-
ent role? Not at all. Ms. Jordan should realize she now has a firm
indication that *Love and Demon Rum* is considered a publishable,
marketable property. She has the option at any point up to the
actual signing of a contract to withdraw her manuscript for submission elsewhere. And she knows that Mr. Jones wants the book
—he's not just undertaking it as a favor to her. It is evidently
something that he sees as having potential for furthering his standing professionally. (If Mr. Jones is somewhat ambivalent about
rather than solidly behind the book, Ms. Jordan will probably have
a sense of that early on.) At the same time that Mr. Jones is
sounding her out on her expectations, she should be sounding him
out on company policies that will affect production and marketing

of her book. She should be pursuing a line of inquiry of her own that builds her confidence in Mr. Jones and Better Books and that leads to a better understanding of publishing in general. A publishing contract in the hand is worth at least two manuscripts under consideration, but only if it ultimately does meet needs that are priorities for the author. Ms. Jordan should be to-the-point and open about her needs. In pressing for her priorities, however, she is well-advised to refrain from an attitude that suggests or contributes to an adversary relationship with Mr. Jones. He is frankly in a position to undercut her priorities in ways she is not aware of, and probably will to some extent if she insists on treating him as an enemy.

You may wonder how Ms. Jordan can assure herself that Mr. Jones is dealing with her fairly. Basically she has to rely on the talent she has for recognizing honesty or dishonesty anywhere. She has to listen and watch for a consistency between words and actions. She has to evaluate Mr. Jones's apparent perception of her interests as an author. She has to trust her intuitive sense of ease or unease with him. And then she has to keep in mind that she has the opportunity in the actual contract negotiations to spell out certain arrangements she wants included and to question and ask to have defined any proposed point of inclusion she does not understand. She can also refer to books like *The Writer's Legal Guide* (by Tad Crawford) or *A Writer's Guide to Book Publishing* (by Richard Balkin) for useful impartial advice on protecting her own interests.

NEGOTIATING GENERAL TERMS

Once Better Books agrees with Mr. Jones that *Love and Demon Rum* is a project the house wants to take on, he will call Ms. Jordan to initiate the formal negotiations. The introductions have been made; both parties have already presented their general overview of the situation at hand in light of their respective primary objectives; both have reviewed the background against which they are operating. So in this first call, specific issues will be discussed.

Typically, the first issue discussed is money. How much of an advance is Better Books prepared to pay for the manuscript? How much money does Ms. Jordan want up front? Ms. Jordan and Mr.

Jones have necessarily already touched on this point. Probably
they've indicated sums to each other in terms of approximate
figures. Mr. Jones is clearly at something of an advantage. He will
have a knowledge of what is "realistic" in the case of a book like
Love and Demon Rum. The author is unlikely to have as clear a
sense of what she can realistically expect to get. In his preliminary
presentation to the company Mr. Jones will have won authorization to propose an advance up to a maximum figure he can offer
the author. As a matter of course, he will already have established
in his own mind what Ms. Jordan will accept. She may actually
have stated a minimum. Ideally, from his perspective, he'll have
an area of discretion between the authorization and acceptance
figures that he can use as leverage on Ms. Jordan. It does happen
fairly often that a company authorizes an advance figure lower
than what an author has named as the acceptable minimum. In
that case the editor has a rougher time of it.

For the sake of understanding what areas of leverage exist elsewhere for the editor, we'll suppose that Mr. Jones has been told
he may not offer more than a $7,500 advance and that Ms. Jordan
has indicated she considers $10,000 her minimum figure. What can
he do to clear this hurdle? The possibilities are numerous, including any or all of the following—and perhaps a couple more:

▶ He can simply gamble on the likelihood that Ms. Jordan will
   give in on the issue because of the fear of losing a chance at
   publication, a fear endemic among first-time authors. That is
   to say, he can put it in blunt terms of "take it or leave it."

▶ He can take advantage of the ambiguities of his position and
   slip around to the other side of the bargaining table as Ms.
   Jordan's confederate, working out possible counterproposals
   with her that might be tried to induce the company to raise
   its ante. At the same time, as company spokesman, he will be
   alert for a possible *quid pro quo* concession to offer the company as a carrot.

▶ He can try a ploy I've found successful on occasion—hit Ms.
   Jordan with an even lower figure than $7,500, say $5,000, so
   he can then psychologically lead her *up* to the authorized
   figure rather than remain focused on the difference *down* from
   $10,000.

▶ He can rely on the sense of rapport he's established with Ms. Jordan so that she comes to accede to the figure because it assures her of being guided through an often arcane process by someone she intuitively trusts and respects. Better the confidence of having a dedicated, capable editor working in partnership with you than the uncertainty attached to going to a "stranger."

▶ He can point to the company's reputation and marketing ability to convince Ms. Jordan that ultimately she will reap the greatest possible financial and prestige rewards through Better Books.

▶ He can table discussions for a time, pleading that consultation will be required for change in the figure from his side. Then he can let time and imagination work in his favor. In most cases, the author left dangling hasn't an alternate prospect to fall back on. If the editor simply calls once a week to reiterate "no new developments," the author will often give in out of fear that the entire project may be dropped if negotiations aren't concluded promptly. That does sometimes happen to authors whose projects are seen as "iffy."

▶ Mr. Jones can also play off any fear on Ms. Jordan's part that there may be another, similar project in the works somewhere else. Subject focuses are evident in the publishing industry, with similar ideas frequently being developed contemporaneously but independently at different houses. If the house were to discover that another house had a book on sex and alcohol under contract, Ms. Jordan's manuscript might suddenly have no appeal whatsoever for Better Books.

Whatever he does, the fact that his position as a professional makes him more aware of what's going on than is Ms. Jordan makes it likely that what concessions are forthcoming will be made from her side.

But Ms. Jordan does have a range of response she can rely on to try to get her way on this issue. The controlling factor, however, is the sense of risk she attaches to any of these and the degree she imagines and fears the possibility the deal may not go through if she is not acquiescent. Were she a best-selling name author, this shoe would be on the other foot, but in her case it's not. This contract is one Ms. Jordan considers her big break. Still, she may be able to work the following tactics to her advantage:

► She can try to engage Mr. Jones's sympathy and win support from him in his role as her spokesman and confederate. She can cite the value of her time, her expenses, her financial needs in general, her disappointment and the threat of disillusionment altogether. Although editors hear enough sob stories to make them skeptical, now and then every editor finds himself commiserating with an author he feels a liking for. Depending on Mr. Jones's in-house clout at Better Books, if motivated he might well be able to fight for and win the extra money for "his" author.

► She can play as much of a waiting game as she dares, indicating she's got to think it over and sort things out. If Mr. Jones really feels *Love and Demon Rum* will be a substantial success for any company with sense enough to sign it up—if he feels an alternative publisher could easily be located—he will probably make a push for the extra money.

► She can simply say $7,500 is unacceptable. However, if she plays the "take it or leave it" game, she has to realize that in this situation the risk is greater for her than for him. Other people are offering Mr. Jones manuscripts for publication all the time. This isn't his only project. It probably is her only promising prospect. But for the same reason noted just above, Mr. Jones may still be susceptible to this ploy.

► She can stress the sales potential and marketability of her book, the fact that she will prove a significant asset to the house. Because she has no established track record at this point, however, she has to keep in mind that this is likely to be purely speculative from Mr. Jones's point of view.

► She can accede with conditions. She can indicate readiness to give in on the issue, using that readiness as leverage for winning a return concession, either immediately or later. (The concessions that she can work for include possible commitments on the part of the publisher relative to publication date, minimum first printing, guaranteed promotional efforts, advertising budget, and/or special sales arrangements under which she can buy copies of the book at a greater than usual discount for resale through her own nonbook trade channels.)

It's best that she use the leverage immediately, or the threat implicit in conditional acquiescence—"otherwise I won't go along on this issue"—may become unbelievable.

Included in the general terms negotiated with the amount of advance moneys are the regular royalty rates and the division on income from licensing subsidiary publication rights (serialization, paperback reissue, book clubs, TV and film, foreign language editions, etc.). Arrangements here tend to be somewhat standardized within the industry, but Ms. Jordan is still well-advised to look after her own interests. Mr. Jones still has the same advantage over her.

NEGOTIATING THE FINE POINTS

The negotiations on the contract's financial terms may be concluded before a draft goes to the author. But once an oral agreement has been reached on the basic terms, a draft contract ought properly to be sent the author with all agreed-upon and proposed terms spelled out in detail. I always prefer sending out a contract with the money figures already in place. I feel it provides a subtle psychological advantage for the editor in negotiating the fine points that can still pose problems on the road to signing the contract. Besides that, authors tend to view resolution of the money issue as a prerequisite for considering a contract agreement, so inevitably they do not expect to be confronted with the document itself until such resolution. It could be advantageous for them to receive it earlier. They might discover areas of compromise they could play on in negotiating the money issue.

Virtually all publishers have preprinted contract forms with a multiplicity of "standard" provisions spelled out in minute detail anticipating a host of possibilities, some of which are fairly improbable, some of which are integral to the relationship between publisher and author but will still read like Greek to the average first-time author. Here and there are blanks for indicating obvious variables like name and date, title, advance amount and payment schedule, royalty rates, and subsidiary rights income division. Everything else is precast "boilerplate." Paragraph upon paragraph describes obligations and responsibilities of the contracting parties

in a wide range of eventualities. Issuing as it does from the publisher, it is to be expected that it reflects the publisher's point of
view rather more than the author's. While the preprinted forms
suggest to the inexperienced author that there is little room for
negotiation on fine-print particulars, there are always points where
modification is possible. Significant provisions in the boilerplate do
reflect points of necessity from the publisher's perspective, however, and if Ms. Jordan questions or seeks to amend these, she will
be told firmly that these points are not negotiable.

Ms. Jordan, in our situation here, has to feel her way through
the contract to some extent, particularly if she hasn't thought to
check one of the references previously cited as available. Even if
she has, she realizes that she still has to rely on Mr. Jones to be
honest and open in his responses to questions she raises. Whatever
she does, she ought not refrain from asking questions lest she
appear ignorant. The truth is that in this situation she *is* ignorant.
And the only way not to fall completely victim to that is to ask
questions and listen carefully to the responses. If Mr. Jones is
immediately truculent or on the defensive, that will provide her a
clue to whether he is as trustworthy as she hopes he is. If he
explains the rationale or effect of contract fine print patiently and
clearly, she will find herself reassured. She will feel, and probably
correctly, that he is not opposed to helping her as he can with
points that she finds problematic, suggesting possible amendments
that he knows are acceptable to his management and that will
protect Ms. Jordan's interests somewhat better.

If Mr. Jones particularly looks forward to working with Ms.
Jordan professionally and enjoys the rapport he feels established
between them, he is very likely already to have modified some of
the negotiable boilerplate to her advantage. He's on fairly safe
ground so long as he doesn't try to set new company precedents
with Ms. Jordan's contract and stays within the guidelines generally established within the company. He may even insert a supplementary clause to cover some point of import to Ms. Jordan that
would otherwise not be covered. (Many authors are so focused on
what *is* in the contract fine print that they fail to consider what
the contract overlooks or deliberately omits.) As long as he takes
care not to compromise company interests in areas of vital import,
he's unlikely to get into trouble. He can always offer as defense that
the author asked for or insisted on the change, secure in the

knowledge that this explanation will routinely be accepted nine times out of ten in areas that are not strict priority for the company.

The tactics available to either Mr. Jones or Ms. Jordan when negotiating contract fine points are pretty much the same as those available when negotiating money issues. Mr. Jones remains at something of an advantage, but Ms. Jordan has some tactics available to her than she can use to good effect. Furthermore, Mr. Jones knows that the completion of contract negotiations marks a beginning more than it does an end. He will as result of the agreement be working with Ms. Jordan over the period of the next several months at least. Since he prefers a comfortable relationship of mutual respect and trust, he will tend to avoid compromising Ms. Jordan's interest in any fashion that will become painfully evident to her later and impede subsequent cooperative endeavor.

USING A LITERARY AGENT

Had Ms. Jordan engaged a literary agent to negotiate for her, the process would have proceeded differently. The agents' network of contacts throughout the publishing industry would have Mr. Jones dealing more immediately with his possible concern that the project might be sold elsewhere if terms are not satisfactory on the author's side. The agent would have a clear enough sense of publishing convention to sort out the boilerplate provisions susceptible to modification in the author's interest. He ought to know what supplementary terms to add to the contract on behalf of the author. For Mr. Jones the negotiation would be simpler in the sense that he'd be dealing with a party speaking the language of the industry and understanding the company's operation and needs. It would be more difficult by virtue of having to deal with a more informed opponent likely to be more hard-nosed in insisting on points of priority that might conflict with the publisher's preferred policy.

So in Ms. Jordan's position she'd have been better off to have an agent negotiate for her, right? Well, possibly—but not necessarily. For one thing, the agent intrudes a separate set of priorities into the process—his own. That can sometimes result in conflicts that might otherwise not have arisen that can work to Ms. Jordan's detriment. The agent might not go over the contract as carefully as Ms. Jordan herself would, odd as this might seem. Although they are in the minority, fortunately, some agents are concerned primarily with the major money issues, which affect their eventual income, and don't as attentively consider other factors, that can work a hardship on an author. A best-selling author friend of mine who is represented by a long-established agent recently confessed that her agent had allowed a very restrictive option clause to stand in a contract that effectively ties the author to a publishing house she fervently wishes to dissociate from. Besides that, every house's contract has its own hidden pitfalls. An editor negotiating with an agent is less likely to warn of those, figuring the protection of the author's interests is the agent's responsibility. In my own work, I've several times alerted unrepresented authors with whom I felt a strong sense of rapport to a fine-print royalty computation pitfall that agents with whom I negotiated contracts completely overlooked. So Ms. Jordan could actually come out better on her own than with an agent. If you ask what the odds are on that, however, I'd have to confess she'd probably be more secure if she worked through a conscientious agent.

NANCY EVANS

Nancy Evans, a writer and editor, is coauthor of *How to Get Happily Published* (New American Library, 1978). For *Publishers Weekly,* she wrote a series called "Who Does What in Publishing," in which this article appeared. She has also written for *The Writer, Ms.,* and *Family Circle,* among other publications. Ms. Evans is managing director of Sensible Solutions, Inc., a consulting firm that specializes in marketing midlist books. Along with John Leonard, she is cohost of *First Edition,* a TV show about books, sponsored by the Book-of-the-Month Club. She is a member of the Authors Guild, the National Book Critics Circle, and PEN.

•   •   •

Line editing is what some authors complain they get none of. Editors who actually put pencil to paper to affect matters of substance, style, and organization are, rumor has it, a vanishing breed. Perhaps, though, the breed is not disappearing but simply self-effacing. Line editors, it seems clear from research, are characteristically reluctant to emerge into the limelight for fear of distracting attention from their authors, and as a result, their work is little known and their praises are only privately sung.

The five line editors interviewed here—who get high marks from the writers they work with and from their peers in publishing—share several traits besides a tendency to downplay their role in the creative process. Optimists all, perfectionists all, each has the ability to make writers draw on resources they never knew they could command.

LINE EDITORS:
THE RIGOROUS PURSUIT
OF PERFECTION

ANNE FREEDGOOD—FINDING THE SOFT SPOTS

Most editors agree that it takes two to edit: an editor who believes that a good book can be made better and a writer who is serious about his or her prose. With a lesser writer or a nonwriter of the celebrity/public-figure stripe, an editor is reduced to one part English teacher—correcting grammar, writing "awk" in the margins—and one part rewrite expert—putting a fresh piece of paper into the typewriter and redrafting whole sections. This word-processing role is one that the editors we talked with try their best to avoid. It is not what they mean when they talk about "editing." Editing occurs when you're working *with* a writer, not *for* a writer. For Anne Freedgood, executive editor of Vintage Books and Modern Library at Random House, a successful editor-writer relationship is really a matter of trust.

Since trust can't very well develop between two people who don't respect and believe in each other, Freedgood is exceptionally careful in selecting which writer she will take on. She feels that she must love a manuscript (she is reluctant to consider proposals on the ground that there's too much room for irreconcilable differences to develop between the time a proposal is submitted and the time the finished manuscript is delivered), and that she and the writer must have a shared vision of what should be done in that manuscript's best interests.

"I try to establish the fact that I see the book basically the same way that the author does," explains Freedgood. "Because there's no point in trying to turn a book into something the author doesn't visualize it as. So if the writer says, 'Oh, no, the end is my favorite part,' when I don't think it's convincing, then I'm not the right editor for the book. It's better to know that at the outset than to get into problems later."

Freedgood is determined to avoid imposing her own ideas on a writer's work. When an editor finds herself doing that, she says, "it means you're not in the writer's world. You're not understanding what the writer's trying to say. It's like drama critics who review a play not for what it is but because it isn't what they think a play about that subject should have been. Book critics are guilty of that too. But the editor's job is to stick with the author on what it is that the author wants to do, and to think that it's worth doing.

"A writer who listens to your every comment as if you were God," Freedgood explains, "well, that makes it much too scary to be an editor. But people who are interested in writing, not just in getting published, will put up a fight, even in the beginning of their careers, if they don't agree. And they should."

Manuscript and writer having been screened and accepted, Freedgood will read the manuscript a second time after revisions have been made and a third time if another set of revisions is needed. But that's her limit. "If you read a book too many times, particularly one by an inexperienced writer, you go totally dead. It's very hard to tell whether a point has been made or not because you think it was made somewhere, but where?" To avoid losing perspective, Freedgood, like most editors, discourages authors from submitting material chapter by chapter. Although hand-holding may prove helpful to the writer in getting the book done, it prevents the editor from ever experiencing the book as a whole.

As Freedgood describes the line editing process, "It's finding a place that's soft and then raising the question to the author. You might say, 'I'm not convinced here. I don't see how you got from here to there. What are you trying to say in this paragraph? The order here is confusing. Are you sure you shouldn't introduce this factor before that factor? This is where you lost me. This is where I got bored. This, I think, you've already covered.' You find the confused places and then you ask the writer what he can do about them. You don't go and rewrite them."

A now classic example of a soft spot came to light as Freedgood edited Mary Gordon's first novel, *Final Payments*. What Freedgood couldn't swallow was that any woman in the 1970s would embark on a sexual life without doing something about birth control. Even if the cloistered heroine wouldn't think of it herself, argued Freedgood, certainly one of her friends would clue her in. And so, at Freedgood's suggestion—simply stated, "Really, Mary, this is silly"—Gordon wrote one of the scenes (Isabel's visit to the gynecologist) for which the book received critical acclaim.

Talking of another scene that Freedgood felt would not be convincing to the reader, she notes, "I just kept Mary at it until she got it clear." The significant word here is "just," for it indicates most editors' attitude toward their contribution to the finished product. As in the fine art of the Socratic dialogue, where the lessons are not taught by the teacher but discovered by the student, editors raise the provocative, leading questions; writers go home to follow the leads where they will.

On occasion the leads can cause a marked shift in direction. Take, for example, Elizabeth Hardwick's recommendation that Gordon change her novel from the third person to the first. "I wish I could say that I had said it," Freedgood says with a smile, adding, "Sometimes it comes to you while you're reading the book and you'll say, 'But you've ended with what should be the beginning,' which is what I did once with a novel. Of course, if the author doesn't agree with you, that's the end of the brilliant idea, although you may get the totally erroneous feeling that you are writing a book." Freedgood laughs. "Then you say, No, No. You just thought of something to help somebody else. You haven't written that book at all."

JAMES D. LANDIS—MATTERS OF TASTE

First to admit that editing is a tough way to make a living despite what myths of glamour may suggest, William Morrow's senior vice-president and editorial director, Jim Landis, ushers through the largest list of titles of any of the editors we interviewed: thirty-six per year, compared to an average of ten.

Landis's office hours, like those of most editors, are devoted to making and receiving phone calls, checking jacket designs, page proofs, catalogue copy, courting and consoling writers, arguing with agents. "I think there's a theory in publishing," Landis speculates, "that editing is, if not counterproductive, at least not as

productive as hustling. You're not going to make money editing
the way you will make money discovering someone who needs to
be edited. That is the job the publisher is most interested in—
soliciting and reading and acquiring manuscripts."

Still, Landis regularly carries six manuscripts home in his duffel
bag at night, some of them under consideration (twenty may arrive
in one morning), but many of them books already acquired. If five
manuscripts under contract arrive the same day, which is possible,
given the size of his list, Landis feels compelled to attend to them
all immediately. After all, to each author his or her book is all-
important. And Landis, a sometime writer himself, appreciates
that. The upshot is that he frequently edits more than one manuscript at a time, a practice not followed by many editors.

Nor do most editors begin editing as soon as they pick up the
manuscript, but Landis skips the typical lay-of-the-land first reading, and he feels his method works best for him, having reached
that conclusion after reading manuscripts as many as twelve times
in the course of editing them when he first started as a jittery
compulsive kid. Dynamo-style, Landis approaches each manuscript with a battery of three writing instruments. There's the blue
pen for copyediting—"I did copyediting once, so I tend to edit bad
grammar and misspellings automatically"—and for making notes
in a steno notebook (each book gets its own notebook). Then
there's the red pen, to emphasize comments in the notebook either
for Landis's attention or for the writer's (the notebook will be used
to guide discussion when Landis sits down with the author to go
through the manuscript). And finally there's a mundane pencil for
making queries in the manuscript's left-hand margins. (Landis
confesses he can come up with quite a few queries and thinks he
set world records with a 1,200-page manuscript which averaged
six queries a page, bringing in a grand total of 7,000-plus questions.
How did the author handle it? He listened, very patiently, acknowledged the correctness of some of the points Landis was
raising, made very few of the changes, and then in a whirlwind of
author's alterations followed most of Landis's other suggestions on
his own terms.)

Most editors encounter an author who says no from time to
time. And when a writer says no to a recommendation, there is
very little an editor can do or should do, Landis feels. "I have a
rule," he says. "You ask once. You don't hammer away unless you

really have an objection. Your job is to point out what you feel. If the author doesn't agree, you go on to the next query." If the passage the editor criticized and the author refused to change is eventually held up to ridicule by reviewers, many an editor will feel vindicated. But no matter what he's thinking, says Landis, an editor should never say I told you so to the writer. "The point is, it's bad to talk about right or wrong when it comes to matters of taste. And once you get away from split infinitives and dangling participles, that's what editing involves—matters of taste."

Landis refuses to discuss his contributions to specific books—insisting all credit belongs to the authors—but he does stretch his standard operating procedure. Like any informed reader, he says, he will note the obvious snags in the texture of the book—an inconsistency in character, a climax that comes too soon or too late—like a dentist finding the possible cavity and putting a question mark on the picture. Beyond that, there's fine tuning which Landis calls the editing of language. "You scrutinize every word in relation to every other word," he explains. "You want to see whether the language works. For instance, the English language tends to break down rhythmically into triads. People tend to write in threes. 'He took off his hat. He took off his coat. And then he sat down.' Now if you're aware that the rhythm is very often in threes, you might realize that it's this triadic pattern which is driving you crazy and preventing the book from flowing in the right way. If you're aware, you point it out." It's the editor who is aware of the greatest number of things happening in a book, Landis feels, who is most able to be a helpful critic.

Says Landis of his working sessions with writers: "You say this is wrong only when you can't say this is right. It's as if you're supposed to stamp everything: This is right. A lot of good editing is acknowledging that the thing has been done well."

Landis likes to solve problems right away ("If I think a word is wrong, we sit there and dream up the right one; it may take an hour"), although obviously if an entire chapter needs to be over-hauled, the writer will have to take it home to work on.

What if the problem is tone? "If it's flat-out inappropriate—a tone of Euripidean gloom for a social comedy—there's a real problem," Landis admits. "But if it's a matter of the tone being off, the editor has to put his fingers into the book and work on the language. So you'll take one sentence and ask yourself, Why is it off? By analyzing one sentence or paragraph, doing a microcosmic job, you can help the writer revise."

In Landis's view, the questions the writer desperately wants answered, and the questions the editor must respond to, are: What is it like to read this book? Does the writing work as an exciting reading experience? Where are my loose ends? "That's one thing writers like most," says Landis, "the editing of loose ends. They want them tied up because they know that very often they lose control over a book. That's a great fear they have. That's why when they get close to an editor they tend to become dependent, because the editor is usually the first reader they trust to tell them what their book is like."

JEANNETTE HOPKINS—TOUGH TASKMASTER

Jeannette Hopkins is tough. Balderdash to allowing the writer to have the last word. Hopkins stays in there fighting long after most other editors would concede. She does not simply pose polite questions: Don't you think we could be a bit clearer here? She puts a writer through a grilling that's reminiscent of cross-examination during doctoral orals; giving the right answer is not enough—you must defend your answer, citing sources.

The analogy is apt because Hopkins's writers are primarily academics in search of a wider audience. An editor for thirty-three years, and now director of the Wesleyan University Press, Hopkins was never interested in doing the frivolous, commercial book. Her commitment to the serious book, the book of ideas, and her less than enthusiastic interest in balancing her list with more popular titles led her in 1973 to set up shop as what she calls an "independent editor." She has created her own job, and it's virtually unique in the business.

What Hopkins set out to do was to get hired on a one-book basis by different publishers. That way she could do the books she wanted—if house X didn't want one, she'd take it to house Y—and she wouldn't have to lose any author because of lack of enthusiasm by any one publisher for that author's next book. To her surprise, the three houses she approached—McGraw-Hill, Pantheon, and Stein and Day—chosen for their different styles, accepted her immodest proposal.

She then asked literary lawyer Harriet Pilpel to draw up a contract to cover the unprecedented arrangement. Hopkins's responsibilities included bringing in a book, working with the author on the manuscript, reviewing the copyediting and sample pages, writing jacket copy, seeing proofs, checking the index, consulting on publicity—in short, doing everything an in-house editor normally does. In addition, she would have use of copying machines and the mail room, and expenses (travel, phone, entertainment) would be paid. In turn, the publishers agreed to pay her an advance against a percentage (usually 2 percent–5 percent) of royalties. Hopkins is *not* an agent, she emphasized throughout the interview. Although many of her writers are unagented and Hopkins does in effect place their work, her financial contract is completely separate from the author's.

On the whole, she explains, her advances are modest (sometimes 10 percent of the author's advance or a flat fee), and except in the case of a best-seller, Hopkins figures she's cheaper than an in-house editor since she's paid only for what she produces—"I'm not paid for going to meetings or for the books I reject," she comments, "and I pay my own overhead."

With a three-year stipend from Harper & Row (where she was an editor for nine years) to edit the books she had previously signed up there and one-book contracts from the three houses she approached, Hopkins then added Yale University Press to her list, and during the first six years she was out on her own, she made deals with a total of twelve and edited sixty titles.

Hopkins frequently begins work with her authors at the proposal stage, often calling for three or four drafts. Then, once a manuscript comes in, revisions on it are extensive as well. To a well-known and much-published political scientist, Hopkins sent a ten-page single-spaced critique outlining the main thematic problems with his manuscript (she notes minor problems on the typescript itself). The letter moves from matters of organization ("There is not a pervasive, consistent thread of argument that the reader can resist or welcome or question along the way. I wish the thread were more clearly drawn") to matters of style ("Some professional language while understandable nevertheless lacks vividness, simplicity, and strength and, therefore, fails to interest or engage the reader. I have in mind a word like 'interact' ") to specific criticisms of each chapter ("I expected rather more far-reaching insights here"). Although criticism from Hopkins is apt to be more severe than that most editors are willing to give, she is careful to soften the blows with diplomatic words: "perhaps," "I am inclined to think," "sometimes," "in my view."

In her scrupulous way, Hopkins responds not only to what is present in a manuscript but to what is *not* there. Often she will draw up what amounts to a semester's heavy reading list designed to challenge the thesis, to make the writer clarify, if not alter, his or her own position. Meanwhile, Hopkins herself will be reading around in the appropriate literature to check the facts, to bone up on the field so she can carry her half of the dialogue. "It's like going to college," she says; it's one of the pleasures of editing nonfiction; and it may demand more time per book than some editors spend on their entire list.

Having experienced the Hopkins total-immersion technique, Christopher Lasch—author of *The Culture of Narcissism*—now refuses to be published without her. Hopkins's account of her involvement with Lasch's work may indicate why.

"To begin with," she recounts, "I read the book in the first place —which is something that doesn't always happen these days. Unfortunately, too often secretaries and editorial assistants are doing the work for editors. So I read the manuscript, wrote him a fifteen-page letter, going through chapter by chapter, making comments and suggestions. One chapter did not feel particularly strong, so there I asked, had he read this book and that book. And we argued about his position on women."

Arguing is not the same as imposing ideas, Hopkins points out. Still, she wasn't sure how Lasch would take it: "He's very independent." Well, he did revise according to her suggestions, but with the delivery of the revised manuscript came a note asking that she please not make any more suggestions. "But I did have a few more"—she laughs—and Lasch acted on them.

MARIAN S. WOOD—LESS IS BETTER

Marian S. Wood, executive editor at Holt, Rinehart and Winston, wonders if line editing is being supplemented by what she calls typewriter editing—thanks to the instant book and the nonbook. "People who describe themselves as typewriter editors are doing the kinds of books I'm not interested in," she says. "When I'm committed to a book it's because the writer has a quality, a resonance that should make it unnecessary to put the manuscript through the typewriter. I never do it. When I was a junior editor I had to do it because I was working with nonwriters. There's nothing flatter than an editor's prose."

Less is better is Marian Wood's cardinal rule. A good line editor does not rewrite the manuscript; she provides answers to the question: What's wrong? Wood's answers usually take three to four single-spaced pages. This character is flat, she may say. This one doesn't make sense. You lose your tension here. There are too many peripheral characters early on. I don't understand the point of this part of the plot. I think you may be repeating yourself here.

Since her emphasis is on what's wrong, not on what's right, her phrasing of criticism is crucial. "The worst thing," says Wood, "is for the author to cave in. So you preface your criticism by saying, 'This is the way I read it. I'm not God. I could be wrong.' And when I put a change in the manuscript, I'll preface that by saying, 'I put this in to show you what I think is wrong, not that this change is definitely right.' "

Different writers need different things from an editor. And it's the editor's job to adjust to the writer, not the writer's to adjust to the editor. "Some writers use you as a sounding board," Wood explains. "Others are perfectionists and won't show you anything but polished prose. Some give you a rough draft. And I mean a rough draft. The only time I might lay down a ground rule is with someone who isn't a real writer. I'll have it in the contract that they'll work in pieces to make sure they're on the right track. There's nothing worse than having the whole manuscript come in unacceptable."

Rhoda Lerman, most recently author of *Eleanor,* is one writer who works in pieces, not because she needs to but because she wants to. "She'll send me in a batch of pages and they're not even numbered." Wood has been with her on three books and talks like a delighted parent about her progress. "To watch the development of a writer like Rhoda is mind-boggling. Rhoda had decided to coauthor a nonfiction book about Eleanor Roosevelt. Now Rhoda's not someone who can write nonfiction, but she insisted. She sent in a section and I said, 'Rhoda, I don't want to discourage you but . . .' " There's no way to force an idea or approach on a writer who's worth her salt. But there most certainly is a way of skillfully encouraging them to come over to your side—the goal being that when they do come around they'll have the distinct impression that they've come up with a totally original idea.

A few months later, Lerman wrote: "Okay, I'll do a first-person fiction account," and thus the idea for *Eleanor* was born. "She brought in the first chapter," continues Wood, "which is now the middle, and I swooned. She's a very serious writer. When I say something is flat, she'll go right at it."

Wood sees Lerman as an example of the kind of writer who is now creating a renaissance in fiction, which in turn is revitalizing the quality of editorial life. As editors point out again and again, great editing is not possible without great books to edit, particularly great works of fiction. Happily, though, many writers working today are dealing with fundamental moral issues and looking at the novel as a form of communication *and* art, convinced that the two are not mutually exclusive.

"I see nothing wrong with a book reaching a large number of literate Americans," Wood declares. "After all, Dickens sold to 'ordinary' people. So you have to ask yourself what the hell happened with fiction? I think in the '60s there was a lot of sterile prose that did not speak to people's lives. It wasn't simply that people didn't have the time to read. It was that the writers themselves weren't taking enough time. I think they're taking that time now, and they're addressing important issues. They're asking: What does this relationship mean to me, to me and my father, to me and my children, to me and the world? What would it have been like to go through Eleanor Roosevelt's travails? Do they have meaning for people today? Yes, because the writer addresses the fact that the old roles are no longer acceptable, but the new roles are still very strained."

If serious books take time for the writer, they also take time for the editor. Wood handles ten to twelve titles a year. Although she has earned a reputation as a great line editor, she figures she spends only 5 percent of her time actually editing manuscripts. "That's because," she explains, "to be honest and fair to the author I have to spend most of my time coordinating things and seeing to it that everything goes through on schedule. In fact, that's the only area where the author should really depend upon you—for jacket design, catalogue copy, the timing of pub date, and the like. But for an editor to act like the prima donna and make the writer dependent on her, that's terrible. It's not your book. You are not the person to take the credit."

The real skill in line editing, Wood elaborates, involves the subtle change, the small change that does not violate the author's style but results in a discernible improvement. "To play a sentence so that you change one small word and it's done. What an ear and head it takes to come up with the author's style. To be able to do that it's got to be that you've been raised reading books. I can't think of any other way to explain it."

PAT STRACHAN—COMPULSION FOR PERFECTION

"The function of editing is to discover what the writer is trying to do," says Pat Strachan, executive editor at Farrar, Straus & Giroux, who apprenticed to Robert Giroux for three years. "And as soon as you determine that, you try to help him or her to do it a little bit better—in the book as a whole and sentence by sentence. As an editor, it's your job to notice what's not clear. You're the only objective reader other than the copy editor before the book gets published. That's the importance of the role. A writer's spouse or good friend knows more about the writer than the words convey, and the editor knows very little other than what the words convey."

Strachan is as perfectly clear about how she goes about performing her function. "When the manuscript comes in, I read it once and sit on my hands and lock up all my pencils. The first reading is an attempt to read as anyone would read, not as an editor would. So large things may bother me as I turn the pages, but if I don't remember them by the time I'm finished, then perhaps they didn't bother me enough to require change.

"The communication with the writer at this point is basically positive. After all, if one is working on the book, one most likely admires it. And it may be the last chance you have to praise the writer. Because after the second reading, all the questions start coming. It's unproductive to be negatively critical if you haven't yet expressed your good feelings about the book.

"Also, I prefer not to make any sweeping definitive statements because on the second reading, which is the nitty-gritty ten-page-per-hour reading, I may find that some of my first impressions were invalid or that they're simply very complicated and must be approached gingerly. That's the point at which I start making specific suggestions, after thinking them over carefully. I have the usual tag system for queries. If something is wrong, I just cross it out and make it right. In any case, I discuss it with the writer.

"I think an inexperienced writer's main faults are overwriting and overexplaining," notes Strachan, "whether it be using too many adverbs or being unnecessarily graphic. Their didactic strain tends to put the reader off. An accomplished writer really doesn't underestimate his audience. One needn't say how a character said something, for example; one need only say that he said it. It's a matter of showing rather than telling."

Editing poetry, which Strachan also does, calls on a different set of intellectual muscles. Strachan's poets include Derek Walcott, Thom Gunn, and Seamus Heaney. Her main concern with their work, she says, is punctuation. "Although our copyediting department is spectacular, it would be impertinent to ask them to punctuate a poem correctly because the meaning and the music interact so intricately that one really has to discuss it with the poet. It's interesting: some poets care about punctuation tremendously; some have to be coaxed to consider it. When there's an unconventional syntactical structure, the punctuation can indicate what modifies what. Every once in a while there's a straining for rhyme with a dangling modifier—which is a no, no, no. And unless you were absolutely familiar with what the poet is trying to do, you might not even notice there's a dangler. But another rhyme will have to be found. I get along with the poets I work with well enough so that they can say, 'It must do,' back to me. I might argue a little bit. With poets I almost never edit for content."

Queried about the effects of her work, Strachan responds with the traditional line editor's disclaimer. "I'm of the opinion that a good book is not going to be made great by an editor," answers Strachan. "A good book can be made better and a great book can be made greater. It's only a polishing process. It's after all the writer's book. So he always wins. As important as the reader is, the writer is more important. I think E. B. White in *Elements of Style* said that a true writer plays to an audience of one. And usually he really does, and one has to understand that. It's what makes each book special."

If editors are reluctant to take credit for work they actually perform, it must be a relief to talk about handling the work of writers like John McPhee and Tom Wolfe, since in these cases the "Aw, gosh, I really did nothing" pronouncement is absolutely true. For writers of the highest caliber, Strachan considers herself nothing more than a glorified expediter.

But glorified expediter or hard-working editor, a line editor's real satisfaction derives from her own compulsion to improve the improvable. "It's a compulsion to strive for as much perfection as you can possibly attain in a book," says Strachan of the primary motive in performing the job. "Whether it matters in the long run, in terms of sales—probably not. Whether it matters in terms of the immortality of the book—definitely not. I'm sure Dickens and Shakespeare didn't have anybody like me around. Maybe someone wishes *Bleak House* had been cut in half. On the other hand, it hasn't been, and the book has survived. One can't be too self-important about the role."

All this self-effacing behavior must have its limits, and finally, sweet relief, Strachan admits that, yes, sometimes she very definitely feels needed. Quick on the heels comes the classic but. "But," Strachan qualifies, "I don't like the image of a Maxwell Perkins who makes a writer. And I'm sure he didn't engender that image himself. He'd probably be shocked to hear himself classified as a virtual co-writer."

Like all the editors we talked with, Strachan gives much of the credit for her ability to line edit to the house she works for. Not only did the house give her editing guidelines, it encourages her to take the time to edit. At Random House, Freedgood says it's the meetingless environment that's conducive to editing—Landis's sentiments exactly about Morrow. As for Marian Wood, she cites the fact that most of the people at Holt have been there for years; they know how to work together well; it makes life easier for her.

Of Farrar, Straus & Giroux, Strachan says: "There is a tradition of line editing here. And undoubtedly there always will be because the younger people learn from the older people. I think at other houses there is often an acquisitions editor who does the acquiring and an assistant who does the actual editing. Perhaps there are books that aren't edited at all, and I'm not too quick to criticize that. But the point is that here the house allows the time so that when a manuscript comes in it is not assumed that it will be rushed off to production. If I worked for a house where that was the expectation, I might do it now and then. But I'm glad I don't have to."

RAYANNA SIMONS

Rayanna Simons, a writer and free-lance editor, spent four years as first reader for Macmillan.

●   ●   ●

Who reads the unsolicited manuscripts that come pouring "over the transom" into publishers' offices? Does *anyone* read these unasked for —often unwelcomed—manuscripts by unknown writers? Someone did, until recently. That someone was called a first reader or, less classily, the slush pile reader. Did the first reader ever find the Great American Novel in the slush pile before going mad or blind? Did *anything* ever get published that was found in the slush pile? For the answers, read Rayanna Simons's uncommonly witty account, written especially for this anthology, of her career as a slush pile reader. It will make you laugh, but it will open your eyes to the difficulty of ever being published in this way. Today the reading of the slush pile is more haphazard, depending on the whim of editors and editorial assistants whose eye may be caught by what looks like an interesting manuscript. The slush pile has one very valuable purpose: it is a great training ground for the aspiring editor to gain experience, to learn how bad bad writing can be, and how different and exciting something of promise can be. Like panning for gold, every once in a great while the slush pile reader came up with a genuine twenty-four-carat nugget, and it could mean the start of a career as an editor and a way out from under the slush pile.

SLUSH

Slush . . . Soft mud . . . brought to the surface by the trampling
. . . refuse grease and fat from cooking . . . trashy and usu.
cheaply sentimental material (as in a book, newspaper, or film):
RUBBISH, DRIVEL, MUSH.

Webster's Third New
International Dictionary

Several years ago I was offered the job of first reader in the Adult
Trade Book Division of Macmillan Publishing. I was peculiarly
qualified for the position: I was a writer, slightly manqué; I had
spent years as a free-lance reader for magazines, television, movie
companies, and paperback houses; I had an interdisciplinary
M.A., a warm heart, and a dangerous tendency to look on the
brighter side of things. I also believed, with Aldous Huxley, that
it takes just as much work to write a bad book as a good one, and
that whoever made the effort deserved, at least, a kind word—even
if the kindest words one could muster were "please learn to spell,
punctuate, construct a sentence, think coherently, find some other
way of making a living." I also cherished the pre-Copernican belief
that the written word was very nearly sacrosanct and that countless unsung Miltons, Prousts, Faulkners, or Joyces were out there,
somewhere, waiting for the light of *my* recognition to shine upon
them. In other words, I was perfect for the job: an educated
masochist in the throes of advanced megalomania.

My reception was unusually cordial, albeit, I thought, a little
shifty-eyed. There was, I was told, a Problem; nothing serious, of
course, but nonetheless . . . A large "backlog" of unread "material" had "accumulated," with which the Trade Division was
unable to cope. All that was necessary was to look at it, see that
it got the proper form rejection letter, and return it to the poor
noodle who had sent it. That small obstacle overcome, I could then
proceed to more meaningful tasks: reading manuscripts for the
editorial staff and delivering myself of Solomonesque judgments.

There might, my inductor continued gaily, eyes glued to the ceiling, just might possibly be something I might find worth reading and calling to the attention of the editor in chief, though not bloody likely. However, you never can tell. . . .

The "accumulation," I discovered, was one that would have caused the Collier brothers great rejoicing. Too late I recalled the dreadful fate of Fulgence Tapir in the Preface to *Penguin Island:*

The walls of the study, the floor, and even the ceiling were loaded with overflowing bundles, pasteboard boxes swollen beyond measure, boxes in which were compressed an innumerable multitude. . . . I beheld in admiration mingled with terror the cataracts of erudition that threatened to burst forth . . . like a waterfall on a mountainside in April. . . . Swamped up to the knees . . . Fulgence Tapir grew pale with fright.

"What a mass of art!" he exclaimed.

Three months and two visits to the ophthalmologist later, some semblance of order had been established, but at (to me) a dreadful price. Like a demented termite, I had plowed through a Chichén Itzá of manuscripts, letters, and first chapters. There were single poems written on grubby scraps of paper with PRINT THIS scrawled at the top. There were ponderous doctoral dissertations, gouty with academese; there were countless stories of maiming and miscarriage (of all kinds, including justice), frequently handwritten and accompanied by gory newspaper clippings. There were hundreds of letters beginning, "This is going to make *you* a bundle," followed by long, lurid tales heavy with incest, rape, dark practices, Communist perfidy, and diabolism.

There were letters (accompanied, of course, by many pages of manuscript) from widows threatening to sell the ancestral manse in order to pay a vanity press to publish the diaries of late, unsung husbands; there were self-help books from people who'd obviously not read their own work; there were cookbooks that began: "My son, Junior, and my friends think it is time I shared my cooking secrets [lots of Cool Whip, Miracle Whip, and Jiff] with the world." There were huge bundles of paper tied with rope, works quite beloved of their authors, rich in obscenity, bigotry, injustice-collecting, despair, and religious mania. There were almost illiterate, heartbreaking autobiographies from incarcerated felons demanding justice and/or prison reform. There were fumbling, agonized stories from Vietnam veterans trying to purge themselves

of obsessive memories, guilt, and confusion. There were crazed
science-fiction fantasies and tales of abduction by extraterrestrials.
There were letters that began: "Dear Sir or Madem: I have wrote
a book . . ." There were stories of autistic and mongoloid children;
there were heroic accounts of overcoming cancer by chewing
kitchen matches. It was a cross-section of the ills of an entire
society, a horrendous mass confessional with just one (now)
stringy-haired, blurry-eyed, frockless female priest in residence.

Then there were the phone calls. The all-time favorite, recol-
lected in tranquillity, went something like this:

CALLER: Do you publish books?
READER: Yes . . .
CALLER: I'm a manic-depressive.
READER: Oh. Have you written a book?
CALLER: No, I've been too depressed. But they're changing my
medication. . . .

Each day I dug myself out of a terminal moraine of human
misery and ineptitude, and each morning discovered that it was far
from terminal: for every truckload which went bye-bye, another
arrived to take its place. *Miss Lonelyhearts* now read like *Rebecca
of Sunnybrook Farm.* In remote corners of the U.S. (and Canada
and England and India and etc.), people were sitting in libraries,
closets, trailer camps, cells, tract houses, university dorms, and
packing crates, writing books and sending them to *me.*

But in every thousand or more manuscripts there was *something.* There was no discernible pattern, nor any predictability as
to when something interesting or promising would surface, but it
did happen. From the avalanche of cries, threats, and assaults
upon one's consciousness, leaping over the barricade of form rejec-
tions and boundless ennui, came an astonishing amount of good
writing. In the earliest stages of my purgatorial employment I was
so slatheringly grateful for the slightest semblance of literacy that
I frequently found myself reading something to the bitter end, only
to discover that I'd been seduced by a new IBM, a nifty typeface,
an artful beginning. Slowly I grew canny, wary of what Nabokov
called "fast typing and slow thinking." My eyes (when I could
open them) were now permanently narrowed: I had become as
suspicious and watchful as a security guard in a bank.

I had been rooting around in the "mire brought to the surface
by trampling" for about six months when *The Conquest of Death,*

by Dr. Alvin Silverstein of the Department of Science at Staten Island College, arrived. It was a lively, thoughtful manuscript which affirmed the value of science if *rationally* applied to human and societal problems, a plea for the application of technology to the preservation rather than the destruction of human values. It's still selling, in six languages. Several months later, an eloquent, powerful book turned up. It was *The Struggle That Must Be,* by sociologist Harry Edwards of the University of California at Berkeley, and it addressed itself to the ambiguous and deceptive role of the black athlete in America. It was acquired by an editor who shared my enthusiasm. From Colorado came a superb novel of suspense with genuine political content, written by two young political scientists, Thomas Kirkwood and Geir Finne—*The Svalbard Passage.* The first printing sold out in one month and the rights were bought by a movie producer. A book about the *Wall Street Journal* was bought by our editor in chief. Two cookbooks, *Cheesecake Madness* and *Aunt Mary's Kitchen,* came next; and a lyrical first novel, *Rajac,* by Ms. Stanley Spain (a young woman with two small children who lives in a small town in North Carolina), made the fall list of 1982. And for each book actually acquired, there were at least half a dozen more that I, were it possible, would have been proud to publish.

Despite the statistics that we are a country suffering from functional illiteracy, we seem to be producing an extraordinary number of imaginative, interesting writers. The problem is that they can't get anyone to read what they write.

Which is hardly news to anyone. Publishing is suffering from one of the most violent upheavals in its history, in transition from a modest, gentlemanly pursuit to a mass-market, high-profit-oriented industry. Editors find themselves scrambling for the writer-clients of high-powered agents; if a writer has not yet been published, he will have an agonizing time finding an agent who will find him an editor to *look* at his work. And to ask an editor, deluged with paperwork—who is responsible for the acquisition, editing, and (increasingly) promotion of twelve to thirty books a year—to read the work of a new writer is to ask the impossible: there simply aren't enough hours in the day. What amazes me is the eternal optimism, the willingness to suspend disbelief (and whatever else they are doing), that editors are capable of, and the genuine delight they take in talent that comes in over the transom.

It's the enthusiasm shown by cops successfully delivering a baby in the squad car en route to the OB ward.

Judging from the flood of stale replays of last year's "page-turners" that wend their weary way back to the warehouse whence they came, perhaps it is time to disabuse ourselves of the presumption that New York is the literary navel of the world. It is not. Across this country there are many, many gifted writers who have no access to anyone in the publishing establishment competent to read their work with an open mind, or to encourage talent which in time might bring a new vitality to publishing books. The vitality and talent do exist, but much of it will die of malnutrition, starved to death in the slush pile. It cannot be unearthed by overworked editors, harried secretaries, or precociously cynical graduates of various publishing programs. There's no reason unsolicited manuscripts can't be read with care and responsiveness: One less bad book bought in the vain hope that it will make it in the supermarket or the movies or television pays for a first reader with a decent education and the awareness that a good book can issue forth sans the midwifery of an agent.

Everyone is no doubt weary unto death of lamenting the passing of great editors like Maxwell Perkins, who seemed to have had time to read everything and did so with the ferocity of a locust attacking a rice paddy. But it would be wise to remember that Perkins believed that "optimism and curiosity" were indispensable qualities for a good editor. Granted that sloshing around in the slush can be wearisome and profoundly depressing; but so is reading the abysmally turgid "blockbuster" you're stuck with on the red-eye to California. For, every now and then, beset though the first reader may be by Fulgence Tapir's complaint, a message gets through like a signal from an unimaginably distant galaxy: *I am a Writer.* Which makes it all worthwhile.

AUTHOR'S POSTSCRIPT: In September 1982, some months after the above was written, Macmillan eliminated the position of first reader: unsolicited manuscripts were to be returned unread to their authors. To the best of my knowledge, Macmillan was the last major publisher to employ a full-time in-house first reader.

CHARLES SANTINO

Charles Santino was the editorial assistant to four editors at Dodd, Mead when he wrote this essay especially for this anthology. Since then he has worked briefly for Richard Curtis Associates, a literary agency, and has gone on to free-lance as both writer and agent. He has authored two books scheduled for publication: a collaboration with noted horror novelist Michael McDowell and a reference book about comic-book art.

•   •   •

A common starting place for aspiring editors is the post of editorial assistant. More than a secretary, less than an editor, a first cousin and sometimes twin to the slush pile reader, the editorial assistant fulfills all these roles. Charles Santino evokes the hectic life of an editorial assistant and delineates the many duties the job entails. Every editorial assistant does not have exactly the same responsibilities that Mr. Santino had at Dodd, Mead, but the requirements are pretty similar at most publishing houses. It's a tough, demanding job, but one that offers great opportunities for the dedicated editor-to-be. Sometimes the opportunities are earned; sometimes they come through luck or chance. But if you want a career as an editor, being an editorial assistant is a great spot from which to see what lies ahead. It may be a lowly spot, but as Mao Tse-tung said, "The longest march begins with a single step."

THE EDITORIAL ASSISTANT

At the end of my first day as an editorial assistant, senior editor Peter Weed (then of Dodd, Mead, now of Congdon & Weed) asked me to read a mystery novel in manuscript form that we'd received from a literary agent.

I was flattered to get this kind of assignment so soon. I was eager to make a good first impression and to show Peter how my background as a reporter, copywriter, and reviewer for various publications, and as a reader of popular fiction, had paid off.

I probably read that book more analytically than any before or since, sizing it up against books by Larry Niven, Karl Edward Wagner, and other popular writers whom I enjoy.

The book was poor. The next day I gave Peter a long verbal report, explaining the story's plot flaws, weak characterizations, and so on. Because I was the first reader, I guessed that Peter wanted to make me feel welcome and that the book would be sent through a battery of experienced editors who might find some commercially appealing quality that I had missed.

Peter said, "Okay, thanks," and stuffed the manuscript into a padded mailing bag to be sent back to the agent.

This quickly put certain aspects of publishing into perspective for me. What was apparent that very first day was that a staggering work load requires rapid decision-making. Because of this, and especially in a small, sparsely staffed company, every able mind will be enlisted, allowing assistants to take on a variety of responsibilities. In my case, this happened quickly.

Within six months after starting as an editorial assistant, I was encouraged to acquire and edit books as long as it didn't interfere with my regular duties. I did this for over two and a half years. At editorial meetings I presented ideas for projects, mostly ideas I created rather than books I solicited from literary agents, since I didn't have time to cultivate and work with the network of agents as full-time editors did. Despite my obligations as our sole editorial assistant, I was in most respects treated as an equal.

A former editorial assistant, now a full editor, told me that her experience was different though she held a similar title (editorial secretary-assistant). Her basic duties were secretarial, but she soon began reading manuscripts for editors and later she copyedited books that had been acquired by her bosses. She occasionally had ideas for books, and coincidentally submitted an idea at a time when an editor was leaving the company. She was promoted on the basis of her performance and that proposal, and she inherited nearly a dozen projects from her predecessor. She didn't have the gradual transition that I underwent.

Another former editorial assistant said that although he had many secretarial duties, he also got involved in getting permission from other publishers to reprint certain material in his company's books, selecting artwork for covers, handling authors' questions about the preparation of their books, acquiring lists of names for direct-mail promotion, and more. Eventually, as a favor to his overworked bosses, he began to edit manuscripts that had been acquired anywhere from six months to two years before. He let his bosses know that he would like to acquire books for them, and would continue to function as a secretary so that they wouldn't have to hire an additional person. He got a raise and a new title (assistant editor–editorial assistant).

The duties of the editorial assistant, and the transition that he or she makes to editorship, are not standard; everyone has a unique story. The most unusual aspect of my experience is that the first manuscripts I worked on were projects I had acquired, rather than books passed on to me from other editors. The editorial assistant can hold that title for a year to four years, depending on promotions, firings, and departures above him, or her, as well as the financial status of the company. If the editorial assistant shows an ability to deal with the complexities of editorial work, he or she will eventually graduate to a full editorship.

Here is my full job description and my comments:

▶ General typing (correspondence, jacket flaps, catalogue copy) —I usually typed for two of four editors, but even that had me typing a few hours each day. If you can't type, learn. Most companies want at least fifty words per minute.

▶ Logging in manuscripts—We had green cards with white duplicates for recording author, title, agent (if any), addresses, editor assigned to the manuscript, etc. The green card went with the manuscript, the white one was filed.

▶ Taking the minutes at editorial meetings—The trick is to get down what's important. Sometimes a half-hour speech can be recorded with a single sentence.

▶ Making out check requisitions for author advances after editors' authorizations—This was part of my job description, but the individual editors seemed to prefer doing it themselves— filling out a form to get an author his or her advance.

▶ Helping to write catalogue and jacket copy (at request of editor)—This rarely happened. Usually it meant just copyediting the editors' copy as I was typing it.

▶ Xeroxing; filing; forwarding mail to authors; returning manuscripts to authors and agents—All self-explanatory.

▶ Handling special tasks, such as checking *Books in Print* for books on the same subject as projects under consideration, and doing market research for the preparation of editorial reports—This was the most open-ended of my duties, and the most interesting. For example, we received a proposal for a book on the preparation of résumés. I was asked to see what was currently available and how it stacked up against this proposal. In the first bookstore I visited, I found sixty-five books on job hunting in general, and twenty-six on the preparation of résumés; fifteen of those were identical in format to the book we were considering. The proposal was rejected.

▶ Determining whether unsolicited manuscripts should be given to an editor and rejecting those that were obviously unpublishable.

▶ Doing first readings on submitted manuscripts at an editor's request, if my time permitted.

After that first mystery, my time rarely permitted. Editors read proposals sent to us by agents and I dealt with the slush pile of unsolicited manuscripts and proposals. Many of the proposals that publishing companies receive do not come from agents. Part of my job time was spent opening mail addressed either to the editorial department or to specific editors, who, recognizing certain pieces as "slush," passed them on to me. This amounted to about one hundred pieces a week. Some contained outlines for books, others partial or complete manuscripts. In three years I considered perhaps fifteen thousand proposals.

All this was interesting for the first two months, and then the novelty of so much bad writing wore off. It became obvious that there was next to nothing in there worth publishing; in my time as editorial assistant we published just one book that came from the slush pile.

The work load of assisting four editors demanded that I spend a minute or less considering most proposals. Determining whether someone can write or has a good idea for a book is surprisingly easy. (My favorite from the slush pile was a revised script for *King Lear* in which everyone lives happily ever after because Shakespeare's ending was "a downer.")

Working for four editors, among whom there was no official pecking order, demanded tact and an even temper. Most editorial assistants answer to more than one editor. When our editorial staff doubled, I wondered how it would be possible to accommodate them, as just the original two editors kept me very busy.

Luckily, I worked for a polite and reasonable group of people who understood that I could sometimes get four concurrent assignments, all of which demanded a day's work. I tried to let each editor know what I was doing for whom and how long it was going to take. By managing my time as well as I could, I was able for the most part to do what needed to be done in the time allowed. If your bosses feel that you are doing the best job you can, they will generally be sympathetic to your situation.

Being a good editorial assistant has more to do with a person's skills of organization and diplomacy than it does with being able to spot a masterpiece. My main concern was to spare bosses as much work as possible—by anticipating their needs, keeping people they didn't want to talk to away from them, gradually taking on more responsibility as I earned their trust, making myself available and "on call" as often as possible, running lots of errands that weren't covered in my job description, and generally being reliable.

Often the editorial assistant will be ready to move up to a full editorship when there is no room for expansion in the company. One must then make the tough decision to look for another job, as much as one may be enjoying the current position. If the person is qualified, especially if he or she has acquisitions experience, there should be a position elsewhere as an assistant editor or something similar. Here again, titles are vague and will have different meanings from company to company. The main concern is making a step up, both in salary and in responsibilities. By taking your time, contacting your acquaintances in the industry, and letting potential employers know you're available, you'll be called to interview for appropriate jobs as they open up.

The type of person best suited for editorial work will obviously be well-read and have an interest in the written word. Of course, willingness to put in long hours, and a sense of purpose and dedication, are needed for any career. Most important, I believe a good editorial assistant (and future editor) should have the widest possible range of interests. The editorial assistant should have a good sense of popular taste and know how to evaluate a proposal in terms of its appeal to that taste. Finally, he or she should know how to strike a balance between quality and commercial appeal in recommending projects to the editor or editors of the publishing house.

A word about money. Publishing has a deserved reputation for low pay. It takes many years for people in publishing to make a comfortable salary, and very few get rich. Many supplement their salaries by free-lancing, doing anything from proofreading to writing novels to ghostwriting other people's books.

Advice about managing your career: If you want to edit trade books, don't settle for a position with a textbook or reference house "for the time being, just to be in publishing." I spent eighteen months in a large reference house where everyone wanted to work in trade. Reference experience won't always impress a trade house. What *will* impress an employer is the ability to use a word processor, as more and more publishers find word processors to be indispensable. Awaiting employment in publishing, you can earn good money working part-time as a word processor operator, while looking for a career job.

At its best, the post of editorial assistant is a proving ground where a young person interested in publishing can learn whether the industry is really what he or she wants as a lifetime career. If it is, then being an editorial assistant can be an excellent starting place: it can bring you into a working relationship with just about every department in the company. It's not an easy job, but I've found publishing to be a career that seems to have chosen me as much as I chose it.

PAT GOLBITZ

Pat Golbitz is a vice-president and senior editor at William Morrow & Co., where she acquires and edits both fiction and nonfiction. She has also worked as a paperback editor handling originals and reprints, and as a paperback copywriter.

•   •   •

Ms. Golbitz's love and enthusiasm for the many aspects of her work as an editor are evident in every line of her lively, personal, and informed essay, written especially for this anthology. Proclaiming herself in the very first line to be a "guardian," she betokens the wide range of her felt responsibilities to her authors and their books. From that commitment flows Ms. Golbitz's devoted, insightful shepherding of the book through the various processes that occur between her first acquiring the manuscript to the birth of the book itself, an effort that can take many months of dedication and hard work on the part of both author and editor. Ms. Golbitz's essay is a short but very practical course in the intensive and extensive involvement of the editor with the author, the book, the publisher, and the reading public. She makes clear as she details each step in the publishing process that the editor's input is at every phase crucial to the development and eventual success of the book; and that while the editor-author relationship can be tender or tough, it is always based on the editor's respect for the author as the creator of the work and for the integrity of what the author has created.

ON BEING A SENIOR ACQUISITIONS EDITOR

As a senior acquisitions editor for a trade hardcover house, I am the guardian of each book I buy from the time it first appears as a proposal on my desk until it sits on a bookseller's shelf, waiting for a reader to be captivated enough to buy it.

I wear a lot of hats in the course of a working day: I am a buyer, negotiator, seller, writer, editor, decision-maker. I approve, reject, confer; I work with every department within my publishing house —sales, art, copyediting, production, publicity, advertising, subsidiary rights. I am always looking for new books to buy, so I have lunch and dinner with agents and keep up my contacts within the industry. Each day in my job, I use every talent I have and all the experience I've gathered through the years. That's what makes it fun, exciting, a continual challenge. In this I am like every other senior editor. We are a special breed, and yet we are as different from each other as the books we publish. We're individualistic, even quirky, but we share one thing: we like our work. We'd be crazy to do it if we didn't.

I believe that being an editor is one of the few remaining jobs that are totally encompassing. As did most of us, I started on the road to being an editor back when I learned to read. That was the first step toward what has become a lifelong addiction—a love, a hunger for books. So an editor is someone who gets paid to keep his "habit," to do what he or she needs to do more than anything else—get a daily "high" on books.

Loving books is not enough; there's a great deal of expertise involved in the job of being an acquisitions editor, and in thinking about what I do every day, I've decided that the easiest and simplest way to describe a complex function is to break it down into three major parts: getting the book, working with the author, and marketing the book.

GETTING THE BOOK

Acquisitions

The first job of an acquiring editor is to buy books. We always look for the big ones, but we also pursue the others—good new novels, interesting nonfiction, special-interest books, and backlist books. We try to anticipate trends. If I buy a project from an outline, it will be almost two years—sometimes more—before the book is published. The author will take about a year to write it, then it takes nine more months to go through the production process before it is ready to publish. If I consider buying a book on a subject that is of high interest at the moment, I must be aware that by the time the book is published there may well be many similar books on the shelves. So an editor must be a bit of a futurist; we must foresee what will continue to interest readers a long time from now. Fiction doesn't usually present this problem—a good story is a good story forever, although tastes in fiction follow trends as well. But nonfiction, unless it is highly personal, risks being outdated at publication day.

An acquisitions editor receives many manuscripts, and turns down most of them for various reasons. And some of the manuscripts the editor wants to consider for publication are turned down by the publishing house. Thus, only a small percentage of manuscripts submitted to a publisher wind up as books under their imprint. Furthermore, books are sometimes lost in auctions to a higher-bidding rival house. (But more about auctions later.)

No acquisitions editor simply waits for submissions to arrive. We meet with and entertain agents and authors and build a network of contacts in our search for books. A lunch can be the most important event of an editor's day. There's a kind of etiquette to an editor-agent lunch. Very often you are meeting someone who had been a voice on the phone, so you spend most of your lunch getting to know each other and leave the business for last. The editor picks up the tab—it's a seller's market! If the agent has nothing for you at the moment, or nothing that interests you, still a connection has been made. This connection will be maintained through phone calls and repeat engagements. And someday the agent will send you the very book you were hoping for—the one you were destined to buy.

All editors have had the frustrating experience of wanting a certain kind of book and not finding it. Many a book gets its start when an editor and an agent toss an idea back and forth across a lunch table. I remember telling one agent about a book I wanted to find because I wanted to read it (I figured if I'd like it, so would lots of others). He happened to have two authors who had *lived* the book I was talking about. Two years later, I published their novel. All editors have had experiences like this. We are great idea collectors—a couple of lines of newsprint can spark a whole book concept—and if we are lucky and tenacious, and if the idea still looks good the next day or week or month, we'll be able to match the idea with a writer.

Before senior editors at Morrow buy a book, we prepare an editorial evaluation, a memo comprising a description of the proposal and a set of figures based on publishing costs and projected sales. This memo is submitted to the publisher with the proposal, which can vary from an outline of a few pages to a full manuscript. Usually the proposal is read by one other member of an editorial "board," which at Morrow is most informal and consists of the president, the publisher, and the marketing director.

Sometimes, high-priced projects are bought rather differently because competition for good properties is fierce. When a "name" author or a big book becomes available, the acquisitions editor brings it to the attention of the house, but it is the house itself that must gear up and present its best publishing package. Whenever there comes my way a book of which several other houses are in hot pursuit, my job, after presenting my evaluation, is to muster the forces of the house. I arrange for the author and agent to meet with the president, the publisher, the heads of marketing, sales, and rights. There will also be subsequent meetings with the publicity and advertising departments. When the agent calls me to say the author has chosen us, it is a decision based upon the author's sense of the entire publishing house and a belief that that house will do the best publishing job for the book.

But you can't win all the big ones in this kind of business. I think perhaps the happiest situation in which editors can find themselves is to have bought a book *before* it was big. And this is why every acquisitions editor values that network of contacts and keeps it strong. When that new, unusual author appears at the agent's door, you want the agent to pick up the phone and call *you*. When you feel that tingle of excitement (a combination of intuition, experience, and ESP) upon hearing of a new project, you want to be the first one in. I've always believed that a whole lot of luck is involved in nailing that special property, and I still think so. But I must admit that it's been the network—the group of agents, authors, colleagues, and friends—that has provided me with some of my "luckiest" chances. Your contacts are what *allow* you to be lucky.

Auctions

An auction is one of the most exciting games in the business. It's like poker, except in a book auction you get to see the cards, not the players. There are strict rules. The auction is played in rounds in which each publisher, in proper order, makes a bid. The first bids are recorded and round two starts with the agent returning to the first bidder to tell what the top, last bid was. A few players get knocked out in the first round, when subsequent bids put the price beyond their purses. Round two gets down to the really serious bidders, out for the high stake. The rounds slow down now, as the players take time out to discuss strategies, hold meetings, redo figures, make important phone calls. The sponsoring editor goes back to the agent with the decision of the house. The agent orchestrates it all, releasing bid information but keeping the identity of the rival players absolutely secret. Sometimes auctions continue into the next day, with the agreement of the players. And sometimes agents simply decide on their own to extend the auction, but they risk losing their top bidder, who may withdraw an offer rather than give competitors time to rethink their strategy and possibly make an offer that will win the book.

There's only one winner, of course, but I find that I get caught up in the game. Winning is marvelous, but even when I lose, I've had an exhilarating time.

Contracts

If you win the auction, you've won just one battle. You could still lose the war negotiating the contract that will buy your book. I approach every contractual negotiation as though preparing for friendly combat. And in truth, the agent and I are well-mannered adversaries: the agent is acting to protect the author and I act to protect the publisher. At certain points in negotiation, as each of us strives to achieve this protection, our interests may conflict. But this conflict is temporary, for if we each negotiate well and reasonably, we will end up in an alliance that will best serve those we represent.

Let's say I won a book in an auction. The advance for the book (money paid by the publisher against future royalties) has been agreed upon. Still to be negotiated are the payout date or dates of the advance, the size of the royalties (the percentage of the list price of the book the author receives), delivery dates of the manuscript, options, subsidiary rights splits, other sales rights, and the territories in which the publisher can distribute the book—all the basic terms of any contract, excluding the fine print.

All goes well until the agent asks for something I can't give or I ask for something the agent can't give. When such an impasse is reached, we will both retreat and maneuver a way around it. I try to hold something in reserve—something I can give when I can't give way on the specific issue causing our difference. That something can be as small as an author's approval of cover art and copy or as big (if the case warrants) as a better subsidiary rights split for the author. Usually these concessions are small on both sides, a kind of two-beat pause in a courteous minuet that allows the other partner to catch up. Notice that my metaphor has changed from war to dance. But it does seem that a dance is ended as negotiations conclude satisfactorily. Editor, agent, and author now join hands and take a well-deserved bow for executing some very tricky steps. But soon the "music" of publishing starts up again. And this time the agent leaves the stage—sometimes to wait just offstage in the wings. Now the dance becomes a pas de deux between editor and author. Almost always it is an improvisation springing from the talents and chemistry of these two artists as they create together that work of art called—the book.

WORKING WITH THE AUTHOR

For me, the heart and soul of my profession is working with the author. To divine and heighten the author's vision, to help authors achieve their best efforts and then in the end to hold a book in my hands—how wonderful! But the editorial process is not always a joy. It can be a tedious job: cutting portions of the manuscript away with a pen, making notes in the margins, telling the author what goes wrong and why. And sometimes reading my comments and hearing my opinions can be a difficult experience for an author. But it's all part of my contribution to the process of getting a book to be as good as it can be. Every writer, no matter how talented or famous, needs an objective eye on his or her work. That's the editor's role: to supply that objectivity, coupled with commitment and expertise.

Editing the Manuscript

I approach every manuscript as a reader. I look forward to being entertained and involved. As long as that happens, my editor's pen is at rest. I'm enjoying the story! Then, when something goes wrong—I'm bored, things don't mesh, the logic is off, the integrity lost—that's when I go to work as an editor. The story has hit a snag and I've pinpointed a problem. With my red pen (for high visibility), I define the problem and suggest solutions. The easiest way to describe the editorial process is to break it down into three stages:

Structuring   This is the first step, the laying out of a coherent road map for the book. It is often done before the author starts work on the actual manuscript. Sometimes a first draft needs restructuring when it takes a direction that leads to a dead end. Author and editor at this point are still dealing with generalities of concept and plot. The strokes are broad and rough; the fine detail comes later. But for now they work together to trace a new route for the progress of the book and convert that dead end into a smooth highway.

Cutting   I like to compare this to a sculptor who can see the figure within the marble; he needs only to chip away the excess stone to reveal it. Cut away a speck here, a chunk there, and you can see the story becoming tighter, tauter, more shapely. Almost every manuscript improves with judicious cutting. It is the nature of many artists to be excessive (call it creative energy), and the job of an editor to keep the book within its natural bounds. These cuts, done after the structure is solid, leave no holes in the story line or the characterizations.

Line Editing   In this last stage, the editor pays attention to details of style. Has the author expressed himself in the most effective way? Can a confusing sentence be made clear? At this point, an editor deals with a writer's style, and I always use extreme caution. If I make a change, I try to do it in harmony with the author's voice and in keeping with the integrity of the style or point of view. (All such changes, of course, are checked and approved by the writer.) In most cases, I do a minimum of line editing on a manuscript. After the structural changes and cutting have been satisfactorily completed, heavy line editing usually isn't necessary.

These three stages are not always clearly divided. Sometimes they are done all together in one draft. And sometimes, but very rarely, a manuscript doesn't need any editing. It's perfect as it is and can go right into copyediting.

Copyediting

After the manuscript has gone through final revisions, I send it on to the copyediting department. If the writer employs any deliberate peculiarities of punctuation or grammar, I write a memo informing the copy editor. The copy editor then goes over the manuscript literally word by word, correcting errors of spelling, etc., suggesting more proper usage of terms, writing directions to the printer in small and miraculously legible handwriting. When copy editors have a question concerning content, they flag it with a yellow or pink or green tag. These questions can regard research ("Is Oxville in Tennessee? Couldn't find it in the atlas") or logic ("Do you want Harry to be in New York at 2:00 P.M. *or* San Francisco at 2:30 P.M.? See pages 23 and 78"). I marvel at copy editors' ability to deal with such fine detail and never lose sight of the larger shape of the total manuscript.

When the copyedited manuscript is returned to my office, my assistant calls the author and the copy editor and arranges a time for them to go over the manuscript together. I do not become personally involved with the copyediting process unless there are unusual problems. Sometimes I am asked to arbitrate an author's and a copyeditor's disagreement. Sometimes I will make a decision in the author's absence.

Writers and Editors

I work differently with different authors. With some I can work at a distance, through phone calls, letters, editorial notes, and manuscripts. Usually there is at least one conference, if only so editor and author can meet. There are other projects, though, that go more easily when I am on the spot. I have two very talented young coauthors who send me chunks of their manuscript as they write it. When I have collected a whole first draft, I fly off to wherever they are. We meet at a borrowed cabin or cottage (where they can get away from *their* phones too) and settle in for a few days' intensive work. From early morning until evening, when we stop for dinner and relaxation, I work on my desk-sofa while the two authors hit away at their typewriters at opposite ends of the room, deeply into revisions. Papers are as thick as fallen leaves. We walk on them, sit on them, push them away to make room for cups of coffee—and have found that the safest place to keep the important stuff is *under* a table. When I fly back to New York, I have a final draft ready for the copy editor.

I meet with another author at her home for a morning or an afternoon. We discuss not the manuscript, which she hasn't yet begun, but the outline, which she had previously sent to me. There are no papers flying about here. It's all talk and ideas as we carefully check the plot outline for weaknesses and strengths. We are both pacers, and when excitement is high, back and forth we go, trying not to bump into each other. Trouble spots are avoided before they occur and this way the first draft requires very little revision. But not all writers can work well from an outline; I've learned that most writers are very uncomfortable with outlines, hate them, in fact. They think of them as boundaries to hem them in.

I do all my editing at home. I need the solitude of a quiet, closed room with no ringing phones and no interruptions, my feet up, nothing distracting me from the total concentration I need for this work. There are few efforts so focused, so exclusionary of everything else, as editing a manuscript. My mind works on many levels:

as a reader (Am I enjoying this and why?); as a trouble spotter (Something wrong here—what?); as a diviner (What is the author getting at?); as a problem solver (Can this be put right? How? Where?). Then there is the overall concept of the book—its integrity, its organic structure, symmetry, and the relationship of its parts—which concerns me with each page I read. Editing means entering another person's mind and anticipating its thoughts, imaginings, mysteries, and surprises until the editor shares that space not as a stranger but as something of an alter ego.

The majority of editorial conferences take place in my office, where I go over the first draft page by page with the author. I write directly on the manuscript and return this so the author can ponder my suggestions as he or she rewrites. Sometimes my assistant will type my notes and comments, to provide the author and me with a record. Usually by the second draft the manuscript is in good shape and just needs some fine tuning. Sometimes a third draft is required, but I rarely go on to a fourth draft. By that time it usually means the author can't do it and I can't help anymore.

Sometimes authors *can't* do the job. They get hopelessly lost in the writing of the book, or turn in a manuscript that's so far off the mark I feel it can't be fixed. It's always a sad thing to reject a manuscript that's under contract. I do it very reluctantly, and only after I'm convinced there's no other choice. I have never tried to salvage a manuscript by calling in another writer, because I feel that the author's "voice" and personality are essential to a book, giving it the magic breath of life. To bring in a doctor-writer would simply create a species of the undead.

A good editor can work miracles with a writer as long as that life-giving spark is present. Give me someone with a voice and a vision, and I can help that writer, however unpolished or unskilled, create a book. My friend and colleague editor Lisa Drew said it perfectly. Responding to a fledgling author's question at a writers' conference, Lisa said, "If it's there, we'll get it. If you've got it, we'll get it out of you. That's a guarantee."

Let me say a word here about the scope and limits of the editor's role. We become intimately involved in the creation of a book, but don't forget the final responsibility for the book is the author's. It's his idea, his baby; it's his name that will be on the cover, and he who will stand alone in the cold wind of criticism and be judged. (Every once in a while a nasty critic will also review an editor, and this infuriates me. What do they know of an editor's hard work? For these reviews are always bad; I have yet to see a critic praise a splendid job of editing! When a book is good, authors get all the credit, as well they should. But it's outrageous for a critic to blame the editor when panning a book.)

The author assumes all risk with his authorship and should have the final word about what goes into his book. In a standoff between editor and author, the author wins, always. The editor can then decide not to publish. I have seen it come to this in only one case, where the author was advised by our lawyers to make changes and refused.

Usually there's no impasse and no adversarial antagonism. Editor and author work toward a common goal and often the most valuable thing I can do for an author is to make him aware of something he doesn't know he knows. I can suggest solutions, but what I really hope to do is jog the author's mind to come up with his own brilliant solution, for an author's inspiration is truer than anyone else's.

My respect for writers—for their skill, their drive, their talent, and the sheer stamina they need to write a book—is deep. They deserve the best from me and from everyone involved in the launching of their endeavors.

MARKETING THE BOOK

The Marketing Meeting

The marketing meeting is the very first time a book comes to the attention of the house since its purchase. Usually a year, sometimes more, has passed. During that time only the editor has been aware of its progress. The manuscript has been completed and is now scheduled by its editor for the upcoming list. The number of books an editor publishes per list can vary from three or four to six or eight, and sometimes higher. At Morrow we have three lists, fall, winter, and summer.The atmosphere of Morrow's marketing meetings is quite informal. They are attended by the publisher, associate publisher, and rights director, head of marketing, sales manager, publicity, advertising—and the editors who present their books. Informal or not, what happens at these meetings is crucial.

Here the first publication plans are made; initial print orders are decided, budgets are allocated; promotion and advertising strategies are devised. The editors' enthusiasm and conviction and the skill with which they present the special properties of their books will help set the books on their proper course. Every editor has his own way of preparing for these meetings. My way is to put a piece of paper in my typewriter and let my mind focus on what is unique, extraordinary, and wonderful about a particular book. These resultant notes will become the basis for future catalogue copy, flap copy, and sales conference presentation. I gather information about the authors, their backgrounds, and their publishing histories. The more specific I can be and the more details I can provide, the more helpful I am to the staff whose job is to market and sell my books.

The Cover

Shortly after I present the new list, I have a conference with our talented art director, Cheryl Asherman. I describe the books to her while she takes notes. We discuss various design and illustrative approaches: What should the cover convey? Do we want a graphic cover? Is there a symbol within the story that can be used as an illustration? Should the book look impressive, romantic, masculine, feminine? Cheryl and I begin to create in these first stages the outward image of the book that will stay with it for the rest of its life.

I give Cheryl a copy of the manuscript plus a description of all copy to appear on the front and back cover and spine. Next I see preliminary artwork. More often than not, the artist has got it right the first time. But occasionally it has to go back to the drawing board until Cheryl and I are satisfied. Then it goes on for further approval to the marketing director and the publisher. It's always a special thrill when I see a cover for the first time. Like print, it gives a book validation. It makes it real.

Catalogue Copy

Editors at Morrow all write their own copy and all of us groan when we're reminded that catalogue copy is due. Still, the editor is best equipped for this job. These are our babies, unread and

unknown by anyone else. Bound galleys and photocopied manuscripts will be distributed to marketing and sales, but that is yet
to come. The catalogue is the first written public description of the
book and its main thrust is toward the booksellers, offering a
quick, provocative sketch of books it is hoped they will want to
stock for their customers.

Flap Copy

If catalogue copy sells to the bookstores, flap copy sells directly to
the consumer. The customer with the book in his hands is looking
for a reason to buy. The best chance you'll have to cinch the deal
is right there on the inside flaps of the jacket. Again, all Morrow
editors write their own flaps. There's a trick to it: I try to give a
true picture of the book without giving anything away. I never,
never tell the plot. I go for effect rather than detail, tantalize rather
than reveal. I think flap copy should be as provocative as perfume
ads and promise almost as much. I try to give the customer the
idea that this book is something wonderful to curl up in bed with.

Advertising

Advertising plans are begun in the marketing meeting, when the
budget is allocated and various media outlets are decided upon.
The advertising director sends a copy of a rough pasteup of the ad,
usually written by an outside agency, to the editor for approval.
If the editor feels the ad misses or if there is new information—
a quotable review, for instance—we can revise the ad ourselves or
ask for revisions from the agency. If the book is special or especially important, the advertising director and the editor will often
have a brainstorming session before sending it out to the agency
with our specifications.

Publicity

The publicity department handles all authors' bookings, promotional releases, tour schedules, review copies, and print media. I
set up a meeting between my author and the publicity director, and
make sure that publicity has all the information that can be useful
in promoting the author's book. Sometimes I am able to suggest

a special approach. For instance, a novelist of mine is a major figure in the preservation of animal wildlife; a novel alone won't get her on a talk show, but *that* might. There's a lot of give-and-take among publicity and editorial, and spur-of-the-moment meetings are often held to discuss the progress of an author's promotion. The editors approve press releases and receive copies of their authors' tour schedules.

The Sales Conference

This is the big push. Here the editors present each of their books on the season's list to a gathering of Morrow's national sales staff. This happens three times a year—in April, September, and December. The conference for adult trade books lasts two full days. The new catalogues are distributed among the field representatives, who comprise the major part of the audience that each editor speaks to. I admit that this can be a tense and nervous time for me, and I suspect for a lot of other editors. We have about five minutes in which to pitch the book, fire the sales people with the same enthusiasm we feel, and give them handles that will help them sell our books to their customers. God forbid we should bore the audience! There is a great urgency to do right by our books and give them a proper send-off. During these two days, the Morrow editorial and marketing staffs have lunch, and sometimes supper, with the sales staff and field reps. This gives us a chance to really talk to the sales force we see only three times a year—the very people who will take the books we've sponsored with hard work and high hopes, and carry them directly to the buyers and readers.

The conclusion of a sales conference means that the "babies" created by my authors, which I have midwifed, are now ready to make their way in the world. I love them and wish them well, but already I am working on my new list and eager to make sure that its books, too, have a happy, healthy, and successful life.

With all the professionalism required for the job, so much of a senior editor's work is intuitive. I believe that intuition is a combination of experience and observation, so deep within us that it's felt as a gut instinct, give or take a little "magic" that defies explanation. And maybe even that magic can be explained as a passionate interest in what you do and a great pleasure in the results of your work. The magic comes from the dedicated spirit of the enthusiast. I've tried to describe here the professional aspects of the editor's job. That professionalism can be learned, but every true professional carries the amateur within. And perhaps the amateur's excitement and joy are the most important parts of the editor's art and craft.

BETTY A. PRASHKER

Betty A. Prashker is vice-president and editor in chief of Crown Publishers. Prior to coming to Crown in 1982, she was vice-president and associate publisher at Doubleday. She has also served as senior editor at Coward-McCann, and as a copywriter for Denhard and Stewart, an advertising agency that specializes in book publishing. Ms. Prashker has never lost her enthusiasm for reading, which, next to tennis, is her favorite hobby.

•   •   •

Just what does an editor in chief do? The answer is: everything. The editor in chief builds her own list of books, guides the other editors in the development of their lists, manages people as well as budgets, works to ensure that both the profitability and the quality of the company's publishing program stays high, soothes disputes between editors and authors, editors and agents, and editors and top management, worries where the next list of books is coming from and how to get the most out of the books that are currently being published. The responsibilities are endless; the time to fulfill them, unfortunately, is not. So priorities must be established. What makes for a good editor in chief, someone who can handle crises, conflicts, success, and failure? Ms. Prashker says it best in this entertaining, authoritative article, written especially for this anthology. "A good editor in chief needs to be warm and cool; creative and businesslike; a leader and a follower."

A LIFE IN THE DAY OF AN
EDITOR IN CHIEF

Book publishing—particularly hardcover publishing—is a mysterious business. For decades we have been trying to take out some of the mystery and put in some science—with varying degrees of success. We have tried to predict our profits—and losses—with more accuracy. We have developed systems, generated printouts, and hired MBAs. But the author and the book remain the all-important foundation of our industry, and so does the editor. The editor is the author's liaison to the publishing house and represents the publishing house to the author and his agent. The editor can be crucial in helping the author produce the best possible book and in coordinating the activities within and without the house that surround the book's publication.

Most publishing houses have editors in chief. The titles vary and so does the job description. Is the editor in chief simply a megaeditor who inspires by her example, handles the most important books, and is charged with the responsibility of acquiring the authors that will illuminate the reputation and the balance sheet? Is the editor in chief the arbiter of the problems that can arise between author and house, the nurturer of young talent in a writer or an editor, a charismatic personality who can attract editors and authors to the publishing house, a hand holder, a slave driver, a serious careerist, a leader, a follower of the most junior member of the staff who has a good idea? An administrator? A creator?

The answer is all of the above and probably more. My first job in publishing was at Doubleday, where I worked as a reader and receptionist in a small editorial department that was headed by LeBaron R. Barker, Jr., who had come to Doubleday from Houghton Mifflin. Lee was very Boston. He was the epitome of cool. His decisions were as crisp as the attached white collars he wore on what I am sure were custom-made shirts. He ran what we called "Book Meeting" in a determined, sometimes impatient fashion, but he was always ready to listen if he detected passion in an editor's presentation. An OK book just wasn't enough. He wanted, demanded and, often, got the extraordinary. The first time he backed a book I wanted to publish, I felt that for the first time I understood the meaning of the phrase "peak experience." He was my role model, and although there was no way that I could truly turn my particular temperament into his Boston Brahmin cool, it didn't stop me from trying. And it's good that I did try, because grace under pressure should be cultivated by those who want a career in publishing.

It is important for an editor in chief to remain calm in what can be difficult circumstances; to be tactful when explaining to an editor that the book he wants to put under contract is not going to be approved; to soothe the author whose book has just been savaged by the *New York Times*. The editor in chief may have to arbitrate disputes within the publishing house, put out fires and mend fences with art and production departments who feel editors make difficult demands upon them, with a publicity department that can't put up with authors and editors who insist that certain books get prime attention. An editor in chief must have the courage and confidence to face top management's questions about profit and loss, and having faced the questions, develop a plan to improve performance. I have gone through many highs and lows with various publishing houses and have greatly admired those leaders who can deal with adversity and retain humor and vigor.

Cool and calm are important, but, paradoxically, so is warmth and energy. The second editor in chief for whom I labored was, and is, one of the great figures in publishing: Ken McCormick. When I began working at Doubleday, Ken was in the army. It was just after World War II, and he had not yet returned to his job as editor in chief. Lee Barker was acting editor in chief and had done a superb job. Ken's ebullient personality was totally different, and so was his work style. Yet the two men complemented each other in a wonderful way and made a most effective team. It was Ken who taught me the importance of enthusiasm and optimism, the importance of looking forward, not backward. The importance of persistence. Ken's ability to put a good face on almost any kind of situation is well known. I remember his comment in an editorial meeting about a public figure he had been pursuing for years. Ken was convinced this man could write a fascinating book, and had sent him countless letters. He had also tried to approach him through mutual friends. Nothing seemed to work. But Ken persisted and finally he did receive an answer, in which the gentleman stated that under no circumstances would he be persuaded to write a book. As Ken announced this in the editorial meeting, he said, "At last he is responding." Two years later, Ken had the man and his book under contract.

The ability to spot talent is an important quality in an editorial job; the ability to match talents is a quality that the chief editor must acquire. Not all writers can work with all editors. A project that is taken on with great enthusiasm by an editor may bog down because the chemistry isn't right. The editor in chief must be prepared to step in and assign the author to another editor or even to herself. Although most authors I know would rather work with an editor who has the most feeling for the book and can get the best out of the author and out of publicity, sales, and subsidiary rights, occasionally authors feel they must work with the house's top editor. If the author wants the chief, the chief should be prepared to step in.

Once the talent is spotted, it has to be nourished. Just as authors work well with some editors and not so well with others, editors work well with some editors in chief and not at all with others. And some publishing houses really don't emphasize the role of the editor in chief at all. At Random House and Morrow, for example, the editors work on their own; their projects are not sifted through editorial meetings. The editor in chief apparently must approve requests for contracts, but does not mix in too much with the activities of the other editors. There are some editors who like to work this way, others who prefer closer contact with the editor in chief or publisher. I prefer the latter system. As an editor, I found the discipline of presenting my ideas and authors at an editorial meeting a good way to make sure that what I was proposing was something on which I had done my homework and about which I felt confident. Editors always want to publish many different books and that tendency can be difficult to control without some kind of review and evaluation. As an editor in chief, I like to listen to ideas, plots, and plans in a somewhat formal meeting where opinions can be traded, and where the editors get a sense of the interests and resources of their colleagues.

A publisher's list is a reflection of the judgment and taste of the editorial staff. As the editors change, so does the list, and the chief editor must review and evaluate the list to see if the balance is right and to work with the editors to maintain that balance. The editor in chief must know what books are under contract for future lists as well as have a sense of what kinds of books people are going to want to read in the next few years. How many books on diet, beauty, making money, and enjoying sex can the market sustain? And what share of that market can the house maintain? These are all questions that must be discussed with the marketing staff as well as with the editors. It is the chief editor's responsibility to make sure that out of a list of one hundred books a year, fifty are not novels set in Hollywood or high-fiber-diet books. On the other hand, she must be aware of the strengths of the house and publish to those strengths. If the house is known for its popular fiction, of course it makes sense to add to that strength and build new authors. If the house is weak in popular fiction and there is a desire to publish more effectively in that area, the editor in chief must make sure that the novels acquired are strong contenders and that they are launched with vigor and excitement.

Once the book is under contract, what is the editor in chief's responsibility for its content? If the book is by one of the authors she is handling, the responsibility is total. If the book is handled by one of the staff editors, it seems to me there is still a responsibility. It usually isn't possible for the editor in chief to read all of every book that is published by a house—unless the list is very small. But she should read all the major books, all the fiction, and at least part of each of the nonfiction books. Different houses have different styles of operation, of course, but if someone takes on the title Editor in Chief, that person must make sure that all the books are well edited. There can be varying opinions on style, organization, length, and the like, but the chief editor should make her opinions known and discuss with the sponsoring editor any changes that need to be made. And if the book is unpublishable, it is up to the editor in chief to see that the book is appropriately revised or rejected as unsatisfactory.

What about competition between editors in the publishing house? How does an editor in chief deal with a number of editors, all searching for publishable material? There is a certain amount of competition in any publishing house, with editors keen to sign on books and to get advance money and promotion and advertising budgets for those books. There is bound to be some pushing and shoving and special pleading. Quite often an editor's enthusiasm is not completely shared by sales and promotion. Compromises must be made. Ken McCormick's ebullience and support for his staff editors, his willingness to listen, and his determination to foster an atmosphere of cooperation were part of my training. I remember well, some years ago, bursting into Ken's office, furious that a book I was handling was not given the attention I thought it deserved, and leaving Ken's office with a well-developed plan to use other methods for the launch. There are many ways to bring a book to the attention of those who might want to read it. And those ways are not always generated by another department. Ken taught me not to give up, not to depend on others, and to generate my own ideas. To draw on my own experience and imagination, on a network of opinion-makers, to start the fabled word of mouth that can create the crucial difference. He taught me to be entrepreneurial. I believe that is a quality all editors need. The editor in chief most of all.

The entrepreneur's instinct also comes into play in editorial matters. What if you're faced with a fall list that lacks a major book by a major author and there aren't bagfuls of money available to try to win the next "big" novel at auction? A resourceful editor in chief will know what possibilities already exist on the list and will be able to build a book that is not a natural best-seller into one that has that potential. The building process will often have a great deal to do with the presentation and energy that surround the book. It will be up to the editor in chief to provide the energy and to mobilize other departments behind the book.

Administration? Some do and some don't. I know chief editors who find administration a bore and hate the process of salary review, attendance, office hours, vacations, offices (windows or not), support staff for editors, dealing with personnel departments, and the like. Others revel in what one of my bosses once called "playing office." As in all things, there is a happy medium. In a small house, administrative duties are minimal. In a large house, where the work style is more formal and structured, it can become a noticeable part of the working day. And the top editor can find that attending to administrative detail can steal time from authors, list building, and publishing. The editor always has to fight the temptation to play office and to eschew its spin-off game, office politics. But on the other hand, the editorial staff must be watched over and encouraged and supported in their dealings with authors and with top management.

My feeling is that the boss is as good as the people around her, and I would much rather spend some time with an editor with whom I have worked, trying to solve a problem, than lose the editor and spend months courting other people, who may use my interest to better their situations at rival houses. Nothing has made me happier than to see one of the editors on my staff grow and develop, produce some interesting books, gain confidence, and do the job. The future of publishing is in the young writers and the young editors, and I want to be part of that future.

I expect a lot from the editors with whom I work. The managing editor has got to keep the traffic moving smoothly. The senior editors need to be heavy hitters, experienced in working with authors, in line editing, and in combing the sources of supply— agents, other editors—to bring in good material. A good senior editor should also have the capacity to someday step into the top job. Younger editors should be attending to the younger writers, spotting trends and telling the senior people about aspects of our society that have not yet been covered by books.

When I began working in publishing, editors sat in quiet rooms reading complete manuscripts in a leisurely fashion and deciding yea or nay. The atmosphere is very different now. Editors have to be aggressive in seeking out authors and ideas. The Xerox machine ended the era of the single submission. There is hustle and there is bustle and the editor must be part of it, must move through it and emerge with the right book at the right time. Decision-making must be based on good ideas and good writing, but other information is required as well. Are there other books on the subject? Has the writer a contract with another publisher? Has the subject been overtaken by events? The editorial team is part of the information-gathering process and an editor in chief will be heavily dependent on that information. How, specifically, are these duties performed, in what context, and what pace?

Here is a more or less true-to-life day in the life of a particular editor in chief:

8:30   In the office at my desk, reading the *New York Times*. I find it hard to begin the working day without at least a quick perusal of the *Times*—beginning with the book page, followed by op-ed, features, business (got to know what the economy is doing), and last of all, news. I get ideas from the *Times,* but most important, it's my only addiction.

9:00   The art director arrives with a third version of a jacket for a lively book on American life in the fifties. What we are looking for is a type style and image symbolizing the fifties in vibrant colors that will stand out on the bookshelves. What we've gotten is a couple of dead sketches. The new one isn't right, either. Back to the drawing board!

9:15   I try to collect my thoughts in preparation for the editorial meeting. One of the editors comes to discuss a negotiation with an agent. The agent received certain concessions on a previous contract, she wants similar concessions on the new contract. Will we go along with the request? I say no. What we did for the other book should not in any way set a precedent. The other book was by a writer with a track record. This is a contract for a first novel. It's apples and oranges, I say. The editor nods. Looks unconvinced and leaves.

9:30   Editorial meeting. We start promptly, even though one or two people are late. Some of the editors bring in manuscripts and proposals. Others carry coffee. We discuss projects. A fine writer who has published three successful novels with another house has decided to try her luck elsewhere. Several publishing houses are reading the first draft of her new novel, *Ziggurat.* The agent has set a closing date for offers and has also asked interested publishers for first-print guarantees and advertising and promotion plans. We discuss the novel. The sponsoring editor is very enthusiastic. He doesn't think it is perfect, but he does think that with certain revisions it will be first-rate. He knows the author, has met with her, and is confident that the house will be proud to publish *Ziggurat,* that we will get good attention for it, and that it will be profitable too. Another editor has also read the manuscript. She found it interesting, but unfocused. She is not sure what story the author is trying to tell, what point she is trying to make. She is not at all confident that the novel will be well-received by the critics or that it will sell. Our subsidiary rights director, who attends the editorial meeting, points out that the paperback edition of the author's last book had disappointing sales. I ask what the sponsoring editor has in mind for an advance. At least six figures, perhaps mid-six figures. I agree to read the novel over the weekend. The gears shift. Another editor speaks. Do we want to consider a proposal for a new book on Frank Sinatra? Maybe, but will he cooperate? Will his friends? We all shake our heads. How about a book called *How to Attract a Mate*? The author is a professor of anthropology at Stanford and has some good new theories. The editor describes some of them. There are questions. Demonstrations. Interest. It sounds promising. We discuss half a dozen projects. The managing editor, who is responsible for scheduling and general troubleshooting, lists the number of manuscripts that are late and reminds us that we are approaching the deadline for the winter list. Fact sheets—giving pertinent information on the books for production, sales, and promotion—are also due, including some of mine. We end the meeting with a general discussion about the state of the industry—not very good; the kinds of submissions we are getting—a few interesting manuscripts, but a lot of mediocre stuff as well; the state of our list—terrific for the immediate future, but in need of some top-drawer nonfiction. We discuss ideas for books, possible authors for those books. We learn that two books we declined last week have been signed by other publishers.

11:30   The meeting is adjourned. I return to my office, to find several telephone messages. An agent has called. He wants to know whether we are going to make an offer on a project he sent over last week. It is on "multiple" submission and the "closing" of the auction is this afternoon. I wonder if I'm going to have time to read the material. I remember that one of the editorial assistants had written a favorable report. There is a message from an author whose book is on the fall list. She is working on her copyedited manuscript and is upset by the changes the copy editor has suggested. Another message, this time from a British publisher who will be in New York for a couple of days and wonders whether we would be interested in a book on Victorian needlework. I try to return some of the phone calls, searching through the various piles on my desk for the proposal that must be decided upon this afternoon. I am not a clean-desk person. I have three separate piles of paper on my desk: Emergency, Priority, and Get Done. I do not find the proposal in any of the three, but in a Super Emergency pile I have put in a special place. I take a quick look at it while I set up an appointment with the British publisher.

12:15   I'm due for lunch at 12:30, fifteen blocks away. I sign an expense voucher for one of the editors, who is on his way to Boston to talk to an author who has self-published some charming cookbooks. Since I am having lunch with an agent I haven't seen in some time, I grab his client list for review in the taxi. Just as I am about to leave, one of our senior editors comes in. "Got a minute?" She looks pale. I want to say that I have to run, but I don't. She tells me she has decided to resign. Maybe leave publishing. Maybe leave New York. I nod. I smile. I say I understand, but perhaps she should think it over and we should talk it over at some length. I don't really have time now because I must leave for lunch. She seems relieved. We make a date to talk tomorrow. I rush to lunch.

12:45   I am fifteen minutes late. The agent is just this side of real anger. I apologize. I hate being kept waiting myself. I also hate being late. Once we order lunch, the tension eases. He asks what our big books for the fall season are. I ask what his current best-sellers are. I tell him we have a fine list, but we are on the lookout for interesting nonfiction. He tells me about some of his new clients. Some sound interesting. Some not. I tell him about one or two ideas I have for nonfiction books, about a novel I think should be written. We gossip a bit. I tell him I may be looking for an editor. He suggests two very good people.

2:30   I am back in the office and have a half hour before my three o'clock marketing meeting to look at the proposal that needs to be decided on by this afternoon. It is for a book by a well-known journalist about the effects of gossip in shaping government policy. The writing is lively, some of the ideas thought-provoking. On the other hand, the idea doesn't really seem strong enough to warrant publication in hardcover. It strikes me as a subject that would work very well as a controversial article for *Esquire* or *New York* magazine. The agent doesn't seem upset by my decision, when I call him at five minutes to three.

3:00   Marketing meeting. The meeting is attended by the editor in chief, the publisher, the directors of sales, advertising, promotion, and subsidiary rights, and the production manager. Since it is two weeks before the yearly convention of the American Booksellers Association, we discuss which books will get preferred treatment, which authors we wish to have in person, and which booksellers we will want to entertain. As editor in chief, I represent all the editors in my group and through them all the books. I try to give them all a fair chance. In the end, only a few books will be featured. The winnowing process takes time and sometimes tests tempers. I make a case for one of the quieter novels. The others agree that it is a book of quality and that it should get special treatment. We discuss advertising budgets; which authors should tour; which should be forcibly prevented from touring. The production manager tells us we have to make a decision on the print order for one of our major novels. It's a long book, and if we think we are going to increase the printing, she needs to reserve paper. Subsidiary rights reports that one of the books on which we were expecting substantial reprint moneys has been getting a disappointing reaction. The publicity director says that a review in the *New York Times* is expected momentarily. She hopes it will be favorable. So do I.

5:15   The marketing meeting breaks up. I meet with the production manager and the publisher to discuss printings on half a dozen books that were not covered in the meeting.

6:00   I head for a cocktail party in honor of a British agent. It's a beautiful spring evening and the party is in the ground-floor garden of a charming town house in the East Seventies. People are sipping white wine and looking very relaxed. I wonder if that is the way I look. I sip some wine too. I wonder if my senior editor is really going to leave.

I hope she decides to stay, but if she doesn't, I know I will find someone good to replace her. There are wonderful people in this business. Writers, editors, publishers, even agents. I feel relaxed. It is the end of the day.

But of course the day doesn't usually end at the cocktail hour, because most editors will be carrying the ever-present briefcase or tote with a manuscript or two to at least dip into before the next day. And the editor—junior, senior, or chief—always carries with her the hope that the next manuscript she reads is going to be the one that will set the heart beating, the adrenaline going, generate the excitement that makes it all worthwhile.

It would be impossible to try to cover everything an editor in chief does: the variety, the range of problems and challenges, the housekeeping aspects of the job as well as its creative highs, and its disappointments. The strengths and weaknesses of the man or woman who fills the job will determine which aspects of it will be emphasized. A good editor in chief needs to be warm and cool; creative and businesslike; a leader and a follower. On reflection, there is one quality that I think is indispensable: the ability to deal with paradox.

PAUL FARGIS

Paul Fargis is president of The Stonesong Press, a book packaging and publishing consulting firm. Mr. Fargis has been responsible for the development of several best-sellers and has had wide experience not only as an editor and publisher, but also in such areas as sales promotion, publicity, acquisition, and strategic planning.

• • •

Is there a new type of editor on the scene today? Yes; one of the most innovative editorial developments in recent years has been the emergence of the producer/packager. As Paul Fargis points out in his stimulating essay written especially for this anthology, the producer/packager provides a creative editorial and production service that can give a publisher's list a newer, fresher look and free the staff editor to give more time to house-originated projects. The producer/packager is usually a former staff editor who wanted more independence, more responsibility, and freedom from the confinements of corporate life. The producer/packager creates an editorial idea, finds an author to execute it, creates a proposal, and finds an editor who wants to take it on for his or her list. The producer/packager then can produce anything from a manuscript to a finished book—depending on the acquiring editor's needs. For the editor who yearns to be "almost a publisher," and who is a self-starter, the role of the producer/packager seems ideal.

THE EDITORS WHO PRODUCE

If a blurb is the sound made by a publisher, then pizzazz is probably the noise that comes from a book producer. "Pizzazz" describes the peculiar combination of enterprise, orchestration, imagination, and enthusiasm essential for the producer of books—a person who is at once developer, editor, financier, and promoter.

There seem to be a number of different notions and a good deal of misinformation in publishing about what a producer or packager is and does, and even (in some old-fashioned quarters) why packagers or producers exist. The first thing one ought to know about them is that many prefer to be called book producers, the label adopted by the recently formed American Book Producers Association. "Packager" seems to describe an individual who merely wraps books or puts them in cartons. A few of us don't like the term "book producer," either, because it implies that we only manufacture books. In this article, though, "producer" and "packager" are used interchangeably.

The number of books being created by book producers and the recent attention they have been getting in the media have prompted some people to suggest that their name change again. As printers became publishers, it is said, so also should book producers become co-publishers. The book producer has at least half the normal publishing responsibility and brings the project to the point where it can be "made public." The publisher, in such a cooperative venture, prints and/or sells the book. Both the responsibility and the risk are shared, and that, to my mind, is co-publishing.

A book producer/packager is an individual or a firm that has an idea for a book, finds and aids the people who develop and write it, and sells it in any stage, from finished manuscript to finished book, to a publisher or another source of distribution. An agent who provides authors with ideas and editorial assistance in return for higher-than-normal agent's fees can be called a book producer. So can a free-lance editor who, in return for a portion of the advance and royalty, reworks, molds, and rewrites a manuscript until it is in publishable shape. Or a book producer could be the person who takes existing texts and/or illustrations (from a magazine or art catalogue, for example) and repackages them in book form. Generally, though, book producers develop new ideas for books and take the responsibility and risk of delivering acceptable camera-ready mechanicals or bound books to a publisher. And, generally, trade-book producers have a certain combination of editorial and marketing abilities (or access to them) that are not common today in many publishing houses, where an editor's time and talent are spent on acquisition and routine editing, not on in-depth development.

Most book producers are tiny companies and they operate out of small quarters with overhead and productivity that would be the envy of any cost accountant in corporate publishing. In a sense, packagers are more editorial than market oriented. By that I mean that more editorial effort and skill goes into creating the physical book than into selling it to a publisher. However, book producers very often have the special marketing savvy to get their books sold in all kinds of nontraditional outlets. Danceways has been able to sell its books in stores that sell ballet clothing; Tree Communications sells books in gift stores; the Stonesong Press (my company) works in mail order; The Benjamin Company in premium sales; and James Wagonvoord sells large numbers of books to book fairs. All these companies are run by creative editors who first develop the idea and then market it. Nowadays that creation and the complete marketing follow-through by an editor would be close to impossible within most trade publishing houses.

One way to explain what a book producer does is to follow some books from conception to delivery. What happens? First there's an idea, and that usually comes from reading and mulling over a lot of different subjects. For example, after seeing a number of books about prescription and nonprescription drugs and then being curious about a drug prescribed for my daughter, I realized there were no reference books that tell parents about children's drugs and their side effects. I contacted several medical writers, examined literature about drugs and medical reference sources, and decided on the necessary content and format for a book.

One writer (of four approached), whose work I liked, agreed to do some sample sections for a fee that would be nonreturnable if the book was not sold—a kill fee, in other words. That same fee would be applied against his earnings if the book was sold.

I drafted a proposal for the book. The proposal and the samples were sent to seven publishers who I thought would have the marketing and publicity skills to make the work a success. I explained what kind of advance and royalty I wanted, and included all material I could gather about the need for the book, its market, etc. Six publishers responded with interest; one said no. There were questions about content and costs, discussions about terms, and then an agreement with one publisher on the advance, royalty rate, and other terms. *The Pediatric Guide to Drugs and Vitamins,* by Edward Brace, was sold to Delacorte, which elected to take the edited manuscript, not mechanicals or bound books. Up to the point of agreement on a contract, the stages in the book producer's sale would be the same as for the delivery of mechanicals or bound books.

For a publisher who wants mechanicals, the producer edits, copyedits, sets type, proofreads, pages out, indexes, and pastes up repro copy. The producer would quote a figure to the publisher for these expenses with an allowance for overhead. Because overhead and expenses of corporate publishing are so much higher, the producer's figure is often lower than the publisher can match. Usually, the contract will call for the producer to stay within that figure. Hearst, for example, contracted with me for a work entitled *Kit Houses by Mail,* a compendium of houses that can be assembled by a handy do-it-yourselfer. I had allowed a margin for error in my estimate, and as it turned out, the typesetting was lower than I expected but the artwork and photostats considerably more expensive, leaving me, when mechanicals were delivered, within thirteen dollars of the quote!

Crown is probably the publisher that has the most experience with and understanding for packagers. They have bought a considerable number of finished books from packagers, including the best-seller *The Joy of Sex.*

I have supplied both finished books and manuscripts to Crown. When they contracted for *In the Beginning,* a Stonesong Press book by Isaac Asimov, they elected to buy finished books. I handled the entire production of the book, using free-lance help where it was necessary for design, copyediting, proofreading, jackets, etc. The R. R. Donnelley company's tailor-made production system allowed me a wide range of choices for paper, binding materials, and jackets. Crown participated in the decisions on such things as jacket design and editing, but basically they depended on and worked with me to produce the book.

When the producer delivers finished books, he has quoted a price (as with the mechanicals) for delivering a certain number of bound copies to a publisher's warehouse at a fixed cost per copy. Technically, until those books are delivered in acceptable form to the publisher, they are owned by the producer. This is the fact that makes some individuals shy away from book production as a part of packaging. The investment risk in producing 25,000 copies of a book are great. One mistake in printing or paper or color could literally lead to the end of many a company.

When deciding how and in what form to buy from a packager, in-house editors should know that most producers are quite flexible about what they can deliver. If the price for bound books is too high, an editor should not hesitate to ask about buying mechanicals or film. Sometimes the producer would prefer to deliver edited manuscript. Of course, this will usually not be possible when a considerable amount of color work is at stake or a large international print run is being put together; the producer's terms stay firm. But on a typical black-and-white trade book, the producer can usually accommodate the needs of a publisher.

Because of the huge number of books published each year and the ever-increasing burden of overhead (often created nowadays by mergers and acquisitions), many publishers, particularly the larger ones, have come to rely on the outside editorial and art sources that packagers can offer. Such out-of-house services are far less costly and time-consuming than in-house staff. How many trade editorial departments, for example, can afford staff people whose only job is picture research, or part-time people who can make calls (as my company recently did) to over 150 different manufacturers of do-it-yourself materials?

While some American packagers have full staffs of people to handle editing, design, production, and accounting, most packagers are one- to three-person operations. At The Stonesong Press, where I've been packaging for the last few years, I'm not only the editor and sales director, but also the production manager, bill collector, and receptionist. We small packagers will farm out copyediting or proofreading and have an accountant check the ledger and do our taxes, but one or two people will do the typing and filing; research all the ideas and write out the initial proposal; find an author; sell to a publisher; handle the accounting debits and credits; arrange for jackets, typesetting, paper, printing, binding, shipping; and pray. Typically, we'll have between two and ten projects under contract and others cooking on the back burner.

On the other hand, trade editors employed by publishing houses probably handle fifteen or more titles a year and simply do not have the time or the assistance to work closely and frequently on their own ideas for books. The editor may suggest an idea to an author, but will not stay personally involved with its development and maturation. An editor-packager, on the other hand, not only comes up with the idea and the writer, but also is the mentor and the wordsmith who sees it to fruition. Perhaps that kind of involvement is the reason why many book producers come from former editorial positions in publishing houses. It is also a key reason why trade departments save time and risk capital by working with packagers.

I think the major difference between the in-house editor and the editor-producer is that the producer's time is spent almost solely on his or her books. A couple of months after I started out, I realized that I had not been to or called a single meeting, had not sought an approval for anything, had not written one memo, read a single printout, or phoned another department in the company. I was doing everything and it was easier and took less time. Time was the wonderful difference. Time to think an idea through, time to look things up, weigh alternatives, talk to others. What a luxury it is and how much difference it makes, particularly when starting out.

For the beginning producer, the proposal to the publisher is all-important because he or she has no reputation. The novice must be able to prepare an enticing but accurate description of the book. And cost estimates must be right, because increases from the publisher are very unlikely after the contract is negotiated. Carter Smith of Media Projects, Inc., who started creating books in 1969, goes so far as to say: "For the first five years, you had better be able to write exciting, attention-getting proposals, because your stock-in-trade is ideas until your finished books have sold well."

There are other significant differences between the producer and the publishing house editor. Here are just a few:

- ▶ The producer-editor creates almost all the book ideas he or she is working on.
- ▶ The producer-editor will share in the royalties received for the books—indeed, will *depend* on the money and will put up the money to get the project going.
- ▶ An in-house editor's project can be vetoed by the editorial board or the sales department, whereas the producer can take the project to many other sources until he or she finds a publisher.
- ▶ A small producer's livelihood depends on his or her skill and knowledge of almost all facets of publishing: contracts, selling, rights, editing, production, design, finance, etc. Indeed, the packager completes about 80 percent of the publishing functions, whereas the in-house editor handles 15–20 percent.
- ▶ Another difference is money, and there the publisher's editor has the advantage. When one is backed by the budget of a large department or company, there is room for monetary alternatives and errors. But when one's own mortgage money or grocery bill is at stake, the perspective is more pragmatic and each dollar in the budget is spent more judiciously.
- ▶ Last, the producer is usually motivated to be in business by the chance at the independence and authority that go with being one's own employer.

Richard Gallen of Richard Gallen Books was quoted in *Publishers Weekly* as saying: "If publishers were doing their job well, they wouldn't need independent book producers. . . . There aren't enough creative editors in house to think up the ideas. So they need us!" I think that's partly true, but would add that we also make the job of in-house editor easier because we deliver a manuscript or book that is already edited, even edited to fit what an editor requests. And when an in-house editor is developing an idea, he or she can turn to a packager for complete follow-through.

There are two sides of the book-producing business that I don't like. One is the selling of a proposal and the other is "doing the numbers." When I offer a book and I don't sense interest and excitement from the receiver, I'm inclined not to push and dangle enticing thoughts about promotion ideas and glamorous sales. I suppose I might add more fanfare to my show-and-tell, but I wonder how much difference it will make in the long run, especially if I end up overselling one of my books.

Doing the numbers . . . Do I really have to tell you about that side of the business? I am not a numbers person. Division and decimals, split plant costs and such, are dull exercises for me. But of course, I have to do them and do them right if my project is going to make any money. I'm sure no one figures out a profit-and-loss sheet the way I do, but it suits me fine. Here's my system: First, I figure out how much money I want to have when I've finished. That sum is my gross profit and includes my overhead. Gross profit minus overhead is my net profit and the figure I want to make when I have finished the project. In other words, I normally cannot rely on future royalties or rights income to cover basic costs.

The profit plus all costs divided by the number of copies to be bought by the publisher equals the amount I can quote as a cost per copy. The same profit plus costs is the figure I need to get as an advance against royalties on a project if I am to deliver a manuscript.

If I stick to those basics and properly forecast expenses and cash flow, I can keep paying myself a salary.

There are many risks and problems for book producers, particularly the very small ones, but as in earlier times, it is basically easy to hang out a book producer's shingle today. Capital and competition are two obvious headaches for the producer. I had heard about and given lip service to cash flow when I was on the publisher's side of the fence, but didn't really appreciate what it meant until I went into business for myself. I still detest doing my bookkeeping, but it has taught me about the cost of money and given me a more hard-nosed and careful respect for where it will be spent.

Competition won't go away and will probably increase among producers. Already we are learning to be leery of trendy ideas that may be on the drawing board of other packagers. It isn't just the occasional similar book that makes things competitive, though. It is also the increasing number of new producers. More and more individuals are producing books in one form or another—a very healthy sign for publishing in general, since it shows that creativity and diversity in books can still flourish and enhance the growth of trade publishing.

JOHN THORNTON

John Thornton is the associate publisher and editor in chief of Facts on File, Inc. He has been editor in chief of the trade paperback lines of New American Library and of the Washington Square Press imprint at Pocket Books. Prior to that, he worked on trade paperbacks at Schocken Books and at the New York Graphic Society.

•　　•　　•

Mr. Thornton offers a concise but thorough history and review of the ever-changing world of trade paperbacks in his lively, witty essay, written especially for this anthology. He discusses the many guises and sizes of the trade paperback, its various audiences, its special placement between the hardcover book and the mass-market paperback in terms of pricing, readership, and marketing, and what lies ahead for this chameleon-like aspect of publishing. Of especial interest is Mr. Thornton's categorization of how editors turn out the vast diversity of trade paperbacks: where they come from, how they are created, how they are marketed. It is a particularly innovative, "wide-open" area of editing, and for an editor fortunate enough to have the chance to create exciting new trade paperbacks, the prospects can't help but look good.

THE TRUTH ABOUT TRADE PAPERBACKS

There are really two questions to be answered in learning the truth about trade paperbacks: What *are* trade paperbacks? How do editors turn them out? Both are questions of some complexity, but given the phenomenal growth of this particular form of book publishing in the last decade, they deserve patient, careful answers. Since no discussion of the editing of trade paperbacks in the 1980s can take place in a vacuum, it is essential to begin with a short if sweeping history of the trade paperback.

The evolutionary forebears of the trade paperback are, on the one hand, the inexpensive hardcover editions of popular and past authors, known in the book trade as cheap editions, and on the other, mass-market paperbacks. Cheap editions were for the most part a late nineteenth (in England) and early twentieth (in America) century form of book publishing, a by-product of the effort in both nations to achieve mass literacy through compulsory education. Some examples of these books still exist today, in the editions of Random House's Modern Library or J. M. Dent's Everyman's Library or Oxford University Press's The World's Classics. Priced at about half the going rate of more expensively produced editions, they provided generations of readers with first-rate reading material at prices even poor scholars could afford. In format they tended to be portable, functional, and a bit plain.

The mass-market paperback, like so many aspects of American life in the late twentieth century, has its origins in World War II. While it is true that in the mid-1930s Sir Allen Lane in England issued his first Penguin books and that in the summer of 1939 Pocket Books in New York began selling the first true mass paperbacks, it was the wartime desire to distribute cheap reading materials to servicemen and women at home and abroad that gave this special form of book publishing an opportunity for rapid growth that has scarcely abated in over forty years.

The great virtue of the mass-market book is that it was able to break free of the staid cultural conservatism of the traditional book publishers. Colorful covers, cheap prices (twenty-five cents at the beginning), and the willingness of national magazine and newspaper distributors (whose combined outlets totaled ten to fifteen times the number of bookstores in the country) to take them on not only resulted in the death of the pulp magazine but established a distinctly new kind of book. Unfortunately, the stroke of genius that fastened mass paperbacks to the habits and demands of the magazine business has contributed to the current stagnation of this marketplace. It may be that the mass paperback, like Neanderthal man, will prove to be an evolutionary cul-de-sac, while the trade paperback, the Homo sapiens of books, with its remarkable ability to take on new characteristics and to adapt to changing conditions, will prove to be the fitter survivor.

Meanwhile, during the Second World War, a national mobilization of immense proportions took place. Men and women from every conceivable economic and social milieu were dislodged from familiar surroundings and exposed to new worlds of opportunity. Accordingly, when the war ended and the GI Bill of Rights was enacted, young men and women began to enroll for higher education in unprecedented numbers. The American university system, which before the war chiefly served a small, wealthy ruling class as a way station to prominent positions in government, finance, or the professions, found itself bursting at the seams as middle- and working-class students came to claim the fruits of victory.

The provision of inexpensive paperback books to these new student readers offered publishers a golden opportunity as well. Suddenly the idea of selling the important books of the age—and of the ages—not just to the tiny coterie of elite readers that had been the book publishers' only customers for centuries, but to an ever-expanding, college-educated readership, became a real possibility. Thus, it was out of the combination of the tradition of inexpensive hardcover editions of great books, the appealing, inexpensive format of the mass paperback, and the greatly enlarged demand for general books of literary fiction and serious nonfiction that the first trade paperbacks were born.

Who published the first trade paperback? It's really not worth the effort to trace exact paternity here. Suffice it to say that by the time the 1950s were over, a dozen or more new imprints were alive and healthy. Some are no longer with us, like Grosset's Universal Library (in which the first edition of *Editors on Editing* appeared in 1962) or Apollo Books (lost, like its parent, T. Y. Crowell, in the publishing-house merger mania of the 1970s). Other imprints are now permanent—even venerable—fixtures in the flashy, slippery world of contemporary trade paperbacks.

Among the best-known of this first generation of trade paperback imprints (with parent hardcover publishers) are Anchor (Doubleday), Vintage (Random House), Meridian, New Directions, Torchbooks (Harper & Row), Dover, Noonday (Farrar, Straus & Giroux), Viking Compass, Rinehart Editions (Holt, Rinehart & Winston), Harvest (Harcourt, Brace & World), Schocken, Beacon Press, Dutton Paperbacks, and Modern Library College Editions (Random House).

Almost without exception, the content of these books was the same as that of the traditional hardcover; in fact, both editions were often printed from the same plates. Their subject matter was traditional too: poetry, theology, history, philosophy, humanistic science, and so on down the roll call of the humanities curriculum. These books clearly reflected the needs of their academic customers.*

In format, too, these books reflected their parentage and therefore came in two shapes—the standard hardcover trim sizes (6" × 9", 5½" × 8", etc.) or the standard mass market paperback size (4¼" × 7"). Big and small trade paperbacks were printed on better-quality book paper, which may account for the synonym "quality paperbacks." The prices of these books fell midway between those of hardcover and mass paperback books (this is largely still true today), as did the typical quantities in which they were printed.

The natural outgrowth of placing such books in the hands of so many student readers—who were also receiving significant doses of mass-market paperbacks on their own—was to change the aesthetic preferences of a whole generation of American readers. Far from graduating—literally and figuratively—to hardcovers after

---

*Also worthy of mention are the trade paperback lines of university presses, begun for similar purposes at about this time, notably Chicago, California, Harvard, Princeton, Johns Hopkins, and Yale.

college, these new readers created a demand for new kinds of trade paperbacks. And just at that moment—somewhere in the mid-1960s—two trends came along to aid and abet this demand.

The first was a by-product of the social and political upheavals of the 1960s—the emergence of a countercultural press. Using any and all materials, formats, and graphic notions that were ready to hand, the "underground" publications of the late 1960s and early 1970s were remarkably diverse and eccentric. Whether Day-Glo newspapers from Cambridge, broadsides from Berkeley, or adult comics from God knows where, the variety of homely, odd, and generally outrageous pamphlets, posters, magazines, and leaflets that were spawned had no precedent. Freedom in content and form were being proclaimed from every quarter.

The first trend, then, was the growth of the small, independent press, whose output of books reflected the individuality and flair of its publishers. The drab imitation-dust-jacket covers on trade paperbacks gave way to more colorful, playful, and creative images. The plain pipe-rack trim sizes were still in favor, but now were mingled with square, oblong, magazine-sized, spiral-bound, or even giant-sized (e.g., *The Whole Earth Catalog*) trade paperback books.

"Alternative" seems to be the word most descriptive of these publishers. For every traditional book on health care, they would publish an alternative book on acupuncture or holistic healing; for every standard cookbook, an alternative book on Zen bread baking or tofu eating; for every mainstream guide on child rearing, an alternative guide to home birth or raising children in a commune.

Some presses were devoted to fine arts, others to poetry or minority or feminist protest; still others to cosmic consciousness or regional concerns. The net result was a wonderful infusion of fresh blood into the gently hardening arteries of the book-publishing Establishment.

This general loosening up of format and graphic styles, coupled with the strange new content of the small-press publications, did not escape the notice of the older publishers. Their continuing search for and exploitation of novelty took no different course in this instance, and by the early 1970s, not only had the most aggressive small presses worked out distribution arrangements with many New York publishers, but the latter began selling their own entries in the Aquarian Age trade paperback sweepstakes. By the

end of the decade, virtually every major hardcover publisher had
either begun or revitalized its own trade paperback imprint. (A
side effect of these oversized paperbacks was the shipping, shelv-
ing, and display problems they caused. The bookstore-fixture
manufacturers realized their own windfall from the changes that
were going on.)

One of the factors that made possible all this growth in sheer
numbers and varieties of books was a second trend, alluded to
above: the appearance of chain bookstores. There are now between
one and two thousand of these stores (B. Dalton, Waldenbooks,
and Doubleday are among the largest), and they account for perhaps one of every four books sold in bookstores in this country,
a notable fact when you consider there are twelve to fifteen thousand other bookstores in competition.

So just when new kinds of books and customers came along, new
kinds of bookstores came along too. Specializing in careful inventory control, fast turnover, best-sellers, and economies of scale
available only through centralized buying, they have learned to
take the quirky, humorous, and unusual offerings of the new-style
trade paperbacks in stride and turn them to considerable advantage. The preferences of a handful of astute trade paperback buyers
for these chain stores and their equivalent numbers at select large
urban or university-town bookstores have made the trade paperback "revolution" a reality.*

But amid the gay profusion of exotic new trade paperbacks—
rock books, wok books, schlock books—what became of the older
types? Actually, they were still around, if you looked hard enough.
Of course, much of this sort of academic trade paperback publishing has retreated steadily to the precincts of the university and
professional publishers, but it continues to represent a small but
nonetheless significant part of the continuing trade paperback programs at most hardcover houses with trade paperback lines. Reliable and with improved appearance, such books form the backlist
backbone of many an imprint.

Thus, by the 1980s, the old-style trade paperback, however
prestigious, was emphatically *not* where the speculative money

---

The New York Times Book Review began publishing a weekly "Trade Paperback
Best Sellers" list (which in turn was discontinued at the end of 1983 in favor of a
combined mass-market and trade paperback list entitled simply "Paperback Best Sellers"; roughly one-third of this list continues to be devoted to trade paperbacks).

and action were for publishers. Instead, the aim of most trade paperback programs today is to be the first out with the trendiest and to hope that, since every book is a kind of lottery ticket, one is holding a few winners. The reasons for this change of attitude may be part of a larger trend in American life and culture to seek homogeneity where once there was diversity, or the entry of the slick mass-market houses into trade paperback publishing—most notably in the 1970s Ballantine Books, Avon, and Bantam Books —or the human tendency of booksellers to buy surefire books accompanied by ambitious promotion plans rather than modest titles accompanied by none. But regardless of the reasons, the bookshelves are groaning and the book racks are spinning with books, and what have been aptly termed nonbooks, on diets, cats, exercise, beauty, and still more cats. Selling the most copies of the fewest titles is a game devised by the mass-market paperback publishers, but it is increasingly becoming the only game in town. And given the fickle buying habits of booksellers and of the general public, it is turning out to be a most dangerous game.

At the outset, I mentioned that answering two questions would get at the truth about trade paperbacks. Now that a short history —at least, as well as I can make it out—has been sketched in, it is time to find out how the editors who bring you trade paperbacks manage to do so.

Understanding the editorial side of trade paperbacks depends on where you look and whom you look at in this line of work. I doubt that there are more than a couple of hundred editors in the whole publishing industry who specifically work on trade paperbacks. (It should be noted in passing that when all is weighed in the balance, the differences between the functions of a trade paperback editor and those of a hardcover editor—certainly up to the final stages of marketing and selling the books—are negligible. A good hard-cover editor can easily become a good trade paperback editor and vice versa.)

My own experience in acquiring and editing trade paperbacks began with the traditional nonfiction academic trade paperbacks. It was about eighteen years ago, at a small, family-owned publishing house in New York, Schocken Books; later, I worked on large-format illustrated trade paperbacks at the New York Graphic Society in Boston; finally, I have acquired, edited, and published a wide variety of trade paperbacks at two of the largest mass-market publishers, New American Library and Pocket Books.

I believe that the possibilities for successful, interesting publishing depend to a very great extent on three factors—the weight of prior history at the publishing house where the editor works, the taste and capability of the editor himself, and pure, blind luck. The last factor is the hardest to predict and to accept, but it is nonetheless operative in all phases of trade publishing. For every book that has a phenomenal success, there can usually be located any number of similar books published obscurely just before and any number of unsuccessful imitative books published just after. When a book becomes a transcendent best-seller, it is rarely the result of conscious prior activity on the part of an editor or a publisher. It really does just happen, and the publisher acts as best he can on the unmistakable demand for the book.

This is not to say that hard work and adroit publishing skills don't pay off. Rather, since I don't believe there is a formula for finding and publishing books that will become best-sellers, I think the best way to examine the process of editing trade paperbacks is to average out all the particulars in order to look at the general, universal steps involved. Whether you are editing trade paperbacks at a small press in Southern California, a university press in Indiana, an established hardcover house in Boston, or a mass-market house in midtown Manhattan, there are certain features common to the enterprise.

In the beginning is the idea, and answering the question Where do editors get book ideas? is daunting. The ultimate answer merely begs the question, because it is that book editors just do somehow come up with book ideas. Nonetheless, if we look at the results of those ideas embodied on the shelves of bookstores, it is possible to trace most books back to certain basic sources. These are, in ascending order of excitement for the trade paperback editor:

Reprinting Public-Domain Books   Dover Books has excelled at this biblio-curiosity sort of publishing for over thirty years now, and many other publishers devote a small part of their list to it as well. Doing this kind of book on a regular basis requires a solid background in library research, bibliography, and a knowledge of the out-of-print book business, but it can pay off. There are numerous beautiful trade paperback facsimile editions that have sold hundreds of thousands of copies over the years. There may be a whiff of the rag-and-bone trade about this sort of book recycling, but for those who love it, there is nothing quite so satisfying as a clever, royalty-free reprint.

Reprinting of or Simultaneous Printing with In-House
Hardcovers   In the last decade, the retail price of hardcover editions has doubled, but in the minds of many a customer, the fair price of a book has not. Accordingly, another reason for the success of trade paperbacks has been their relatively reasonable cover prices (as noted earlier, usually somewhere between hardcovers and mass-market paperbacks). Most trade paperback editors at hardcover houses work in concert with hardcover editors to plan the eventual or simultaneous publication of a hardcover project in paperback. In many ways, this is a sound approach. It assures the book of the reviews it must have (if it is a serious work and not a "how-to" or "self-help" book that any customer would readily recognize at a glance in a store) to excerpt on the paperback cover, which validate the book and explain it and encourage its purchase. It also offers the budget-conscious a book that can be afforded, even if it sometimes means waiting half a year or a year until the hardcover sale has ebbed.

Buying Paperback Reprint Rights of Hardcover Books
This sort of trade paperback has become increasingly hard to do, since virtually all the major hardcover publishers now have their own trade paperback lines and routinely feed their own hardcover titles into them for a second life. Consequently, when there is auctioning of paperback rights on newly published hardcover books, until recent years a phenomenon restricted to the mass-market publishers with their fabled acquisition budgets, it is now readily participated in by the more active trade paperback imprints, no matter how close their ties with a hardcover parent.

Often an editor will spot a potential "lead" book on another publisher's hardcover list and will inquire about buying paperback rights. If several other reprinters call with the same question, the stage is set for an auction. Profit-and-loss projections must be compiled and a decision must be made about whether it is worth the risk of overpaying at auction for a book that will not only be bought in large quantities initially but will be reordered as a back-list title for years to come. This kind of speculative buying, since it often takes the editor out beyond the three-mile limit into un-charted waters, is not for everyone, but it can be an exciting and potentially profitable way to add titles to a list.

The Original Trade Paperback   This is the commonest type of trade paperback in contemporary publishing—or at least the type that receives the most attention—and editors put them to-gether in several ways:

The Packager —There are dozens of independent groups who combine ideas—their own or those of a publisher's editor—with book packaging, book writing, illustrating, typesetting, and other production skills, to deliver more or less finished books to order. If an editor wants a book on the latest punk-rock star or on aerobic exercising, he can call a packager and thereby save substantially on in-house costs, both in overhead and in personal wear and tear. The best packagers are sensitive to the editor's needs for the book and the best editors always keep a firm grip on what the packager is doing.

The Agent —Most trade paperback editors who work with agents find they are more interested in original hardcover projects than in trade paperbacks. The reason is partly one of age—most established agents are older and more in tune with hardcover publishing—and partly one of fiscal prudence. Though more paperbacks (mass-market and trade) are sold in bookstores, the hardcover dollar volume still exceeds that of the paperbacks. Moreover, the possibility of first placing hardcover rights on a property, with the eventual sale at auction of paperback rights (for large sums of cash), holds an almost mystical fascination for most agents. Nonetheless, among the younger agents there is a growing awareness that trade paperbacks are the books of the future, and they often do turn up with some first-rate projects.

The Unsolicited Submission —This is the least likely route by which an editor can latch onto a worthwhile project. The quality of most blind submissions is abysmally low. Most experienced authors do find and use agents to do their submitting for them, so unless an editor is willing to waste a lot of time looking for a very little, wading into the slush pile is not to be recommended. (That said, I must add that some years ago, Helen and Scott Nearing's wonderful book on homesteading, *Living the Good Life,* which sold about 200,000 copies in hard and soft editions, came to me unsolicited one day in the morning mail.)

The Original Idea —These can truly come from anywhere, even possibly from outer space. Watching television, reading obscure newsletters, attending subcultural events, talking to friends, relatives, and interesting strangers, traveling around the country or abroad, getting a tip from an old author, from a sales manager, a bookseller, or even—rarest of all—from a fellow editor: all these are tried and true paths to new trade paperback projects. Original ideas tend to result in the most satisfying books because in a special way they are one's own, even though it must be conceded that successful contemporary publishing is preeminently a group activity.

Once the editor has hatched an embryonic book idea, the next step is to build a consensus among those charged with decision-making (or with *not* making a decision, as often seems to be the case), about whether and how the book should be done. This usually involves the careful preparation of a profit-and-loss statement that purports to forecast the sales performance of the book. Such documentation also helps everyone concerned to think hard about the right length, format, number of illustrations, etc., since these are factors that condition the impact of the eventual finished book on its audience. In addition to hard figures, this stage of decision-making involves a fair amount of buttonholing after meetings, cajoling in the corridors, and trading favors with colleagues. The main thing is not to leave unaccounted for some factor, like permissions costs or a sales manager who always says no after lunch, that might appear out of nowhere and send your hopes up in flames.

If the go-ahead is given, the scenario for publication proceeds in typical fashion. The negotiation of the contract takes place with author or agent or publisher, and the agreements are drawn. Next, the manuscript is written and the illustrations are gathered, the editing and necessary rewriting are done (in some large outfits, the editor who acquires the project does not always do the manuscript editing), the design and cover are prepared, the publication date is set, the catalogue copy is written, the sales presentation is made, the orders are taken, the advertising is chosen, the books are shipped, the fingernails are chewed, and (one always hopes) the cash flow is begun.

Perhaps I have slighted the routines of book publishing in the foregoing paragraphs (in truth, there are dozens of books and courses and ways to find out how books are made). I have done so for this reason: to emphasize how crucially important the *editor's personal effort* is at each and every stage of this progress from acquisition of property to sale of finished books. Unless the editor perceives himself or herself to be in fact a publisher in miniature —not just a Zorro with a blue pencil—the book in question is doomed. The buck can never leave the sponsoring editor's desk. If a poor cover design is done, it is the editor's job to get it changed; if the print run is set too low or (rarity of rarities) too high, it is first and foremost the editor who must work to get it corrected.

This total involvement on the editor's part has always been true of good publishing, but never truer than now. The annual production of new titles—hardcover and trade paperback and mass paperback—is staggering, reflecting the common belief that since no one knows with certainty what will sell, the more books you put out for sale, the better are your chances one *will* sell. The modern chain bookstore resembles nothing so much as a supermarket wherein not one but twenty brands of the same product are offered. Making the naive consumer choose your book begins to be possible only if you as editor have tried mightily to keep the underlying concept and value of the book in sharp focus for everybody standing on the bucket brigade between author and reader. If the editor has been an indifferent collaborator, a lackluster cheerleader, and an inept strategist, the chances are overwhelming that the book will go belly up onto the remainder tables a season or two after publication.

Publishing is a business of exceptions rather than rules, a truth that gives both pause and hope for the coming years.

What is the future of the trade paperback? It would appear to be steadily increasing in sales and prominence in the small world of commercial publishing, if the known indicators are examined. The audience for trade hardcovers is shrinking, as prices increase, as the hardcover aesthetic ceases to dominate rising generations of readers, and as the slow acceptance of original paperback books by reviewers proceeds apace. The flexibility of format and the especially colorful packaging most trade paperbacks have seem to make people reach out for them in a bookstore. (On the negative side, the 1980s opened with widespread retrenchment in the publishing industry, as rising overhead costs, poorly aimed publishing programs, a downturn in the national economy, and the end of the great period of expansion of chain bookstores coalesced into forecasts of gloom and doom.)

On the up side, as younger, business-minded editors might put it, there is a new generation of readers for trade paperbacks. Students, the traditional customers for trade paperbacks, in their intense pursuit of vocational goals, are steering a course away from the liberal arts and toward economics, business, law, and the utopian vistas the personal computer has painted. Publishing programs, of course, spring up like crabgrass after a shower to meet their needs with a luxuriant new growth of trade paperbacks on everything from résumé writing to software programs on how to use your hardware.

And so, despite the arrival of the two-paycheck marriage, the competing diversions of television watching and magazine reading, and the sheer exhaustion of trying to survive the special ordeals of urban life in late-twentieth-century America, trade paperbacks have indeed found their own ecological niche, and their readership seems assured, even loyal. If a forecast is wanted, then I predict that the next edition of *Editors on Editing,* the 2001 edition, will feature another article telling the latest truths about trade paperbacks.

MEL PARKER

Mel Parker is a senior editor at the Berkley Publishing Group, acquiring both originals and reprints. He was formerly a senior editor at Playboy Paperbacks.

●　　　●　　　●

Writing with uncommon warmth and enthusiasm, Mel Parker captures, in this lively essay, written especially for this anthology, the excitement, competitiveness, and satisfactions of being a mass-market paperback editor.

Covering the special responsibilities of both the paperback originals editor and the paperback reprint editor, Mr. Parker takes us along on the search for the book—whether a hardcover reprint or a paperback original—"born to be a paperback," the book destined for success in a big, profitable, commercial way.

Mr. Parker speaks of the editor's role in dealing with subsidiary rights directors when buying hardcover books for paperback reprint, and he discusses authors, marketing decisions, cover art choices, sales efforts, costing, and estimating print orders. Authoritatively and comprehensively, he escorts the reader through every area in which the paperback editor works. Of especial interest is Mr. Parker's discussion of the joys and pleasures peculiar to the paperback originals editor and the paperback reprint editor—where they are the same and where they differ. All in all, his article is an excellent and informed overview of the editor's role in one of the most dynamic and ever-changing areas of publishing.

BORN TO BE A PAPERBACK

It's Monday morning, time for the weekly editorial meeting at a mass-market paperback publishing house. As is the custom at most publishing companies, the editors gather around the conference table to discuss the business of the week: recent acquisitions, closing dates for upcoming paperback reprint auctions, and new submissions. But soon these mundane procedures give way to a kind of excitement. After the editorial director concludes the general business and asks the first editor what he's presenting for the week, the editor enthusiastically describes his book, and ends his presentation by saying that his book is "born to be a paperback."

Suddenly everyone realizes that this is no run-of-the-mill book being presented. There's an instantaneous unspoken communication among the editor, the editorial director, and the other members of the editorial committee: the group realizes that the editor, who usually calls his shots carefully, might very well have a hot property on his hands. By saying that the book he's presented is born to be a paperback, the editor isn't operating on instinct alone. On the contrary, the committee realizes that he's probably thought very carefully about the market for the book.

But what *are* the qualities that make a hardcover book or a manuscript "born to be a paperback"? First and most obvious, the book has to be a "good read." But by what standards? By the standards of the *mass market.* And what does that mean? It means the book must appeal to and be accessible to the greatest number of people.

The mass market is made up of many specialized markets. For instance, there's a category romance market, a male adventure market, a British mystery market, a Westerns market, a science-fiction market, etc. But the blockbuster mass-market paperback, the book that most paperback editors look for, goes beyond specific categories to embrace one of three major markets loosely defined by gender: the women's market, the men's market, and the "cross-over" market. Think of authors like Danielle Steele for the women's market (which embraces roughly 70 percent of the total market); of Robert Ludlum for the men's market; of James Michener, James Clavell, and Leon Uris, whom men and women read with equal enthusiasm. The books these authors write are "born to be paperbacks" because the stories they tell have great popular appeal to one of these blocs of readers.

It's a given that the "born paperback" is commercial, timely, and accessible. If it's a woman's novel, it must give the greatest number of women the kind of story they may be looking for at the time, either (1) fantasy entertainment like *Scruples* and *Master of the Game*—books with generous dollops of sex, glitz, glamour—juicy reads about self-reliant women who take on the world on their own terms; (2) historical romances, which offer women escape to another time and place; or (3) women's problem novels, stories that address the issues women care about today—coming to terms with the loss of a love, relating to a loved one, finding a job, or building a career, searching for identity amidst a maze of options.

If it's a man's novel that's "born to be a paperback," it might resemble books by authors such as Robert Ludlum, Ken Follett, or John Le Carré. These big books always treat the big issues, the big threats, the big conspiracies—so it's natural that many of these novels move in the direction of international intrigue, where the fate of nations (and often the world) is at stake.

Finally, there's a grand "crossover" book like *Roots, Exodus,* or *Shōgun.* Read by men and women both, these modern epics and family sagas are probably the most quintessentially mass market in that they generally contain elements that will appeal to everybody—colorful characters and places, romance, intrigue, great family dynasties, war, peace, the making of nations. It isn't surprising that these books, more than any others, sell in the millions.

But what about the literary quality of a "mass-market read"? Don't editors talk about the quality of the book? Of course they do. But basic editorial quality should be a *given* before the book is presented to the rest of the house (although many publishers have made lots of money with books of no quality but the right "elements"). The editorial director of a mass-market house may forgive certain flaws in a highly commercial reprint or original property, but few editors worth their salaries will knowingly publish books that are poorly executed from page one to the end. As in any kind of publishing, good books generally sell better than bad books. It's another given that word of mouth can make or break a book.

Still, the most successful paperback editors are concerned first and foremost with the *market* for the book. If the editor can't first identify the market for the project, he will have a hard time convincing the committee that the book should be bought. To complicate matters further, aside from markets separated by gender, mass-market editors also think about markets according to *means of distribution.* Rack-size mass-market paperbacks are distributed to the public in two basic kinds of outlets; for the sake of simplicity, let's call them supermarkets and bookstores. Mass-market paperbacks are generally sold to supermarkets by way of a national distributor, and they are sold "direct" to bookstores by the publisher's own sales force.

So when an editor says a book is born to be a paperback because not only is it a great women's read but it will sell in both supermarkets and bookstores, he's saying that the book will be a winner through its appeal to two kinds of readers: women shopping for groceries, who get the "impulse" to buy such and such a paperback, and women who go into a bookstore knowing pretty much what they want to read. The editorial director may press the editor by asking, "Is it primarily a supermarket book?" And if the editor says yes, that's good. The paperback house often would rather invest in a book that is primarily a supermarket book, because the greatest number of paperbacks are still distributed through supermarkets, convenience stores, and airports, and if you can reach that market with your terrific women's, men's, or crossover novel, then you're in business.

But what if an editor proposes a wonderful family saga, but it's set in England, with characters whom average readers will find a bit distant, and language that's wonderful but a bit too advanced for most readers? What if an editor says this is really only a "bookstore" paperback, with little chance of wide distribution in supermarkets? Well, then the committee may very well table the project. Because while direct bookstore distribution is becoming more and more like supermarket distribution through the growth of the highly successful chains such as Waldenbooks and B. Dalton, to label a book a "bookstore only" book is to stigmatize it. Although some literary novels like Anne Tyler's *Dinner at the Homesick Restaurant* become highly successful "bookstore only" paperbacks, they do so because they've already established themselves as hardcover best-sellers.

What this should suggest is that a mass-market editor's understanding of the market is at least as important as his literary judgment. So how does the editor spend his day searching for that elusive mass-market paperback best-seller? Generally by wearing two hats—as a reprint editor and an originals editor. As a reprint editor, the editor will generally "cover" a number of hardcover houses—that is, he's responsible for knowing the lists of those houses; assessing the suitability of specific books on those lists for reprint in paperback; and learning what's still in manuscript at the hardcover houses, in the hope that he'll get that treasured first look, and if he and the paperback house love the book, receive the opportunity to make an early offer and thereby preempt the auction.

However, one of the frustrations is that preemptive bids are rarely possible, particularly for potential best-sellers, simply because if a paperback house publishes the work of a best-selling author, that house usually has an exclusive option to bid on the best-selling author's new work. Then, if the paperback house and the hardcover house come to terms, there's no auction. And one of the great boring moments of a paperback editor's day is the time, during lunch with a subsidiary rights director of a hardcover house, when the rights director runs through his catalogue, pointing out all the books that are unavailable because another house has an option on them.

So if preemptive bids are rare because the option system prevents editors from invading other publishers' turf, what is it exactly that makes reprint editing interesting? What skills are called into play? Well, one of the ways to become the option house for a best-selling author is to be the first paperback publisher to reprint his work. That's where pure good instinct and good judgment come in. In these instances, the paperback publisher takes a risk on an unknown quantity, but if the author is successful, that house has begun to build an equity in the author's future.

More often than not, however, most paperback reprint deals involve a different speculation—not so much whether the book is right as whether it's affordable. Say it's January and the editor is at lunch with a sub-rights director. They go over the spring list of hardcover books; but more important, the editor notices a book in the upcoming fall rights guide of hardcover projects in development. It's an obvious "hot" property, the one "born to be a paperback." The hardcover house hopes the book is going to be successful and doesn't want to show it until the book's momentum has begun to build, but in the end, the editor convinces the hardcover house to give him a first look at the manuscript. Naturally, the book is sensational, and the editor goes back to management and then offers the hardcover house a high floor bid for the book, say $200,000. By that time, the manuscript has become a Book-of-the-Month Club main selection, with first serial rights sold to *Cosmopolitan,* plus a movie deal with Paramount. Since the hardcover house in question is now convinced that it has a book that will do very well in paperback, it isn't rushing the auction date, but will wait until after publication for the book to hit a few national best-seller lists so that they can get the highest possible price. While this is going on, other paperback houses are preparing profit-and-loss statements and getting the book read to decide if they'll "show up" at the auction (though auctions are held by phone), and how high they'll bid. Soon after the book hits the *New York Times* best-seller list, a closing date is established, and auction day arrives. The paperback publisher who set the $200,000 floor has a 10 percent topping privilege—that is, if the final bid goes to $500,000, he can bid $550,000 and get the book. Rules for the auction (there are a number of different formats) are established by the auctioning house, and then it's a war of nerves.

Suddenly, after a day-long escalation to a bid of $660,000, one of the paperback houses makes, in the words of one of my colleagues, a "kamikaze" bid of $800,000, and thereby discourages other bidders from staying in the auction. The auction is over and the top bidder gets the book. What about the paperback editor who noticed this project in the first place, went crazy to get a first look, and secured a large floor bid from his company for the book? What has he gained? Probably nothing, except perhaps the excitement of participating in a nerve-shattering auction. In the end, either the editor is going to be angry, knowing he's lost a valuable book, or he's relieved that he didn't involve his own house in the kind of high-priced venture that was finally too expensive anyway.

Where, then, is the fun and challenge of reprint editing? It's in foraging for the less obvious but nonetheless "marketable" book. It's not a million-dollar blockbuster; it's a book you can set a modest floor on, then back to an advance guarantee of, say, $50,000 when every other paperback house drops out, and then proceed to make into a book that hits the *New York Times* paperback best-seller list because the book is terrific, its market easy to identify, its packaging potential clear and direct. It's the book everyone overlooked; maybe there was a modest book club buy, some good prepublication trade reviews, some serialization. But it was never a high-profile project. Then, all of a sudden, the book in hardcover gets on the best-seller list—maybe for a few weeks. And you own a book on the *New York Times* best-seller list for only $50,000, probably one of the best reprint properties to own.

And then there's "category" foraging, another kind of high-profit publishing. Say the paperback publisher has a category program—a military history series, for instance—where the initial distribution is modest but the cost of publishing is low. Well, if the paperback house is smart enough to spot the books early, buys them for small advances—in the $3,000 range—prints 50,000 to 75,000 copies, and sells 50,000, it will do fine.

Foraging for that good buy; making a small book a bigger book —these are some of the real pleasures of reprint editing. Not to mention that the reprinter is also buying a predeveloped package. First, the book has been edited, and if the paperback house is lucky, well edited. That's a tremendous time-saver for editors whose individual output sometimes approaches fifty to sixty titles per year. Second, the book can often be photoreduced, rather than reset, for reprinting in paperback, a cost-saver that may help the editor convince his superiors to spend money in other, more productive, areas, such as promotion. And if the book has been reviewed, advertised, selected by book clubs, serialized in magazines or newspapers, and the author has gone on tour or created other kinds of publicity and promotion for the book, the book has already imprinted itself in the paperback buyer's mind as a book with some visibility. If the bookseller has heard of the book, he's more likely to order its paperback edition—the $15.95 book now $3.95—in greater numbers, and sell the book more aggressively.

But there are also some obvious frustrations in reprint editing. For example, the hardcover success that doesn't "translate" as a paperback, the best-selling literary novel that effectively reached an "upscale" hardcover-book-buying audience but might go over the heads of the mass-market audience, who want to be entertained more often than challenged. Or there are the perils of timeliness: the monumentally successful diet book that went to the top of the best-seller list, stayed there for thirty weeks, and then failed as a paperback after medical findings on the dangers of the diet were released.

And finally, the worst frustration of them all—overpaying for a reprint property. In the excitement and competition of a high-stakes paperback auction, the art of bidding sometimes becomes detached from the object of everyone's affection—the book. Will this masterpiece for which five paperback houses want to bid over a million dollars make money for any of them? It is possible; often these big-money books do make big money, but publishers rarely reveal when the big-money books *lose* big money. And sometimes a string of big-money losers can mean the end of an editor's job and a paperback house's existence.

So if there's ever a time when an editor has to be concerned that he's bidding for a book that's "born to be a paperback," it's during the big-money auction. If he's not convinced of the book's market-ability, he has no business being in the auction. There's an old piece of wisdom that I like to remember whenever I consider what to pay for a book: You really know you're maturing as an editor when the money you're spending for your company feels like money you're taking out of your own pocket.

But when all the pleasures and frustrations involved are tallied, there's one thing that reprint editing *doesn't* offer—and it's critical to the psychic well-being of many editors in the business. I'm referring to the creative interplay between author and editor, the pleasure of helping an author communicate what he or she is trying to say, and participating in the process of making books.

Many editors in the paperback business find the satisfaction of creative (and often very profitable) work in editing paperback originals. Here's where all the traditional editorial functions come into play: contracting for a manuscript or proposal, providing editorial feedback in the form of a "revision" letter, and doing structural and line editing work on the manuscript to prepare it for the copy editor and the production department. Very much the skills employed by the general hardcover editor.

Editing paperback originals is probably the most labor-intensive side of paperback publishing, and sometimes the most frustrating. Some editors call it dirty work—that is, sleeves are rolled up and hands get dirty as the editor sweats away over a problem manuscript. Editing demands a high degree of concentration, and at the end of working on a long book, editors are frequently physically exhausted.

In addition, the originals editor is, again like the hardcover editor, an in-house "book producer," who goes beyond the structural and pencil editing stage to be a kind of impresario for the book: suggesting cover concepts, trying to get the book endorsed or reviewed, and supporting marketing efforts by being the book's principal spokesperson—the one who writes the title information sheets and sales presentations. The editor has to convince his colleagues that this original manuscript is really first-rate—a winner—and if they would only make it a lead title for the month, they'd see how profitable the book is going to be. But it's a struggle, for the editor doesn't have a prepackaged property complete with sales figures, book club adoptions, and reviews, as he would for a reprint book. Therefore, he has to convince his house—by getting readings, by circulating the messy manuscript—that the book is every bit as good as, if not better than, the reprints recently bought from a hardcover house.

And then there's the frustration of trying to find the perfect cover for a paperback original. Originals do not have a high recognition factor, and a poor cover can ruin a book's sales. Although paperback originals are beginning to get some review attention, publishers must rely on striking covers to get the consumer's attention. The average supermarket rack offers hundreds of books to choose from, and your book must dazzle to stand out; that's a brutal fact of life in the paperback business. The cover package is also important for reprints, but for originals it is absolutely crucial. If the cover is lifeless, amateurish, downright unattractive, one that does not press the right emotional "buttons," there's a very good chance the book will never be picked up by the consumer.

Among the pleasures the paperback originals editor experiences is an author's developing his skills and sometimes even making money. There are many successful authors who have written paperback originals, such as John Jakes, John Saul, Roberta Gellis, V. C. Andrews, and Janet Dailey, one of the most successful authors in the world today. And the profits an editor helps make for his author, he makes for his publisher as well, because dollar for dollar, paperback originals—as either lead or category books —are still often extremely profitable. The costs of an original—at least before the author becomes a superstar—are modest compared with the prices sometimes paid for reprint properties. Let's say the editor has taken a chance on a first novel—one that has enormous commercial potential—and has paid the author an advance of $10,000 against a royalty of 8 percent. The unit cost per copy is kept reasonable, and if the publisher prints, say, 300,000 copies of the book and sells 200,000 at $3.95, the profits can be extremely impressive. And since most publishers of paperback originals attempt to control many of the subsidiary rights to the book—though this income is often split with the author—the potential for additional income can make the profit picture even brighter.

A profitable paperback original emphasizes the importance of finding the quintessential mass-market book—i.e., the book that's "born to be a paperback." The publisher, lacking the high visibility of a hardcover best-seller, will have to create a paperback best-seller from scratch. The publisher can't rely on reviews; the original must be the kind of wonderful book that generates excitement within the house and then good word of mouth among consumers. Finally, the publisher has to be imaginative in putting the right cover on the book, catching the consumer's attention, and "closing the sale" at point of purchase.

But despite these difficulties and challenges, when an editor overhears two people at a paperback display say to each other how much they loved the best-seller he's edited; or when "his" book is on nearly every blanket on the beach, or being read by many people on the subway, it all seems worth it. At moments such as these, he realizes that maybe he was right ten months ago when he said that the book now being bought, read, and enjoyed was "born to be a paperback."

FAITH SALE

Faith Sale is a senior editor at G. P. Putnam's Sons. She joined Putnam's in 1979, after two years as a senior editor at E. P. Dutton. For more than a decade before that, she was a free-lance editor, reader, copy editor, proofreader, consultant for publishers, agents, and a book club. She was also senior editor of *Fiction* throughout its life. Her editorial apprenticeship was served at Alfred A. Knopf, Inc., and the J. B. Lippincott Co.

●   ●   ●

"I see my role as helping the writer to realize his or her intention. I never want to impose any other goal on the writer and I never want the book to be mine," says Ms. Sale in this affecting and instructive essay, written especially for this anthology. Displaying the very necessary editorial qualities of sensitivity, tact, discretion, enthusiasm, and dedication, Ms. Sale takes us through her involvement in the editing of two very different novels and her editor-author relationship with two very different kinds of novelists. She shows us the importance of the editor's guidance of the book through all the stages of its gestation: art, copy, sales, reviewers, catalogue copy, publicity, etc. Above all, Ms. Sale reveals how vital patience and conviction are in her day-to-day work as an editor, and how important it is to strike the creative balance between her editorial contribution and the author's own creativity and integrity.

EDITING FICTION

A cold Monday in January 1983. I got to the office at about nine-fifteen, and before I had hung up my coat Paule Marshall was on the phone, calling collect from Iowa. *Praisesong for the Widow* —her third novel and fourth book, the first to be published in more than thirteen years—was on the brink of publication. She was calling to confirm the dates when she'd be in Washington next month to deliver a lecture and do some publicity for the book. I told her the date of the party–book signing Doris Grumbach (whose last two novels I edited) was planning and assured her that I had seen to the consignment of books Doris and her partner wanted to have on hand at their small bookstore. We talked a bit about other possible book signings in Washington and in New York the following month, and then I told her the news I was bursting with: *Praisesong* would be receiving an "unqualified rave" (a "grapevine" term—no one I knew had actually read it yet) review by Anne Tyler in *The New York Times Book Review.* Paule lost her gravelly first-thing-in-the-morning voice then, even began to sound a bit giddy, and promised that the news would keep her warm through one or two Iowa winter days. Telling a writer news like that (which I had carefully, deliciously hoarded till the end of the conversation) always makes me feel a bit misty, and as if I'm doing something right.

What I mean is that I choose the manuscripts I want to publish simply by how I respond to them. If the prose gives me a thrill, the images make me tingle, I want to—sometimes even feel I *have* to—publish the writer. I don't try to outguess the American book-buying public or the book clubs or the paperback reprinters—none of those could be regarded as predictable anyway. Instead, I believe—and my experience so far bears it out—that if I think a novel is strong and writerly, some few thousand readers are bound to agree with me, and at least sometimes a book club or reprinter will too. I am not talking about big-money books, obviously, but I do mean the serious, thoughtful fiction that reviewers tend to pay attention to.

Shortly after that phone conversation with Paule, our advertising manager came around with the layout of an ad for her book. He and I had decided that in this case it made sense to time the ad to coincide with publication, rather than to wait for reviews for a "quote" ad (we decided this before we'd heard about the Anne Tyler review): *The New York Times Book Review* had recently run a how-I-became-a-writer piece by Paule and we wanted to keep her in the public eye for greater recognition when the book was available; and one can never be sure of getting great reviews. Besides, if the reviews did turn out to be wonderful and the book began to sell well, we'd probably be able to swing an ad for the daily *Times*.

Next came a drop-in visit from our national accounts manager, who had just returned from a trip to B. Dalton to sell the titles that would be published at the start of the next season's list (March, April, May publications). He came to say that he had breached both timing and protocol to make a special pitch for a novel I would be publishing later that spring. The breach in timing was simply that the book would not normally be mentioned until his trip to sell the second half of the list (June, July, August); the breach in protocol was calling it to the attention of Kay Sexton, who writes Dalton's weekly newsletter and who is usually contacted by our publicity director or, sometimes, our publisher. He did it because the novel, *Oral History* by Lee Smith, had become something of a personal campaign for him and his colleague, the field representatives' manager, both of whom had read the book in manuscript and taken an unusually active role in titling it. Their immediate boss, the sales manager, had thought that "Oral History" did not have the lyrical ring of the author's previous novel, *Black Mountain Breakdown,* and might be misperceived as nonfiction; but these two were prepared to go to the mat to defend "Oral History" as the perfect and only title for the novel. The author, incidentally, came up with about ten alternatives in her eagerness to accommodate the objections, but was mightily relieved that her original choice was upheld. I had always liked the title, but, like the author, wanted to be sure we had something that didn't start out with a negative from those who had to sell it. (Note: As it turned out, Dalton's fiction buyer read *Oral History* in bound galleys and placed an order for 2,600 copies—which was anywhere up to ten times what one might expect for a "quality" novel and which was later increased by his management to 3,200.)

Next I had to catch the publicity department up on the details of Paule Marshall's trip to Washington, as well as plans for a party the house would be chipping in for and I'd have to speak at in New York, and to find out what else they had heard about forthcoming reviews—the *Washington Post* and the daily *New York Times* both did, in fact, come out before the Sunday *Times Book Review,* one stunningly favorable, the other respectful. Just to keep up to date, I called inventory control to check stock. I like to be ready to nag the publisher, Phyllis Grann (who *does* stay right on top of these things, but never minds a bit of encouragement from me, she claims), about reprinting; and a second printing was ordered the next day.

All this still didn't take me much past ten o'clock, before most of the outside calls started coming in. Many are from agents— maybe five a day. That day included three agents discussing contracts in the works. All were for fiction: Donald Barthelme, Thomas Farber for his first novel, and a first novel by a nurse, which I bought on the basis of a sample chapter and outline. There was one call about the timing of *Redbook*'s condensation of *Oral History* (to verify that there would be no conflict with our publication date, which must come afterward), as well as a discussion of a fiction manuscript the agent wanted to send me. Each of these required a trip somewhere in the house: to the contracts manager to check a more or less routine legal point; to the publisher to ask for some unprecedented contract item (and it seems every contract has at least a sprinkling of these); to the subsidiary rights director to double-check the timing of the book club publication of *Oral History* (the first club selection for this author of five previous books; it was an alternate selection of the Literary Guild), which is what our date is predicated on, and to keep him current on *Redbook*'s plans to condense the novel. Like other executives in the house, he is likely to be on the phone or otherwise occupied, and it sometimes happens that we end up chasing each other back and forth over the course of half a day before exchanging some little bit of information.

Other in-house business that day included a visit from someone in the production department asking me to select materials for the

binding of a forthcoming book. This always entails a bit of noo-
dling around with colors and textures to try to accomplish something that looks good, matches the jacket, and does not go over
budget.

I always decide—with help, if it is volunteered, from the production person—on the spine binding, the sides, and the type of
stamping for the spine and, sometimes, the front. (Often I will
choose a blind-stamp—no foils, just an indentation—of the author's initials or signature or an ornament used inside the book.)
This can take anywhere from fifteen minutes to a couple of
(spread-out) hours; sometimes it even waits on samples ordered
from a binder, especially in cases where colors are hard to match.
And, too, I check (this day, with a different production person) the
design of the title page, half title pages, and the type for spine dies
for each of my books (usually six or seven a season). Another
branch of the production department sends around mechanicals
for jacket flaps and back copy, which I also check (having written
the copy, approved or invented the design, checked roughs and
revised galleys); and I see these again when they come in as blue-
prints before the jacket is finally printed.

This morning I made one quick trip to talk to the art director
about the photographs Donald Barthelme had requested for the
jacket art of his next book. Jackets must be in the works well ahead
of the season—anywhere up to nine months before a book's publication—because they should appear in the catalogue, which is
printed three or four months before that season even begins. So
while I am in the throes of publication of Paule's fall 1982 book
and preparing for the spring 1983 publication of Lee's new novel
(and other books), I am doing jacket requests and writing catalogue copy for Donald Barthelme's stories for November 1983 and
Tom Farber's novel for January 1984 (and others).

Another item was a few minutes' chat with another editor about
a nonfiction proposal I had read for her. This kind of personal
editorial discussion is unusual, occurs maybe once a month,
though proposals circulate for written comment at the rate of three
to five a week. Then came a twenty-minute visit from a Swedish
publisher to hear what forthcoming titles I had that he might be
interested in publishing.

It is not often that any editor, even an editor most identified with
fiction, as I am, does only fiction, nor do I imagine anyone would

want to be thus limited. The "quiet" day in question had a couple of matters relating to nonfiction projects. One was uncharacteristic: a trip with our new house lawyer to the sales manager so the lawyer could learn how our books are distributed in a state where one of my authors—and, of course, his publisher—was being sued by a member of the Ku Klux Klan. The other, which I worked on after five-thirty, when things start to wind down and one has a prayer of finding a few consecutive minutes to think, was to study and answer a letter from Joseph Heller's lawyer to his agent about our contract for a book Heller is going to write with his friend Speed Vogel about Heller's rare illness. I had gone over most of the points with our contracts manager, some with the publisher, one or two with our lawyer, and now I had to frame our responses as thoughtfully, politely, and cooperatively as I could—without acceding to a number of them.

Throughout the course of this day, I had flipped through one British publisher's catalogue to see if there was anything I might want to consider for U.S. publication, and managed to scan the latest issue of *Kirkus Reviews,* to get a glancing look at what other houses were publishing, who was doing books I had passed up, how other house titles were being received. I also read through the reviews of my books sent up from the publicity department. The first reviews come from *Kirkus, Publishers Weekly,* and *Library Journal,* in advance of publication, with the others peaking in the few weeks surrounding publication, when there can be a dozen or more, but they may stretch over a whole year. My assistant and I made photocopies of all the reviews for each author and each author's agent. (This was yet one more duty of my assistant, who screens all my phone calls; types contracts and jacket requests and catalogue copy and letters; fills out all check, book order, and messenger requests, and other in-house forms I don't even know about, as well as Library of Congress and ISBN forms; prepares manuscripts for press, doing character counts, front matter, production memos; and reads most manuscripts submitted to me, as well as her share of the mountain of unsolicited manuscripts, proposals, and queries sent to the house.)

That was the day—call it nine-fifteen to six—and it could be regarded as absolutely typical, except for the solitary lunch. About once a month, I don't have a lunch date—two hours or more with an agent, a writer, an editor from another house, a film story editor, or at a PEN committee or an AAP committee or the Women's Media Group, or maybe with someone from the house —and manage just to eat quietly at my desk, reading. This happened to be one of those days. But the peace never lasts very long. This absolutely typical day in the life of an editor included absolutely no editing. In fact, it included nothing that would even suggest where a book comes from.

One afternoon in the summer of 1981, as I was leaving the office, I picked up a page-long report my assistant had written about a manuscript and about thirty-five pages of it she had clipped to the report for me to read. (I, and most of the editors I know or know of, do all manuscript reading and editing outside the office. The summer happens to be my best time for this, because instead of my usual ten- or fifteen-minute bus ride, I spend at least three and a half hours a day, four days a week, on a relatively comfortable and quiet commuter train and one whole working day at home in the quiet country.) My assistant's report said, at considerable length and with noticeable fervor, that this manuscript had interested her a lot, but that while she thought I ought to have a look, she wasn't sure I'd want to publish it. I saw what she meant in those first thirty-five pages. It was a very immediate-sounding novel about a woman with a lymphoma. True, there was some backing and filling, the story was not as tightly worked out as I thought it should be, and it had a central character, Mona, who was not quite likable enough. But the writing was strong, the central issue compelling, and it had an irresistible first line: "Hannah was my best friend until her father killed her mother with the bread knife when we were eight." The next day I told my assistant that she was wrong that those pages were all I'd need to read, and for the weekend I took the rest of *The Fourth Stage,* Gail Albert's first novel.

I was drawn intensely into the story of this woman's plight, which was as much about her struggle to understand why/how she was the one to be stricken as it was about her pursuit of a cure. But how, I wondered, could I publish it, how offer a novel about cancer to a book-buying public that has indicated in unmistakable terms that what it wants is to be entertained. Before I decided what to do, and while I dodged the agent's urgent pleas that I make up my mind, I asked my publisher to read it. She admired the work but told me I was on my own. Despite an encouraging reading from the publicity director, I feared an uphill battle for house support—the enthusiasm from people in other departments which is then conveyed to sales reps and from them to the people who buy from them, and is conveyed to book reviewers for good attention. But the agent persuaded me that I just had to tough it out —in effect, that I *had* to publish this book. That is a credo I learned from the late Henry Robbins, one of America's most distinguished editors, although I also picked up from him its flip side (literary birth control, you might call it): "Do I *have* to publish this book?" He also taught me something he claimed to have learned from Robert Giroux, one of America's all-time finest editors: the distinction between *willed* and *felt* in a novel. A keen reader can spot the difference between a work whose narrator and characters are boldly moving toward a predetermined goal, boxed in by the author's clear determination to get a message across, and a work that unfolds in a fluid, spontaneous way, with its own sense of inevitability. The definition always holds, I find, and there is no question about Gail Albert's work: it is felt.

Now, then, let the editing begin. Many other editors prepare an editorial letter suggesting what might be fixed where and how, etc., which might simply be responded to point by point or might result in a revised manuscript with the suggestions incorporated or rejected. But I believe the editing of a novel is an organic process, just as the writing of the novel is. I think the most beneficial and certainly most comfortable and enjoyable way for me, and the one by which I can learn most about how a writer works, is for the editor and writer to meet and talk about everything—the characters, the structure, the plot, whatever names one chooses to put on these elusive elements that make up a novel. This way I can determine how close the writer feels to the material of the novel, how sensitive about changes, how vulnerable to outside suggestions, how open to specific solutions, as opposed to more general hints about where the problems lie. We can sometimes throw possibilities at each other until neither of us can possibly remember who came up with the solution that turned out to work. Most of all, I can come closer to an understanding of the writer's intention: I see my role as helping the writer to realize his or her intention. I never want to impose any other goal on the writer and I never want the book to be mine.

It was clear right at the start that Gail Albert was exactly the kind of writer for whom this approach works best. She wanted to hear everything I had to say—and as I recall, she didn't say much, mostly listened very thoughtfully—and then she went away to make it all her own, changing Mona into a more sympathetic person, eliminating some telegraphing, excising some soggy portions.

It came as little surprise to me that she would be eager to latch onto possibilities for improving her novel and to do the fixing on her own. I had expected her not to be someone who would assume she had finished her part of the work. There are other first novelists, more often than not very young, early twenties, and wild-eyed with ambition of another sort. "What about the parties?" they will ask when I try to direct their attention to the rewrite the novel cries out for. "Will I get on television?" "Can my book be published before my next birthday so I can still be only X years old?" Or there are those who will defend outrageous coincidences and unlikely behavior by saying, "But that's how it really happened." I have learned only since Gail's book was published that she had made one of her characters who was based on a real person believable by portraying him as less saintly than he is known to be in real life.

Gail turned in the revised first section just about when she promised it—it did represent what I considered a real improvement, and she felt better about it too—so I scheduled the publication for about ten months thence, at the very beginning of October. I wanted the novel to have enough time for in-house support to be mustered but still to come out early enough in the season not to be overwhelmed by the blockbusters that are likely to proliferate once October is well under way.

Many publishers like to allow a full year from delivered manuscript to published book—indeed, they build in a cushion of up to eighteen months in many cases. Our house is accustomed to producing books a bit more quickly; I have done a book in three months, with concentrated, not even round-the-clock, effort, but that means greatly increased pressure—i.e., split-second timing—for editor, copy editor, proofreader, typesetter, compositer, printer, binder, publicist, shipper. In planning publication with even a normal schedule, allowances have to be made for the calendar: December, for example, is out for any book that ought to be given review attention or that needs to be unpacked and on display in the stores before Christmas; the months of July and August and January and February are problematic for certain types of books because they're too late in the selling season for sales and publicity enthusiasm to be maintained in the face of an oncoming fresh new list; on the other hand, most books that are destined for major attention tend to dominate press attention in September and October and March-April-May; so a bit of wisdom, a lot of magic, and a modicum of happenstance go into the scheduling of many books.

After Gail revised the first section, she felt she had gone as far as she could on her own; she had, after all, accomplished the major general transformations. So I took the whole manuscript and started digging in for specifics, finding the precise places where the pace slowed, where false leads seemed to be introduced, where extraneous characters or scenes appeared. I suggested—in the margins or on notes on a separate sheet and later orally—cuts or reordering of pages or paragraphs, sentences or words; alterations in dialogue, single word changes; and I spotted repetitions, faults in chronology, inconsistencies in character. We met for several hours to go over all of my comments, more or less sketchily, and then Gail took it away to ponder. She was back in a week with some changes made, a few rejected, and a number to discuss, plus several carps of her own. We spent the better part of a day talking over anything that had been spotted but not resolved. Then I took the manuscript home to clean it up—to make it clear and unambiguous for the copy editor (and then the typesetter) and to make it neat and readable for copying so it could be sent out to book clubs and read in the house. This task is usually performed by an editorial assistant, but I felt so close to this book, as I often do with books I edit, that I did not want to entrust it to anyone. Also, I knew that there might be some unfinished matters that I would discover only when I was alone with it, and sure enough, I made a number of phone calls to Gail that weekend to clarify/argue/plead certain points.

I specially requested a copy editor who I know has a sensitive ear for fiction and who used to be a nurse (just in case, I thought, for the cancer sections—as it turned out, that was an unnecessary precaution), and she did a careful and affectionate job and then spent a full day with Gail going over her queries. I was in and out of their meeting, playing mediator on anything they couldn't agree about. It's not ordinarily considered a sign worth heeding in the business when a copy editor admires a manuscript, but that is the one person who can always tell the truth, who has no ongoing connection with the project. Someone from the sales department is in effect promising orders when he says a book is good, a publicist is implicitly predicting reviews or TV appearances, a sub-rights person is expected to substantiate a judgment with a sale to a book club or reprinter, but a copy editor is finished with the book and offers (rare though it may be) only a personal opinion. This copy editor is someone whose opinion I respect, and she thought very highly of the book.

By this time—winter—things had started moving. We had, finally, arrived at a title. *The Fourth Stage*—which I felt applied only to the lymphoma and thus did not not begin to describe a novel that was also about family and work and childhood and neighborhood—was not a very evocative title. The author dutifully phoned me every few days during that period with one or two suggestions—and I had my assistant running to *Books in Print* to see if they might have been used recently—until before too long she came up with what was unquestionably the perfect one: *Matters of Chance.* With that solved, the jacket artist could go to work (incidentally, she, too, was very moved by the book) and have something by March, in time for the catalogue—to go with the copy I had to write (with a great deal of help from Gail). The catalogue had to be printed before our May sales conference, where I would talk about the novel for five minutes (or preferably less) to the assembled sales representatives and everyone else involved in any part of the selling of our books (i.e., publicity, advertising, library sales, sales promotion).

When the manuscript was set in type in April, the author had her last chance to read it before finished books. I will sometimes read the galleys (again, not a standard job for an editor) if I have not been intimately involved in the copyediting process and want to make sure that nothing has been missed; I always look over the author's corrections and frequently transfer those corrections to the master galleys. (Our copy chief *allows* me to do so because she knows that I, unlike most of the editors she works with, have had copyediting and proofreading experience; that is also one of the reasons I choose to do it—I often don't trust anyone else to do it well enough to suit me.) Some people regard me as strange or overzealous for doing for my books what others are expected to do, but as my publisher said when she saw me working on some galleys (of an earlier Lee Smith book, in fact) one day, "Oh, you *care* about that book." I always insist on at least a brief look at every stage in the production of the books I edit: I see page proofs, repro proofs, and blues (and I must say that I almost always find at least one little mistake that hasn't already been caught).

Gail was very sparing in her corrections in galleys, the typesetter had done a remarkably clean job, and the whole production process went without a hitch.

What remained for me to do was to send out bound galleys to people who might offer comments to be used on the jacket or in the publicity release that would go to reviewers. The release was written in the publicity department, but I checked it and, in this case, had to send it back for a number of rewrites. Bound galleys —which are simply the first, uncorrected proofs of the type, photocopied, cut up, and bound into a booklike object—cost a publisher more, copy for copy, than bound books. And the return on them, in the form of quotes to be used on book jackets, in publicity releases, or in ads, is often very skimpy. Consequently, we send very few and choose those few very sparingly. I always consult my authors about bound galleys: are there well-known friends who can be counted on? Who would the dream blurbers be? Who in a specialized field is likely to come through and be respected? We make up the short list, then I try to write personalized letters to the people we've selected. It's almost always a disappointment, but there are those times when just the right comment comes in to make the whole enterprise worthwhile.

Gail Albert was a first-time writer; her adult life had been spent not among writers but in research laboratories. We tried one scientist, who did offer a (belated) comment, and a few writers, of whom one was too busy writing her own book to take time out to read Gail's and the others never bothered to respond. I gave bound galleys to one book review editor (duplicating—or you might say reinforcing—the publicist's job), which did pay off in the form of a well-placed review later on.

In the meantime, the production process moved along. The galleys were made into page proofs, and the production manager and I spent hours—and I mean hours—poring over ornament books, trying to find the perfect decorative item. (We had earlier chosen the type and general design together, postponing the choice of ornament.) He ended up making a very special effort—probably, I think, because he knew how special this book was to me—by preparing the ornament by hand so that elements were added to it with each new section of the book, building to something quite elaborate at the conclusion.

By summer, things were pretty much out of my hands. The various stages of the book's production had been checked, fussed with, released. I had spoken to a couple of people I knew at a book club (again, doubling up on someone else's effort—this time the rights department), and they had read and admired *Matters of Chance,* but a first novel can be an even riskier proposition for a club than for a publisher.

Sometime in August, the *Publishers Weekly* review appeared: a rave. This created a new surge of enthusiasm in the house, as it provided the first outside confirmation of our opinions of the book. A skimpy projected print order (about 4,000) was made a bit less skimpy; the publicity release had a strong quote to lead with; the book began to exist in the world outside.

Reviews appeared close to publication date (October 5): the *Washington Post,* the *New York Times,* both daily and Sunday, with clippings from smaller papers trickling in—about a dozen in all, most favorable, some questioning or carping. And then the Book-of-the-Month Club decided to use the book as an alternate selection in the winter, a rare honor for a first work of serious fiction. I was enormously pleased. Gail was shyly proud. The months passed, a few more reviews came in, some reprinters started looking at the book, I watched the slowly creeping sales figures. In February, the American Book Award nominations were announced. One of the nominees in the first-novel category was *Matters of Chance.* I was elated; Gail was dumbstruck.

Alas, even this couldn't budge the reprinters over their fear of fiction that has cancer in it, so the book never found a second life in paperback. Nor did its hardcover existence succeed in breaking the 4,500 mark. But this novel lived, we all gave it our best shot, and we'll all be going back for more—the author, the house, and, of course, the editor.

The specific novels I have talked about here were all successful in certain terms. Both *Praisesong for the Widow* and *Oral History* were well and widely reviewed (in the case of Lee Smith, my biggest problem—and we should all have such problems all the time!—was sorting through all the superlatives to put together the very, very best so they'd fit on the back of a single book jacket), sold twelve to thirteen thousand copies, had reprint sales to strong houses. In short, they made their marks and have become recognizable to readers in the know. They and *Matters of Chance* all earned back their advances against royalties. And as far as I am concerned—and the house agrees—they justified whatever efforts were made to publish them.

I am utterly convinced that these examples look rosy not because I am prettying up their stories. The rosiness comes from meeting expectations. If all participants take passion as a given in publishing serious fiction and rely on experience (and a certain amount of luck) to set expectations, we can all end up more or less happy. And we might be bringing some pleasure to more and more readers and helping to build a future for more and more writers.

JAMES WADE AND RICHARD MAREK

James Wade graduated from Harvard College in 1962 and has been working his way through publishing ever since. He has held sales and editorial positions at Blaisdell Publishing, Ginn & Company, Harcourt Brace Jovanovich, Macmillan, Co., and David McKay Co. He founded Wade Publishing Company in 1975 and worked as a co-publisher with The Dial Press and Dell Publishing under the Dial Press/James Wade imprint. In 1978 he merged his company with Rawson Associates to form Rawson, Wade Publishers, until it was reorganized to become an imprint of The Scribner Book Companies in 1982. Since then he has served as a senior editor at Crown Publishers.

Richard Marek started in publishing at Macmillan when Peter Ritner was its editor in chief. Following Peter, he moved to World Publishing in 1969, became editor in chief of The Dial Press in 1972, started his own imprint, Richard Marek Press, for Putnam's in 1977, and has had his imprint, St. Martin's/Marek, with St. Martin's Press since 1981.

•   •   •

"We believe that the editor has one primary responsibility, one loyalty, and that is to the *author's book.*"

This is the theme of this important, practical, and knowing essay, written especially for this anthology. James Wade and Richard Marek distill the wisdom of their many years in publishing to present a wide-ranging discussion of the special problems and pleasures of editing nonfiction. They stress the particular need in editing nonfiction for "clarity, organization, the efficient conveying of ordered . . . information." And they point out the need for strict fact-checking and for seeking the advice of experts and legal opinions when necessary. The special role of the editor demands that he not assume an expertise in a field when that assumption is unwarranted and could harm the creation and success of the book. Messrs. Wade and Marek go on to offer many extremely valuable tips for the proper editing of a manuscript. Above all, they emphasize that the editor is not a collaborator. The author needs the honest, objective eye of the editor to suggest, to guide, to recommend clarifications, and to help in any way possible to achieve the most effective and creative expression of the author's intent. Never should the editor confuse his role and responsibilities with those of the author. Wade and Marek sum it all up best when they say, "An editor edits. A writer writes."

Give all you can as an editor to the limits of your expertise and experience, be an effective advocate of the book in every department of the publisher, remember your responsibility to the reader, the author, and above all, to the author's book. "If the book is brought into the world with love and attention and thought and passion and understanding, then you have been the right editor for it, no matter what its fate."

EDITING NONFICTION:
In the Service of One Book and Many Readers

For our mentor, Peter Ritner*

———————————◆◆◆◆———————————

We learned early in our careers that a good nonfiction editor must be capable of being interested in just about everything. And so we have edited, among others, books on aerobic dancing and high-fiber diets; on autistic, normal, and extra-bright children; on Alexander the Great and the British spy Anthony Blunt; on American, Russian, French, English, Italian, and Chinese history; on American furniture and UFOs; on all major wars of the twentieth century; and on a multitude of individuals, both good and evil.

In short, the uniqueness of a good nonfiction editor is that he or she is *not* unique. The chances are, such an editor will have a liberal arts education, a catholicity of tastes, and patience, perseverance, pluck. In most respects, he or she resembles the fiction editor (indeed, in most houses, editors edit both fiction and nonfiction), but is different from, say, the music editor or the science editor in that while the nonfiction editor may have some knowledge of an author's field, he or she is not an expert in it.

However, a good nonfiction editor is one who quickly learns the

---

*Peter Vaughan Ritner (October 6, 1927–October 27, 1976) was managing editor of the *Saturday Review,* then a senior editor and editor in chief at Macmillan. He worked with authors ranging from Michael Harrington to Albert Speer, Ronald Clark to Theodore Sorensen. He was larger than life physically and intellectually, with a dazzling mastery of history, science, music, and many other fields. He wrote two nonfiction books, *The Society of Space* and *The Death of Africa,* and published several novels. His sudden death shocked and saddened the publishing community. So many were his gifts and talents that they were almost too much for any one person. And what a wonderful, exciting, maddening, unforgettable teacher he was, to us and to many other editors active in senior positions in publishing today.

proper use of those who *are* experts in special areas. One begins, inevitably, with lawyers. Hardly an issue of *Publishers Weekly* lacks some kind of legal horror story—libel, invasion of privacy, plagiarism—and the origins of many such horrors lie in the failure to use an expert properly or at all. Your (and your lawyer's—house or outside council) concerns begin where the author's warranty leaves off. In general publishing practice, the author is the creator of the work and thus assumed to be *the* knowledgeable authority on whatever aspect of baseball or biology is in the manuscript. In the case of biography, certain automatic precautions are mandatory. How many of the people in the book, even minor figures, are living? Depending on what the author says about even a minor individual, is it libelous? Does it invade that person's privacy? Are that person's thoughts and emotions "fictionalized"? E.g., "As Captain Smith stood on the burning deck, he thought, 'Maybe I should have checked the fire extinguishers.'" If Captain Smith *told* the author that he did indeed think about fire extinguishers, and even better, if the author has it on tape, got the captain to initial each page of the transcript, and then initial pages of the manuscript bearing on him (so as to indicate that he was properly quoted *in context*), then one is probably safe. (We say "probably" with good reason. In a biography of a famous American family, one member of the family stayed at the author's home for weeks, duly initialed pages of manuscript—and then claimed to have said not a word of it! No suit came forward.) As you gain editorial experience, you will know when a manuscript requires a formal legal review. Don't go to counsel lightly—the lawyer's meter ticks away at a high rate. But *never* ignore your instincts and prudence. Attention to legal issues is essential, but you cannot utterly ensure against unpleasant surprises. That's why you pick authors carefully, look at their credentials, previous books, and reputations. And that's why there is a warranty clause in the contract—you are not a mind reader. But you are a professional sworn to exercise "due diligence."

Sometimes, in a terribly specialized work, it is wise to secure the services, for a reasonable honorarium, of a vetter or referee. The author's identity need not—in fact, *should* not—be revealed to the referee, and vice versa. A good outside expert will almost always do more than you ask him or her to do—check facts, suggest clarifications, or raise useful critical points—and contribute to making the book as good as the author can and wants to make it. Even the greatest sages and authorities accept (and profit from) the referee system as used by scholarly and professional journals. You must decide when you think a work requires such outside scrutiny. Having the humility to know your own limitations is vital—if you aren't sure, pay the money and get the right expert. Your house will not have cause to regret the money spent and you will be employing the right resources for the job you can't do on your own.

There is, we think, a dangerous or at least stormy life awaiting editors who mistakenly begin to believe that they *are* experts. Some editors are indeed experts in certain fields and bring unusual support and insight into working with authors. But such relationships are exceptional in trade publishing (they are necessary and common in textbook publishing), and when it comes to books for lay readers, it is usually an advantage to be a general, or lay, editor, to act as average reader, to ask the questions that the interested but nonexpert book buyer (the *audience!*) would have asked if the editor had not asked them first. (The most common question asks for a clarification of jargon, but we've asked historians for dates, archaeologists for maps, how-to authors for diagrams, and *everyone* for definitions.) A good editor is a reader's advocate, and if he or she can't understand what an author means—in a sentence, a paragraph, or sometimes, lamentably, in the better part of a book —then it is highly likely that the audience won't understand, either.

We believe that the editor has one primary responsibility, one loyalty, and that is to the *author's book.* He owes some loyalty to the author as well, in that at all times he must tell the author the truth; but he is *not* the author's friend (although *some* compatability is essential, too close a relationship can ruin objectivity and disintegrate painfully if the book does not succeed), he is the *book's* friend—and he must not superimpose his own philosophy or his own style on the author's.

No editor should labor under the delusion that he or she is a collaborator. A collaborator belongs on the other side of an editor's desk. True, the editor can give the author direction—what the editor, as reader, would want to know—but he should not "improve" a manuscript by infusions of editorial prose or invention. The editor asks the author to clarify; he does not himself clarify.

The editorial pencil is properly employed in asking questions, in making corrections, and in pressing for revisions that match the author's expression to the author's intention as nearly as the author can manage it. (If the author is incapable of rewriting satisfactorily, the editor may then take a crack at it, with the author's approval, or a collaborator may be hired. If everything fails, the editor can cancel the contract and ask for a refund of the moneys already advanced.)

There is nothing glamorous or magical about the proper use of an editorial pencil. Such work demands a great deal of time and rigorous attention. Georges Pompidou once remarked, "Conception is much more fun than delivery." If the author suffers all the pains of giving birth—and all authors do—then the editor will sympathize, for he or she soon learns about the long hours and late nights of the midwife, one who works at home rather than at the maternity ward that the public imagines publishers' offices to be.

While the editor must inevitably end up as midwife, he is often present at the conception. These days, most nonfiction books are sold to publishers while they are still in outline form; or, somewhat less frequently, the editor thinks up an idea and commissions an author to write it—first looking in *Books in Print* to make sure there is not too much competition, and then finding the author through an agent or from his or her previous writings in the field. (The editor-generated book was more prevalent ten years ago; editors have become lazy.)

The criteria for acquiring (or "signing up") a book have been presented in many other books and articles. We simply wish to emphasize here that an editor's "bet" can be tested well before acquisition by soliciting the opinions of colleagues, not only in the editorial department (these, in fact, are the most suspect—"I'll like your idea if you like mine") but in the sales and subsidiary rights department as well. The solicitation of such second opinions is part of the operation of any publishing house, no matter its size, and any editor—particularly any untried editor—willing to fly in the face of general commercial disagreement ("The book won't sell") had better be right at least two times out of five ("See—the book *did* sell") or begin thinking about another profession. For beyond his responsibility to the book and to the book's author, the editor has a responsibility to the publishing house that employs him, and he must make money as well as assist in making art.

Even in this age of committees, the process of acquisition starts with a single editor and, for better or worse, when the final profit and loss is drawn up, ends with that editor. [In publishing, victory may indeed have a thousand fathers, but defeat has only two parents—the author and the editor who accepted the author's book for publication.]

No matter how a book is acquired, it is imperative that every resource in the publishing house be employed to arrive at a very, very educated guess as to how the book will fare when—after conception, sometimes many years after—it becomes a printed reality. Many editors rely on their own instinct, but this essential alone is not enough. The tough questions *have* to be asked: "Are there other books on the same subject recently put out by other houses?" "In a time of recession, will a reader really want to pay $19.95 to learn about the subject?" "Is it too expensive to do a mailing to the interest group most likely to want the book?" "Is the author likely to get on television shows?" "Is the book really as good as the outline promised?"

Most of these questions ought to be asked at conception, and too often aren't; but conditions do change, and at time of delivery they must be asked again. And while the editor, among others, should do the asking, the answers should usually come from the more objective departments, and those answers must not be disregarded. Sure, we can give you dozens of examples of books thought by everyone save the author and editor as bound to fail that did in fact succeed. But for each of these, there are ten that the editor and author (sometimes even with the agreement of the marketing arms of the company) thought would succeed which did in fact fail. The good editor will let realism temper enthusiasm, but on the other hand cannot let prudent enthusiasm flag. Time and time again, the tightrope trembles, and there is no safety net below. In only rare cases do we know "for sure" what we have; almost all books perform above or below our expectations once they are published. Were this not so, there would be many more rich authors and relaxed editors!

If you do not tolerate a certain level of anxiety over a considerable length of time (say, an entire career), then you are probably not constituted to be an editor. Editors and publishers take gambles every day. The gamble is at its greatest in serious fiction—the only way to determine how many people want to buy and read today's equivalent of *Moby Dick* is to publish it and find out. The odds in nonfiction publishing can be minimized, but even with improvement in communication between publisher and public, bookstores and marketing department, there is still more than a small element of risk and there is surely a large element of luck. We suspect that as long as human beings write books to be read by other human beings (that is, as long as there are human beings!), Fortuna will play her role, if only because public taste is as changeable as New England weather, and the market research that will tell Procter & Gamble which toothpaste to push is too expensive to be tried on anything so one-of-a-kind as a book. This is, of course, the reason so many of us are frustrated by publishing every day and continue to love it with all our hearts.

Once the outline is acquired or the book commissioned, the waiting starts. Sometimes, children come on a bit early in their gestation, but few books are delivered prematurely. Some are delivered by caesarian section, generally when the book is about an ephemeral subject (one usually better left to newspapers and magazines than to books), or the urgent requirements of cash flow or other business exigencies demand its publication before it has been fully edited. Few of these deliveries are happy ones.

Normally, the author is late—by weeks, months, or years—in delivering. The anxiety of author or editor or both to get the book finished may lead to an agreement between the two to work on the book in installments—chapter by chapter, for example—but our advice is to do this as infrequently as possible, for one should have an idea of the whole before editing an individual section. Sometimes it is a good idea to work on a neophyte author's first chapter just to make sure of style and tone, but the best editing is done with the whole manuscript in hand. In nonfiction, and more often in fiction, something planted in the first sections might look silly standing alone but make absolute sense in the context of the whole book.

Editors must always be sensitive to the peculiar situation of the writer, a person who sits alone in a room facing a typewriter, often, even in nonfiction, revealing for eventual public scrutiny his innermost self, passions, obsessions, and fears. Thus, the editor must serve as a sympathetic sounding board, empathize with the author's stormy moods and irrationalities, and lend encouragement and support of a general sort. But he should try to give very little specific editorial advice during the book's formation, lest it come back to haunt him when he is finally able to see the whole manuscript.

Most authors do, eventually, deliver an entire book. There are some (happily, not many) manuscripts that, when they come in, suffer from such a gulf between conception and realization that they are "hopeless"—at least in the editor's eyes if not the author's. In these few cases, the editor must simply reject the book, hoping to get some or all of the advance back and trying to find for the author another publishing house, where the book might be better received.

In recent years, the question of a manuscript's "acceptability in content and form" has too often become the subject of litigation. This is particularly likely to crop up when the advance paid is substantial, but an author's self-esteem can, understandably, also trigger a lawyer's letter in response to a rejection. If there is an arbitration clause in the contract, then publisher and author can pursue that generally less complex and expensive means of resolving a conflict. But prevention of litigation or arbitration is devoutly to be wished. We have, to our best knowledge, not rejected manuscripts on frivolous or unfounded grounds. In fact, a rejection is a confession of defeat most editors hate to make. But again, we insist that no one person is absolutely *right* about any book. The phrase is a familiar one in rejection letters written to agents and authors in response to submissions: "We don't feel the book would be right for our list." Well, there is in that stock phrase a lot of collective experience, intelligent guesswork, and honest admission of incapability to see the right way to publish the book. One must, however, be a good deal more specific in rejecting a contracted book—and one must be guided by one's lawyer in saying enough and not too much. Editors are generally comforted by the knowledge that most of the books rejected after delivery do find other publishers and have varying fortunes. The rejecting publisher-editor was no more "wrong" than the editor-publisher who contracted the book after its rejection. An author who insists on a house proceeding with publication in the face of that house's grave and reasonable reservations is weighting the odds against the book's success. As for the few "hopeless cases"—well, remember "hopeless" *Moby Dick*?

However, in the vast majority of cases, the manuscript will not be "hopeless," and the editor will set to work. Ideally, the editor should hide out in a room with no telephone and read the book straight through. Without a pencil. The first reading of a manuscript gives the editor an overall view, an assimilation of the entire text that will endure through all the modifications of perception induced by subsequent readings, a map of impressions that will both set the editor's attitude toward the book and decide the course to be followed in the editing.

Apart from the first decisive mapping of the book, the editor must try to arrive at a clear appreciation of what the author intends to accomplish through the cumulative effect of line upon line, paragraph upon paragraph. This is a bit hard to do if, in the curious fashion of some publishing houses today, the handling of the book is given to *two* editors. One is commonly called the acquisition editor (or, in the mordant phrase of Robert Giroux, the editor known by the place at which he lunches), the other the in-house or pencil editor. In our opinion, the institutionalization of such a practice is pernicious. The acquiring editor is the one who has had those many early discussions with the author, who *knows* the author, whose own idea might have spawned the book. *This* editor is the one who should do the line work (apart from the crucial copyediting tasks), for in a sense, he is right when he goes to those lunches and describes the book as "his." The use of an editorial pencil makes the claim truly valid.

The first, straight-through reading of the manuscript enables the editor to act as audience. But the second reading, this time with pencil in hand, will give the editor far more detailed knowledge of every part of the book, built up by line-by-line consideration of the text. Such readings will bring out structural weaknesses: whether, for example, an entire section of the book should come earlier or later than it does now. And it will bring to the fore the larger questions of style, of effect on the reader.

The editing of fiction and the editing of nonfiction have many similar rules and skills. But the great difference between the two is this: in fiction, one is dealing with a kind of *raptus,* a literal "carrying away" of the reader on the wings of the author's imagination and narrative. Thus, the editor tries to help the author enhance that very special effect a novel has on a reader, who is transported into another world that is half perceived by the reader and half created by the author. This act of cooperation is unique to novelists and readers and one not shared by, say, those who write and read most expository nonfiction. In fiction, writer and editor are concerned with a kind of magic (or, if one is a Platonist, illusion). In nonfiction, one is concerned with clarity, organization, the efficient conveying of ordered, available information. But in either sort of editing, the less seen of the editor's hand, the more successful the editing. The pencil is there, in both cases, to *suggest* cuts when things drag a bit, to *suggest* a more precise word, to *suggest* ways of more economical exposition or heightened dramatic effect.

Different authors will want to work in different ways, but we try to edit the whole book before sending it back to the author (after which there's usually a meeting so the author can be absolutely clear on the requested revisions), for the same reason that the author should submit the manuscript whole, rather than chapter by chapter. And if the editor isn't convincing? If he or she can't persuade the author to change? Then the editor must try again, given that his or her reputation, as well as that of the publishing house, is to some degree affected (we find it a good ploy to warn the author of adverse reviewer reaction—writers are often more scared of critics than of editors). And if the author remains adamant? Then the editor must decide whether to accept the book as is—or cancel the contract.

A book, considered as a discourse, is written to inform or persuade a particular group of readers. The level of discourse, the author's selection of words and phrases, contributes to that highly complex, distinctive way of saying something which is termed style. And as we've noted, while the editor must bend all his or her powers of analysis and understanding to see how that style works (or, more important, when it falters), the editor has no business playing teacher. Of course, the editor must say when he or she thinks an author's style falters, but it is the author's own voice that must dictate the book; the editor is there to *learn* about language —language different from his or her own. Deferentially, the editor can *suggest* that the author might consider this or that alternative, but it must be an alternative consistent with the style of the writer. Heaven help the editor who is bent on "improving" a style, with the author's help if possible, but without it if necessary. Such editing is futile at best, arrogantly destructive at worst. An editor edits. A writer writes.

When the editor approaches the House of Books, he finds in-
scribed above the door the admonition: "Be Bold, Be Bold." On
the frieze inside, however, is written the admonition: "Be Not Too
Bold." Editors must follow just such a discretionary path in dealing with each book. The very uniqueness of a book is what draws
editors to editing. Imagine being paid to be taught new tricks each
day by a decidedly motley but often inspiring group of teachers!
Editors tend to contract the sort of books they themselves enjoy
reading. Or books that touch on their avocations and obsessions,
from sailing to cooking, trout fishing to particle physics. Thus,
sensibility and interests—narrowly special or sprawlingly diverse
—condition what editors actively seek out.

Good editors never stop learning, and never tire of finding and
getting interested in or excited and actually changed to some
degree by fresh ideas and new subjects. Resisting the invitation to
change and expand even the inventory of one's fairly superficial
knowledge is a sure sign of editorial sclerosis. Yet the most important learning, as far as the editor's proper work on behalf of the
book is concerned, is acquiring more practical understanding of
how every element in publishing works, from accounting and
fulfillment operations through text and jacket design, to promotion
and advertising. A good editor will try to give his or her appropriate suggestions to colleagues who work in the many areas that
comprise the publishing house: ideas for the look of the jacket, for
example; special sales opportunities the sales department might
have overlooked; promotion ideas such as headlines for ads or
offbeat reviewer mailings. An appreciation of your limits and the
territorial sensitivities of your colleagues in other departments can
save you from being a pain in the neck. But you as editor are the
publishing person who knows the book best, so you can and should
have a lot to say about the fate of the book once it leaves your
hands and is "put into production." Even if you *are* a pain in the
neck, never forget that you are the book's servant; *it* comes first
—and besides, it is *your* neck that is often sought afterward if
things go wrong.

Still, be not too bold. You depend on your colleagues, as they
depend on you, to do the job right. A good publishing house is
good throughout, from the art department to the comptroller's
office, from the editorial room to the mailroom. All publishers—
and as an editor you ought to think like a publisher because,
organically, that is what you are—know that Fortuna smiles on

those prepared to recognize and exploit her gifts. Any editor knows that such preparation requires equally passionate commitment from those with whom he or she works every day and to whom he or she turns over the book after the editor's and author's valediction. You owe all your colleagues the most truthful, experienced evaluation of the book at conception, the widest midwifery you can manage at delivery, and a combination of enthusiasm and solicitude as they and you prepare it for its entrance into the world.

If the book is brought into the world with love and attention and thought and passion and understanding, then you have been the right editor for it, no matter what its fate.

HOPE DELLON

Hope Dellon is a senior editor at St. Martin's Press, with a particular interest in mysteries. She worked as Joan Kahn's assistant at Harper & Row and joined St. Martin's in 1975.

•   •   •

Ms. Dellon takes much of the mystery out of the art of editing mysteries in this informed and witty essay, written especially for this anthology. She discusses her criteria for judging a good mystery and what makes for an exceptional one, the special editing problems faced by the mystery editor, the pleasures and pitfalls of editing a mystery series, the changing tastes of the audience for mysteries, and the place of the mystery novel on the publisher's list. All in all, enough clues here to help the aspiring mystery editor begin to develop a personal taste and style and, it is hoped, to find the next best-selling mystery writer.

EDITING THE MYSTERY NOVEL

"The first person you should think of pleasing, in writing a book, is yourself," Patricia Highsmith, author of *Strangers on a Train* and other classic thrillers, advised in her guide to *Plotting and Writing Suspense Fiction.* "If you can amuse yourself for the length of time it takes to write a book, the publishers and the readers can and will come later."

Happily for the mystery editor, the first task in editing mystery novels is much the same: to find books that he or she enjoys. While this may sound too easy and pleasant to be true, it is actually the most effective way to approach the dozens of manuscripts that will come your way once the word gets out that you are still buying mysteries in a tight market. The remainder tables are piled with books that had "all the elements" for success and yet were so flat or mechanical that they were failures. If you do not genuinely respond to a manuscript—if you do not find it lively, original, and compelling; if, no matter how much you admire the ingenuity of the plot or the richness of the prose, you are reluctant to pick up the story once you have put it down—chances are that the public will feel the same way. But if you do find yourself staying up late to read one more chapter or hoping that the author writes a sequel immediately, the chances are equally good that other readers will share your enthusiasm.

This assumes, of course, that you have a basic liking, preferably a passion, for mysteries—that, unlike Edmund Wilson, you *do* care who killed Roger Ackroyd. While it is possible to discover the pleasures of mystery fiction late in life, most editors and authors seem to start early; I remember that the first "adult novel" I ever read (I believe I was in the fifth grade) was Agatha Christie's *Seven Dials Mystery* and that I was unable to study for exams one college term until I had finished Dorothy L. Sayers's *Gaudy Night.* (Before that, of course, I watched *Perry Mason* and read Nancy Drew books. Dilys Winn, founder of the Murder Ink bookstore in New York and "perpetrator" of the book by that name, writes: "For years I attributed the first mystery to Carolyn Keene, Nancy Drew's creator, even though I knew full well a gentleman named Poe deserved the credit. I'd read Keene first, and according to my personal mystery chronology she rated the honor.") Neither editing nor writing mystery fiction, or indeed any kind of fiction, can be undertaken cynically—"I hate this sort of thing, but the morons out there should like it"—with much hope of success.

A good many distinguished writers have tried their hands at mystery fiction, T. S. Eliot, William Faulkner, Ernest Hemingway, C. Day Lewis, Somerset Maugham, and George Bernard Shaw among them. Perhaps inspired by this tradition (or possibly by the impulse that makes soap operas so popular on college campuses), many teachers and scholars come up with murder mysteries— usually, these days, cautionary tales about the perils of denying a worthy professor tenure. In addition, mystery writers tend to be voracious mystery readers; Howard Haycraft cites an extreme example in his history of the detective story, *Murder for Pleasure,* reporting that "S. S. Van Dine read more than 2,000 stories before he tried to write one." Whatever the reason, the standard of mystery fiction submitted both by agents and directly by authors seems markedly higher than that of, say, romances or science fiction. Surprisingly many of the detective manuscripts I read are publishable, with serviceable writing, workmanlike plots, mysterious wrongdoers who are properly unmasked at the end, and sometimes even an interesting setting or a clever twist. Yet I turn down books like this every week. Often their cover letters tell me the authors are trying to write "in the tradition" of A. Conan Doyle or Raymond Chandler or John D. MacDonald or anyone else they admire. Usually, the books are pale imitations of the real thing, but even if they are a bit better than that, it is difficult to work up much enthusiasm for novels that do not offer anything fresh. The most promising authors are those who know and love the tradition in which they are working but who find some way to, in Ezra Pound's phrase, "make it new."

There is much to be said for that tradition, which offers its readers considerable satisfactions. Its essential attributes, I believe, are readability, pace, reasonable fairness to the reader (the crucial piece of evidence should not be withheld, except perhaps in a thriller, where the emphasis is on the chase rather than the puzzle), and the convincing creation of an orderly universe in which questions are answered and wrongs put right. (The last may have something to do with the excellence and popularity of mystery fiction during the Depression, when the idea of a just world must have seemed particularly attractive.) These elements will make a mystery competent; in order to stand out, it needs something more: charm, complexity, exceptional writing, engaging characters, emotional intensity, a brilliantly conceived puzzle, a unique and intriguing background. (Howard Haycraft cites "B. J. R. Stolper's humorous 'recipe' for the tasty police novel: ½ Sherlock Holmes, ¼ P. G. Wodehouse, ⅛ sheer adventure, ⅛ anything you know best." When an author can take the reader inside, say, village life or horse racing or banking or even apartheid in South Africa, the result can have a particular fascination.) Obvious as it may sound, I also look for mysteries that work as novels, that have, in addition to the mystery itself, a plot in which the protagonist resolves some aspect of his or her own life in the process of solving the crime. In the end, though, it is impossible to characterize exactly what I am looking for, since the real find is the book that demonstrates an unimagined turn that the mystery novel can take. By the time one can spot a trend in mystery fiction, it is usually a good idea to move on to something else. While the first three mysteries featuring women private detectives may have a certain panache, the thirty imitations that cross your desk begin to appeal less and less and will seem even staler when they make their way into the marketplace nine or ten months later.

In considering a new author, a mystery editor is usually fortunate enough to be able to base his or her decision on a completed manuscript (it is unusual for most editors to have a complete manuscript upon which to base a decision whether to accept or reject)—fortunate because, while it is often easy to tell from a few pages or even an opening paragraph whether there is an interesting writer at work, it is considerably trickier to predict whether that writer will be able to keep the story moving. Reading a manuscript straight through gives you the opportunity to find out exactly how the pieces fit together, to check if your attention begins to wander, and to judge if it is satisfying or otherwise to learn at the end that the butler did do it after all. Most important, it gives you the chance to see the book through a reader's eyes, which is invaluable in both selecting and editing a manuscript; your "gut reaction," while you are still looking at the whole forest before concentrating on the trees, is the most useful data you have to work with. Provided that you have a partiality for mysteries and enough experience to give you confidence that reviewers and readers will share your taste more often than not, the choices are frequently obvious: a suspense novel that can keep a jaded mystery editor passionately interested is clearly worth acquiring.

There are, of course, borderline cases: manuscripts that seem promising but flawed. Whether or not you decide to take on such books will usually depend on your perception both of the quality of the work (just how good would the book be if the flaws were fixed?) and of the willingness and ability of the author to undertake major revisions. If you do have doubts about a manuscript and yet want to make an offer, it is crucial to discuss your ideas with the author as early as possible, certainly before the contract is signed, lest both editor and author get a shock when each learns what the other has in mind. When possible, it is helpful to get a detailed letter or revised outline from the author in advance to make sure the two of you are thinking along the same lines. There are also numerous instances when you will be asked to make a decision on the basis of a synopsis and sample chapters. If the proposal comes from a first novelist, it will generally have to be pretty dazzling; agents and authors seem to realize this often enough to keep such submissions down. If you have read previous books by the author, however, it is often possible to judge an outline fairly reliably, especially if you have developed a successful working relationship with him or her. The one advantage of considering a book at this stage is that it enables you to point out possible weaknesses early, before they have been carefully, sometimes inextricably, woven into the story.

Having read a manuscript straight through, one sets out to edit it as one would any novel, reading it a second time, slowly, with a mixture of respect and skepticism. While you are convinced that the book is special—and it is important never to lose sight of this in talking to the author about any rough spots you may find—is there anything that gets in the way of your enjoyment this time through? Sometimes the book's particular virtue can give rise to difficulties; for example, the aspect you like best is its insider's view of the legal system, but the author uses so much jargon that you find yourself feeling excluded rather than drawn in. Or the narrator's cynical, worldly voice, which is attractive on page one, begins to grate halfway through the book, when you realize that you are being kept at arm's length from the character. Probably you will find yourself asking questions: Would the hero really walk out on the heroine at that moment? How *did* the murderer leave the door locked from the inside? Is it convincing for the detective to make that startlingly brilliant deduction from the evidence provided? Does this sentence say what the author means it to say? On the principle that other readers may share the editor's reservations, loose ends, inconsistencies, awkward phrases, developments that may be possible but are not probable should all be brought to the author's attention—*not* simply changed to suit the editor's taste —as gently as possible. In many instances, the editor's response is the first chance the author has to learn, in detail, how his or her work strikes a reader other than his family and friends; it is also a chance to resolve any difficulties before reviewers and readers (voracious mystery readers can be aggressive letter writers) point them out. When shown their work from this angle, most mystery writers are eager to plug up holes and clarify points of confusion, and their solutions to problems are almost invariably more imaginative than any their editors could come up with.

Mysteries may differ from certain other sorts of fiction in their emphasis on plot. As Dorothy L. Sayers put it, "There is one aspect, at least, in which the detective-story has an advantage over every other kind of novel. It possesses an Aristotelian perfection of beginning, middle, and end. A definite and single problem is set, worked out, and solved; its conclusion is not arbitrarily conditioned by marriage or death." Curiously enough, however, while each detective novel must come to a tidy conclusion, it also has an unusual potential to end up as part of a series. Whereas sequels to most types of novels are apt to be disappointing, many mystery writers have gone on to deepen their characters and tackle more ambitious themes as a series develops, perhaps because the plot— which necessarily involves something other than the protagonist's inner life—leaves only so much room to explore personal issues in each book. As an editor, one is excited by the prospect of discovering a new "series character," usually a detective, but there are pitfalls. For one thing, each book must stand entirely on its own, which means you must try to put yourself in the position of an uninitiated reader every time. Occasionally you will find that an author is deliberately leaving some unfinished business to be dealt with "in the next book," and it is your task to try to persuade him or her that there will be little interest in the next book if this one leaves readers unsatisfied. Sometimes the author will neglect to fill in necessary background about a series character, presuming, for instance, that everyone knows all about the detective's feelings for his ex-wife. (This can be a sign that the series is running out of steam, which is another possibility the editor should keep in mind.) On the other hand, editing a series can give you the great luxury of discussing possible directions with an author when you both know the characters extremely well. Once in a while, you may even get to watch a kind of magic taking place. As James McClure writes in *Murder Ink:* "I believe the mystery series writer has more in common with the alchemist—beyond such superficialities as a dim, dusty workroom littered with manuscripts and sobered by the odd skull—than is generally conceded. . . . [By the third book] my Afrikaner detective and his Zulu colleague, illusory beings I'd personally summoned up, seemed to have become independent of me and my powers. Not only that, but they'd moved out into the real world, where a section of the reading public, albeit a small one, had placed them under the protection of the law."

The sales record of mysteries in general, and consequently the tangible rewards for writers and publishers, is unfortunately not cause for rejoicing. While there are a few highly visible, hugely successful living authors (and many more dead ones), even they have usually had to build an audience slowly. Agatha Christie's first novel reportedly sold around two thousand copies; much more recently, Patricia Highsmith cautioned aspiring writers that "a first book is a luxury, more of a luxury than a trip to Europe." Hardcover first mysteries, like most first novels (except for a handful of heavily promoted "big books"), are extremely difficult to advance to bookstores, sell mostly to libraries, and usually net under five thousand copies. In light of these gloomy facts, a mystery editor's most difficult job may well be persuading the house he or she works for that mysteries are worth publishing at all. To give a mystery its best chance in the marketplace, the editor can pull all available strings to make sure it has a handsome design and jacket (while being careful not to push the already high retail price any higher), send it out to notable people who might be willing to give advance quotes (writers and others; I once got a quote for a mystery set in a bird sanctuary from the president of the National Audubon Society), perhaps push for an ad or two—more in the hopes of attracting reviewers' attention than in the belief that anything short of a prohibitively expensive ad campaign is likely to drive customers into the stores—and then hope the reviewers will like it as much as the editor does. (In the U.S., at least, no talk show wants to interview a novelist until *after* the novelist is rich and famous.) If the reviews are positive enough, if readers begin telling their friends that here is a genuinely exciting discovery, and if the author and editor—mostly the author—can work to make sure that the second and third and fourth books are as good as, or better than, the first, then the author can begin to build a following of surprising size and conviction.

Finally, the greatest service that you can do the house, the author, the reader, and yourself is to be as rigorous as possible in both selecting and editing manuscripts. In extraordinary cases such as that of Joan Kahn, whose imprint on a novel of suspense has been a guarantee of high standards for many years, an editor's reputation can help to attract new authors of similar excellence and become a selling point all its own. For most of us, the place to start is with books that meet our personal criteria—which is, as it turns out, where many writers begin (Agatha Christie said that she wrote her first book because her sister complained she couldn't find a "*good* detective story"). In part, this means telling the truth, even the unpleasant truth, as one sees it. Harriet Vane, the scholar-turned-detective-novelist in *Gaudy Night,* says that she would "lie cheerfully" about "anything . . . except saying that somebody's beastly book is good when it isn't." With as much tact and compassion as possible, you must try to draw the same line, knowing that you can't do the right job of either editing or publishing a book unless you start with honest enthusiasm. There are risks, of course —you may love a book everyone else hates and turn down another book someone else will publish successfully—and there are times when you have to compromise. But to the extent that you are able to attract and publish the mysteries that come up to your highest expectations of the genre, you will be doing your real job—to recognize, aid, and abet talent where you find it.

DAVID G. HARTWELL

David G. Hartwell has been a science-fiction editor and critic for almost twenty years. He has been a consulting science-fiction editor at Berkley/Putnam's and New American Library. He was director of science fiction for Timescape Books (Pocket Books) from 1978 to 1983. In 1984 he became consulting science-fiction editor for TOR Books. He is also director of science fiction at Arbor House, and has been a Hugo Award nominee for Best Science-Fiction Editor in 1982, 1983, and 1984. He has written a nonfiction book on science fiction, *Age of Wonders.*

•   •   •

Mr. Hartwell provides a remarkably in-depth look at the very special world of the science-fiction editor in this wide-ranging article, written especially for this anthology. He defines the concept of "category" publishing, of which science fiction is an important component, and shows how science fiction today is an outgrowth of the old-time pulp magazines. Mr. Hartwell is particularly fascinating and informative in his discussion of the close and intense world of the science-fiction enthusiast. With great acuity, he examines schools of science fiction, style, the stringent economics of publishing science fiction, the unpredictability of science-fiction audiences, and their values, likes, and dislikes. A certain rueful quality in Mr. Hartwell's essay suggests that, in terms of recognition and status from the publisher for whom he edits, the science-fiction editor's efforts are not always appreciated. Or as he puts it, "An editor or a writer is generally indulged as harmlessly crazy, a not very threatening nut, for devoting a career to SF." Intense, emotional, Mr. Hartwell's essay offers an unusually intimate look at the deep bonds that exist among the science-fiction editor, his art, and his audience.

EDITING THE
SCIENCE FICTION NOVEL

Almost all mass-market paperback editors are specialists, often multiple specialists. This has been subtly enforced upon the industry by the distribution system: paperbacks are brought to the mass market through the national magazine distribution agencies as a secondary aspect of their business. Although the growth of the paperback bookstore is a force for change in the last fifteen years, the magazine distributors still dominate. (As one wag informed me early in my publishing career, all the distributors went to high school together in 1939 and they haven't learned anything since.) Paperback companies publish books monthly (as do many magazines) and the unsold books are stripped of their covers and destroyed, while the covers are returned for credit. But further than that, as the selection of titles offered each month has evolved, publishers have established monthly slots to compete with and replace the older pulp magazine categories with which the distributors are familiar.

In bookselling, and therefore publishing, a category is a kind of publication separated out from "general fiction" to reach a special audience. Categories are shelved separately in bookstores or consigned to a special area on a mass-market rack so that readers can find what they want without shopping further. A category is a response to a specific audience demand. Obviously, the known factor of a preexisting audience, even if you don't know precisely the demographics of the audience, guarantees a certain minimal level of success for books appropriately placed in the category-selling section.

It is lower than the top of a mass-market list that you find the "categories," the mysteries, Westerns, Gothics, romances, occult nonfiction, groups of books for special audiences who are in some way identifiable markets, most of them analogous to the fiction categories filled by the pulps years ago. And most senior editorial personnel have had experience in buying and editing and publishing category fiction when they rise to specialize in the best-seller category, the category of flash and rewards at the top of the list.

As a fiction category in the publishing world, then, SF is only a specific case of "the categories." Hangovers from the heyday of fiction magazines, the Westerns, mysteries, and Gothics are specialities that have fallen upon difficult times in hardcover and paperback, times from which SF (and romance) seems to have escaped, and only partially. For years there were notable specialists in category editing in both hardcover and paperback, some identified with only one category, some experts in several categories (Donald A. Wollheim, one of the first—and certainly of longest tenure—SF specialists, is also a Western specialist). Now most of the categories are comparatively low-sales sidelines from which the senior editorial staff has risen.

Editing for a specialized audience is considered limiting by the greater part of the publishing community, and whether truly limited or not, category editors occupy a lesser position in community esteem than general editors. This is probably another legacy of the pulp days, when pulp editors were considered a lesser breed, engaged in commerce to the virtual exclusion of any literary values (and this was usually true).

The freshman editors who are most often given "some categories" as their first assignment in publishing strive to rise out of that position as rapidly as possible to escape "typecasting." There are, to the best of my knowledge, no full-time distinguished career specialists in the Western field among the editorial ranks, while most mysteries are edited by young men and women under thirty with the title of associate or assistant editor. The great generations of mystery editors have passed, with the great ages of popularity of mystery and detective fiction, once the profitable mainstay of most major publishers of fiction. Most mysteries are not considered important books, don't sell as they used to in earlier decades, are not published in such numbers as before, and are separated into best-sellers (a few) and trash (the rest). Right now, there is a whole new generation of specialist romance editors, producing the category of fiction that dominates the early 1980s. Their books are hugely successful.

Yet over the recent decades, SF has maintained for a number of publishers a significant and growing share of the mass market in particular. And this has fostered the careers of a certain number of new specialist SF editors, Judy Lynn Del Rey, Edward Ferman, Terry Carr, George Scithers, and myself among them; specialized agents such as Virginia Kidd and Kirby McCauley; and specialized illustrators, including Kelly Freas, Vincent DiFate, Jack Gaughan, and Michael Whelan. In spite of the malaise of category publishing in general, the environment has fostered a strength through separateness.

As the writers and editors know, if a work of SF succeeds well enough so that people outside the traditional audience must pay attention, then it will either be discovered to be not really SF but literature (e.g., the works of Ray Bradbury in the 1950s, Kurt Vonnegut in the 1960s, Ursula K. Le Guin and Stanislaw Lem in the 1970s) or be condemned as trash with literary pretensions. This is a heavy load for editors and authors to bear.

An editor or a writer is generally indulged as harmlessly crazy, a not very threatening nut, for devoting a career to SF. Certainly there is an audience for the stuff, but someone who wishes to be taken seriously does not associate with category fiction except perhaps at night, when one flirts with the socially unacceptable.

It is important to understand the popular origins of fantasy and science fiction to put the present state of the art in perspective. SF is reviewed separately from other literature, is written, edited, and marketed for a select cluster of overlapping audiences, who go to special sections in bookstores and libraries to choose their reading matter. Science fiction, although it is published in hardcover, trade paperback, and mass-market paperback, is a pulp category long ago identified, and the mass presentation thoroughly dominates its publication in all forms. Readers know that their favorite category is not literature as it is fashioned by the dominant practitioners of our day, that it is just pop culture, but of a very particular kind which they seek out.

SF has such a specifically "nonliterature" image that the general reader will never attempt to read a work that is so identified. It is not too extreme to say that SF is so far from fashionable literature that it is identified and defined in the public consciousness by its worst examples, from degraded B movies to the lurid and/or livid cover art of its magazines and paperbacks (a sometimes tiresome leftover from the era of pulp magazine fiction). Ironically, this tradition of packaging even the most careful and literate SF as antiliterature is comforting to the core audience, an identifiable market, predominantly male (circa 60 percent), predominantly under age twenty-one (circa 70 percent), who habitually buy and read almost nothing but SF. Many of them are part of "organized fandom," the international community of fans who publish amateur magazines, run large and small conventions, write letters, and influence the marketplace in many ways. They have chosen to reject the self-consciously literary. One violates conventional packaging at the grave risk of offending the central audience.

There is a peculiar community aspect to the SF field, though, which provides extraliterary support to editors and authors. The SF world is conscious of its separateness from the rest of literature and of publishing and has its own culture, which reveres the "pros" who write and edit. Not only writers but also editors are well-known public figures in this culture, which even has its own awards for editing (the "best editor" Hugo Award, presented annually by the World SF Convention; the Locus Award, given by the readers of a leading fan magazine). Both author and editor have a direct line of communication to a significant portion of the people who read what we produce, who praise and condemn through an international network of amateur publications (the fanzines), through conversations at the frequent conventions held nationwide, and through a number of systems of peer awards and public honors.

It is my impression that editors in no other field have the constant opportunity to interact with knowledgeable readers who approach with sincere praise for the entire publishing program, all or most of whose books they have carefully read and winnowed. They will even buy you a drink sometimes, while they tell you which books or parts of books they did or did not like. This is always informative and frequently not unpleasant—they have bought and read them, after all. It is harder on the authors. The isolation of this culture has led to the characterization of the SF field by some insiders as a ghetto, by others as an exclusive country club.

If there is a single commandment for the SF editor, it must be: you cannot ignore the established SF culture and its standards. Many young SF editors have truncated promising careers over the years by raising the banner of the avant-garde in the SF microcosm, only to find their books or magazines without a core audience. A whole group of revolutionaries in the mid-sixties in England and America, under various rallying cries, declared the death of "old" SF and the birth of "speculative fiction." These groups of writers and editors are now remembered as the "new wave." Most of the editors associated with that movement are no longer active, although the movement did have a crucial influence on SF for fifteen years, partly by focusing the reactionaries.

All editors worth a nickel wish to improve the breed, by selective acquisition and individual editing. Yet the recurring idea that SF should become literature by replacing the clear, journalistic prose standards of the genre with one or another fashionable stylistic mode alien to the audience has, to date, invariably alienated the audience. Only sophomoric hubris can lead one to believe that the core audience has no defined tastes and can be won over by stylistic sophistication.

Yet one of the challenges for an editor working with SF is that a wider range of stylistic effects is permissible in a work of SF than in any other form of category fiction. Every significant SF author has a strong and individual style, for good or ill, that is the author's trademark, and with which the editor must deal (and especially protect from insensitive copyediting and proofreading). One must identify the strengths of radically differing styles of SF and preserve them. At best, you may find yourself editing a manuscript on a level equal to the stylistic sophistication of the best contemporary literature. These golden moments occur all too infrequently in any editorial career, but are possible in SF.

Presently, three out of four SF specialists have college degrees, but I know of no SF editor with a science degree. Among the earlier generations of SF editors, most were self-educated—and even John W. Campbell, the great magazine editor, never completed his science degree at MIT. So by rule of thumb, the primary qualification for an editorial job in SF is wide reading—and comprehensive familiarity with writing—in the field. Knowledge of literature is optional, though useful. An enthusiasm for the wonders of science is immensely helpful. The degree of your publishing experience, or a detailed appreciation of the everyday realities, the nuts and bolts, the crafts and finances, can make you or break you.

Fortunately, the SF culture, fandom, is a good practical training ground and has spawned a majority of the practicing specialists in publishing today, as well as many major authors. And most of them knew one another as fans before they were professionals. They learned about publishing in the fanzines, and through letters, and in conversation at conventions.

Dozens of first novels are published every year in the SF field, the short story is alive and well in the SF magazines and in slick markets such as *Omni* and *Playboy,* and the creative ferment and conflict within the SF culture is constant, fueled by the continuing changes in contemporary science. Universal competence in all the sciences is beyond the reach of even the most committed SF editor, and because the author chooses the special scientific content of the work, the editor must always be prepared to query new ideas and technical polysyllables, even at the risk of momentarily appearing an innocent to the author. For SF is founded upon what is known to science. One may speculate beyond what is known when writing SF, even to building great cathedrals of improbable speculation, but one may not contradict what is known without shifting the work into the realm of fantasy, where anything is possible and nothing is probable. SF authors sometimes write, and SF editors publish, fantasy, but the difference must be clear.

Fantasy and science fiction are closely allied in publishing, since both categories posit worlds that are not reality. The SF editor is most often a fantasy editor as well. Yet the most useful view for the working editor is to consider fantasy as conservative and pastoral, and SF as radical, technological, urban. There is a spectrum of variations, especially considering that for at least the last half century, many of the same authors have written both, a legacy, again, of the pulp magazines, which published both in the early twentieth century, before the battle lines were clearly drawn. There are several good histories of this period, the most useful of which perhaps is James E. Gunn's *Alternate Worlds* (Prentice-Hall, 1975). Due to the historical yoke between SF and fantasy, the fantasy and SF category audiences are linked and often cross over the boundaries between the two, especially for favorite authors. As always, the presentation of the work as one or the other must be clear, the cover art a blatant declaration which tells the bookseller where to position the book so that readers who head straight for the fantasy and SF section will find what they prefer.

SF art and packaging is a direct descendant of magazine cover packaging. There have now been dozens of colorful books devoted to SF art, which feature various present and historical styles, giving many theories, but the common thread I see is that SF art is vivid, colorful, and depicts a scene or image that declares at first glance the futuristic or fantastic nature of the book. The art may range from abstract and surreal to magic realism, but the appeal is escapist.

The artists who paint these blatant declarations are generally a happy lot, often well-paid (packaging is such a crucial marketing element), and even more, aesthetically satisfied. It is common for a cover illustration from an SF book to be nominated for major awards in the field of illustration, and it is common among the better illustrators to hear one declare his or her preference for SF work, because it is easier to "get away with good art" in SF than in any other realm of commercial packaging in publishing (the painted-to-format romance cover is hardly enough to keep the mind alive). And furthermore, the illustrators have the best of both worlds, being valued members of the SF culture, which has regular honors for them.

I find myself, as I write, returning frequently to the SF culture to explain some of the peculiarities unique to the career of the professional SF editor. I recently attended a party in celebration of the annual Nebula Award ceremony, thrown in California by the Science Fiction Writers of America. In attendance were several book dealers, a number of editors, several agents, a scattering of artists, reviewers, at least two typesetters who are regular readers, and of course a large number of writers, over a hundred of them. More than half the writers had never published a novel, some had only sold one or two short stories. It occurs to me that I have not encountered such a cross-section of people involved in an area of publishing anywhere other than at a science fiction event, and not only that, I could attend a similar event in the SF field two dozen times a year somewhere in the U.S. and expect to find a variant of the same party, even at a regional convention run by a bunch of teenagers and some older fans in Baltimore or Nashville or Seattle or Boston or Philadelphia.

The benefits to an editor ought to be evident. One becomes knowledgeable about the majority of young writers all over the country before they are ready to write novels. And because you are known in the community, writers and agents know your taste and reputation and will make an informed decision when they send you a manuscript. Although there are some agents knowledgeable in the SF field, many young authors submit their manuscripts directly to editors and perhaps get an agent after a book or two is sold. I know of no other area in publishing today (again, excepting romance) where editors are expected to read unsolicited manuscripts, and do, and often buy them.

Buying and editing and publishing is the daily work of an editor, and I find this so in SF work. My greatest problem, which I expect (not without a sigh) is a permanent job condition, is to communicate information about science fiction to people who neither read nor understand it but whose technical assistance and enthusiasm is vital to the successful publication of the book. Most often, difficulty in communication is the result of mistaken emphasis— people tend to fix on the familiar—so if I ask for art or copy on a trip to Mars with a small crew of men and women, I get lots of emphasis on the men and women and none on the trip to Mars, which is of course the main point for the science fiction audience.

The magazine editors who formed the SF field—Hugo Gernsback, John W. Campbell, Anthony Boucher, H. L. Gold, and a number of others—set standards for author-editor relationships that still hold sway among professionals in the field. The basic assumption is that there is never enough really good SF available to publish. Every editor must constantly and of necessity work to bring along new writers, and established writers must help, sponsor, and give moral support to new writers (and they do, much more so than in other fields, because there has always been enough *in-field* attention for everyone).

Yet the majority of published SF is not acceptable to readers outside the core audience and never will be as long as the SF culture I have delineated coheres. The SF field has established a variety of prose techniques eminently successful for communication from author to reader within the confines of the field, which is the primary aim of all written science fiction. Communication to outsiders has always been considered secondary. Without broad reading experience in the field, through which one learns the specific reading protocols of the genre (those preconceptions about the literal meanings of words and word patterns which identify a text as SF), you can't tell whether you are reading good SF or bad— or fantasy that looks like SF.

I said earlier that the author invents the science in his story based upon whatever specialized knowledge he has or can research for his purposes. This is true, but on a day-to-day basis both writers and editors are operating within the framework of a common literary language which has evolved within the genre since the 1920s. By the early 1950s, SF had developed a useful repository of cliché locutions. Phrases and words such as "space warp," "hyperspace," and "hyperdrive" can be used in any SF story to lend scientific verisimilitude (and that old SF flavor) without explanation or lengthy rationalization because other writers in the genre have already explained and rationalized them, often in great detail, in many other stories. The core readership of SF already knows what the terms refer to, how they work, and can fill in the rationalization from reading experiences they have in common.

An author of SF can devote more concentrated attention to his thematic concerns, what is new and different and essential in his work, by taking his characters on a *spaceship* (one of the earliest of the cliché words) equipped with *hyperdrive* (generally, a faster-than-light space drive) through *hyperspace* (that abnormal space through which a ship on hyperdrive travels) to a distant and alien planet. Author and editor may know nothing at all about how the characters really would travel, but the clichés get them from here to there and the real concern is the characters and the environment and their thoughts and feelings and interactions.

Still, you must be aware that the specialized clichés do have a literal meaning, are not nonsense words or supernatural explanations. The text is to be taken literally in an SF story, not metaphorically; the ability to do this is the basic imaginative leap required of a reader or writer or editor confronted with an SF text. Working with such a text requires certain forms of editorial concentration and experience not far removed from what is required by a work of poetry or avant-garde fiction. I have been the editor and publisher of a contemporary poetry magazine, *The Little Magazine,* since 1965 and I find that contemporary poetry has a similarly specialized audience, body of techniques and conventions, and image of opacity to outsiders. Editorial familiarity with a large body of contemporary work is a sine qua non. The inner consistency of the work and the artistic goals that it sets for itself position the work vis-à-vis the rest of the field and dictate your editorial stance.

As in every fiction-publishing endeavor, the majority of what gets into print in the end is ephemeral and mediocre, done to fill slots in the distribution system, to keep the sales force busy and the voracious readership, if not fully satisfied, at least somewhat entertained, and to maintain the authors as they build up to masterpieces planned or hoped for. The editors who work in SF know all this and persevere and are generally happy. I am fortunate to be among them.

PAUL ANBINDER

Paul Anbinder is president and publisher of Hudson Hills Press. Mr. Anbinder started his book publishing career at Dover Publications, where he first worked on illustrated books. He then served as editor in chief of Shorewood Publishers, a firm specializing in art books, before moving to Harry N. Abrams, Inc. (probably the world's largest art book publisher), of which he subsequently became president. Before founding his own firm, he was director of special projects for Random House and Alfred A. Knopf, and vice-president in charge of the trade paperback program at Ballantine.

•　　　•　　　•

Some illustrated books are works of art in themselves. The creativity and dedication of the editor of illustrated books are explored in this detailed, authoritative, and highly informative essay, written especially for this anthology. Mr. Anbinder discusses the very special editorial skills that go into the editing of an illustrated book. He describes the importance of such critical steps as finding the right photos for the text or vice versa, designing the layout of the book so that text and photos interrelate, cropping and sizing photos, assuring the highest quality of reproduction, and many other crucial factors that go into the creation of an illustrated book. This type of editing may not be for everyone, but for some people, as Mr. Anbinder says, "editing the illustrated book represents the most interesting and challenging aspect of the publishing profession." It is a field well suited "to those inclined . . . to a career that combines the literary and the visual."

EDITING THE ILLUSTRATED BOOK

There are many types of illustrated books: books of fiction and general nonfiction to which illustrations have been added for decorative effect; textbooks and instructional books in which the illustrations are necessary to amplify the text, or are even a key part of the text's exposition; and books about essentially visual subjects, where the illustrations are absolutely essential to the content of the book. This essay is concerned only with the last category.

Within this category—or even, narrowing it further for the purposes of this discussion, within the category of books about the visual *arts* (photography, painting, sculpture, architecture, the graphic arts)—illustrated books may take many forms. At one extreme is that much maligned icon of our age the "coffee table book," which can at its worst be a pretentiously produced object with a text that might generously be called an excuse for stringing together a collection of illustrations. At the other extreme is the illustrated book with a substantial and scholarly text which is truly amplified, illuminated, and enriched by a series of illustrations.

However, appearances can be deceptive in this field. The fact that an illustrated book is large and beautifully produced is no guarantee that its editorial content is weak. The fact that a book has a modest, scholarly appearance, with lots of densely set type and dingy gray illustrations, is no guarantee that its editorial content is sound.

In fact, as the book-production revolution of the past few decades has made good reproduction quality and lavish production values more available, there are many magnificently produced "coffee table books" that are not only a sensual pleasure to hold and to behold but also a joy to read, not to mention a lasting contribution to scholarship in their field. You can't tell a book by its package!

Editors of illustrated books also fall into several categories.

Some, basically "word people," come from a literary, journalistic, or academic background, as do editors in all areas of publishing, find themselves either drawn by their own tastes or assigned by fortuitous circumstance to illustrated books, and proceed to develop an expertise in this speciality. Others come from a visually oriented background, perhaps graphic design or art history, and find that they have an affinity for the written language as well. Whatever their backgrounds, successful editors of illustrated books combine the usual talents and aptitudes of all book editors with a highly developed visual sense and, ideally, a well-grounded knowledge of the visual arts.

The editor of illustrated books should also be fully conversant with—and sympathetic to—the work of design and production people. I had the good fortune to begin my publishing career in the editorial department of Dover Publications, where I was encouraged to take a book-production course. I subsequently worked closely for a number of years with Harry Abrams, whose own approach to art-book publishing was essentially a visual one, and who saw to it that I was exposed to every aspect of book design and production. Thanks to that background, now that I manage my own publishing firm I am able to serve as de facto art director and production manager.

The editor of illustrated books must work closely with the designer in determining how text and pictures will relate, in terms of both overall balance and specific layout decisions—which illustrations must be juxtaposed to specific portions of the text and/or to each other; the relative importance (and thus the relative sizes in reproduction) of various illustrations; how illustrations will be cropped; whether illustrations may be "bled" off the page, leaving no margins.

The editor must work closely with the production specialist in determining how the editorial aspects of the book can best serve and be served by the physical format in which the book will be manufactured—and here, of course, questions of budget are often factors in the decision-making process.

How many illustrations will be reproduced in color? Will the color plates be ganged in separate inserts or signatures, requiring that cross-references be added throughout the text, or can they appear throughout the book, precisely where they are needed to accompany the points of the text that they are meant to illuminate?

Perhaps the answer will be a compromise between these extremes.

How many illustrations are to be reproduced in black and white? Will they be printed in regular offset, in duotone offset, or in gravure; if duotone offset, will the second color be a gray-black, a warm brown-black, or a cool blue-black?

Do some of the illustrations lend themselves to reproduction across two-page spreads, or perhaps as gatefolds? If the former, how can they be made to fall at the centers of signatures, where they will be least disturbed by the gutter (the space—and fold—between facing pages); and if the latter, how can they be made to fall at the ends or centers of signatures, which are the only locations where a binder can practically accommodate them?

All of these questions rightly fall into the domain of design and production people, but the editor should understand that the decisions also help to determine how well the book works editorially, and should make every effort to be helpful in seeing to it that they suit not only the designer's aesthetic concept and the production person's budget but also the author's intentions.

A manuscript for an illustrated book needs, at minimum, exactly the same editorial work as any other manuscript: checking facts, consistency, sense, organization, and comprehensibility, plus copyediting and styling. Similarly, the editor will be involved, as all editors are, in checking material at every step of the production process: galleys, layouts, mechanicals, perhaps even printer's press proofs. Again, in addition to looking after those aspects of accuracy with which every editor is concerned, the editor of illustrated books will be using these checkpoints as opportunities to make certain once more that each illustration has been sized and cropped properly, that each illustration is accompanied by the correct caption, and, always, that the look and physical quality of the book properly serve the author's intentions.

The editor of illustrated books must also be prepared to deal with many items peculiar to this area of publishing. In some cases, the editor will be involved in determining what illustrations are needed; seeking out the sources for them; and arranging to purchase or (if photographs of the type—black-and-white glossy or color transparency—and quality needed already exist in the source's files) rent them or have the subject specially photographed. The editor must also secure the necessary reproduction rights, sometimes from the same source as the photograph itself but often from a different source entirely. This work often requires enormous reserves of patience and tact, not to mention good instincts, since there is no uniform, clear-cut law covering reproduction rights to the visual arts in this country. The original artists, the owners of works of arts (whether institutions or private collectors), newly established agencies representing artists' rights (much as ASCAP represents composers' rights), and photographers who photograph works of art for reproduction—all vie for a fee, an acknowledgment, and/or the right to determine whether and how a particular work of art may be reproduced. The editor may also be responsible for compiling a list of photograph credits to be printed somewhere in the book.

The editor of illustrated books needs to work not only with the basic text but also with captions for the illustrations. The editor will be involved—along with the author and designer—in deciding what form the captions will take. Will they be straightforwardly factual, simply listing data about the items illustrated? Will they be more expository, perhaps repeating brief pertinent passages from the text? Or will they be "deep" captions, containing significant information not included elsewhere in the book?

The editor of illustrated books must check for consistency between the text and the captions. When both have been prepared by the author, there are less likely to be problems, but captions must sometimes be prepared by the editor from information supplied by picture sources, and it then becomes necessary to query and resolve inconsistencies.

Even authors of illustrated books can be careless in terms of visual evidence, or confused about so basic a matter as right versus left. So the editor must check each illustration against both the text and the captions, so that if the author describes something as appearing on the right side of a painting, it is in fact on the right side, or if the author describes an inscription as reading "Excelsior," it does not in fact read "E pluribus unum." Authors of illustrated books are no more or less prone to errors than authors of any other types of books, but since the visual evidence is on hand to embarrass them in any such errors they make, the editor must make the extra effort to check that evidence scrupulously.

Another area requiring editorial checking overlaps with the production department. If the author describes a passage in a work of art as being a vivid crimson, the editor must make sure that it so appears in the transparency, and that it is ultimately so reproduced in the printer's color proofs.

Still other special problems arise in connection with international coproductions, which, because of the economics of such projects, are most commonly illustrated books. If the editor is working on the originating edition, on which foreign-language editions will be based, he may have to take into account the other publishers' needs with regard to translating the original manuscript, particularly if the exigencies and economics of coproduction dictate that all the different-language editions must be produced at the same time. The editor on such a project will see to it that the designer does not call for type to be dropped out of the backgrounds of illustrations, especially color plates, since new color separations would then have to be made for each language edition. When I was director of special projects at Alfred A. Knopf, we copublished the Metropolitan Museum's immensely successful *Tutankhamun: His Tomb and Its Treasures.* The book had been designed and produced by the Metropolitan with no thought of foreign-language co-editions, but when we succeeded in licensing several of these, much of the book had to be redesigned to eliminate type dropped out of illustrations, in order to simplify their production.

The editor working on an American edition of a book that is originating elsewhere will have to be concerned with having the manuscript translated and with all the aspects of editing a translated manuscript that an editor of any kind of book may encounter. In addition, the editor will have to ensure that the English-language text will fit into the space allotted by the designer of the original edition, with the usually unalterable sizes and positions of the illustrations, since the English-language version may vary dramatically in length from the original in another language. Some flexibility may be available through changing the type sizes, but not as much as is available when publishing a non-illustrated book, where it is a simple matter of adding or subtracting a signature or more if the text in English runs longer or shorter than the original.

Depending on the language from which the translation is done, other problems may be encountered. American publishers of illustrated books seem to be more concerned with the accuracy and substance of their texts than publishers in some other parts of the world. Publishers in the Romance languages especially seem to be more interested in the stylistic flourishes of the writing, in texts that fly off into the empyrean of poetry or philosophy, than in texts that present well-organized information pertinent to the subject matter of the book.

For me, editing the illustrated book represents the most interesting and challenging aspect of the publishing profession. I heartily recommend the field to those inclined, as I am, to a career that combines the literary and the visual.

JANE ISAY

Jane Isay began her career in publishing in 1963 as first reader at Harcourt Brace Jovanovich. She spent fifteen years at Yale University Press, beginning in 1964 as an editorial assistant and ending in 1979 as executive editor. She then moved to Basic Books as associate publisher and became co-publisher in 1980. She was made a vice-president of Harper & Row, establishing a division of electronic and technical publishing.

• • •

In this sensitive and authoritative essay, written especially for this anthology, Jane Isay offers some excellent practical advice on the creative, productive, and rewarding relationship between the editor and the scholar. Discussing how to present the author's scholarship in the most lucid, readable, and effective manner, Ms. Isay outlines the best use of the many elements of a scholarly book—methodology chapters, subheads, illustrations, notes and footnotes, chapter openings and closings—and she describes the importance of the final chapter as the "author's last chance to convince and excite." Ms. Isay concludes by remarking: "The working relationship between scholar and editor can be exciting and taxing at the same time. So long as the editor can serve multiple masters—the material itself, the author, and the 'reader over your shoulder'—then the work is likely to be also fruitful and challenging."

EDITING SCHOLARS AND
SCHOLARSHIP

"You're unlike any editor I've ever worked with," an author recently told me. "My other editors have always had a book in mind and tried to get me to write that one. You, on the other hand, listen very carefully to what I have learned and what I want to say, and then you offer strategies to make the material come out as *I* wish it." This author had put his finger on what I conceive to be the difference between editing scholarly and nonscholarly books. For the scholarly writer and editor, the quest is a joint one: to bring as much out of the research as possible, to make the work as elegant and sophisticated as it can be, and to create its intellectual and literary setting. What differentiates this kind of work from other kinds of editing of nonfiction is that there are three parties present: the author, the editor, and the research data findings. Instead of being able to focus on the author's preferences, or the editor's ideas, we begin with the research, attempting to understand its quality, its importance, and its problems.

So the first rule of scholarly editing is: *You have to understand the research.* That rule is easier to carry out if you know something about the subject matter. But even if it is unfamiliar, a good editor can catch on quickly. The best teacher is usually the author, who is generally delighted to talk for hours about his field. Intelligent questioning makes any author happy, and is often the beginning of the relationship of respect that is so essential to the task.

A corollary of rule one follows this argument: *You have to respect the work.* If you don't, then your suggestions about what to leave out and how to frame the book may be perverse—and the author will quickly learn to mistrust your suggestions, even if on occasion they are good.

Understanding the research and respecting it doesn't mean that you have to buy all of it forever. When a researcher, for example, called his study of grown men a theory of adult development, I kept reminding him that since he'd studied only men, he couldn't claim "adult." He agreed and made that clear everywhere in his book—and now he's studying the other half of the human race.

Sometimes an editor's inability to make heads or tails of a manuscript is crucial. I recently received a tremendously important study from a distinguished pair of social scientists. As I pored over hundreds of pages of almost unintelligible writing, I knew that somewhere in the research, somewhere in the minds of the authors, there were findings, there were conclusions, and there was wisdom. But for the life of me, I couldn't tell what and where it was.

When the author called to find out what I thought, I had to admit utter puzzlement with the manuscript. So we sat down together, in order for me to show him what my problems were—and what I couldn't understand. Each explanation the author offered in person, and in speech, was clear and fascinating. Almost simultaneously, we reached the same conclusion: He had to reclaim his own voice, and he would follow his instincts more readily. We reviewed every page of the manuscript, and he took copious notes. When, two months later, revisions came in, I was delighted to see that the author had really understood my problems and had addressed himself to them. I couldn't lay out a new literary style for him, or a new organization. But I had shared with him what was going on in my mind, and he readily responded to the problem. Losing one's voice is a very common problem in scholarly writing; it's usually caused by being overwhelmed by the amount of data or the scope of the research.

However the questions are posed, whatever the subject of the analysis, the connection between author and editor has to be clear, real, and mutual. If an author accepts too readily the suggestions for revision that I've tossed off informally, then I begin to worry that he is too malleable; if someone gets the feeling that I don't respect or like him, then there's no way in which anything I say or do from then on is acceptable. I have watched myself being too hard on a manuscript, not being fair enough to its merits in the author's presence, and I have seen the ebb of good feeling. Once lost, it rarely comes back. The editor has to be very careful to be certain that the problems or criticisms are framed in a context that is friendly both to the discipline and to the person. Since we desperately need each other—the author wants the help of a good editor to improve the book and to gain the confidence of the publishing operation, and the editor needs the author who alone can write this book—we have to find ways to work together.

I have dwelt so long on the relationship between editor and author because it really is fundamental. The mutual respect, the common view of the problems, the joint efforts to solve them, and the drive to make all things happen, all come from that relationship. Sometimes the contact is daily, and sometimes monthly or yearly; sometimes the phone rings constantly, and sometimes not at all. The frequency and intensity of contact range widely. But the connection between us is the lifeline of the editorial process.

Although the problems are always different, there are some tricks of the scholarly editing trade:

- ▶ Organize a book so that the most generally interesting comes first, and the most specific comes last: imagine the reader walking into a cornucopia.
- ▶ Never let the author of a work of research think of it as a mystery story, with the conclusions coming in the last chapter. The more the reader knows about the author's suppositions and conclusions, the more easily the reader can take in and evaluate the arguments of the book. Since you can peek at the end of any book, there's no advantage to keeping the interesting data for the last—and every advantage in letting the reader in on the point of the book early.
- ▶ Methodology chapters belong in appendixes. And the authors of scholarly books should always be allowed to put into the book—in appendixes if necessary—information and data that they really do think is crucial. It is suicidal for an editor to insist that a researcher jettison the heart of the research. We have to be inventive and creative to figure ways to keep it in. Here again the cardinal rule works: Least general goes last.
- ▶ Conceive of the various elements that go on a page as allowing the author to write or speak in different ways. For instance, part titles and chapter titles can really frame the way the reader views the book.
- ▶ Subheadings can be helpful pointers through a long and difficult argument or narrative. Sometimes, in the effort to find the

right subheadings for sections of a long chapter, the author will begin to see that the organization of the chapter can be improved, so performing an editorial act of finding subheads can serve a formal end—forcing the author to look once again at the order and presentation of the argument.

Illustrations—graphic or numerical—should be viewed as a way of speeding the reader through the text, and are suspect if they impede the reader. Some authors prefer to present their information in both ways—in words and in numbers. If length is a problem—as it often is with scholarly works—then the author should choose the most economical way in which to present that information. Any information that can be expressed in as much space in words as in numbers should be said in words. Sometimes a few numbers can tell a complicated and interesting story in themselves, and they should be allowed onto the page of a scholarly book. But if they do appear there, they should be presented in as clear and simple a format as possible, and the importance of the findings should be sketched out in the text. Illustrations of a graphic sort can and should, whenever possible, appear on the page that discusses them. The technology of offset printing allows this, and there is no reason to bunch illustrations in sections, unless they belong there for intellectual reasons—sometimes they need to be compared, sometimes different pictures are referred to repeatedly and in different parts of the book.

Footnotes belong in one or both of the following places: at the bottom of the page, or at the end of the book. They never belong at the end of the chapter, because it is the hardest place for the reader to find them. If they appear at the end of the book, this simple technique is a big help: running heads should say "Notes to Chapter X, pp. 00–00." That way, if the reader doesn't remember the number of the chapter, the page number will do the job. What goes into the footnotes depends on the demands of the book. Sometimes footnotes simply cite sources. When research includes original sources, those notes may be the most important intellectual contribution of the book and should never be slighted. When notes refer to well-known works of a secondary nature, they should be used sparingly. When they contain nuggets of argument and insight, they should always be considered as candidates for inclusion in the text. If the author and editor agree that the footnote is a genuine digression, no matter how interesting it is, then it should remain a footnote.

Whether notes belong at the foot of the page or in the back of the book is still disputed. I believe that some footnotes do belong at the bottom of the page, even at the risk of making the book look less readable. My principle of footnote location comes from Alvin Eisenman, professor of graphics at Yale, who said that the point of having a note on a page is so that the reader can ignore it! When some juicy notes are interspersed with reference notes, and they are all at the end of the book, there is no way for the reader to know whether or not to flip back when a note turns up. I'd rather segregate the reference notes at the end and leave the interesting ones on the page. Never, in a scholarly work, should the note numbers disappear so that the reader has to flip to the end to find out whether or not there is a footnote. Once when I was trying to sell a very scholarly book to a magazine, I tossed off a comment to the editor that the footnotes were almost as interesting as the text. He ran an article based on ten of the most interesting nuggets that appeared in the notes.

One kind of note that must always be excised: the defensive footnote. Scholars, especially when they are treading on new ground and are afraid of the reception of their ideas, tend to cover themselves with references, attempting to show that no book has gone unread and no issue ignored. This makes for boring and irritating reading, and we hope to convince the author that the research is strong enough and the argument persuasive enough so that they require no defense tactics.

▶ Openings and closings are crucial elements for editorial guidance. The beginning of a scholarly book should always be written last, framing the book in the widest appropriate perspective and giving a preview of the arguments and conclusions. It should never be defensive, but can disarm critical readers and reviews by stating precisely what it claims to achieve—and what it doesn't.

▶ Chapter openings have a similar character, and they can guide the reader to both the chapter's place in the argument of the book and to its internal organization. Scholarly authors are best advised to avoid reviewing the literature at the start of the chapters, since that stops the flow of the argument and is usually a defensive move. The tendency to recapitulate what comes before and what will follow has to be watched carefully.

▶ Chapter closings are another art: they should somehow achieve a high note of excitement and form a bridge to what follows, encouraging the reader to turn to the next chapter. Good chapter conclusions make it much easier for the reader to retain a sense of location within the book. It is often hard not to get lost in a long and deep work, and the author and the editor can keep the reader always knowing where he is and where the book is going.

▶ The final chapter is the author's last chance to convince and excite. This element of the book can depart in style from the rest: it may take on a polemic tone, a lyrical one, or a questioning one. Here the author decides what the reader should take away from the book, and sets both tone and content for the ending. One superb book on the Bible ended rather abruptly, as the author had finished writing all his chapters. I asked him to remember the closing services on the Jewish Day of Atonement, a moment when the last rays of the sun filter through the windows of the synagogue and the struggles of self-assessment and repentance come to an end. "Think of that closing service," I said to him, "and write me a few pages at the end of the book, adding rest and reflection to your brilliant and arduous writing." He did that, and imparted a special feeling to an already beautiful work.

Questions needing further thought and study often belong at the end of a book; the author can get one last crack at bringing home the major thrust of the argument—this time without the careful accretion of evidence. It often gives the author a sense of accomplishment and satisfaction to sit down and write those last few pages, easing him into the time when the intense work on the book is beginning to come to an end. Authors may feel at this point that they really have written a pretty good book, have said something worthwhile.

What I have discussed here are all large topics, ones to be agreed upon between editor and author. Since most of this work is done by the author and not the editor, it is best to cover all these topics before the manuscript is in its final draft. In most cases, the editor has the opportunity to see the book before it is ready to go to copyediting, even if the author sometimes doesn't expect it to get sent back to the typewriter. The time spent on these tasks, on solving the intellectual and practical problems of a scholarly manuscript, is well spent, because it can often make the difference between a monograph and a work of serious nonfiction. Trust and admiration are essential, because no self-respecting scholar will go to that kind of effort just because some publisher said so.

The working relationship between scholar and editor can be exciting and taxing at the same time. So long as the editor can serve multiple masters—the material itself, the author, and the "reader over your shoulder"—then the work is likely to be also fruitful and challenging.

JONATHAN GALASSI

Jonathan Galassi joined Random House as a senior editor in 1981. He began his publishing career with Houghton Mifflin in 1973. Mr. Galassi is the poetry editor of *Paris Review* and has published a number of books, including his translations of Eugenio Montale's selected essays, *The Second Life of Art,* and his most recent book of poems, *Otherwise: First and Last Poems.* In 1984 he won the prestigious PEN/Roger Klein Award for Editing.

•　　　•　　　•

Originally written in 1980 and revised for its appearance in this anthology, Mr. Galassi's essay is a thoughtful and passionate defense of the importance of the literary editor to the continued existence and profitability of the general commercial publisher. He discusses what qualities the literary editor should have, how he should pursue the acceptance of the superior work of literature within the commercial publishing house, how to fight for the proper attention for the book, and finally, how to be optimistic even in the face of the declining rate of literacy. It is altogether an inspiring essay, reflecting the deepest commitment to publishing's highest standards and most enduring values.

DOUBLE AGENT:
The Role of the Literary Editor in the Commercial Publishing House

To some observers today the phrase "literary publishing" is a contradiction in terms. Literature, after all, is essentially an expression of the spirit, a human activity without quantitative dimensions. Publishing first of all is business (publishers make up an important arm of the modern "communications industry") and the publisher's primary concern, of necessity, is survival in the marketplace. And since most major publishers today are either part of the diversified portfolios of large corporations or are themselves big companies, survival for a publisher means having rates of profit and growth which are commensurate with those of the other businesses that are its counterparts and competitors on the stock exchange. As a result, the trade publisher today tends to behave like other big businesses and treats its product, the book, as a commodity to be exploited like a new brand of toothpaste or cereal or whiskey.

This approach works well enough for certain kinds of books, particularly those that have readily identifiable large markets due to the timeliness of their subjects or the visibility or popularity of their authors (in the publisher's eye, the writer is an "author," a subcontractor who manufactures the publisher's product). What I am concerned with here, however, is the publishing of serious books, books that can be said to make some sort of real contribution to human knowledge or understanding; I am especially interested in new work that, by virtue of its originality or difficulty or very newness, is not assured of an immediate, predictable audience. The first novel, the essay in cultural criticism by an unknown or a foreign writer, the book of poems or stories, are high-risk ventures for modern publishers who have inherited the overhead of big business along with its management techniques and managers, and who have become increasingly reluctant to invest even very modest sums in projects that promise little in the way of immediate return.

Because of this reluctance, more and more "marginal" or financially unpromising "quality" publishing is being undertaken by small and university presses, and at times it seems probable that eventually most serious writers may first be published in this manner. If that day comes, trade publishing will have become nothing more than the calculated marketing of slickly packaged materials, another "leisure time" industry, as it is already seen in some quarters, unconnected to its own past or to the intellectual and cultural roots of the society it purports to serve. For the time being, however, most trade publishers continue to devote some part of their resources to the presentation of new talents whom they believe to be important or promising, and I am convinced that despite the pressures of the contemporary marketplace they will continue to do so. I believe "literary" publishing must remain an essential activity for any trade publisher who can see beyond the short-term balance sheet and who understands that remaining in touch with and encouraging what is original and new is vital for his own future.

But how does the meritorious but problematic literary work find its way into the highly competitive world of commercial publishing, where it is if not always precisely unwelcome, usually only tolerated? The responsibility for the presence of this kind of book on commercial lists usually rests with the surprisingly large group of editors in trade publishing who are interested in writing for its own sake, who do not agree with one of their glamorous colleagues that "there is no such thing as a good book that doesn't sell," who persist in the conviction (which is not always supported by the evidence) that really important books do in the end find their audience. Some of these editors are highly valued by their employers, who recognize the usefulness of their contributions and who have seen that some of the writers they sponsor do eventually become popular. Others are embattled, at odds with the companies they work for; sometimes they become embittered, quit or lose their jobs, and leave publishing altogether.

It is not easy to be a literary editor in a commercial house; nor

is it easy to become one. When the aspiring editor comes to publishing with the aim of being involved in the presentation of important new work, he or she is immediately confronted by the domi-
nating profit motive of the business. From the outset, if he makes
the mistake of revealing his ambitions to those he meets who are
already in publishing, he will be discouraged from pursuing them.
He will be told that publishing is commerce, that most of it has
nothing to do with literature. He will learn that within the publishing industry the adjective "literary" is usually a synonym for
abstruse, artsy, Brahmin, gnomic, highfalutin, or academic, and
that the highest praise that can be bestowed on a book is for it to
be called "commercial." The would-be editor may be momentarily
thrown by all this, but he will not quite be able to believe it, and
if he perseveres in looking for work, if he is smart enough to stop
talking about his more rarefied interests and concentrates instead
on his enthusiasm for books of all kinds, eventually—if he is
persistent enough—someone will give him a job as a secretary or
an editorial assistant. And if he learns quickly, educates himself in
the politics of the business and shows an aptitude for the work and
a willingness to do it, he will sooner or later find himself in a
position where he is able to express his own interests and even at
times to act on them. And he will come to realize that although
the publishing industry is often suspicious of "literary" works,
enormous prestige is still attached to their publication, and that
this prestige, which is a commodity second only to money itself in
the world of publishers, can be a most effective weapon; for many
(though certainly not all) publishers still feel that the publication
of an important book validates their existence to the reading public
and their peers, and to themselves as well. Many of them still feel
in some visceral way that the publishing of significant books is the
real purpose of their work. Some deep love of books drew them
to publishing in the first place; and though this love may have been
thwarted by experience, and may even be the source of their cyni-
cism about literary publishing, something in them still wants to be
convinced of the importance of a new writer's work; for they know
that nothing is as thrilling as the discovery of a new writer of
potential importance. There are scores of editors in commercial
publishing today who have successfully learned these invaluable
psychological lessons, and who have been able to make the trade
publishing machine work to accommodate serious new work at

least some of the time. In doing so they have contributed greatly to the liveliness and strength of American publishing.

What does it take to be an effective literary editor in a trade house? Apart from courage, tenacity, good humor, and tact, the primary requirement seems to me to be an educated and well-defined taste. This does not mean a closed mind; obviously, the more wide-ranging and inclusive an editor's interests, the better equipped he or she will be to respond to really good new work. But an editor should have ideas of his own about what he thinks is important and why. He should be aware of other cultures and traditions than his own and should constantly be replenishing his reservoir of experience through the exploration of new areas of interest. If his values are well grounded and well developed, he will not be duped by pretentious works that are neither salable nor useful, nor will he lose touch with what he believes to be important when he confronts the skewed values of the corporate environment, where salability is often the determining criterion of judgment. What passes for literature in the publishing house may at times strike the editor as high-class hackwork or worse; and what he feels is important or exciting may not always be seen as such by his confreres. Often he will have to keep his real opinions to himself. If he is sure of what he thinks, however, and is willing to trust his own instincts, he will be prepared to act when something of real value does come along.

This intuitive taste is the bedrock of the *yin,* or passive, aspect of an editor's job. Along with it should come something comparable to what Keats wanted for the poet: a kind of "negative capability," a capacity both to see the writer's work objectively, as it would be approached by a common reader, *and* to understand it subjectively, from the inside, as it must be felt by the writer. This dual way of appreciating the work—empathy with its creator combined with dispassionate critical distance—is the second intuitive quality necessary in an editor. If he has it, he will always approach a writer's work, even work that is not to his personal liking, with a respect for its particular integrity and an appreciation of its specific aims; he will not be tempted to refashion a writer's work to suit his own idea of how it should be written.

The complementary *yang,* or active, side of an editor's work begins with reconciling the writer's sense of his book with the reader's needs. If the editor feels changes are necessary to clarify or point up the writer's intentions, he must be able to persuade the writer of their advisability; he must inspire the writer's confidence and trust. And then he must be able to turn around and do battle for the book within the publishing house itself.

With the writer the editor is collaborator, psychiatrist, confessor, and amanuensis; in the publishing house he must be politician, diplomat, mediator. He is a double agent. Since he represents the publisher (who employs him) to the writer, and the writer (to whose work he is committed) to the publisher, his loyalties are inescapably divided, for though these interests should ideally coincide, they often appear to be or actually are in conflict. Within the publishing company the editor is in competition with his fellow editors for the always limited resources (time, money, and manpower) of the organization. This is true for any editor; but the literary editor's role is especially tricky since the book he is interested in seeing succeed is often likely, because of the apparent limits of its potential market, to command the least degree of voluntary commitment from the publishing machine. Having agreed, often reluctantly, to take the book on, and with little hope for immediate financial reward, the publisher expects to spend as little effort and money on it as he can, imagining that the book will "find its own way"—i.e., that its author and editor will go away and be quiet and not cause trouble.

Often the literary editor will have to be content with the very minimum of effort the organization is willing to spend on such books. In the publication of poetry, for instance, where the potential readership is small and dispersed, it is doubtful whether a poet's work can be effectively promoted by a publicity campaign, and the most the editor can really ask is a few ads in literary reviews.

But there are other books which are more susceptible to a publisher's efforts, and in order to be effective in getting his company to work for these books, the editor must have the respect and confidence of his colleagues. He must be able to speak their language; he must make them feel that he is fundamentally one of them, and that his goals and theirs are actually the same, though they may assume different guises. The literary editor, if he is to succeed in his aims, must be seen as a significant, not a secondary, figure in the overall affairs of the company. He needs to master the financial and technical dimensions of the business; he should be able to carry his own weight financially, through the editing of other types of books if necessary; and he must be able to demonstrate to his superiors that the serious works he wants to publish will in fact benefit the organization: in visibility and prestige, as backlist properties that will sell well over time, as investments for the future. Sometimes, as a well-known literary editor once said to me, he has to lie, has to make claims he doubts will be proven true. But he cannot lie effectively unless his earlier predictions have been accurate at least some of the time.

Once the editor has established that his judgment is reliable and that the books he is interested in publishing do stand a good chance of being noticed, he will be in a much better position to wheedle, cajole, kvetch, scream, beg, and plead for the kind of special attention that careful publishing requires. This involves painstaking consultation and checking with everyone involved in the process of publication: art director, copy editor, designer, publicity and sales departments, and, outside the house, reviewers, critics, other writers, other editors, bookstore buyers—with anyone, in fact, who will listen. The editor who makes himself a nuisance—who is an agreeable but constant and demanding presence—is probably the editor who is doing the best job for his writer's book.

This can be lonely and frustrating as well as time-consuming work, and still the editor's best efforts can lead to disappointing results, for the truth is that much literary publishing is bound to fail in the short run (and the short run is how businesses measure success or failure). The argument that publishers' backlists are rich in works that sold slowly at first but have continued over time has been used again and again to convince a reluctant publisher to take on a chancy book, and I believe, as must anyone who is committed to this kind of work, that the relatively small risks that intelligent literary publishing involves do generally pay off in the long run. But there are good books that do not sell, even in the very long run.

Often when such a book does prove to be a modest financial success, it remains problematic for the contemporary commercial publisher, for the economies of scale of high-gear commodity publishing today are not compatible with the much smaller risks (and gains) a serious new writer's work usually involves. The most successful houses have developed efficient mechanisms for the distribution and marketing of their books, and the size and expense of these mechanisms require big, highly salable properties to keep them occupied, and ever-larger revenues to justify their size. Expertise in marketing eventually brings these houses many excellent writers whose reputations have actually been established by smaller publishers, where the new writer's book represented less of a relative drain on the company's less sophisticated machinery. Thus the larger publisher, like any big business, tends to reap the fruits of his smaller, often more adventurous but necessarily less efficient competitor's ability or willingness to take a chance on a new talent. The predictable consequence is that more and more of the smaller publishers are being forced by economic necessity to imitate the policies of the larger companies, or are themselves being absorbed by them.

All of this seems to bode ill for the future of the literary editor in commercial publishing. And yet, as I have indicated above, I believe that the publishing industry will have to continue to find ways to encourage a new writer. The whole superstructure of publishing as we know it depends on this trial and error, this vital spadework of introducing new work, whether it is done by the smaller commercial publishers or by the even smaller small presses. The publisher relies in the end on the work of the serious editor, the person who is interested in books not as momentary properties but as ideas with a future. The serious editor is the one person in the publishing organization for whom the long view is his basic stock-in-trade, and if he is perspicacious his employer can profit from his initially unpopular decisions a decade or a generation hence. If the publishing industry cannot find room for new writers, eventually it will have nothing to publish.

This is why it seems to me that the doomsaying about the future of literary publishing is exaggerated. True, the immediate prospects for the publishing of serious books do not seem bright. But how easy has it ever been to publish such books? Literary history is peopled with great writers—Joyce, Frost, and William Carlos Williams, to name only three—who struggled for years to find publishers; it is crowded with great books—*Walden, Moby Dick,* the novels of Italo Svevo—that were virtually unread for years after they were published. In fact, it is probably easier for a writer to get his work published today than it has ever been. The number of poetry books published annually in this country, which is supposed to be hostile to or uninterested in poetry, is staggering. And the proliferation of writers (and of writing programs to "teach" them) seems geometrical. As always, the number of the really talented remains small, but the fact that so many people in our visual culture still want to write seems to indicate that there are also still readers.

Certainly the audience for serious books is limited, and it may be shrinking. Yet the market for commercial books has its limits too, and recently the sales volume not only of hardcover books but of mass-market paperbacks as well has been declining, while sales of trade or quality paperbacks have risen. If it is true, as it seems to be, that literacy itself is on the wane, then commercial publishers are battling for shares of a shrinking market, and the effects should be felt more definitely in the sale of books for the mass of readers than among the much smaller but relatively more constant audience for serious books.

In fact, it seems possible that in time the market for the really commercial book—the suspense novel, the romance, the how-to manual—may shrink to a fraction of its current size. When recipes can be beamed onto the kitchen wall at will and the Regency romance and the thriller have been replaced by Huxley's "feelies," the publishing industry as we know it will have been absorbed by bigger, more sophisticated mass-media cartels. Yet there will still be a group of hardy nonconformists who read, write, and live by fiction, poetry, biography, criticism, philosophy. And they will still have publishers, though they may work in radically different ways from the way we work now.

Technology is bound to revolutionize reading as it is already changing how we write. Perhaps readers will pay a fee to screen the work they are interested in on their home computers, ordering an actual book to be produced (on demand) only in the comparatively rare instances when a permanent copy is desired. This may mean that the writer's work will never again be forced "out of print"; it may also mean that books as we know them may cease to be everyday objects and once again become remarkable, as they were before the invention of movable type; however it is distributed, though, the writer's work will remain essential.

For writing is simply the elucidation of ideas, the most complex, supple, and sophisticated means of expressing experience that man has yet devised. The word remains our intellectual currency, our surest way of explaining ourselves to each other; and the publisher, the purveyor of ideas, remains fundamentally dependent on the man who can express himself on paper, who extends the capacities of the language and points the way. All the publisher can do is follow, with his bevy of interpreters, popularizers, and rip-off artists. He may begrudge the truly original man or woman a place in his scheme of things, because the truly original man is by nature ahead of his time, and therefore not immediately "commercial"; but if the publisher is intelligent he recognizes that the serious writer's work is the heart and soul of his undertaking. Everything the publisher does depends on the writer's gift, his inimitable spark of intuition, genius, creative intelligence.

This is what the serious editor makes it his business to recognize, to nurture, and to promote. And that is why I believe there will always be some kind of place for him in the publishing business, as long as it survives. He will never be rich, and he may never feel really at home or appreciated, but he belongs and needs to be there, because he and the writers he devotes himself to will still be at work when the idea of books as entertainment and as big business has gone the way of the serialized novel and the illustrated weekly.

ANN BENEDUCE

Ann Beneduce began her career in publishing in 1957. She has been a children's book editor since 1960, when she joined the J. B. Lippincott Co. From 1960 to 1980 she held top editorial posts in the children's book field at World Publishing Company, T. Y. Crowell, and William Collins Publishers (the American subsidiary). Since 1980 she has been editorial director of Philomel Books, a division of the Putnam Publishing Group. Philomel Books is Ms. Beneduce's own imprint, and it is devoted to quality trade books for young readers.

●   ●   ●

"Editing children's books is not really a game for children. It is a serious, multifaceted, demanding profession. Neither is it any more 'fun' than any other kind of editing, though it is in some ways more rewarding," says Ms. Beneduce in this warm, insightful essay, written especially for this anthology. Displaying great joy and dedication to her craft and to her readers, Ms. Beneduce discusses the special pleasures and responsibilities of the children's book editor: working with artists to create books of beauty as well as value; making sure that the vocabulary level is right for the age of the reader; creating books that will be read for pleasure, whether fiction or nonfiction; being aware of the book's effect on the child's mind in terms of moral and ethical values as well as factual authenticity; originating books that will permit children to "try on" various kinds of personalities and lifestyles. Ms. Beneduce's deeply felt essay tempts one to quote from it at length. I'll content myself here with just one more quote: "If we expect them [the children] to change our world for the better, we must not infect them with adult fears or disillusionment; we must instead offer them insight and inspiration." Read on and discover the very special delights and demands of the children's book editor.

PLANTING INFLAMMATORY IDEAS IN THE GARDEN OF DELIGHT: Reflections on Editing Children's Books

One of the unspoken hazards of being a children's book editor is the head-patting syndrome. This occurs in social situations, such as a dinner party, when you respond to someone's well-meaning inquiry as to what it is you "do." A momentary silence descends, while everyone feverishly searches his or her brain for a suitable comment. Then one person helpfully says, "Oh, I just *love* Dr. Seuss!" "What a *fun* job!" cries another. Like the character Tree-horn, you feel yourself shrinking to the size of a two-year-old, while cringing from these verbal pats on the head from the grown-ups with whom you have been allowed to mingle.

But editing children's books is not really a game for children. It is a serious, multifaceted, demanding profession. Neither is it any more "fun" than any other kind of editing, though it is in some ways more rewarding. Still, the adult reaction to children's books —the sense that the world of children's literature is a cloistered garden of delight—is a response to which attention must be paid. For it is this sense of joy and wonder and, yes, even *fun* that one tries, as a children's book editor, to find and foster in the works one will publish for young readers. School workbooks and text-books are in a specialized class apart, and we are not concerned here with these. But the children's trade book is created for the young person's *voluntary,* recreational reading. It is meant to be read for pleasure. This pleasure may be derived from literature of various kinds and at various age and interest levels. There are fairy tales and fantasies, realistic novels and stories, books of riddles, games, and jokes, poetry, both light and serious, and beautiful picture books. Informational books offer pleasures of a different sort. "How to" books may provide tips on sharpening one's skills at baseball or building a home computer. Other books deepen a child's understanding of nature, politics, or history. There are even picture books to teach toddlers how to count to ten, or to tell time. Throughout the wide range of subjects and styles, the challenge is consistent: every children's book published has to have that special joy-producing ingredient that will make it stimulating to the growing aesthetic and intellectual capacities of young readers.

The term "children's books" covers a broad area. Children as an audience range from newborn infants to sophisticated high school seniors, and their interests and reading skills vary widely. Even the tiniest infants benefit from—indeed, *need*—verbal and visual stimulation. For them there are cloth or board books to play with, chew on, take into the bathtub or sleep with, as well as picture books and stories for parents to read aloud and share with them. Then come more complex picture books and "easy readers" for the six-, seven-, and eight-year-olds, who are just beginning to read independently. Next come the eight-to-elevens, the so-called middle-aged children. This group wants more grown-up-looking books, still fairly simple to read but offering a broad spectrum of subjects in both informational books and in fiction, which at this age level includes romance, adventure, fantasy, science fiction, and realistic novels about children like themselves. The category that once was named "teenage books" is now read by this pre-teenaged audience, while the actual teenagers read what are called "young adult" (YA) books. Young adult fiction is becoming more and more similar in subject matter to adult books, with the difference that the protagonists are still in their teens.

Editing books for such a diverse readership is a protean task. Some editors find they prefer to specialize in one or another of the categories or age levels. Editing picture books, for instance, calls for a different sensibility and training from that required for doing young adult science books. Most children's book departments are big enough to have several editors, and to allow each of them a degree of specialization. The editor in chief, however, needs some expertise in all these areas, and in a small company may indeed handle the entire range. The diversity of skills and interests demanded to edit and produce such a variety of books is insurance against on-the-job boredom!

The basic technique of editing children's books is similar to that of editing any kind of books, and there is much valuable guidance to this in other parts of this volume. Every editor must work within a reasonable budget to produce a certain number of books of a particular character and quality for a specific range of readership, and to promote and market them in such a way that they will bring a financial profit to both the author and the publisher. This is an oversimplification, of course. Selecting the manuscripts and projects, negotiating contracts, working with authors and artists to help them bring the project to its best form (involving substantive editing, line-by-line editing, copyediting, lay psychoanalysis, nagging, and hand-holding), supervising the format, design, and actual production, overseeing the advertising, promotion, publicity, and sales, keeping track of royalties and subsidiary and foreign rights sales, checking on inventory and fulfillment of orders—all these are also part of any editor's job.

The most obvious difference between the work of the children's book and the adult book editor is in the audience. The reading skills and interests of children vary much more widely than do those of adults. But the principal factor that distinguishes the work of the children's book editor is his or her special *responsibility* to the intended reader. Children are sensitive readers. Their attitudes are still in a formative stage. This means that editors have a duty, in addition to maintaining high standards of quality in a novel or a factual book, to consider its effect on the child's mind, personality, and character and on his or her developing interests. Such things as avoiding racial stereotypes and sexism are also serious concerns of the children's book editor. This is, again, because the child's mind is open and vulnerable. Adult books containing these biases are published all the time, and are read by people with matching prejudices, for the most part, or by persons with well-informed views who can evaluate these negative opinions and deal with them. Children, however, are most likely to accept what is written in a book as true, and therefore such books can be harmful to them. It is the editor's job to guard them from misinformation.

For the same reason—because the child believes in the reliability of the printed page—factual books for children are generally much more carefully vetted than similar books for adults. Most editors have them double-checked by outside experts in the field concerned—mathematics, ornithology, history, or whatever it may be —to avoid passing on inaccurate information to young readers.

Reading skill and vocabulary vary at each age level, and the children's book editor must be sure that these factors have been taken into consideration by the writer. Some authors find it very difficult to adjust their writing to the age level of their prospective young readers. Children are just as intelligent as their elders, of course, but they have not lived as long, so they have not yet acquired the range of information or the complexity of language needed in order to understand a text written for adults. However, it is very important not to let an author "write down" to them, or patronize them. There is almost nothing a young reader cannot understand if it is carefully and clearly set forth. If a new word is used, it should be defined. If something is mentioned that the child is unlikely to have learned previously, a sentence or two can be added to fill in the background. Short sentences are more easily read than long ones. And short words are more direct and easier to understand than long, Latinate locutions. On the other hand, if a long word is exactly the right word, it should be used, and its meaning made clear. To use a vocabulary restricted to words on school-graded lists would be a mistake, as there would be then no opportunity for a child to expand his or her language skills. Editors must be sensitive to the differences in reading levels, and make sure that the books they publish really communicate with their intended readers.

I am often asked what training would be useful to someone thinking of entering the field. Some things would apply equally well to someone planning to go into other areas of editing—training in literature and the arts, and some time spent in one of the many good publishing courses and workshops available now. For editing children's books I would add some training in child psychology and developmental psychology. The essential factor is a real interest in children, a deep and urgent curiosity about all fields of learning, and a wish to convey the joy of learning and discovery, as well as an appreciation of the arts and literature, to young people.

Another question frequently asked is why most children's book editors are women. There are two reasons for this, I think. One is that all things concerned with children have been traditionally considered the special province of women, as part of their nurturing role. Fifty years ago, when children's book publishing was in its infancy in this country, women were naturally considered to be the people who would know best what was suitable to foster its growth and development.

But there is another reason. The male editors and publishers who dominated the field of adult books felt that there was something less serious about children's books, something intellectually inferior, and they were not really interested in the field. Since they made it difficult for women to enter the adult realm of publishing, which men felt was their "turf," women who wanted to move upward into responsible positions in publishing had to enter through the back door and move up where they were permitted to do so—in children's books, cookbooks, mystery stories, crossword puzzle books, and the like. This was certainly true even when I began to work in publishing. Now that children's book departments earn as much as or more than their adult book counterparts in many publishing houses, success has removed the stigma from the category, and male editors are much more numerous in children's book departments than was formerly the case. (And the situation in adult book departments has also changed quite drastically over the years, so that there are now many women in the upper echelons of editing and publishing of adult books, a reflection of the change in society and values as a whole.)

Children are eager to explore their world and their futures; they are seeking their own identities and possibilities. Books allow them to "try on" various kinds of personalities and lifestyles. If we expect them to change our world for the better, we must not infect them with adult fears or disillusionment; we must instead offer them insight and inspiration. In our children lies the whole potential of the human race. Children's book editors, like all who deal with the aesthetic and intellectual development of children, must take seriously the responsibility for giving them books that contain the ideas and motivation they need to fulfill their aspirations—and our own.

Since children's books are written by adults, there is often a tendency on the part of the authors to use their stories to foist their own adult preoccupations on children. Fortunately, most writers of children's books have someting of real value to share with their young readers. Their books, in all their variety, celebrate such things as humor, beauty, fantasy, truth, courage, friendship, and creativity. Others, however, may be fearful, angry, or disillusioned. Every editor has received, and rejected, hundreds of variations of the story of the lion who escapes from the zoo, only to discover his newfound freedom to be so frightening that he hastens back to the safety of his cage. However cleverly disguised, their message is clear: Don't try to be independent; settle for security, no matter how confining.

Some cases, however, are less clear-cut. A well-known artist once brought me a brilliantly innovative picture book in which the very small reader was supposed to search through ingeniously die-cut pages for a hidden surprise, at the same time learning such concepts as *above, below, through, behind,* etc., as well as shapes: *round, square, triangular,* and so on. But the prize at the end turned out to be a pirate's chest filled with jewels and coins. Beautiful and clever as the book was, we were dismayed. Would a toddler really be thrilled to find a box full of coins? Are children that young already money-oriented? Or was this just a transference of the artist's own secret wish? And is a pirate's cache of stolen loot really a suitable thing to offer anyone as a reward? These were the questions we raised to the artist. Fortunately, he is a man deeply concerned with the effect of his books on small children, and he understood at once. Within a few days he had solved the problem perfectly. In his revised version, the child reader searched through the die-cut pages for a birthday gift that had been hidden by his parents. The present awaiting him at the end of the book was an adorable puppy—a totally appealing gift on just the right emotional level for a small child.

One of the unique pleasures of being a children's book editor is working with such artists. There are many wonderful artists to be found today who are creating sensitive and innovative picture books, the kind that really encourage a child's creativity. Good illustrations can stretch the imaginations of children and expand their visual vocabularies. Books like those by the Japanese artist Mitsumasa Anno—his alphabet books, his counting books, his wordless but very articulate journey books—these open new worlds. Maurice Sendak opens different doors: his pictures reveal our inner world of dreams and emotions, a world familiar to children and adults alike. These are but two of the many brilliant artists on the picture book scene today. Working with artists and illustrators is not usually a part of adult book editing, but it is one of the joys of editing books for children.

Of course, while keeping in mind the best interests of the child who is the ultimate consumer, the editor cannot ignore the financial aspect of publishing. To do so would be unfair to one's employer, and also to the author and the reader. One must have a sense of the marketplace; the market is the barometer of the consumer's real concerns. However, in the case of children's books, producing books with an eye *solely* to financial return cannot really be called editing; it is just product processing. And these products—these listlessly manufactured nonbooks—can harm young readers either actively or, more subtly, through boredom. Edith Hamilton has said that the mark of an educated person is his or her ability to be set on fire by an idea. Books for children should be "inflammatory" in this sense. Anything less robs children of the powerful magic of a dynamic involvement with the right book at the right time—a significant experience every literate adult can remember.

EDITOR/AUTHOR
CORRESPONDENCE

JENNIFER CRICHTON

Jennifer Crichton is a writer who has covered the publishing world extensively for *Publishers Weekly.* She has also been published in *Ms., Seventeen, Book & Author, Outside,* and *Diversion.*

• • •

How do editors and authors communicate in today's high-pressured publishing houses? Is it all on the phone? Do editors still take the time to write long, detailed editorial letters to their authors? When is it more effective to use the phone? What is the phone definitely *not* good for? These are the questions raised and answered in Ms. Crichton's lively and sometimes surprising review of the state of today's editor-author correspondence.

Some editors rely on the telephone just for socializing and to confirm editorial suggestions already made in a letter. Some feel that the editorial letter is useful, as Roger Straus, president of Farrar, Straus & Giroux says, as "a frame of reference so there's no misunderstanding or misconception." And recent court decisions make it clear that editors should maintain a detailed, comprehensive, step-by-step editorial correspondence with the author. Why? If the editor decides to reject the finished manuscript and ask for the return of the advance, he or she should have ample evidence of careful editorial guidance given the author, or else the author might claim that no editorial guidance was offered and that the author was not given a chance to revise the project in order to meet the publisher's standards of acceptability.

Whatever the situation between editor and author, it seems clear that to assure the effectiveness of any necessary revisions and line editing, and for legal protection, it is wise and sensible to put everything down on paper. Not for posterity but for the health of the book and the editor-author relationship.

DEAR EDITOR . . .
DEAR AUTHOR . . .

"I would know Tom Buchanan if I met him on the street and would avoid him," Scribner editor Maxwell Perkins wrote F. Scott Fitzgerald in 1924. "Gatsby is somewhat vague. The reader's eyes can never quite focus on him, his outlines are dim. Now everything about Gatsby is more or less a mystery, i.e. more or less vague, and this may be somewhat of an artistic intention, but I think it is mistaken."

"I myself didn't know what Gatsby looked like and was engaged in & you felt it," Fitzgerald wrote back. "If I'd known & kept it from you you'd have been *too impressed with my knowledge to protest."*

The Fitzgerald-Perkins correspondence stands as a document of collaborative thinking. Perkins's letters are politic yet forthright, self-effacing yet firm. In their steady tone, they complement the mercurial nature of Fitzgerald's letters, which sweep from heady elation to the lower registers of despair. The exchange is a record not only of creative effort but of the development of an enviable friendship as well—the two perhaps inseparable and both marked by trust, respect, and affection.

The example exists. But has the editorial letter, which delves into the flaws and attributes of a manuscript, survived? Much works against it and little fosters it. The postal service is less than immediate, and the phone is used impulsively and without hesitation. Air travel is no longer intimidating and collapses the geographical distance that separates an editor from an author. Heavy work loads at publishing houses, by most accounts, have placed unbearable time constraints on editors and their assistants. Clearly, the letter has suffered.

"The Bloomsbury generation in Europe and the Hemingway-Fitzgerald generation in America were possibly the last about which you could write the kind of literary biography that has been our meat and drink," Viking editor Amanda Vaill believes.

"It's painful for contemporary writers to read something like Virginia Woolf's letters because now so much gets lost on the phone," laments short-story writer and novelist Laura Furman.

But precisely because so much gets "lost on the phone," many writers and editors—not all veterans of the old school of publishing—find that the editorial letter has a value and function that no other means of communication can quite fulfill.

Describing the misinterpretation that often occurs in phone conversations, Vaill draws circles in the air over her head and explains, "It may be that the writer has a kind of thought balloon above his head of what is understood, the editor has another thought balloon, and the two don't correspond at all." Vaill never gives editorial suggestions over the phone, in conferences that too often lapse into "shmooze sessions," but will only elaborate on what she has already stated in a letter.

The very term "correspondence" implies an agreement of meaning, and this harmony may be one of the letter's primary virtues.

"There's a kind of exactitude missing in phone calls," writer Bill Barich (*Laughing in the Hills*) thinks. "You can sit around and talk, have great ideas and be a real genius, but when you have to sit down, think something through, and put it into words, you become a lot clearer and much more responsible."

"I'm guilty, but I don't feel guilty about it, of conducting most of the real business of working on a book through voice," Farrar, Straus & Giroux editor in chief Michael Di Capua says. While preferring face-to-face meetings with authors, he finds the telephone an acceptable alternative. "After working with a writer on several books, you know each other's way of thinking, and the possibilities for misunderstanding are less and less. Perhaps that's an illusion. But if there has been any confusion, it's been kept secret from me."

"There's not some handing of the baton from the letter to the phone call as in a relay race," Farrar, Straus senior editor David Rieff feels. "The phone and letter don't contradict each other, and they're both very useful with different while overlapping functions. The need to have a record of what you've said is still a powerful reason for a letter, and the editorial letter has, to that extent, the value of any business letter."

"So many books now are written on the basis of proposals that a response by a writer to certain queries from us almost becomes part of the proposal," says Vaill. At Viking, as at Dutton, correspondence is circulated throughout the editorial staff. "It's a very clear expression of the editorial *we,* to see how and what our colleagues are doing and how they solve thorny problems when you have a thorny problem yourself," Vaill says. "Even if you haven't sponsored a specific book, you still have a vested interest in how it does."

The editorial letter is a record less in the sense that it's a document to be brought into evidence in a breach of contract suit than as "a frame and point of reference so there's no misunderstanding or misconception," according to Roger Straus, president of Farrar, Straus & Giroux.

"I started out at Macmillan over forty years ago. The editorial letter was a big thing then, and everyone wrote great, long letters. I'm afraid I've written a great too many letters since, but I can't change now," says Howard Cady, senior editor at Morrow, who uses the letter for editorial suggestions and the WATS line for morale. He values the letter as a reference point because when the revised manuscript comes in later, he can recall specific issues that were raised as the manuscript was being written.

The tangibility and permanence of a letter can't be supplanted by WATS lines or lunch dates. As John Donne wrote to a friend (in a letter that appeared in Donne's collected letters in 1620, one of the first such collections), "I desire that you might have in your hands Letters of mine of all kindes, as conveyances and deliverers of me to you. Because they are permanent, in them I may speak to you in your chamber a year hence before I know not whom, and not hear my self."

Mary Lee Settle, author of *O Beulah Land* and *The Killing Ground,* considers this concrete aspect of the letter vital. "The telephone is ephemeral, and people remember things differently," she says. "A letter you hold in your hand: there it is."

Editorial suggestions, expressed in a letter, may be referred to by a writer again and again. Laura Furman observes that notes taken during telephone conversations may not be precise. When working on *The Shadow Line* alone on a Texas ranch, she pinned her editor's letters to the wall. While reminding her where a scene moved a bit slowly or a character was described too hazily, they also served as "a token of conversation, a token of camaraderie and of the outside world. All writers are very isolated, even when they're in the middle of Manhattan."

A letter demands a response in kind. By writing to an editor, the author might clarify thoughts as much for his or her own benefit as for the editor's, and this is something underscored by William Howarth, the Thoreau scholar who wrote *Thoreau in the Mountain:* "When I've worked with Pat Strachan at Farrar, Straus, after sending in a manuscript, the first thing I'd get back was a general letter of response saying, 'I see what you're trying to do, here's what you could do to make it work everywhere.' This would prompt an outline from me on how I could proceed to do what she'd suggested or to defend what I'd done. The process of any composition can make your thought a lot clearer, and in writing a letter to an editor, I've sometimes found what it was I wanted to say in the manuscript."

That letter writing helps focus an idea applies to an editor as well. "The editorial letter gives the editor a chance to refine his or her thought and the writer a chance to reflect on those thoughts," says Pat Strachan, one of the many younger editors who believe in the practice. The letter's relative slowness is directly to its advantage, she feels, adding that "writing is not done on the spur of the moment. One can't expect the editing to go quickly, either."

The slow and private assimilation that a letter affords is a vital alternative to a phone call, which may be intrusive. "There's something awful about picking up the telephone and in effect announcing, 'Hey, I'm in your house, and I hate to tell you, but there's a big problem in the book.' It's difficult to do that," Vaill says. Because one tends to be more careful in constructing one's opinion when writing, a letter may tread more lightly on touchy areas. An editor is dealing with delicate things, Vaill believes. "The work is delicate because it isn't yet written, and writers' feelings about their work, even with the least egocentric writer, are delicate and complicated."

"I'm offering suggestions—writers end up doing what they want and can do," says Knopf editor Victoria Wilson, who finds that most letters from writers are about "little practical things rather than the coming-to-surface of a new book."

As form follows function, many writers find letters their ideal means of communication. An author writing an editor is on home terrain: putting words to paper. David Rieff points out that the material dealt with in letters is the same as that of the entire enterprise. "It's not an accident that a writer writes prose," he remarks.

"We writers tend to be more forceful in writing than we are in conversation," William Howarth says. "There's a certain different kind of persona that takes over when you start to type, bolder and more expressive. All the eloquence gets channeled into the silent relationship with the paper."

"You know that old phrase, 'How do I know what I think until I hear what I say'?" asks Virginia Rich, whose *Cooking School Murders* was edited entirely through letters and complementary telephone calls, with nary a trip to New York to meet with her Dutton editor. "Well, how do I know what I think until I see what I write?"

"Writers used to talk so well, sitting around saying brilliant things, having a salon. Now they seem to be inarticulate, and I certainly am not a good talker," says Florence King, whose novel, *When Sisterhood Was in Flower,* was edited long-distance. "I have absolutely no self-consciousness in a letter at all—it is me at my best."

"I suppose everyone imagines that in the recent past there was more time than there is now," says Joseph Kanon, editor in chief at Dutton, who does much, if not most, of his editorializing in person or on the phone. "Editors are much more involved in the entire publishing process now. You're the person called on by an author or agent for every aspect of the publishing of a book. That an editor just sits at a desk and works on projects no longer holds true—that's just a small part of it."

Even if publishing were a more leisurely profession in the past, speed doesn't always hold first priority in an industry where quality of thought reflects on the products and profits.

David Rieff objects to notions of utility. "This is not the Amalgamated Widget Company," he says. "The course of world culture is not going to alter if most books are published a month earlier or later."

When Viking struggled to synchronize its publication of D. M. Thomas's *Ararat* with its overseas publication, Amanda Vaill found herself frequently on the phone with Thomas in England. "The pages of the manuscript rustled, the phone was stuck in my ear, and those little cash register bells were ringing, reminding me that the phone call was costing the earth." Justifiable as expensive phone calls may be for a best-selling writer like Thomas, the publishing industry "is not ITT," as Rieff puts it. The cost efficiency of letters can't be ignored.

The letter least in threat of extinction is the durable rejection letter. Gordon Lish's colleagues at Knopf view him as the master of the rejection letter. Lish describes his peerless technique: "I'm courtly with relatively unrecognized writers and offhand and wise-apple with very established writers. The task in a letter of rejection is to say no fearfully. The principle is to assume that the person to whom you're sending the letter, if the rejection is not said charmingly enough, will one day get you. But to speak of letter writing is entrameling to the zen of letter writing. The thing is not to think, that's all. One way in which I'm exceptional is that I answer a letter the instant I receive it. If I should think about it or ignore it, I answer it instantly. I cannot help myself."

It's plain that as long as there are writers, there'll be letters written. Writers use letters for therapeutic reasons—to warm up before episodes that may in effect turn out to be drafts. But as letters come into publishing houses and carbons of letters sent from publishing houses stay put, what happens to them? How are they preserved?

House procedures range from haphazard organization to diligently followed plans. One of the most well-developed systems is at Viking. Editors weed out extraneous or irrelevant material from their personal files and give them to an archivist in charge of a central bank of author-editor correspondence files. When staff members need to refer to old files and to withdraw documents from the central bank, they log out the files to protect against disappearance. The archivist also ensures that valuable files aren't sent to the Viking warehouse in New Jersey, where inactive material is consigned to a dormant life of relative disarray.

Most publishing houses, when they find themselves flooded with files, avail themselves of warehouses, an arrangement usually most to the benefit of warehouse owners, since files then become inaccessible to all but the most dogged detective.

"One of my first jobs at Macmillan was to help decide which files were to be thrown out and what was to be kept. It's tragic to think of what I helped throw out—the marvelous source material it would have been!" Howard Cady recalls with regret. "Macmillan published everything Edward Arlington Robinson had written, as well as John Masefield and Rabindranath Tagore." Cady, honorbound as all editors are to leave their correspondence files behind when they move from one publishing house to another, is sorry he didn't snag a "wonderfully sweet letter" written to him by William Butler Yeats. (Tom Stewart, Atheneum's editor in chief, confesses to have taken a Robert Lowell letter received while he was at Farrar, Straus & Giroux.)

A felicitous solution to the storage problem is the donation of inactive files to libraries. Gift arrangements with libraries are often determined by the university affiliation of a publisher and a reluctance on the part of a house to let its files go too far afield. "That we're in New York and accessible, that we're an educational institution and had a manuscript room all set up, and that so many publishing people have gone to Columbia, make such an arrangement almost irresistible," Kenneth Lohf, librarian for rare books and manuscripts for the Columbia University libraries, can happily say.

Bennett Cerf, Columbia graduate, arranged for Random House's files to be given to the university's libraries, and files seven to eight years old are delivered in great bulk every year or so. The papers of Alfred A. Knopf are found at Columbia, as are those of M. Lincoln Schuster and Richard L. Simon. But neither Knopf nor Simon & Schuster have immediate plans to send their files there. Norton ships off files at least twenty years old to Columbia as well.

Boston-based Houghton Mifflin and Little, Brown donate their files to Harvard, where the library that specializes in manuscripts is the Houghton, named for the publishing house's founder. Scribners files find their way to the Firestone Library at Princeton because Charles Scribner II, a Princeton alumnus, felt a close connection with the school.

While some libraries avidly pursue the correspondence files of certain writers to augment their collections, publishing houses rarely break up their files for individual archives. Financial statements are almost never included in the files given to libraries, but otherwise, few publishing houses exercise much selectivity in what is to be donated.

Neither Farrar, Straus & Giroux nor Viking has a gift arrangement with a library, and Farrar, Straus has no such plans for the foreseeable future, principally because "there are certain matters that come up in correspondence that neither the publisher nor writer would want to become public knowledge," Michael Di Capua explains. "The notion of evaluating that through tons of correspondence is horrifying."

Access to Columbia and other libraries is granted to qualified researchers, and publication of letters' contents, which are generally uncopyrighted, requires permission from the library and publishing house. This question is, however, a shady area of the law. Access to files within publishing houses is trickier, particularly since there's no published record of what files do or do not contain. Access, granted on an individual basis, sometimes seems capriciously approved or denied.

In 1979, biographer Marion Meade, at work on a literary biography of Dorothy Parker, wrote to Norton for permission to see Parker's correspondence files. Boni & Liveright, which had published Parker in the twenties, had merged with Norton, and Meade presumed the material was now in Norton's possession. Norton insisted there were no such files, but some time later, an editor granted Meade permission to see what files there were. On opening them, the first thing Meade saw was her letter of request and the subsequent reply that said no files existed.

"People are nervous about strangers going through their files," Meade now says, "especially to help an author from another house. Who are they benefiting? Another publisher." Most publishers have been helpful in permitting access, but Meade contends that the real challenge is getting in the door. "It's helpful if you know someone, preferably high-placed," she says.

Hilary Mills, whose *Mailer: A Biography* appeared in 1982, discovered that the Holt, Rinehart and Winston files she needed had been shipped to a warehouse and were impossible to place. For a look at Mailer's relationship with Little, Brown, Mills requested permission to view his correspondence files. The request was denied. "I don't think they asked Mailer," Mills says. "They're trying to protect their authors, and that makes a certain amount of sense to me."

How valuable is correspondence? Will the literary biography that has been our "meat and drink" die out?

"If someone twenty years hence were to do a literary biography of Derek Walcott or Joseph Brodsky, the letters they've written will be of enormous advantage," Roger Straus thinks. "But there's another resource in addition to letters—a writer's journals. Susan Sontag, for example, writes extensively in her journals, and Edmund Wilson's notebooks, which we publish, are invaluable."

"People who work in this industry should be interested in the preservation of letter writing not so that a future associate professor at the University of South Dakota can pry into the lives of people who'd perhaps rest easier if they were left alone, but because they're beautiful works of prose," David Rieff insists. "Without denigrating my profession, great books are going to get written with or without editors or editorial letters. There are no editors in the American sense in France, and French literature has done quite well over the years."

There is the awful nonexistence of letters that never get written —the complete absence of letters and telephone calls that often attends a writer bound up by a writer's block. "You don't hear *anything,*" Amanda Vaill says in an ominous whisper. "Writing letters becomes a reminder to the writer that something else isn't coming out of the typewriter."

Ed McClanahan, whose first novel, *The Natural Man,* was published in 1983 to glowing reviews, was at work on the book since 1962. "I could not write a letter for years because it was necessary for me to say something about the progress of my book," he remembers. "When I wasn't making any progress or wasn't pleased with my progress, I just couldn't force myself to write letters." But he did finish the book and sent it up from Kentucky to Farrar, Straus & Giroux and found that his publishers agreed to take it. "Now," McClanahan says with a lilt to his voice, "I'm writing letters like crazy."

MAXWELL E. PERKINS

Maxwell E. Perkins joined Charles Scribner's Sons, the distinguished American publishing house, at the age of thirty in the year 1914. He remained with that house until his death in 1947.

•   •   •

Mr. Perkins, perhaps the best-known, most revered (and envied) trade publishing editor of our time, was the editor of Hemingway, Fitzgerald, Wolfe, Lardner, James Jones, and many other of the leading literary lights of the twenties, thirties, and early forties.

Not a man given to satiric thrusts of humor, overflowings of emotion, or deep personal involvement with his authors (except, of course, in the very special relationship with Thomas Wolfe), Perkins derived his power and greatness from his superb taste, which was exquisite without in any way being effete; his unwavering belief in his author; and his rigorously adhered to standards for integrity, craftsmanship, and artistry.

Without taking one whit of praise away from him, let us not forget that Perkins's greatness was augmented by the unusual stable of wild talents he commanded. His "list" was the dream and the envy of all his contemporaries.

In this selection from John Hall Wheelock's *Editor-to-Author: The Letters of Maxwell E. Perkins,* published by Scribner's in 1950, Perkins is revealed in several of his editorial roles: soliciting new material, editing and revising, bucking up the spirits of momentarily dispirited authors, praising new successes, and propounding his beliefs in freedom of expression.

TO F. SCOTT FITZGERALD

Dec. 12, 1921

DEAR FITZGERALD:

Don't ever *defer* to my judgment. You won't on any vital point, I know, and I should be ashamed, if it were possible to have made you; for a writer of any account must speak solely for himself. I should hate to play (assuming V.W.B.'s[1] position to be sound) the W. D. Howells to your Mark Twain.

It is not to the *substance* of this passage[2] that I object. Everyone of any account, anyone who could conceivably read this book, under forty, agrees with the substance of it. If they did not, there would be less objection to it in one way—it would then startle them as a revelation of a new point of view which, by giving a more solid kind of value, would lessen the objection on account of flippancy. (I hate the word. I hate to be put in the position of using such words as "respect" and "flippancy," which have so often enraged me, but there is some meaning in them.) The Old Testament ought not to be treated in a way which suggests a failure to realize its tremendous significance in the recent history of man, as if it could simply be puffed away with a breath of contempt, it is so trivial. That is the effect of the passage at present. It is partly so because Maury is talking and is talking in character; and that is the way men do talk too, so far as ability enables them, even when they fully appreciate every side of the matter. It is here that the question of the public comes in. They will not make allowance for the fact that a character is talking extemporaneously. They will think F.S.F. is writing deliberately. Tolstoi did that even, and to Shakespeare. Now, you are, through Maury, expressing your views, of course; but you would do so differently if you were deliberately stating them as your views. You speak of Galileo: he and Bruno showed themselves to have a genuine sense of the religious significance of the theories they broke

[1] Van Wyck Brooks, American critic, author of *The Ordeal of Mark Twain,* Dutton, 1920. In this book, the influence of Howells on Mark Twain is revealed as, on the whole, a restrictive and injurious one.

[2] In *The Beautiful and Damned* (Scribner, 1922), in which Maury makes light of the Old Testament.

down. They were not in a state of mind to treat the erroneous beliefs of men with a light contempt. France[3] does not so treat Christ in that story of Pilate in his old age. And "Whited Sepulchre" is an expression of a high contempt, although applied to an object which had no such quality of significance as the Bible.

My point is that you impair the effectiveness of the passage—of the very purpose you use it for—by giving it that quality of contempt, and I wish you would try so to revise it as not to antagonize even the very people who agree with the substance of it. You would go a long way toward this if you cut out "God Almighty" and put "Deity." In fact, if you will change it on the line indicated, by that change you will have excised the element to which I object.

I do agree that it belongs in Maury's speech; that it does bring it to a focus. But you could so revise it that it would do this without at the same time doing the thing to which we object.

I hope this gets over to you. If I saw you for ten minutes I know you would understand and would agree with me.

As ever,

TO F. SCOTT FITZGERALD

Dec. 31, 1921

DEAR FITZGERALD:

The letter from Reynolds[4] which you sent and which I return is rather pathetic, but so far as it concerns your writing, I think it represents a temporary condition. The time ought to come when whatever you write will go through and where its irony and satire will be understood. They will know what you stand for in writing, and they do not really know yet. It is in recognition of this that I want very much to have this book[5] so announced in our lists, and so on, that it will be regarded as "important" as well as the other things.

There is, especially in this country, a rootless class of society into which Gloria and Anthony drifted, a large class and one which has

[3] Anatole France.
[4] Paul Reynolds, literary agent.
[5] *The Beautiful and Damned,* Scribner, 1922.

an important effect on society in general. It is certainly worth presenting in a novel. I know that you did not deliberately undertake to do this but I think "The Beautiful and Damned" has, in effect, done this; and that this makes it a valuable as well as brilliant commentary upon American society. Perhaps you have never even formulated the idea that it does do this thing, but don't you think it is true? The book is not written according to the usual conventions of the novel, and its greatest interest is not that of the usual novel. Its satire will not of itself be understood by the great, simple-minded public without a little help. For instance, in talking to one man about the book, I received the comment that Anthony was unscathed; that he came through with his millions, and thinking well of himself. This man completely missed the extraordinarily effective irony of the last few paragraphs.

As ever,

TO RING W. LARDNER

July 2, 1923

DEAR MR. LARDNER:

I read your story, "The Golden Wedding,"⁶ with huge enjoyment. Scott Fitzgerald recommended it to me and he also suggested that you might have other material of the same sort which, with this, could form a volume. I am therefore writing to tell you how very much interested we should be to consider this possibility, if you could put the material before us. I would hardly have ventured to do this if Scott had not spoken of the possibility, because your position in the literary world is such that you must be besieged by publishers, and to people in that situation their letters of interest are rather a nuisance. I am certainly mighty glad to have the chance of expressing our interest though, if, as Scott thought, you would not feel that we were merely bothering you. Would you be willing to send on any material that might go with "The Golden Wedding" to form a volume, or to tell me where I might come at it in periodicals?

Very truly yours,

⁶Published by Scribner, with other stories by Ring Lardner, under the title *How to Write Short Stories*, 1924.

TO F. SCOTT FITZGERALD

November 20, 1924

DEAR SCOTT:

I think you have every kind of right to be proud of this book.[7] It is an extraordinary book, suggestive of all sorts of thoughts and moods. You adopted exactly the right method of telling it, that of employing a narrator who is more of a spectator than an actor: this puts the reader upon a point of observation on a higher level than that on which the characters stand and at a distance that gives perspective. In no other way could your irony have been so immensely effective, nor the reader have been enabled so strongly to feel at times the strangeness of human circumstance in a vast heedless universe. In the eyes of Dr. Eckleberg various readers will see different significances; but their presence gives a superb touch to the whole thing: great unblinking eyes, expressionless, looking down upon the human scene. It's magnificent!

I could go on praising the book and speculating on its various elements, and means, but points of criticism are more important now. I think you are right in feeling a certain slight sagging in chapters six and seven, and I don't know how to suggest a remedy. I hardly doubt that you will find one and I am only writing to say that I think it does need something to hold up here to the pace set, and ensuing. I have only two actual criticisms:

One is that among a set of characters marvelously palpable and vital —I would know Tom Buchanan if I met him on the street and would avoid him—Gatsby is somewhat vague. The reader's eyes can never quite focus upon him, his outlines are dim. Now everything about Gatsby is more or less a mystery, i.e. more or less vague, and this may be somewhat of an artistic intention, but I think it is mistaken. Couldn't *he* be physically described as distinctly as the others, and couldn't you add one or two characteristics like the use of that phrase "old sport"—not verbal, but physical ones, perhaps. I think that for some reason or other a reader—this was true of Mr. Scribner[8] and of Louise[9]—gets an idea that Gatsby is a much older man than he is,

[7]*The Great Gatsby,* Scribner, 1925.
[8]Charles Scribner, Sr. (1854–1930), president of Charles Scribner's Sons.
[9]Mrs. Maxwell E. Perkins.

although you have the writer say that he is little older than himself.
But this would be avoided if on his first appearance he was seen as
vividly as Daisy and Tom are, for instance—and I do not think your
scheme would be impaired if you made him so.

The other point is also about Gatsby: his career must remain mysterious, of course. But in the end you make it pretty clear that his wealth
came through his connection with Wolfsheim. You also suggest this
much earlier. Now almost all readers numerically are going to be
puzzled by his having all this wealth and are going to feel entitled to
an explanation. To give a distinct and definite one would be, of course,
utterly absurd. It did occur to me, though, that you might here and
there interpolate some phrases, and possibly incidents, little touches
of various kinds, that would suggest that he was in some active way
mysteriously engaged. You do have him called on the telephone but
couldn't he be seen once or twice consulting at his parties with people
of some sort of mysterious significance, from the political, the gam-
bling, the sporting world, or whatever it may be. I know I am flound-
ering, but that fact may help you to see what I mean. The *total* lack
of an explanation through so large a part of the story does seem to
me a defect—or not of an explanation, but of the suggestion of an
explanation. I wish you were here so I could talk about it to you, for
then I know I could at least make you understand what I mean. What
Gatsby did ought never to be definitely imparted, even if it could be.
Whether he was an innocent tool in the hands of somebody else, or
to what degree he was this, ought not to be explained. But if some sort
of business activity of his were simply adumbrated, it would lend
further probability to that part of the story.

There is one other point: in giving deliberately Gatsby's biography,
when he gives it to the narrator, you do depart from the method of
the narrative in some degree, for otherwise almost everything is told,
and beautifully told, in the regular flow of it, in the succession of
events or in accompaniment with them. But you can't avoid the
biography altogether. I thought you might find ways to let the truth
of some of his claims like "Oxford" and his army career come out,
bit by bit, in the course of actual narrative. I mention the point
anyway, for consideration in this interval before I send the proofs.

The general brilliant quality of the book makes me ashamed to
make even these criticisms. The amount of meaning you get into a
sentence, the dimensions and intensity of the impression you make a
paragraph carry, are most extraordinary. The manuscript is full of
phrases which make a scene blaze with life. If one enjoyed a rapid

railroad journey I would compare the number and vividness of pictures your living words suggest, to the living scenes disclosed in that way. It seems, in reading, a much shorter book than it is, but it carries the mind through a series of experiences that one would think would require a book of three times its length.

The presentation of Tom, his place, Daisy and Jordan, and the unfolding of their characters is unequaled so far as I know. The description of the valley of ashes adjacent to the lovely country, the conversation and the action in Myrtle's apartment, the marvelous catalogue of those who came to Gatsby's house—these are such things as make a man famous. And all these things, the whole pathetic episode, you have given a place in time and space, for with the help of T. J. Eckleberg and by an occasional glance at the sky, or the sea, or the city, you have imparted a sort of sense of eternity. You once told me you were not a *natural* writer—my God! You have plainly mastered the craft, of course; but you needed far more than craftsmanship for this.

As ever,

Nov. 27, 1929

DEAR SIR:

We have received your letter with regard to ———. We are sorry that you feel as you do about the book—it is far from pleasant to us to have given offense to anybody, and in particular to those who belong to your faith, which we respect. At the same time, you seem not to understand the function of a publisher, nor to attach any importance to one of the greatest principles in the whole world—that which upholds free speech for the sake of the freedom of the intellect. According to this principle any serious and careful book upon any person of importance and significance to the general public should find a publisher; and any publisher who refrained from publication, even if he did not agree with the author's conclusions, because of fear of some particular sect, would be untrue to his profession, and indeed to the cause of intellectual freedom.

You assume that this book is manifestly unfair and irresponsible, but not one single reviewer has thought this. The very opposite has been the opinion of all the leading publications which review books, including the greatest newspapers and magazines of the United States.

It is a part of the American philosophy as expressed in the Constitution—that, except in the most extreme cases, people should be allowed to express their opinions, and that the result of this is to stir up thought and controversy, out of which will emerge the Truth. It is only what is false that is killed by discussion, not what is true.

Ever truly yours,

TO ALLEN TATE

June 27, 1931

DEAR MR. TATE:

I am taking your poems home to read, but I know a number of them already, well, and of course anybody would be proud to publish them. I shall write you more definitely next week, and everything would be very simple indeed if it were not for these detestable practical questions that cannot be eliminated. I am not referring to the mere matter of a contract, for that too would not be difficult, but there is also the serious question of an author dividing his work between two publishers.[10] I think your letter shows that you have considered that, and you would not intend that it should always be divided. And I only raise the question because you should. Our policy has always been definitely to publish for an author rather than to publish individual works, and it has also always been opposed to taking steps to detach an author from another publisher. I am not asking you to discuss these questions with me, but I thought I ought to explain our position, although I do not wish to do that even, in any way that will be embarrassing to you, and I need hardly say that—like any publisher —we should value your name on our list.

I shall write you again next week. It was a pleasure to hear from you, and to receive a manuscript of yours.

Ever sincerely yours,

P.S. I have been trying hard to get proofs of your wife's book.[11] I am pressing the printer for them, and should very soon begin to have them, and then they will go to her rapidly.

[10]Putnam and Scribner. Putnam had published Tate.
[11]*Penhally,* by Caroline Gordon, Scribner, 1931.

TO THOMAS WOLFE

Jan. 21, 1935

DEAR TOM:

I'm committed to Key West now, however impossible it seems to go, and since, when I return, "Of Time and the River" will be a book, I'm taking this last moment to say what I've long been on the point of saying:

Nothing could give me greater pleasure or greater pride as an editor than that the book of the writer whom I have most greatly admired should be dedicated to me if it were sincerely done. But you cannot, and should not, try to change your conviction that I have deformed your book, or at least prevented it from coming to perfection. It is therefore impossible for you sincerely to dedicate it to me, and it ought not to be done. I know we are truly friends and have gone through much in company, and this matter, for my part, can have nothing to do with that, or ever shall. But this is another matter. I would have said this sooner but for some fear that you would misinterpret me. But the plain truth is that working on your writings, however it has turned out, for good or bad, has been the greatest pleasure, for all its pain, and the most interesting episode of my editorial life. The way in which we are presenting this book must prove our (and my) belief in it. But what I have done has destroyed *your* belief in it and you must not act inconsistently with that fact.

As for your preface, there is this obstacle to it at the start: a reader is meant to enter into a novel as if it were reality, and so to feel it, and a preface tends to break down that illusion and to make him look at it in a literary way. But perhaps that is, in some degree, a literary objection to a preface and when yours began so finely I thought you might be right to have it. But when I read more of it today, it seemed to me you did the very things you meant to avoid doing in the novel: you made the book seem personal and autobiographical, and by showing resentment against those who objected to the apparent reality (as the preface implied) of the characters in the "Angel"[12] you opened yourself to the same charge against *this* book and notified the whole public that it might rightly be brought. And of the whole public not a handful can understand the artist's point of view or the writer's conscience. In

[12] *Look Homeward, Angel,* Scribner, 1929.

these, and other ways, I thought, you bared yourself to all the enemies you have and I told you so because I am your friend——

P.S. I thought that woman looked dangerous!

In his answer to Wolfe's twenty-eight-page letter, Perkins had written, on January 13, that he had as yet only had time to glance through it, and so could not answer it properly. He referred to it again, briefly, in his letter of January 14th. The letter that follows was written after he had read and pondered this long and important document in the Wolfe-Perkins correspondence.

TO THOMAS WOLFE

Saturday, January 16, 1937

DEAR TOM:

In the first place, I completely subscribe to what you say a writer should do, and always have believed it. If it were not true that you, for instance, should write as you see, feel, and think, then a writer would be of no importance, and books merely things for amusement. And since I have always thought that there could be nothing so important as a book can be, and some are, I could not help but think as you do. But there are limitations of time, of space, and of human laws which cannot be treated as if they did not exist. I think that a writer should, of course, be the one to make his book what he wants it to be, and that if, because of the laws of space, it must be cut, he should be the one to cut it; and, especially with you, I think the labour and discipline that would come from doing that without help or interference would further the pretty terrible task of mastering the material. But my impression was that you asked my help, that you wanted it. And it is my impression too that changes were not forced on you (you're not very forceable, Tom, nor I very forceful), but were argued over, often for hours. But I agree with you about this too, fully, and unless you want help it will certainly not be thrust upon you. It would be better if you could fight it out alone—better for your work, in the end, certainly; and, what's more, I believe you are now in a position to publish with less regard to any conventions of bookmaking, say a certain number of pages almost, whether or not it had what in a novel is regarded as an ending, or anything else that is commonly expected in a novel. I believe the writer, anyway, should always be the final judge, and I meant you to be so. I have always held to that position and have sometimes seen books hurt thereby, but at least as often helped. "The book belongs to the author."

I certainly do not care—nor does this House—how revolutionary your books are. I did try to keep you from injecting radical, or Marxian, beliefs into "Time and the River," because they were your beliefs in 1934 and 1935, and not those of Eugene in the time of the book. So it did not seem that they could rightly belong in the book. If they could have, then the times could not be rightly pictured, I thought. It must be so. Still, you were then and always conscious of social wrong and that is plainly in the book as you then saw it. There was the Astor story. What was told was not heard by Eugene. It was second-hand, and second-hand material—something told, not heard and seen—is inferior to first-hand. If cutting had to be done, ought that not to be cut? I know your memory is a miracle, but it seems as if you must have forgotten how we worked and argued. You were never overruled. Do you think you are clay to be moulded! I never saw anyone less malleable. And as for publishing what you like, or being prevented from it, apart from the limitations of space, you have not been, intentionally. Are you thinking of "K 19"?[13] We would have published it if you had said to do it. At the time, I said to Jack:[14] "Maybe it's the way Tom is. Maybe we should just publish him as he comes and in the end it will all be right." But if we had, and the results had been bad at the moment, would you not have blamed me? Certainly I should have bitterly blamed myself. I do not want the passage of time to make you cautious or conservative, but I do want it to give you a full control—as it has done in the case of great writers in the past—over your great talent. And if you can stand the struggle, it will. But you must struggle too, and perhaps even more than in the writing, in the shaping and revising. That might be the hardest thing of all, to your nature. You have so much in you, that the need with you is to get it uttered. Then to go back and polish and perfect seems petty, and goes against your nature, I guess.

[13]Section of manuscript removed from *Of Time and the River* but never separately published. "K 19" was the number of an overnight Pullman car between New York and Asheville. This material was later used in *You Can't Go Home Again,* Harper, 1940.

[14]John Hall Wheelock, an editor at Scribner.

Tom, you ought not to say some of the things you do—that I find your sufferings amusing and don't take them seriously. I know something of them. I do try to turn your mind from them and to arouse your humor, because to spend dreadful hours brooding over them, and in denunciation and abuse on account of them, seems to be only to aggravate them. It does no good. You have to suffer to write as you do, and the slings and arrows that strike you from outside madden you the more because you instinctively know that all that matters is your work and so why can't you be left to do it. I understand that. Have you seen me amused by other people's sufferings? You know that was unjust.

Then comes the question of your writing about the people here. I don't want to discuss it, because I agree that you have the same right to make use of them as of anyone else in the same way, and if there is an argument on it the whole thing may be bedevilled. . . . But when I spoke of resigning after we published—and the moment I inadvertently said it I told Miss Nowell[15] she must not repeat it, and she said she would not—I did not mean I would be asked or wanted to resign. That would never happen on any such ground. But it isn't the way you think, and it's up to you to write as you think you should. Your plan as outlined seems to me a splendid one too. I hope you will get on with it now.

There remains the question of whether we are in fundamental agreement. But it is no question if you feel it is not so. I have always instinctively felt that it was so, and no one I ever knew has said more of the things that I believed than you. It was so from the moment that I began to read your first book. Nothing else, I would say, could have kept such different people together through such trials. But I believe in democracy and not in dictators; and in government by principles and not by men; and in less government if possible, rather than more; and that power always means injustice and so should be as little concentrated as is compatible with the good of the majority; and that violence breeds more evils than it kills; and that it's better to sizzle in the frying pan until you're sure your jump won't take you into the fire; and that Erasmus, who begged his friend Luther not to destroy the *good* in the Church because of the bad in it, which he thought could be forced out with the spread of education, was right, though not heroic, and the he-

[15]Elizabeth Nowell, literary agent.

roic Luther wrong—and that Europe is the worse for his im-
petuosity today. I don't believe that things can't improve. I believe
that the only thing that can prevent improvement is the ruin of
violence, or of reckless finance which will end in violence. That is
why Roosevelt needs an opposition, and it is the only serious defect
in him. I believe that change really comes from great deep causes
too complex for contemporary men, or any others perhaps, fully to
understand, and that when even great men like Lenin try to make
over a whole society suddenly the end is almost sure to be bad, and
that the right end, the natural one, will come from the efforts of
innumerable people trying to do right, and to understand it, because
they are a part of the natural forces that are set at work by changed
conditions. It is the effort of man to adjust himself to change, and it
has to be led, but the misfortune of man is that strong will almost
always beats down intelligence, and the passionate, the reasonable. I
believe that such as you can help one change, but that it ought to be
by your writings, not by violent acts. I believe that wealth is bad but
that it should not be confiscated, but reduced by law, and in accord-
ance with a principle, not arbitrarily and in passion; and if it is done
in passion and violence the result will be a new privileged class
made up of delegates of the man or the oligarchy that has seized the
power. But it may be that the great underlying changes will dictate
communism as the best society for most people. Then we ought to
have it; but if we can evolve into it gradually how much better
(though I know many on both sides say that is impossible) than if
we go in by revolution and civil war. At least let us try the way of
evolution first. It seems to me that our Civil War and many of the
great convulsions were caused by extremists on both sides, by those
too hot-headed to wait for natural forces to disclose their direction,
when the inevitable outcome could no longer be resisted. I do not
believe the world can ever be perfect, of course, though it might in
a sense approximate a political and economic perfection if conditions ceased from changing so that a long enough time was given to
deal with known and permanent factors. But this is getting to be too
much of a philosophy of history or something, and I don't think it
has anything to do with fundamental agreement. I had always felt it
existed—and I don't feel, because you differ with me, however violently, on such things as I've said above, that it does not, necessarily. It is more that I like and admire the same things and despise

many of the same things, and the same people too, and think the same things important and unimportant—at least this is the way it has seemed to me.

Anyhow, I don't see why you should have hesitated to write me as you did, or rather to send the letter. There was mighty little of it that I did not wholly accept, and what I did not, I perfectly well understood. There were places in it that made me angry, but it was a fine letter, a fine writer's statement of his beliefs, as fine as any I ever saw, and though I have vanities enough, as many as most, it gave me great pleasure too—that which comes from hearing brave and sincere beliefs uttered with sincerity and nobility.

Always yours,

TO NANCY HALE

June 18, 1937

DEAR MRS. WERTENBAKER:[16]

I got your address from Miss Nowell. I had been asking her about you because I cannot help being impatient to see the novel done, or even to read some more of it, and yet I do not want to keep bothering you and perhaps worrying you about it. But she thought it would be all right if I wrote you, and she told me you were working well. I am delighted to know this. Writing a novel is a very hard thing to do because it covers so long a space of time, and if you get discouraged it is not a bad sign, but a good one. If you think you are not doing it well, you are thinking the way real novelists do. I never knew one who did not feel greatly discouraged at times, and some get desperate, and I have always found that to be a good symptom. Anyhow, I have seen enough of the novel to have no anxieties about the outcome, but rather the very greatest hopes. I hope you will be able to go on steadily until you get to the end.

I hope when you go through here, in the Fall, on the way back to Virginia, you will give me a chance to see you. Maybe by then you will have the manuscript complete.

Ever sincerely yours,

[16]Nancy Hale, the novelist.

TO ERNEST HEMINGWAY

Jan. 19, 1940

DEAR ERNEST:

I cabled you the morning after I read what you sent of the ms.[17]
The impressions made by it are even stronger after the lapse of time.
The scenes are more vivid and real than in the reading. This has
always happened to me after reading your novels, and it is true of
mighty few writers. That Chapter Eight is terrific, and as one gets
further away from it the characters of those different men when they
came out to be killed, and the way they took it, seem as if one had
seen it all, and had known them. It is truly wonderful, the way the
temper of the people changed as things went on and they got drunk
with killing, and with liquor too. The first chapter, or the first eight
pages, had the old magic. Last night, I had to talk about forthcoming
books to the people in the bookstore,[18] and I ended by saying what
a simple thing it was to be a real writer, the easiest thing in the world,
and I was going to give them an example to show it, how anybody
could do it, and then I read them, without saying who had written
it, the first three pages, through the point where Jordan gets his glasses
adjusted, and sees the mill and the waterfall and all. Having him do
that makes the whole scene jump out at you as real as real. I said,
"Why couldn't any of us do that? It's perfectly simple." But of course
nobody can do it. Then I did tell them that they were the first pages
of a novel by you, but I told them nothing else about it. You could
see how even that little bit impressed them all. Well, of course, I am
mighty impatient to see more.

I did not put in about depositing the check for $250 for the sake
of keeping the cable short—Yankee frugality.

I had lunch with Waldo[19] yesterday, and he was in fine form, and
talked awfully well, and so we were much longer at it than we should
have been. But as we went out, we met a man who looked exactly like
he ought to, which does not often happen. That was Sweeny,[20] the

---

[17] *For Whom the Bell Tolls,* Scribner, 1940.
[18] The Scribner Bookstore.
[19] Waldo Peirce, the painter, a friend of Hemingway and of Perkins.
[20] Colonel Charles Sweeny, soldier and writer, author of *Moment of Truth,* Scribner,
1943.

soldier, who said he had had a letter from you, and took it out of his
pocket, but didn't read it to us. I was mighty glad to see Sweeny, and
to see what he looked like.

Anyhow, I think this book will be magnificent.

Always yours,

*The letter of June 17, 1943, which follows, was written after Perkins had
received, and read, a book on writing and publishing which, in the course
of an attack on editors and publishers in general, alleged that Thomas
Wolfe had been the helpless victim of his editors, who had cut and mangled
his work in such a way as to do him, and it, serious injury. Perkins resented
these allegations, not only as regarding himself—for he had been Wolfe's
principal editor and had sacrificed time and health in an effort to help him
—but as regarding editors in general. As Perkins points out, Wolfe's own
letters give the lie to these allegations.*

June 17, 1943

DEAR ———:

I got a copy of your "———" because I heard it contained a furious
attack upon me. It does, and one that is plainly libellous, as Thomas
Wolfe's own letters alone will show. But I found the book such good
reading, upon the whole, that I suppose I now shall read it through.
And I'll enjoy it, for the most part. But I am the slowest reader in the
world, and so hardly ever get to read anything but what we are
publishing. Which is a very bad thing in an editor.

But then I found your chapter called "———," and I thought you
should hear a few facts which are at complete variance with what you
say. One thing you say is that if a manuscript of a novel "did not come
in through one of the big agents" it is condemned "to cursory and
dilatory reading." When we take on a new novelist we advise him to
get an agent for the sake of magazine, dramatic, radio and movie
rights. These he owns, and they must be skillfully handled. But here
are a few of the authors that came to us on their own and got
thorough, deeply interested, and immediate readings:

Struthers Burt   Christine Weston
Scott Fitzgerald   Nancy Hale
S. S. Van Dine   Arthur Train

Robert Briffault   John Thomason
Ernest Hemingway Will James
Marjorie Rawlings   Taylor Caldwell
Marcia Davenport

Most of them still have no agents in connection with book publication, but only for these other rights.

Then you come to tell how ninety percent of the novels published bear "bruises and slashes" from editors. I should say that ninety percent of them are barely touched, and then only in view of such matters as libel and other legal points. The publisher has to take some care in those regards, of course. Even so, I should say that ninety percent of our novels were very slightly changed and that if they were changed it was because the author asked for help, even demanded it, even thought he or she was neglected if it were not given. When it is given, it is given very reluctantly and fearfully because, as you say, the book can only come out of the man. Editors know that mighty well, at least those I am acquainted with.

As for the greater part of Thomas Wolfe's manuscripts being torn out and thrown into the waste-basket, it is not true. Not a page was thrown into the waste-basket. A good deal of what was in "The Angel" was removed, and a great deal of that was used in "Of Time and the River."[21] A great deal was removed from "Of Time and the River" and was used in the two later novels[22] which Harpers published. Almost nothing of what Tom wrote failed to appear in print except much that was so unfinished, as he himself thought, that it could not be published. But that too would have been revised by Tom and would have appeared, if Tom had lived.

As for Tom not being in a position to resist sabotage, why not? He had a contract. We were bound to publish everything he wrote except what was libellous and obscene—what would have endangered him with the law. The truth is that nothing was ever taken from Tom's writings without his full consent. When he could go no further with "Of Time and the River," he brought it to me and asked me to help him, and I did it with very great reluctance and anxiety. Tom *demanded* help. He *had* to have it. No one who did not know him could possibly understand it, but he would get into a state of such despera-

[21]Scribner, 1935.
[22]*The Web and the Rock,* Harper, 1939; *You Can't Go Home Again,* Harper, 1940.

tion that one realized that if he were not enabled to complete his book soon, something very serious would happen to him. He intended to proceed in the same way with Harpers. He called his book, which they made into two books,[23] "finished," when it was not at all. And he knew that, and he expected to work with Edward Aswell[24] as he had with me. What's more, I know Aswell's feeling about the matter, one of great anxiety for fear he would do damage. You seem to know only one kind of editor, and it is not the kind that I know. Certain authors absolutely demand help, and if it is not given them they will go to another publisher to get it. But most real writers do not. Most of them know what they want to do, and do it. Nobody ever edited Hemingway, beyond excising a line or two for fear of libel or other legal dangers.

Then you speak of fun being poked at Tom because of the hugeness of his manuscripts—because he delivered a packing case from a truck. In fact, it was a taxicab. You say he was ridiculed. To my knowledge, he was not. He was admired. This peculiarity of his genius was interesting and was told about for that reason, just as such peculiarities as that of De Quincey, in working in a room until it was so full of papers and books, etc., that there was no room for him and so he locked it up and got another, were told about. It was not ridicule. It was affectionate admiring surprise. When Tom's book[25] came here, it was instantly recognized as a work of genius, and we were all excited about it, and it was read in sections by three of us at once. It was too long, and there was one big cut[26] of about 70 pages at the beginning, concerned with events which did not seem to come within the scope of Eugene's story, for they related to things before Eugene's birth, and remote from Altamont. Tom fully agreed that this cut should be made. I have a wonderful letter he wrote to his old teacher,[27] telling how he came here, and when we mentioned certain passages that were pretty rough he said he would take them out, and we said, by God he wouldn't, that they were

[23] *The Web and the Rock* and *You Can't Go Home Again*.

[24] The editor at Harper and Bros. who was in charge of the publication of Thomas Wolfe's books after he had left Scribner.

[25] *Look Homeward, Angel*.

[26] There were many other deletions of material used elsewhere in later books. This one cut may, in parts, have been lost to print—but not the best of it.

[27] Margaret Roberts (Mrs. J. M. Roberts) of Asheville, N.C. Excerpts from Wolfe's letters to her were published in the *Atlantic Monthly* during 1946–1947.

among the best things in the book. You don't know what you are talking about. Even a good deal of that first part got into the later books in improved form. It is a long and complicated story. It may not interest you, but you have absolutely misrepresented the situation.

As for Henry Miller, I haven't read enough of him perhaps to be a qualified judge, but from what I have read, I should fully agree with you and Bunny Wilson.[28] But I suspect that the reason he cannot get published is that he does not sell. Publishers do have to think about that. It is like a law of nature. They would have to do it even under communism.

Anyhow, from what I have read of the rest of your book, which is a good deal, you have said many right and true things that have not been said before. Editors aren't much, and can't be. They can only help a writer realize himself, and they can ruin him if he's pliable, as Tom was not. That is why the editors I know shrink from tampering with a manuscript and do it only when it is required of them by the author, as it was by Tom. When an editor gets to think differently from that, to think he knows more about a writer's book than the writer—and some do—he is dead, done for, and dangerous. When he thinks he is a discoverer because he doesn't fail to recognize talent—was a jeweler ever praised because he knew a diamond from a lump of glass?—he is a stuffed shirt, and through. But I've known it to happen.

As to libel, I shall look up the law. But I think suit can be brought until one year after the sale of a book has ceased. But my suit would ask no more compensation than would meet the expense, since the purpose would be only to show that what you said was grossly untrue, ignorant, and injurious. On the other hand, from what else I've read of your book—such as that refutation of those silly so-called laws or rules of fiction, since genius can break any law and indeed always does —I think you spoke from misinformation and irresponsibility, and so I should prefer to let the matter lie until—if there is a chance of that —you come to New York and will give me an interview. I don't like quarrels, and I hate the law, but I can't by silence seem to acquiesce in what you have written, for if you now think it is the truth, you will then have grounds to assume that it is.

Ever truly yours,

[28]Edmund Wilson had expressed admiration for the writing of Henry Miller.

Excerpt from a letter to an unidentified author.

I have read a good deal of your novel about the editor. You obviously regard me with contempt for approving the publication of such books as "The Women on the Porch,"[29] although it seems to me that, if one wants to look at it from a moral point of view, it is of value to show what frustration and futility our present civilization produces. But if I were what you had supposed, if I remained the helpless employee of an organization in which I disbelieved, and which I thought was what you think it is, I should be utterly despicable in my own eyes too. That would be the lowest thing possible.

Then, in the end, you have your editor go out for himself as a publisher, on the basis of certain resolutions. One of these is, to my mind, a complete betrayal of his profession—that he will only publish books which will coincide with his own views. If he is that kind of man, let him speak for himself and be a writer. But the function of a publisher in society is to furnish a means by which anyone of a certain level of intelligence and abilities can express his views. A publisher should not be, as such, a partisan, however strongly partisan he may be as an individual. If he allows his partisanship to govern him in his choice of books, he is a traitor to the public. He is supposed to furnish a forum for the free play of the intellect, in so far as he possibly can. That is the whole American theory—that opinions can be given a means of full expression, and that the public, hearing all of them and considering them, will eventually approximate a right conclusion. Every profession has its own particular code of ethics, its own morality, that its members must adhere to or they betray it. And a primary element in the morality of the publisher is that he shall not let his own personal views obstruct the way for the expression of counter-views. I should say that no individual in this House, for instance, is a believer in communism. But when we got so fine a book as "Soviet Communism: A New Civilization," by Beatrice and Sidney Webb, who have been life-long students of social questions, we felt that it was our obligation to publish it. Then the ways of the Russian system would be ably set forth, and the arguments for it, and the American citizen could, from that source and others, form his own opinion. The American idea is that public opinion rules, and the American publisher's idea is that it is his duty to get individual opinions bearing upon issues before the

[29]A novel by Caroline Gordon, Scribner, 1944.

public in order that it may be given the materials from which public opinion may competently crystallize.

Ever sincerely yours,

May 31, 1944

DEAR ———:

Your novel has been read by several of us, and we are very sorry that we have had to conclude that we cannot make an offer of publication. It is quite readable and has vitality, but, in general, it is our impression that you have not yet sufficiently mastered the technique which is necessary to present its thesis impressively and logically. Apart from this general consideration, your conception of publishing houses and their function in society is quite contrary to the reality—at least, you have not established its validity. It is clear that publishing houses, even as churches and hospitals, etc., can function only on a stable financial basis. The ideal of publishing would be a forum where all sections of humanity could have their say, whether their object was to instruct, entertain, horrify, etc. Nevertheless, there are certain rules of quality and relevance, which can only be determined by some sort of selection and this the publisher, representing humanity at large, attempts—with many mistakes—to make. Or, to put it differently, artists, saints, and the other more sentient representatives of the human race are, as it were, on the frontiers of time—pioneers and guides to the future. And the publisher, in the capacity mentioned, must make some sort of estimate of the importance and validity of their reports, and there is nothing he can base this on but the abilities to judge that God has given him.

I realize that our correspondence is futile and had better be ended, but I should like to say, if you'll let me, that I knew from your face that you were an utterly sincere and good person.

We are returning the manuscript to you under separate cover.

Ever sincerely yours,

Oct. 3, 1944

DEAR ———:

It is very hard for me to express a certain uneasiness I feel about ———, because it is really instinctive, though backed by experience.

298   MAXWELL E. PERKINS

It is, first, that books written in anticipation of events and developments often lose a great deal of the relevance they are intended to have because things develop quite, or somewhat, differently.

Another consideration is that a writer does best what comes entirely from himself, and not so well in carrying out the ideas of others. This I know, considerably, from having myself suggested books to writers who had nothing at the moment and wanted to write. Such books were always below their best, though sometimes successful.

A third reason is that the best fiction does not arise out of an idea at all, but the idea, or argument, arises out of the human elements and characters as they naturally develop. And this seems to apply particularly to ———, because her nature is to begin a book without knowing the conclusion, or even the steps of development, so that the development and conclusions come from the situation and the people.

Your idea I think is a good one except for the reasons given above, and they *may* not apply. I cannot tell about it. Apart from an uneasy feeling that comes from these considerations, I should be all for the plan. Anyhow, if ——— wants to do it, as I think she does very much, we could be sure that the outcome would be what we should regard with great favor—even though it fell below her best work. We are for whatever she may do. Anyhow, she has at present to complete "———," and I thought we might be able to see more clearly what the probabilities for "———" would be by the time that was done.

Ever sincerely yours,

TO G. P. BRETT, JR.

Sept. 27, 1946

Dear Mr. Brett:[30]

I am afraid I cannot coöperate with you as fully as I should wish in this matter because I did not read "Forever Amber."[31] I did look it over, to see what it was like, and my impression was that it was an honest piece of work and that, in respect to the great events of the restoration and the character of the King and his brother, it was historically good—particularly the plague and the fire. I thought, too, that the ending was quite admirable. From what I saw of those doings

---

[30]President of the Macmillan Company.
[31]A novel by Kathleen Winsor, Macmillan, 1944.

that might result in what might be legally called obscenity, I should not suppose that there was anything in the book that could rightly be so described. The events were rather referred to as happening, than described. There was no attempt, that I could see, at salaciousness.

That is all I can say about the book because, as you know, a man becomes an editor because he loves books and then finds that he cannot possibly get time to read the books of any other publisher than the one he works for. That is too bad.

As to censorship of literature, while I must agree that there are sometimes books which are deliberately contrived to appeal to vicious instincts, I believe that freedom of speech is the very basis of this nation, and that what damage, if any, may come from such books should be risked because of the much greater damage that would come if the principles of censorship were introduced and progressed. Nobody knows who is qualified to exercise censorship. I have read the opinions of various people of high repute, in the *Journal American* "Crusade" against salacious or obscene books, and most of them seem to me to have no understanding of literature at all. They constantly assert that writers introduced an element of salaciousness, as they called it, into books to make them sell. A true writer never wants to introduce that element. He does it because his book is a revelation of life—and life should be revealed as it is—and he generally hates it just as much as any genteel reader or censor, and generally much more, for he is bound to be a sensitive person if he is a true writer.

Ever sincerely yours,

The Scribner files reveal many instances in which Perkins made similar detailed suggestions, to a great variety of writers, but the following, like one or two other letters of the same sort in this collection, has been selected as representative.

TO MARCIA DAVENPORT

April 28, 1947

DEAR MARCIA:

I think you have written a notable book[32] in a first draught but that it needs, as any book, to be revised. The revision should be almost only

[32]*East Side, West Side,* Scribner, 1947.

a matter of emphasis, for the scheme is right. Having borne the heat
of the battle, you must not fail it now. It is a book about a person,
Jessie, but it is also about New York, and that must never be forgotten. Jessie is a New Yorker who came out of the East Side and the
West Side. In one week many things occur, quite naturally, which
change her life and herself. In telling of these you should always keep
the reader aware of New York, as you mostly do: when Jessie recalls
the past, she should still be aware of the present, in motors, cabs, or
walking, or in bed, or in a bath—as people always are. New York is
a foremost character in the novel. Jessie is in a crisis of her own life,
in New York, but in all her reflections, here and there, she is in the
place she came out of, New York, and is aware of it. So you give New
York, top to bottom, and that alone is a great thing to do. Make Jessie
more aware, as she goes about in cars, cabs and afoot, of the way New
York is, of how Fifth Avenue looks in the haze of afternoon, or
whatever, even when she is lost in the past. This means that you
should emphasize what you have already done. A person, like Jessie,
walks or drives along a street in deep reflection, but is still aware of
how it looks, and of its *quality*. So get that in more, by a touch here
and there, to make this book realize one of its great motives, to give
New York as only an East Side, West Side New Yorker knows it. You
have done this, really, but emphasize it—and the fact that these Park
Avenuers, etc., don't belong to it, don't really like it, but that the
children of immigrants who never got out of it, even Jessie and Mark
and others, do belong and love it and couldn't for long be anywhere
else. So make the book say that, by blending Jessie's present with the
past as she recalls it. The reader must be aware of time and place, as
it is and as she remembers it. That is what you intended, and means
only an occasional reference to give a sense—by sight or smell or
whatever—of a spot of New York. In truth, I only know this from
what you have said and written, so you have done it. But strengthen
it. For instance, you tell of her in a taxicab as being *oblivious* to the
ugliness of the street. I think she should be *aware*. People are oblivious
only momentarily. And in this book that gives New York through
Jessie, you must not have her oblivious unless she has to be—which
would be briefly. I ought not to be telling you, because you told me:
maybe the biggest thing this book can do is to give a realization of this
unique place, New York.

But the book is also about Jessie, who is an indigenous New Yorker,
as her mother, the child of immigrants, was. Her character and talent

brought her into wealth, and into the society of the upper East Side, but never even blurred her sense of reality, her sense of values. Jessie, her daughter, would have inherited and learned that sense of things, and so, as you have it, she would, as she did, have worked. (I think you should have had her work on the *World,* and not on a literary-sounding review.) She gave up working when she married—this should be made plain—which was even more natural for her when the depression made those who had money, or some, feel ashamed to keep a job from someone who needed it. But in the week of the book, and early in it, I think you should show that it was on Jessie's conscience that she was not pulling her weight, as it would be. And at the end of the book you should show, perhaps even in only a paragraph, that she was through with that, that this week of crisis had changed her, and restored her sense of values—those of her mother and, I hope we could say, of all true New Yorkers. Anyhow, New Yorkers are not fooled by any pomps and vanities or by the sinful lusts of the flesh. They know them for what they are, and may like them, but they reverence nothing. Jessie is real and not unhuman, but she is too much always in the right and Brandon too much in the wrong. About that I don't know what you can do, except by having Jessie realize that in some ways she had been exasperating, and by the use of two more outside scenes. You have the one where the two women who knew her recall Rosa Landan. One could say this violated the scheme of your book—that all should be presented through Jessie's senses. That scene is essential, I think. But it would be less obtrusive if you added *two* others, and one of them could be where people commented on Jessie, and more or less unfavorably. But the great thing is to have Jessie come out of this book as a woman different from when she went in. That you must do. She's been through too much to be the same. It was a week of culmination. It must end, must indicate a changed life for Jessie. Must be conclusive.

So much for generalizations—forgive me for telling you what I know you know and most of which you told me—and now to come to particulars. Perhaps for that I should have kept the manuscript by me. But I did make notations on the margin, up to the last hundred or hundred and fifty pages. There was nothing to be said against them, I thought, except that some of the speeches were too long to be natural, though great novelists have made them so and perhaps rightly. Writing, like drawing, is an art, and whatever conveys the *meaning* is justified. But I think, as we are today, that when Mark talks so long among his people, without interruption and a fresh start, or even Jerome Block (who is grand), the effect is reduced, because it seems unnatural. Just consider this a little. If I'm right, a few trifling interpolations, here and there, will make amends.

You say you will have to rewrite the first chapter in the light of the last, and that is right in principle, but I have no fault to find with it. But work it in there that she has worked and thinks she should. And I think there should be more about Matthew Kernan.

I put a note on page 30, which said: "Generalizations are no use —give one specific thing and let the action say it." Can't recall the instance, but it's true. By the way, don't they still have an orchestra on the Staten Island boats—they do on others—and would you be phony to have one play for Jessie and Mark, some old-time song? They could ask for it. Even if not true, I think it would be fair. They have music on the ferry to Blauvelt.

I should have kept the manuscript, but look at notes on pages. When you have people talking, you have a scene. You must interrupt with explanatory paragraphs, but shorten them as much as you can. Dialogue is *action*. You can't take the reader's attention from it much without impairing its effect. Think of watching a duel, with someone explaining the *why* of it. I think this was about Millicent, that there you do too much explaining. The action and dialogue, which is action, should do it. They can't do it altogether, but you don't trust them enough. You must interpolate and explain, but you tend to overdo it.

The truth is you're right, you can't see a book before the end. It must be revised in the light of the end. Now there are two weak scenes in this book, where you were "planting" things that have to be there. They are weak only at the start, where you tell, expositionally, of the various people present. Ideally, you should let them come in and *reveal* themselves in talk and action. You can't, but I think you should trust more to the talk and action. One scene is the committee meeting and the other is the Stillman dinner. (Let me put this in as I think of it: You must make people talk, as they do, in elision. Not, "You will," but "You'll" etc., all through.)

On page 55, or thereabouts, I have made a note that your exposition stops the action for too long, that too much is explained that comes out anyhow.

Lorraine and the dog are very good, and might even be somewhat enlarged upon. She is a real type, all over New York's East Side.

A little thereafter, Jessie is preparing dinner, shelling peas. And she remembers about Brandon and how he had acted. In this, while she is remembering, you should still have Jessie aware of New York.

Wherever you bring in the sounds of the East River, and the scene, you always do wonders, and I don't think you could overdo it.

Chapter 6, page 111. The Stillmans' dinner party. I have commented on this. It just needs to be pulled together and organized. More should be said by the action and the talk. It gets to be all right when Mark turns up, but I think you might make more of Stillman's telephonitis, and if you could explain the characters by what they did and said, in the early part of the chapter, it would be better. Then they go home. Just emphasize New York. Couldn't you make more of their drive up, I think, Fifth Avenue in the dark, in brief description, which you do excellently well. But about Mark and herself, I think you explain what the reader gets by inference. What they say and do tells all. You tend to explain too much. You must explain, but your tendency is to distrust your own narrative and dialogue.

I may be getting out of order, not having the manuscript, but when they have that dinner before the play, you explain too much. Once they get to talking, everything is right.

Now we come to Thursday. My notes say, "Cut down Anna and Sarah somewhat." The cat, Putzl, is good and he, or she, should be brought in several times, later in the story, and not just here.

Now we come to the committee meeting. Make the people come out through talk and act, just as far as you possibly can. Avoid all possible exposition. You introduce characters, such as Althea Crowe, who reveal themselves in what they say and do. But then you stop the narrative to explain what should come out in the movement of the story.

When Mark comes to dine with Jessie, you have the chance to bring out all about her work—the work she did on the *World*—and why she isn't doing it now. She could just simply say it. She could tell why she stopped.

Wednesday. This is where she remembers the agonizing time when, because Brandon wanted it, she was pregnant. Helen Lee comes and, after Helen Lee goes, she remembers. But even here, along with her remembrance, you should keep her aware of the present. It is Jessie *now,* remembering her mother's death.

I think the brief chapter which breaks into the scheme of the book, where Serena and her friend, waiting for Serena's car, talk of Jessie, is admirable. But since you have to have this chapter, I think it would be well, as I have said, to have two other chapters, and in one of them you could have people talk about Jessie in a way to show that she was fallible herself.

Iris's call is good, very effective in showing the aspect of New York life that she represents. If anything, it might be enlarged upon.

Then, when Jessie is in her bath she remembers. This is a good example of what I mean. She would be absorbed in her memories, but still she would be aware of her bath, and of the sound of the river, and of New York. She should realize at the same time, through interpolations of the present, both the past and the present.

Again, after they realize the deadly character of Rosa's illness and go there to dinner, which is good, Brandon wants her to have a child. She agrees to it. This is told in memory and somehow, during those memories, the reader should be aware of what was going on in the present. I forget exactly where she was, but at one time her memories come while she is walking. There, too, I think you ought to break in upon her abstractions with things she notices, so that the reader will be conscious of the present, as she would be, even while the concentration is upon the past. Always the present and New York should be kept in.

I did think that perhaps you overdo Brandon's brutality during the period when she was in all those agonies of pregnancy. I have a note, "Around page 319: too obstetrical and should be cut, and compressed."

Then, we come to her going to market, and that is very good. And then, later, to the theater. There is the dinner party at the night club, before it, and there you begin again with too much generalization. Try to make the people stand out through the dialogue and action. I think they almost would do it alone, but you do not put enough confidence into your dialogue and action.

Then you come to the play. Everything is right with this, excepting that it would be better if you could give some running account of the action of the play. I know what play it was, I suppose, and I realize that you do not want to put that failure before the reader, for the sake of the author. But couldn't you just give snatches of some imaginary play, so as to make the whole thing more actual? Couldn't you invent a play, of which you would only have to give trifles, that was somewhat parallel to the real one?

The Elizabeth Betts incident of the party is extremely good. The rest, I think, might stand compression.

You really know all about this book yourself. It is true that Althea's loyalty—though one knows right away what kind of person she was and that she would be loyal—should be based upon something more than the reader is given. I do think you should account for this, for her strong feeling for Jessie, through Jessie's memory.

I do have some fear that the murder runs too far toward melodrama, but not so much in what quite plausibly happens. But, in revision, I would think of that danger. When Serena Lowdon tells them off, she does it wonderfully. Even so, I would try to compress what she says, because I think she too speaks at greater length than people actually do speak at unless they have been prepared in advance, which she was not. She was speaking out of her emotions and her character, without forethought. I have argued to that effect about Mark's talk to his people, which is very good, as they are, and about Bloch. Mark begins to speak on page 530, I think. I would try to have more questions thrown in while he is speaking.

I have referred to it before. It is on page 593, where you have Jessie oblivious. The story is told through Jessie's senses almost wholly, and she must not be oblivious. You might be, for a block or so, but when you were stopped by a traffic light it would bring you back to awareness of the present.

I have referred to the Staten Island ferry. I hope you can find it rightful to have music on it, and that maybe they could ask for some old New York song. I think you could do it, even if they do not any longer have three-piece orchestras there.

If this book can give the quality of New York and show the wonderful people, mostly the descendants of immigrants, as the real New Yorkers, and also at the same time show the corruption among people of wealth and supposedly of culture, who just live here without belonging, it will be a very great achievement in that alone. It could be simply the story of Jessie, a woman whose life comes to a week of crisis in which she must come to conclusions with all the most important things in her life. That would be enough in itself. But if you can only get all this meaning into it—and it is in it, in fact—about New York, and also the situation the world is in, which comes out when she goes with Mark to visit his Czech relatives, you will have done wonders. To accomplish this, you need only to intensify throughout what actually is there—and I think you would naturally do this in the revision, anyhow. It is largely a matter of compression, and not so much of that, really. It is, as you said, that you can't know a book until you come to the end of it, and then all the rest must be modified to fit that.

Always yours,

June 4, 1947

DEAR ——:

This is in answer to your letter of May 29[33] with regard to certain passages in the tale of Aladdin in "The Arabian Nights." We deeply sympathize, as individuals, with the development of better understanding among all groups, but we do not think that in this country there should be any groups, as was the intention of its Founders, and we deplore, as individuals, the development of group consciousness. While we are, therefore, wholly in favor of the intentions of your League,[34] it does not seem to us as publishers that it would be proper for us to edit a classic of some centuries' standing. Only the author would have the right to do that, it seems to us, and if we did it, we should in some degree betray an obligation to our profession.

Nowadays, publishers are under pressure from all sorts of groups. What if they should trim their books to suit every point of view and every element of religious and racial pride? What, then, would remain of that one relatively free realm left, the republic of letters?

Ever sincerely yours,

[33]A letter requesting the removal, in future editions, of certain passages involving Jewish characters.
[34]The Anti-Defamation League.

HAROLD STRAUSS

Harold Strauss was born in New York City in 1907, and was granted a B.S. magna cum laude from Harvard in 1928. The following year he began his long career in book publishing as editor for Alfred H. King, 1929–1932. He then went to Covici-Friede as production director, 1932–1934; editor in chief, 1934–1938. In 1938–1939, Mr. Strauss served as director of the New York City Federal Writers' Project and editor of the *New York City Guide*. He became associate editor at Alfred A. Knopf, Inc., in 1939, and editor in chief in 1942. Mr. Strauss died in 1975. Among the writers with whom he worked at Knopf were C. W. Ceram, John Hersey, Ruth Moore, John Steinbeck, and Nicholas Monsarrat.

• • •

Taut, tart, perfectionist, with a rich vein of glittering humor, these selections from the editor-to-author correspondence of Harold Strauss display his meticulous taste, wide range of knowledge, and vigorously applied high standards for intelligibility and readability in a manuscript. These are qualities, of course, one would expect to find in so distinguished an editor; they serve, too, as a set of criteria *any* editor might find invaluable.

A FEW NOTES ON POPULARIZING SCIENTIFIC OR
MEDICAL DISCOVERIES:

Excerpt from a letter to a writer [Knopf] subsequently published.

ONE of the most important distinctions between good and bad popularizations is the direct relevance of human interest detail *to the discovery*.

Bad popularizations stress irrelevant detail, such as the discoverer's hobbies or his father's religious beliefs. Good popularizations rest on good sensory reporting, if that is possible; if not, on good research. What did the place in which the discovery was made look like at the climactic moment? Who was there at the time? What irritating distractions were there? What was the weather like, and did it have anything to do with what the scientist was doing that day? What about the physical equipment? Something missing? Some failure? Improvised substitutes? Anything of this kind is useful. It is much better than saying abstractly, for instance, that controlled tests took two years to complete. . . .

Biographical information is of course useful and desirable. In a book, however, it must be handled quite differently than in, say, *Time* magazine. Here the principle is motive impulse. What made Schliemann stop being a merchant and start digging? What made Darwin decide to ship aboard the *Beagle*? Generally speaking, the question of motivation has two aspects: first, why did the particular individual become a scientist in the first place? Second, what put him on the track of his greatest discovery? Was it planned? If so, how and why? Was it accidental? Was it planned in one direction, but ended in a slightly different one?

Admittedly, this could lead to heavy-handed metaphysical questions, or to overly sensational "iffy" ones. But these tendencies, too evident in German popularizations, can easily be controlled. . . .

Both of the above points are subordinate to narrative. Usually a scientific discovery is a process which moves through time, thus lending itself naturally to narrative treatment. A general format for a particular chapter (subject to pleasing variations, of course) might go something like this:

1. A quick, broad sketch of the prevailing state of knowledge at the time, pointing to the crucial unsolved problem.
2. Abortive attempts of others to solve it.
3. Then Mr. X comes on the scene. Why? I.e., what motivated him to become a scientist in the first place, and to embark on a particular course in the second place.
4. The events or steps leading to the discovery, told in as dramatic a narrative *order* as possible, but without excessive verbal embellishments, such as superlatives. In other words, the color and human interest must be drawn from the events, not varnished on by means of the author's comments.
5. The significance of the discovery. *Here* is the place for metaphysics, if you like; for speculations and editorial comment.

Finally, beware of jargon. The common language is much better and more communicative, not only because it does not send readers to a dictionary too often, but because it has more stability. The meaning of a technical term can sometimes be altered by an obscure monograph in an obscure learned journal, but not if the idea is expressed in the common language. In extreme cases, jargon conceals meaning, and the discipline of translating it into the common language often forces a writer to sharpen his grasp of his own topic. Jargon saves words, but squanders time. We prefer to print the extra words.

Letter to a distinguished scientist writing in English, an acquired language, for the first time.

I have now finished the extremely laborious and time-consuming job of editing and rewriting your manuscript and I have sent it to Professor X for his expert advice. But the manuscript is far from complete and ready for the printer. Some things that must be done can be done only by you. A few of these things I have already written you about, and I urgently need your answers. You must go through the entire manuscript again and eliminate all modifying phrases such as "it seems" and "it appears" where they are not strictly required because the scientific evidence is inadequate. The constant use of these phrases makes the manuscript tiresome reading in spots.

Another point on which I have already written you is to request you to recheck your footnotes and references, some of which I have found wrong as to page number and in other respects. You should always refer to an English language edition where one exists, and if the book has been published in England and America, to the American edition, if that was the original one. It is imperative in the English language to use the full name of the author, not just the initial of his first name, as is the continental practice. It sounds terribly pedantic in English if you do follow the European custom. Furthermore I enclose herewith some guidance on the form of our footnotes which must include the title in full, as well as the city, the publisher, the date of publication, volume where necessary, as well as the page reference (see p. 11 of the enclosed guidance booklet).

All these points I have written to you about before, though in somewhat less detail. But what follows is new, and most important.

The first question concerns your quotations from the Bible. I have three versions at home, all different, and none corresponds with yours. I need most urgently to know which version you have used, and to be precise, you had better give me the complete title page or any other information about it, because it apparently is not enough to say "The King James Version" since that has been revised several times. On the whole, I prefer the King James version, because of the magnificence of its style, although the King James version of some of your quotations, particularly Joshua 11:16, is much more obscure than the Revised version. I think the solution in this and possibly in a few other instances is to use the King James version throughout in the text, and add a footnote giving other, clearer versions, when necessary. It can be done here, later, as soon as you tell us which version you have used.

The next point concerns your description of pottery. I am afraid that you have relied entirely or almost entirely upon technical terminology, and that even the most interested general reader cannot follow to the point of visualizing the pottery you refer to. I believe that we ought to be able to visualize the pottery from your words alone, even if excellent illustrations are supplied. I have no objection to the use of the proper technical term if it is accompanied by a vivid description in the common language. This will be very important to the success of the book outside of purely scientific circles. I must ask you to review your own manuscript with this in mind at once.

The word "pebble" presents some difficulties. In English it suggests a stone no bigger than one that can be held in one hand. I am sure you use it correctly as far as eoliths are concerned, but when you reach the age of incipient farming, I am not so sure that you distinguish properly between pebbles, stones, rocks, etc. When you say that the neolithic basements were covered with pebbles, do you really mean rather round stones of the size one can hold in one hand, or smaller; or do you mean *stones,* which conveys to us a meaning of something slightly larger, and of any shape, including a flat shape? For even larger stone objects, the word *rock* should be used, as it should be for the raw material in its natural place, in the earth or on mountainsides.

I must also know at once whether the rock pictures of the desert were invariably carved, or invariably painted, or sometimes painted and sometimes carved. This makes a great deal of difference in giving your style more flexibility and grace, since the concrete active verbs "to paint" and "to carve" in their various grammatical forms ought to be substituted for the one or two terms you use rather stiffly and vaguely, such as "depict."

Another point of the utmost importance concerns only that part of the book covering the period after the invention of writing. I have had long experience in handling works in your field and I can assure you that perhaps the single most fascinating thing to the general reader is the question of primitive or early writing, the various scripts, what they looked like, whether we can read them, how their secret was cracked, if it was, etc. I am afraid you have neglected this point completely. I consider this subject so important and such a sales asset that I would like to urge you to prepare a whole special chapter on it, taking all the space you wish, and supplying line cuts illustrating the different scripts.

We are going to have acute problems with some of your technical terminology, but I have to wait till Professor X finishes the manuscript to write you in detail about this. For instance, I think your term "Indo-Aryan" is not correct in English. I think it must be either "Indo-European" for the language or "Aryan" for the people, but I am not sure about this; I am only sure that "Indo-Aryan" is a term not used at all.

As you will see, when I return the original copy of the manuscript to you for your approval of the rewriting, it has been so drastically rewritten that the carbon copy unfortunately is not going to be usable for anything at all except to convey my detailed questions to you. These questions will cover many things not mentioned in this letter, and I hope you will supply the most detailed answers you can in every case.

As to the book itself, I consider it a major scholarly achievement of which you should be proud. But it also is an extremely difficult book for the general reader in its first half. This raises some interesting questions. In the first place, I may have to go over the early chapters once again, now that I understand the weak spots in your English a little better, and see if I cannot make them a little easier reading for the intelligent layman without sacrificing any scientific accuracy. But there are two things that I would suggest you do in the meanwhile. I assume that you are going to write in English a great deal hereafter, and I must say that your English improves noticeably toward the end of the book. But it still lacks a certain richness and flexibility of vocabulary. It was easy enough for me to correct certain grammatical errors, but it was much harder, because it was risky, to try to inject a greater richness of vocabulary into your prose. I have chanced it in a few cases because you will have the opportunity of checking my revisions. But I think, *both for the purposes of this book and for the future,* it would be a most important investment of your time if you would read Lewis Mumford's new book, *The City in History,* immediately. I know it has been published in England as well as in America, so it should be easily available to you. Actually, it is an immensely long book, but you will only have to read the early chapters, taking the history of the cities through the neolithic. Mumford is not a scientist, and I am not suggesting that you will learn anything of a scientific nature from him. But he is a magnificent stylist, and since in the early chapters he deals with palaeolithic, mesolithic, and neolithic man, I think you will do well to absorb his vocabulary. You may then want to make some further revisions in your own manuscript. You may also find Lewis Mumford's psychological and philosophical speculations interesting, even though you don't agree with them.

Believe me, I cannot stress the urgency of your reading the early chapters of this book too much.

The second thing we must do to help the general reader, and to give us a better chance of publishing the book successfully, is to supply the book with a ten-to-twenty-page introduction, directed outspokenly to the general reader, and explaining to him what he will find in the second half of the book, and even suggesting to him that he may find it most rewarding to read the second half of the book first, and then to pick up the first half. When you describe what is in the second half of the book you should do so in general terms, omitting all references to sources and scientific proof. In the text itself you will of course have to supply the scientific proof, and this is what makes it such difficult going in spots. I have written you about this before and I must say that you have quite literally done what I asked you to do in the first place—taken the reader by the hand and explained to him at all times what was going on. You have been somewhat repetitious at times, and I have deleted a few of these passages where I thought they were not necessary. But this additional help of an introduction is also now necessary.

On the other hand, I must tell you frankly that I do not like your "Conclusion" or epilogue at all. I think perhaps it is the result of the limitations of your English, but as it is written now, it sounds very commonplace and a bit banal; and also sounds quite repetitious. The place to tell the reader why your subject is important to him is in the introduction, not in the epilogue, where he has grasped the point long since, or he would never have read through to the epilogue. I have made some slight cuts here but I want to review the whole thing when you decide what you want to do about the introduction.

In successful books, the text and the illustrations should be more or less independent in the sense that they are independently comprehensible. I don't think you should rely on your photographs to elucidate obscurities in the text, but always try to be clear with your words. By the same token I think that the photographs will need much fuller, non-technical captions. I have made no attempt to cope with the photographs just yet, and certainly not to select them or place them. This is going to be a fantastic job, simply because I don't know with any degree of certainty which figure you are referring to in your figure references in the text, even though you have done a splendid job of organizing the photographs chronologically. No doubt we must allow double the usual time to publish your new book. I think that much of the material, including manuscript, proofs, illustrations, and captions, will have to travel back and forth between us several times, unless by chance you decide to come to the United States about four or five months from now, which will probably be the crucial period.

I have given an enormous amount of my time to this book because I think it is important. In return, I am and shall be quite perfectionist in my requests of you.

I'll write you again as soon as Prof. X has read the manuscript. He's a human dynamo, so I don't imagine he'll take very long over it.

Cordially,

I think you already know from X, a good friend of this house, that we are very much interested in your recent magazine article. It seems to us that this is very well done in itself, but cries for expansion into an 80,000 word book. You whet the reader's appetite. You touch on many dramatic moments that suggest full-scale descriptions. In fact the piece could be considered an outline for a book.

I am of course speaking of a trade book, a book for the general reader. A word about books of this kind. We don't think they should be written down for simple-minded readers. We think they should be just as scientifically sound as the author can make them. At the same time, we like to see technical jargon translated into the common language, and see no reason why sound books need be obscure or difficult reading. We hope that these books will be popular, but that does not require over-simplification. In the case of your prospective book, the inherent drama should create excitement enough to keep the reader turning the pages.

Do let me know what you think of all this. If you are interested in writing such a book for us, we probably could accept the magazine article as a general outline. We then would require from you a few sample chapters to show just how and in what style you would expand the material.

Cordially,

Letter to a very able author who fell short of his own standards. The manuscript was subsequently drastically rewritten and accepted.

You have written a good book—but not quite good enough. As I see it, you are a masterly teacher. Your writing is sober, informed, and wonderfully clear for the layman. You succeed in clarifying some very complex geological situations.

But then, why do we not offer to publish the book? I shall accept your own reference to Rachel Carson as the basis for what follows. You simply do not know how to paint word pictures. You do not know how to evoke vivid images of particular phenomena. You are not the master of what is called good sensory reporting. Now these qualities are not always necessary. But a "blind" nature writer is no nature writer at all, as far as the general public is concerned. I could give you literally hundreds of examples of what I mean. For instance, you say clearly and intelligibly that a [landslide] menaced a certain highway. Are you really going to leave it at that? It must have been an awesome spectacle—and perhaps terrifying to hear, also. Couldn't you spare a paragraph or two to say what it would have been like for a traveler to pass under it on the highway?

In your reference to a mummified sheep, you merely tease the reader. A few more details of what it looked like (and possibly what it smelled like), and about its zoological characteristics, would have helped a great deal.

You quote a very dramatic description by X. This is very effective writing. But you don't do anything of the kind on your own. You are comprehensive, as you should be. But I should think it would be eminently worthwhile to paint the portrait, in the utmost detail, of a dozen or so particularly interesting natural phenomena.

From the layman's point of view, your writing is not at all bad, except that it is badly punctuated, and except that it is sometimes a little repetitious. However, I think your even, pedagogic tone becomes a little monotonous after a while. It is a question of emphasis, of excitement. Where the emphasis should be I leave to you, but it needs emphasis that will lead to more force and color in your writing.

If your book dealt with a major scientific field, it might be possible to work out these problems in detail. But the subject of this book, although it has its own learned journal, is only a fragment of geology, and therefore a portion of a science, as far as trade publishing is concerned. Much as I would like to be able to publish a purely utilitarian book in this field, I don't think we could do it successfully. To be successful, your book must give pleasure as well as information, as the books of Rachel Carson do. Under these circumstances, the best I can do is to write you these generalized criticisms, and return the manuscript to you with many thanks for letting me see it.

It is quite possible that some other publisher will wish to publish it as it is. But if you feel responsive to the comments I made in this letter, so responsive that you wish to rewrite the manuscript drastically with these comments in mind, I certainly would welcome the opportunity to reconsider it.

Cordially,

Letter to a foreign-born novelist writing in English, for him an acquired language. For clarity, the points are deliberately repeated in various formulations.

I have read your revised manuscript and on the whole I think you
have done a splendid job. The ending is now very strong. As I told
you, I want one or two more people to read it before coming to a final
decision, but there is a more immediate problem than that. I think
that Chapter XIII, when the young man makes love with the girl in
the fisherman's shack, has to be entirely rewritten. I have discussed
this with your agent and another reader here, and we all agree that
through a series of accidents the scene has almost the opposite effect
of the one you intended. Because you have been rather vague about
all the physical details of the scene, details which I am sure you have
visualized in your mind but have not presented to the reader, it ends
up by becoming rather ludicrous.

The scene belongs in the book, and is very important in clarifying
the motivation. But it has an entirely uncharacteristic weakness: it is
not visual. Throughout the rest of the book you present wonderful
visual images which enable the American reader to *see* your people
and their land. Please don't misunderstand me. I am certainly not
asking you to write an obscene chapter. Erotic, of course. Obscene,
no. I don't know exactly how to make the distinction to you, but
several of us here feel that it is more obscene to be vague than to be
forthright. After all, this is the first sexual experience for both man
and girl, a moment of deep emotion. This has disappeared almost
entirely from the scene. What are the girl's feelings? This too must be
added, and is perhaps *more important than anything else I have to
suggest*. The way you handle the scene now, the girl is almost a piece
of furniture.

The whole setting is very challenging. No doubt this will be the first
time in literature that anyone has made love in a sardine cauldron.
And for reasons too complicated to explain in a letter, please call it
a *cauldron* throughout, and not a *pot*.

And this is not all. You further compound the ludicrousness of the
scene by confusing two appetites: hunger and sex. It simply will not
do to have the man and the girl eat leftover sardines out of the same
cauldron in which they make love. Why shouldn't there be two caul-
drons? one for each appetite? Or perhaps they could find some leftover
sardines elsewhere in the shack.

Another point: You have had the young man light a fire under the
cauldron a little while before they begin to make love! At that point
the reader doesn't think of the idyllic moment, but worries about
blisters on the girl's bottom. I'm sorry to be so coarse about this, but

these are the reactions you arouse by vague writing. Even the physical positions and movements of the two inside the cauldron are not clear. Furthermore, the fact that the shack is in darkness, and that you don't describe the banked fire very clearly, nor the kind of stove (I believe the Japanese call it a *kamo-do*) being used, all adds to the confusion.

It would be a great mistake to delete this scene, because it adds greatly to the structure of the book. But it must be rewritten entirely, with great care and much more frankness, and very explicitly. I think you will have to provide some dim light from the fire in the shack, and give a much clearer visual description. Furthermore, you will have to prepare the reader carefully for the size of the cauldron. Unless you stress its size, the situation will seem impossible. It would help if the man failed to light a fire under the cauldron, and if it were still kept warm by the ashes underneath. Ashes retain their heat for quite a long time. Then the girl could quite logically climb into the cauldron to keep warm, and the boy eventually, having found sardines elsewhere, could creep in to join her.

I have the feeling that you are rather uneasy about American standards of decency in sexual matters. I think you can be quite frank and detailed about some gestures, provided you maintain the mood of lyricism and purity.

One more detail: What kind of skirt is it that is fastened around the girl's bosom? If your people's skirts do indeed fasten this way, then I think you must lay the groundwork in some detail, explaining just why the boy reached for the girl's bosom to unfasten her skirt. This is part of the general vagueness in physical description.

Another detail: While most American readers will not be prudish about sexual details, some may be quite repelled by the bubbles of saliva on the girl's teeth. There is something particularly disgusting in the description of the saliva as frothy. We associate frothing at the mouth with madness and physical uncleanliness. Perhaps it is chiefly your choice of adjectives, but you do emphasize the saliva beyond all reason. A sentence such as: "With a slight groan of 'Ahoo' her lips parted, and he touched her warmth and saliva" just won't do. There is absolutely nothing wrong about writing such a sentence as "His lips touched the moist warmth of her mouth" or, in certain circumstances, if the man is quite sophisticated, his tongue instead of his lips can touch the moist warmth of her mouth. But when you inject the clinical word *saliva,* you immediately put yourself in a predicament.

I'm afraid a similar problem exists concerning the word *bottom.*

Certainly the cauldron has a bottom, but so has the girl, and no matter how you handle your description of the cauldron, readers will inevitably associate the two bottoms. I am afraid you better do without the word *bottom* entirely, since there are many other words for both kinds of bottoms.

I hope you will excuse me for writing in such detail. Usually language problems are not that complicated, but when it comes to sexual overtones and the free associations that go with them, the problems become unusually subtle and need careful explanation. I have spoken with your agent about this, and we both agree that you simply have to rewrite these few pages before we take formal action on our option. Perhaps the scene should be expanded. Do you need my copy of the manuscript?

> Cordially,

JOHN FARRAR

John Farrar (1896–1974) was one of America's most influential editors. After serving as editor for the George H. Doran Company and later for Doubleday Doran & Company, in 1929 Mr. Farrar and Stanley Rinehart, another Doran editor, formed their own company, Farrar & Rinehart. This partnership ended in 1945 after Mr. Farrar's return from military service. Early in 1946, Mr. Farrar and Roger W. Straus, Jr., launched a new publishing firm, Farrar, Straus & Company, with Mr. Farrar as editor and chairman of the board and Mr. Straus as president. Among the authors Mr. Farrar worked with were Stephen Vincent Benét, Carlo Levi, Wilhelm Reich, C. G. Jung, Robert Graves, and François Mauriac.

•   •   •

This diverse selection from Mr. Farrar's editor-to-author correspondence appeared in the 1962 edition of *Editors on Editing*. In these letters, John Farrar's integrity, idealism, generosity, wry humor, and technical virtuosity as an editor are displayed—to use one of Mr. Farrar's own favorite words (in speaking of pet authors)—"brilliantly."

Both novice and veteran editors will find much to learn from and admire in Mr. Farrar's various approaches to authors and their problems. He can be gentle, cautionary, folksy as a fox, stern, and delighted—it all depends on what the author needs at that moment in his relationship with Mr. Farrar. Whatever his tone, however, Mr. Farrar, one of the last of the editor-publishers of the "old school," maintained the traditions of that great age in American publishing when a firm's list, in the main, represented the personal taste, high standards, and convictions of the editor-publisher and not the characterless compromises of today's many board-and-broker-run houses.

Most of my letters to authors have been lost through the years, buried in the files of other publishing houses or strayed otherwhere. It occurred to me, however, that some of the letters I have written to authors this year might give a picture of how one man, and, to a certain degree, one publishing house, feel about the disarrayed state of current publishing and its effect on the author. It's to be understood that the letters reflect my personal opinions and not necessarily those of my partners and associates, though I might add that we are fortunate in our many agreements.

John Farrar

A question which has interested me for years. I am happy to say that Mr. Richard M. Baker agreed to let us be explicit in our description of his situation.

DEAR DICK:

Your letter of November 15th is one of the finest letters I have ever received, and it made me proud of you—prouder than ever. So far as my own health is concerned, it is all right, except for a bout with laryngitis. You can really rest easy about it; my doctors have always been honest with me, and there is no reason for supposing that they are not, in this case. Naturally, one cannot expect to live forever, but apparently this particular episode has reached a happy conclusion.

For many years I have firmly believed that to keep facts under cover that have a direct bearing on an author's work is unwise from all kinds of points of view. Not to come out right at the start and say that you have multiple sclerosis would mean that, sooner or later, if the book makes the effect I believe it will, or even if it doesn't, many questions will be brought up which will have to be answered.

I suppose there will be some people who will think, as they did with our Dr. Thomas Dooley, that we are, you are, exploiting illness. This cannot be helped. Your own life and ideals are the things that made your book, since it deals so poignantly and in such great detail with experiences and, oddly enough, with experiences that you didn't have. It is bound to excite curiosity, and there is really no possible way to make of you a mystery, since you and your family have so many friends; and, after all, you are not completely isolated from the world. Why people are always trying to pull down the good men of the world,

I don't know. Tom Dooley was dedicated. And how much more important a national symbol he was than, say, Frank Sinatra! I also suspect that he was a saint. Saints were always thorny characters.

I find the same difficulty confronting me with a well-known woman who has written an extraordinary first novel and for some reason doesn't want anyone to know that she has written it. She may indeed put a pseudonym on the book, but it never helps. Sooner or later, particularly in these days of highly personal reporting, it is bound to be discovered. In fact, many years ago, when Lady Jones wrote *Serena Blandish,* anonymously, there was a document, as I remember it, in our safe saying that we were bound not to disclose who had written it. It was not too long, in spite of everything we could do, before it was discovered. Her other writing name is, you'll remember, Enid Bagnold.

The most successful secret of this kind was long, long before and I was not involved in it. Basil King wrote *The Wild Olive* and other great best sellers under a woman's name.

The various Patrick Dennis pseudonyms and games also didn't work for long.

Forgive me if I seem to be writing you an essay on the subject, but I hope you will bear with me, for I took the matter into my own hands, and have put on the back of the jacket the following:

"Richard M. Baker, Jr., was born in Worcester, Massachusetts, in 1924, was graduated from Bowdoin College, and now lives with his wife and five children in South Portland, Maine. He started as a public accountant. However, in 1957 he decided to make writing his career, 'to gamble on writing and leave tax accounting behind.' He is a victim of multiple sclerosis, severely handicapped, and likely to be more so in the future. He does not mind talking of this, partly to encourage other handicapped people, partly because his handicap lay behind the impulse that led him to writing. Mr. Baker has never been to Japan, volunteered for the Army but was only in it briefly. Everything in this strong and compelling book is the result of years of research and of the reconstruction of events and the creation of characters by his powerful imagination."

In this respect, another interesting parallel is that of R. C. Hutchinson, whose first book was about Africa, the next about Germany, and the next about Russia. These were all creations of his imagination, and he had never been to any of these places.

You must, of course, expect the reviewers may spend some time

322   JOHN FARRAR

talking about this, but to repeat myself, I do believe that putting the facts right on the line is the best thing to do.

In the last part of the book (with your permission for cuts), I have toned down the episodes with the Negro girl, and some of the explicit material in the final scenes with Michiyo. It seemed to me and to some other readers here to give the effect of coyness on her part, and almost a feeling of vulgarity. Not that I don't presume that she would have acted in this way, but by this time you are telling a real love story and that is the note, I believe, on which the book should end. I do not think that you will find that it detracts from the power of the story. Of course, I have added nothing.

I would love to have a copy of the photograph, and please do sign it.

All my very best,

Dear Mrs. ————:

Thank you for your kind and appreciative letter. Of course I meant it when I said you could call on me for future suggestions.

You say: "It would help me immensely if you could find time to mention a couple of publishing houses which in your opinion might be interested to see my novel. The agent I tried had not time to handle my work. I do not plan to approach another literary agent, for I have concluded that most agents are concerned only with the Established Name or the Genius. If I had an independent income I would like to found an agency which did not need to concern itself with profit, but could afford to offer guidance and marketing services to writers of promise as yet unpublished. Lacking such an agency I shall send my novel out myself, and would be immensely grateful for any suggestions you might have. I realize that to some extent the book falls into the 'old-fashioned' and 'romantic' categories, and so would find a place on selected publishing lists only. My difficulty: which lists?"

I remember that you told me certain publishers have already seen your novel. Forgive me if I do not dig back into our pleasant, lengthy correspondence to check. Here is a list of eight publishing firms I think might well be interested.

Perhaps it is best in your case to send out the novel yourself.

However, I ought to point out that while agents, too, must make a living, most of them do take an interest in writers of promise. I'm doubtful that a subsidized agency would prove practical or effective from any point of view, any more than would a subsidized publishing house, with the exception of special interest publishing houses such as the university presses. It is true that these days some of the agencies are forced to husband their time because of the high overhead. When they have refused to take you on, I suspect it is honestly because they feel that for one reason or another they could not place your work.

As I pointed out in earlier letters, it is my opinion that what is wrong with your novel in its present form is not that it is "old-fashioned" or "romantic" but that it is, first, too long for its purpose, and that the purpose itself is not clear. You have definite ideas you wish to impose on your readers, and you also wish to write a good story in the Romantic tradition. There is no reason why you should not accomplish this, but somehow you haven't or so I believe. There would undoubtedly be several ways to triumph over this difficulty. Any editor wishing to help or suggest a remedy would, I fear, find you both puzzled and argumentative. This has been true in the past, hasn't it? I can sympathize with your own belief that the book, if published in the form you desire, would find readers. Yet, you have now had a number of professional opinions to the contrary. There is, of course, the possibility that they have been mistaken. Nonetheless, you must face the world of writing and publishing as it is.

From your various letters I do conclude that you are loath to change the novel, or at any rate that your arguments in support of your own point of view incline to be long and complex. This, in itself, can be frightening to an editor or agent.

My hope is that if you do find an editor who is enthusiastic about the possibilities of the novel, you keep an open mind about his suggestions and do not overwhelm him in lengthy rebuttal. Your reply to this will undoubtedly be that it is your book and that you wish it to remain so. I'd be the last person to maintain that books have not been harmed by insensitive and mistaken editing. The dilemma exists and each author must finally decide whether honestly offered criticism can be accepted and made a part of his own thinking and re-writing.

With my best regards,

To a young writer, at work on his first novel.

DEAR ALEX:

Now that I have finished reading the re-written parts of your novel I must tell you how strongly I admire the way in which you have acquired technical skills you did not show in earlier drafts. You and I always knew how well you could write, and how far you can go, but to find that your powerful drive and nervous energy can summon up such disciplined patience is even more exciting than when I first read your work.

One of the things I like first about you, Alex, and about working with you, is that you don't ask for answers but accept hints, run away with them and manage to come up with your own answers.

I have gone over the first chapters carefully again, looking for the big words, the clichés, the repetitions, the usual faults of a re-write done for overall effect rather than detail. This section is, as you know, the most difficult part of the book. (By the way, if you like, it might make sense to call this Part One. There is a real break when Quentin goes back to the South.)

What I like most now in this first part is that you have prepared for all that follows, and yet kept your preparation subtle and almost concealed. You are dealing here with material which is, I suppose, in a sense sensational, and you face it honestly but with good taste and sensitivity. There is a great (here's a word I have cautioned *you* not to use too much) difference between the suggestion and the ability to suggest. Your complicated hero has become understandable now. You do not mean him to be sympathetic, nor can he be, until the last part of the book. Even then, he must remain somewhat of an enigma, a product of the time, but, by Heaven, Alex, you, the author (this seems to be full of exclamation marks, another bad habit I deplore in others. And I don't much care for parentheses either, you'll remember), never pule nor whine! Bless you, for that!

You are giving us fresh material. I don't know of any book like it. You could have written it with ugliness and crudity. Instead, you have chosen to give us the effect without the deliberate coarseness. And there is nothing prissy about your book. When you need a strong word, you use it. Your dialogue is excellent, often brilliant. When you tackle a strong scene, whether it is in the barracks room or the bedroom, it is alive; but always, these scenes, whether they detail the normal or the perverse, are a part of the fabric, belong to the book.

The most important thing left for you to consider now is the texture of your style. In characterization, in the big scenes, in the dialogue, you are yourself and you are damn good. But in connections, in the troublesome "say words," in various other necessary utilitarian paraphernalia of the novel, you stumble. This is easily fixed in consultation. But, of course, you want it also to become part of yourself. That is why I sent you a copy of *Pride and Prejudice* and a copy of Ted Morrison's new book and suggest you read them. You should also read C. P. Snow. There seems to be a singular devil abroad in the schools and colleges these days that suggests a kind of tasteless jargon in the underpinnings of style. This will not ever get you where *you* wish to go and where you shall go!

I look forward to Saturday. We'll tackle Part One to an accompaniment of Beethoven. Happy New Year. May it see the publication of the novel. By the way, everyone, except me, is satisfied with the tentative title. For some reason, it suggests Sloan Wilson to me, and while I respect his abilities, the echo isn't good enough for you.

Ever,

A letter I include for several rather special reasons. For one, the "young writer" is working on his beautiful first novel at the age of seventy-one.

MY DEAR FATHER ———:

It is, I'm afraid, presumptuous of me to write what follows. When you realize how enthusiastic I am about the book, you will perhaps absolve me. There is every chance that I may be wrong about a number of my suggestions. As the book progresses, it becomes the story of a remarkable human being, and that is assuredly one kind of novel. Most of my notes are intended to make the reader, laymen in particular, more aware of Fr. Martin and more concerned over him at an earlier point.

The most remarkable fact to me is that you could, in your first draft, and in your first novel, succeed so well.

I am sorry that I cannot get to the monastery before Christmas, and I realize that since you do not have the manuscript, some of these points may not be clear. Since it is a unique manuscript we must not trust it to the mails, and, besides, as I promised to do, I have made check marks and minor points on the manuscript itself which might be baffling to you. We must have our conversation? Conference? Meditation?

The notes follow. One of my chief difficulties in writing them was one we share; trying not to use the words *fine, beautiful, inspiring,* over and over again.

Hoping that I shall be seeing you before too long,

Faithfully,

Notes on the author's novel

On p. 2, before Fr. Martin visits the communities, it would help if you were to give us a flashback to some childhood episode, some look at his earlier life so that the general reader, the less-informed layman, perhaps, could form a human and simple picture of our hero, so to say.

Also it would be good, perhaps, to visualize the Aunt before she tells him of her vision and to expand this episode by a paragraph or two. It seems to me you throw it away, while with some extension and some use of sounds and possibly colors it would more strongly affect the reader. After all, you and I may have been privileged to see angels and converse with them, but it's not precisely an ordinary occurrence! And "Pillar of Light" is the theme of the book.

The meditation before his "second conversion" could well be expanded. Here, also, some relation of a former episode in his life that had made him "anti-everything" would help.

Chapter II ends somewhat abruptly.

After "This lecture made a great impression on Father Martin's mind," I feel we need to have a meditation or another episode related to outside life. My own preference here would be one of your fine and inspiring meditations.

I have no suggestions for the Requiem chapter. It has dignity, tenderness and depth.

On p. 39 in the lovely Advent and Christmas chapter—and it *is* lovely—at the bottom of p. 39 things would again be strengthened and pulled together if we had a flashback (and I am not at any time suggesting long additions) which would let us see him at another time when he perhaps did not realize that Christmas was "a feast of light as well as joy."

Chapter V. Here again we have a chapter trailing off. I have no specific suggestion. Possibly, again, a personal meditation by Fr. Martin. Possibly a feeling of inadequacy as he thinks of conducting his own first retreat. Possibly wondering if his prayer life is wrong. I'm sure you'll solve this but I'd cut that last sentence. It sounds as though you wrote it because you couldn't quite figure out what else to do.

By p. 66 when the Devil again appears, had Fr. Martin conducted retreats so that he knew how popular he was or does this go back to his former parish work? This should be made clear. If he has had retreats, I believe we should be shown one. Also, to describe which one of the "works" the bishop suggested appealed to him and why?

When he goes home to make his final decision about his vocation, why not a line or two about what sort of friend it was with whom he goes mountain climbing. Did they perhaps pray together?

I have no suggestions on "Profession." It is serene and filled with a sense of devotion. The sermon on "Holy Hope" is strong and, of course, applicable to all Christian living as well as monastic living.

The entire "Jubilee" chapter holds the interest and seems most helpful.

The conference on Plainsong is informative, absorbing and clear. The conference on "Baroque" is, as you know, controversial, but bold and convincing. There are many who will say that the most beautiful of the "modern" churches follow somewhat similar principles and are not like factories. Did you happen to see Kidder Smith's article on church architecture in the new edition of the Encyclopedia Britannica?

The conference on penance is excellent and so is the one describing "Corpus Christi."

Some of the material in the first four pages of "The Guestmaster" is an exact repetition of material used earlier. This is easily remedied by referring to the earlier material, saying that Father Martin used it here, then giving only such points as are new or freshly said. The meditation on "The Way of the Cross" is striking. But again, the end of the chapter is probably too swift; a paragraph or two more about his possible inner struggles would help.

"Holy Week" is graphic, has color and sound. (Forgive a personal note here. It was my good fortune to attend my first retreat at Holy Cross on the Palm Sunday week-end. Your description brings back the wonder and the awe.)

"Problem" is human and revealing. The story of Stephen shows this type of modern rebellion clearly and your appreciation of objective psychiatry most helpful. I could wish you would add a few more words on analysis and psychiatry. So much fun is made of it these days that I hope it will be made clearer and clearer how freeing (at its best) it can be to clear the mind for the reception of the Lord. The sermon on Cowboys and Indians is certainly refreshing!

The "Failure" chapter is poignant. Nothing more needed here!

In "Night" you have succeeded in conveying this terrifying period, so difficult to describe and so difficult to survive. Perhaps you do not need the last sentence.

There is nothing I dare say about "Light." If you are as honest as I believe you are, in spite of your humility, you know that it is truly beautiful.

This young man is gifted and will probably one day write a good book. He did not answer this letter. He had said in his letter to me that a couple of other publishers had seen the novel and, from their letters to him, had obviously not read it. He felt he "deserved" a reaction. Well, I bless him. I hope he lets me see his next book.

Dear ———:

I'm sorry to have been so long writing you about your novel. It arrived at the Club while I was in the hospital. My recovery has been good but the convalescence has been slow, and concentrating on reading was one of the things that was difficult.

I did promise to read your book, I remember, and to write you about it. However, one of the reasons editors don't write authors about their books is not that the editors don't read them but that it is really unfair to write an author what must necessarily be a surface reaction. Unless one is going to work with an author and takes time to study a book, it is impossible to help materially.

The notes on your novel which follow were made *as I read.* You have attempted a most difficult technique in using the first person. You do have talent, and, at times, a vitality in your writing which is impressive. However, many editors would immediately be put off by your inability to spell, your curious use of words which don't exist, and your lapses into ungrammatical writing. Many young people today have these faults, but it is safer to find someone you trust to correct them for you before you approach publishers.

I'm sorry to say that, in my opinion, this novel is unpublishable.

My honest advice is not to try to re-write it but to put it aside and to start on a new one. As you read my notes, you'll discover that I had no idea what you were driving at as I read, and that the denouement was a surprise. Unfortunately I never believed in the girl from first to last.

I'm sending you a copy of Bernard Malamud's *A New Life* which we are publishing on October 4. Malamud, as you may already know, is a writer with original methods and a highly individual style. I am not offering this novel as a model, but you will see that he had some of your problems, and, indeed, some of your ideas.

Sincerely yours,

Notes on the author's novel.

The Prologue a mistake . . . somewhat out of key.

Every now and then you make a curious slip in grammar, such as your use of "graduated" on pages 17 and 19; "like" on page 20. Curious use of "prowess" on page 27. *Like* for *as* on page 55.

There's a somewhat patronizing attitude . . . use of middle-class too often? Chip on the shoulder about the middle west? All right, if it is illuminated by character of narrator, but I don't feel that it is.

You should watch overuse of "a bit." Probably never should use it. Also, a pet horror of mine, although it's being used by many good writers these days: "remain," "enter." Why not "stay" and "go in" and "put" instead of "placed"? After all, you're writing what is supposed to be colloquial style. "Rose" for "got up," p. 62. "Remove" for "took out"; "glanced slowly"? Why not "looked"? you use "glance" too much.

Also, you use curious words, slips for the right word: "obstensively" on page 62. Anyhow, what's an "obstensively pensive mood"? "Plaintiff" for "plaintive" on page 87; and there are many others.

Your editorial parentheses are usually unnecessary, sometimes seem naive, and, in general, your editorializing isn't good. (This might be acceptable if it were not in the first person and we could get some light on this strange young man from other points of view.)

A point about construction: school matters are left out too long. In a couple of the S—— episodes, the book seems lacking in focus. Exactly what are you writing about?

"Demurity," "patulous" (102), "connatation" (109).

Some of your descriptions are good, both of people and of nature. I liked the hunting party. But, frankly, some of them are dreadful! The description of Mrs. ——— at top of page 113 is so overwritten that I'm afraid it becomes comic.

What in blazes do you mean by "sensually-tenor"? Whatever you mean, it's mannered and bad writing!

This whole scene is silly. It might well be a burlesque of a Victorian novel.

You see, by this time, your book is beginning to irritate me. Sorry.

Wouldn't such pretentious people have had at least one servant, even in this day and age?

Mrs. ——— is completely unreal. *Nobody* ever talked like that. As for ———, you haven't made me believe her either. If you're trying to re-do Dante's Beatrice you haven't succeeded.

Amusing touch at bottom of page 128, but most of this story is, believe me, silly, unreal, miles away from what you do best.

Which is—the wild young people. The surprise in chapter XII is good and seems real, and when you get into a scene like this, you do it well. It is as if you knew these people and didn't actually know the others.

Page 139—here is one of your worst parentheses.

Page 142—an example of what I mean by editorializing. "When the soul becomes *accustomed* to a certain vitality," etc.

There is no real preparation for the Lesbianism. It doesn't ring true, and the finish becomes melodrama and, again, is overwritten.

To Dr. Theodor Reik concerning a new book.

DEAR THEODOR:

Here it is, almost twenty-five years since Florence Powdermaker introduced us! Your continuing friendship and loyalty through those years, in spite of (or I like to think because of) the fact that I have been associated with the publishing of your books have meant much to me. I thank you.

Everyone here at the office applauds your outline of the new book, and Roger Straus and I are heartened by the news that you plan to spend more time on it and make it a firm unified work rather than a related series of essays and anecdotes. *The Need to Be Loved* is a fine title. A subtitle would be superfluous. The theme is important, universal in its appeal, and your development of it in the outline shows vigor and the results of your latest psychological thinkings and the extension of your own insights, your work with Dr. Salzberger, and your willingness to stay young. You are always loyal to Maestro Freud, but here, it seems to me, there will be much that is freshly conceived and worth the labor you are expending in doing it.

(I was amused the other day to read that one of the new master race of publishers sent a memo to his office staff forbidding them to use the word "doing" as in "doing a book." Heavens to Betsy, is this not pretentious and pompous? Doesn't a book take a deal of *doing?* Doesn't *writing* take a deal of doing?)

So I'm happy that you're doing this new book. You ask me if I have any suggestions. As always, you will take my reactions to your ideas as amateur. We have often argued over psychiatric and psychoanalytical matters, but never quarreled.

From personal contacts and the confidences of a number of our young friends, it has seemed to me that the shift in parent roles in the last ten years has affected the children, often making them violent, and indeed producing violence in the fathers toward the children. Many young fathers are now sharing in duties which in our youth were considered maternal. The wife plays a more and more dominant role. In the cases we know, the husbands are disturbed, cannot understand what's happening to them, and in some cases, where they can afford it, seeking psychiatric help. There is also the growing importance of the baby-sitter on the domestic front. A psychiatrist friend of mine who specializes in work with children tells me my thinking in this matter is muddy. Probably so, but, nonetheless, if you are not planning to discuss these variations and changes, it might be interesting for you to do so, and you must have much data on the subject. I presume Margaret Mead would find that we are simply changing our tribal customs, or that the change in the apparel of men and women has something to do with it all. Maybe so.

The other point has to do with your discussion of "moral status." Where you first used this in *Listening With the Third Ear,* I thought it brilliant. I believe you were the first to use the term. That men have a limit to their abilities to live according to certain ideals and principles is, of course, true. In many cases, also, it is apparent that requiring themselves to meet standards too high for them could be dangerous to their health and sanity. However, in many cases, I suspect this is a religious problem. In religion, you and I have never thought alike, but respected our differing points of view. Fundamentally this seeking for "moral status" is the sin of pride. In my belief it can be brought to the confessional box as well as the analyst's couch. Moreover, I have known men whom the Lord has helped to reach higher in escaping compromise with sin than, perhaps, their nature allows. You will say that often, certain religious rigors produce the neurotic and the psychotic. I'd point out that Satan also plays his part here. This is complicated, involved and my theology is weak. All I mean to suggest is that you might find it in your heart and conscience to say there are those who believe that unsuspected triumphs of this nature apparently have and can be achieved by the grace of God.

Always with affection,

To an honest and indefatigable literary agent, whom I trust as a friend and admire as an operator.

Dear ———:

I wrote you as follows on September 21.

"We had a very favorable report on ———, but my own point of view is that if everybody else is as sick as I am of this kind of thing, it isn't going to have much of a sale from here on in. I may be wrong. There is undoubtedly a reprint sale here, although I do not think it would be a very large guarantee. Also, it just isn't written well enough. The writing is smooth but completely lacks distinction, and I rather think the ear for dialogue isn't good. Now, here I am, breaking my own rule about giving my opinion in a rejection letter.

Thank you for thinking of us."

Sincerely,

Now you send me back this novel I had previously rejected, along with two others by the same writer. You say that both you and the writer are determined that we should be his publishers. I accept your praise of us and your bow to my own abilities for the care and feeding of authors, as sincere and not as flattery.

However, we must say, "no." Since in this case we are obviously rejecting a writer of exceptional talent, and one who will certainly make a pile of money for some other publisher, I think it behooves me to explain myself. You'll be sending us other manuscripts by other writers and I trust, as in the past, we shall be publishing them.

This man, as you point out, has had much success in his acceptance and publication by a number of the great popular magazines. He is adept, facile, and able to produce a smooth product in a variety of themes and moods. Since I have never met him, it is easier for me to say that I dislike his manuscripts and don't want to work with him. He doesn't belong on our list.

As you well know, I have worked with many authors, and still do, who are considered "popular" rather than "distinguished." In many cases, I disagree with the tags tied to them. In our shop, however, I am perhaps the only editor who addresses himself to this particular problem in publishing, and in order to perform sucessfully I must have a genuine enthusiasm for the work.

You'll be able to find a good home for this writer in one of the huge houses where cubicles are filled with editors eagerly listening to their account-minded business departments and finding satisfaction in the success of the "no-books," the "non-books," or whatever you choose to call them.

I am still actively engaged at the job I like best, which is working with authors and promoting them. But, at this time in my life I have made it a rule to cosset myself by refusing to spend my time on things I plain straight don't like. Our list is a distinguished one. We have managed to keep free of the current phenomenon of big-business publishing; the book stores and our own salesmen expect us to give them books we believe in.

The trouble with this writer is, I believe, that he doesn't feel deeply anything he writes. He is the slickest of the slick. Every great popular writer I have ever known has been emotionally *engaged* in his stories. I do not recognize this here. I may be wrong, but if I am, it is still my privilege to reject this determined suitor.

Forgive me, my dear lady, if this seems to be a rude letter. Perhaps it is. But I'm sure that you, as friend, would not wish me to spend my time on a project that gives me no joy. Let's leave this to the eager youngsters. Someone should be able to set the cash registers jingling with the results of this gentleman's speeding typewriter. But not I, please, not I.

Thank you just the same, for your confidence, your compliments, and your always admired enthusiasm.

My best also to the author in question. He certainly knows his craft, but you may tell him, if you think it wise, that from my point of view he's too crafty.

All best,

To a lady who had read "Letter to an Unpublished Writer" and wrote asking if I would read some of her stories. Part of her letter which came with the manuscript follows, along with my reply.

"Enclosed you will find six of my completed stories which you were kind enough to agree to look at. I decided it would be far better to let you judge half of the work, now, so that you may decide whether or not you are interested in the rest of the collection.

"This will save you the bother of wading through manuscripts you have lost interest in and spare me the ultimate suspense as to whether or not I am going beyond my hopes in thinking that I have something to say to an audience.

"Of course, as you well know, it would be folly for me to say, casually, that a rejection will not bother me. I have worked long, hard hours on these, through a serious illness, childbirth, financial difficulties, through crying children, visiting relatives, friendly neighbors and calls from organizations who want help. All in all, I have taken over a year to write just these six. I have tried to give you different samplings of my style and to be as critical of the final works as any author can attempt to be.

"I have changed, re-written, written again, thrown out, agonized over a comma, an expression, wondered if I could write at all, decided that I was shooting too high above my limitations, cursed even the people I am writing about and have become so involved in their lives that my own seems almost unreal to me. I feel that the stories are finished, but, I am reluctant to let them go, for fear that they will return.

"I have faced the fact that my work may prove unsuitable for your purposes, that my letter may have misled you as to my ability and that you may expect more than I am actually capable of producing. I do know, however, that these are not for magazines: they must have the format of a book to have any impact at all. I have probably made all the errors every eager amateur makes and for this I apologize to you."

DEAR ———:

Let me say at once that I found your stories original and much more than promising. I hope you'll send me the others. Meanwhile I'll hold on to these, if I may. I'm afraid I missed the possibility of seeing you by being caught by troublesome minor ailments. If you are coming down again, please let me know and we'll arrange to have a talk.

Meanwhile, I do have some thoughts about your problem. That your stories would make a book, even with the others, I doubt, quite apart from questions of marketability. While they do show your own personality and style, they differ enough so that I cannot feel them as an effective whole. I am certainly not convinced that some of the magazines would find them unpublishable. I may, indeed, be wrong, but I do think it imperative that you recover from fear of rejection. Forgive me, but that *is* the sin of pride, and you must avoid that particular manifestation of the sin if you are to reach the goal of writing achievement you hope for.

In your case, I hope you'll consent to allow me to ask a good agent's opinion, to ask him whether or not he'd like to undertake to send out some or all of these stories and the others, too, when you send them on.

I wish you could free yourself to write faster, in spite of all the day to day duties to which you and, indeed, most of us are committed. Perhaps confidence is all you need for that. Your humor is excellent, your conception of life's realities and hopes, fine. I have no specific suggestions for re-working the stories. I like them as they are. Occasionally sentiment shifts toward the sentimental, but this honestly does not worry me.

Do let me hear from you soon.

Sincerely,

To one of the best unpublished writers in the U.S., perhaps the best.

DEAR CHRIS:

It was kind of you to send me the statement of how you feel at this time in your writing career. As with everything you write it has sense and sincerity:

The first thing an unpublished author should remember is that no one asked him to write in the first place. With this firmly in mind, he has no right to become discouraged just because other people are being published. He must also remember that only by the grace of the typewriter and the printing press are so many people writing and being published today. If most authors writing today had to write a ms. in long hand, there would be fewer mss. to reject.

Therefore, having been fired by some Muse to dedicate a life in this pursuit . . . much guts will be needed. Guts may also be termed artistic conceit, which is necessary to anyone writing these days. In addition to artistic conceit, if the author be lucky, he will have outside confirmation from people who count and this can be a strong source of encouragement. Often it is the only source of encouragement. He must also be prepared to be buried with his unpublished mss. as a shroud if nothing else happens.

An unpublished author must also know and learn how to evaluate criticism. He must also not be prepared to re-write for every Tom, Dick and Harry. This can often ruin his original ms. Besides, the art of re-writing has to be learned.

Of course, like water finding its own level, if the author be serious and sincere in his intent, he is bound to find an outlet for meeting his public. From time to time there will be crumbs of publication thrown his way, and he must know how to accept them, how to feed upon them and how to treasure them.

All this comes from one who has dedicated more than fifteen years of his life to writing as he must, and from one who is prepared to spend another fifteen years in the same way if it must be. There is no key to publishing and success. Each author carries the question and the answer within himself . . . and of course the key.

You have, of course, had many confirmations of your own belief in yourself: the production of plays in the hinterlands, of television scripts, the enthusiasm of one of the best literary agents.

However, your plays have always escaped (narrowly at times) being produced in New York City, and your novels do not get published.

I once thought that you use such difficult themes because unconsciously you did not want to be published. I've observed this happen in other cases. Many an author dodges finishing his work because he shrinks from the possible disillusionment of publication. I've performed a couple of Caesarians myself. It is not a legend that I locked Hervey in a room at the Yale Club before we could succeed in extracting *Anthony Adverse* from the womb. What a gigantic baby that turned out to be!

You know from ———'s recent letters that had he remained editor in chief of ——— at least one of your novels would have been published. Under different circumstances, I might have sponsored one of them myself, and I think it probable that in its re-written form the one about which I was most enthusiastic will find an imprint either with us or elsewhere.

One thing I have admired greatly over all these years is that you have insisted on writing on your own terms. I'm sure that you are aware that with your imagination and your facility you could have made a good deal of cash by collaboration, by ghost writing, by all the tricks of the trade. You could make the life of Zuzie Swickett or anyone else as interesting as *Little Me*. You haven't done so. If you weren't eating regularly or if you had a family to support I might feel differently. But under the circumstances I applaud you loudly.

As I look forward to the New Year I find myself more and more distressed about the changes in publishing. They are bound to have an effect on authors. Fortunately there are still some publishers who are privately owned and have every intention of remaining so. I thought the Viking Press manifesto of faith after Harold Guinzburg's death was magnificent. What a man he was! And how gravely he deplored the changes in the publishing world. You must know what an inspiration and comfort it is to me that my partners and associates agree, and intend to make every effort to preserve our corporate set-up.

When one reads *Publishers Weekly* with its report on stock-market activities in publishing stocks; when one hears of the shifts of editors and executives from firm to firm; when one sees more and more evidence of the account-minded upsurge in publishing, it is discouraging. People say it is good to have the public know more about the book business. Maybe so. I find dinner parties too often cruel affairs these days when I am exposed to questions about prices and shenanigans and the solidity of this or that house. I don't want to know much about it and I just tell them it's not my kind of shop, that I think it all can't last anyhow.

They talk about new shining merchandise ideas. I can't see that anyone has come up with an actually helpful one in years. They say the type of book published will not be affected by the changes. Nonsense! I've seen publishing house after publishing house succumb to dry rot as the business men got control. Only in rare exceptions can they help transferring to the creative side of the business. Prestige was first affected. Then, inevitably, profits.

There is one comforting thought for authors. In spite of all, the genius will thrive, though he may have a more difficult time of it. Much good honest talent will suffer, both among authors and, indeed, editors. Sooner or later, the business men will wake up and find out that you can't appeal to the imagination in men, without imagination. It is as simple as that.

So, keep on in your own special way.

All best,

SAXE COMMINS

Saxe Commins was an influential, highly regarded editor whose career spanned thirty years in publishing. He began with Covici-Friede in 1929 and worked at Liveright from 1931 to 1933. In 1933 he joined Random House, where he remained until his death in 1958. Among the authors with whom Saxe Commins worked were William Faulkner, Eugene O'Neill, Theodore Dreiser, Stephen Spender, William Carlos Williams, James Michener, W. H. Auden, and Sinclair Lewis.

• • •

The correspondence and publishing papers of Saxe Commins are catalogued and stored in the Princeton University Library. These examples of his editorial correspondence, with S. N. Behrman and about and with Robinson Jeffers, are from *What Is an Editor: Saxe Commins at Work,* by his widow, Dorothy Commins, whose comments are included.

In the letter to S. N. Behrman, note the close reading Commins gives the manuscript, all the while saying that it will be closer still once he and Behrman get together. Commins is enthusiastic, supportive, but determined to get the author to think seriously of Commins's idea to have Behrman write the biography of Max Beerbohm in an anecdotal style. Commins is, even at this early "memo" and "improvisation" stage of editing, giving Behrman a line-by-line critique of his book, one that will be augmented conversationally when they meet, and in future correspondence.

The Robinson Jeffers correspondence is a particularly dramatic instance of the editor's exercising his personal moral responsibility and his responsibility to his publisher in a situation wherein his political views are diametrically opposed to his author's. Commins's comments are fair, impassioned, and yet always sensitive to the necessity of having the author express his deepest views, however unpopular and even reprehensible they may be. His solution to the problem is as valid now as it was then.

. . . Saxe edited Behrman's autobiographical The Worcester Account, which was published in 1954, and following that his biography of Max Beerbohm, Portrait of Max, which was published in 1960. The letters written during the time the Beerbohm manuscript was being prepared add more to the picture of their close working relationship. In January 1954, from Rapallo, Italy, where he was interviewing Beerbohm, Behrman wrote expressing his pleasure at having received a letter from Saxe. He related Beerbohm's delight in Saxe's praise of the old man's wit and his own distress over Beerbohm's enfeebled and lonely life. Four years later, Saxe was writing Sam with his comments on the manuscript.

Now, less than twenty-four hours after the arrival of the typescript, I must tell you that you are getting closer and closer in mood and selective detail to the impressionist portrait of Max both of us have in mind. Your own charm and unmistakable style are strikingly apparent on every one of the tentative forty-six pages, and the material is indeed rich if, until now, only suggested.

I still feel very strongly that it cries for expansion. So far it only hints at its possibilities but I realize that once you put flesh on this skeleton, still a little disarticulated, it will begin to move and breathe and have a life of its own.

It's no favor to you to make so generalized a statement. Unless I can particularize you won't be able to guess what I am driving at. So let me offer, for whatever they are worth, page-by-page questions and suggestions, some sensible, some captious, to be accepted or vetoed, but at least a sort of agenda for our summit talks. To begin:

Page 1. It seems to me that much more can be made of Max's and Herbert's[1] background by elaborating on Julius, Constantia, and Eliza,[2] more or less as you did with the forebears of Duveen.

Also on this page, could there be a little expansion of Max's attitude toward the "theatrical columnists" and why he wouldn't deign to point his silver dagger at them?

Page 2. Would it be possible to convey a little of the prevailing atmosphere in America, particularly in Chicago, when Tree put on

[1]Sir Herbert Beerbohm Tree, Beerbohm's half-brother.
[2]These were, respectively, Beerbohm's father, his father's first wife, and his mother, Julius's second wife.

An Enemy of the People. Here Max's attitude toward his brother's showmanship is clear enough, but what about Herbert and the act he was putting on.

Page 3. Harry Paine's shot at Max suggests the reaction to "In Defense of Cosmetics," but do you give enough of the flavor of the essay itself to make the reader aware of what the shooting was all about?

Page 4. Would it be out of place to write in a sentence or two about *The Yellow Book.* It had quite a history. On this page you do give a little of the flavor of the essay, but I think it would profit by a few more comments almost in Max's own vein.[3]

Page 5. The references to Scott Fitzgerald and Ned Sheldon are dangling in midair. Unless you specify some of the similarities I'm afraid the comparison will be lost. And why not more about Aubrey Beardsley?

Page 6–7. The cracks at Pater are too good to miss. They make me want more. The gem-like flame should be blown on a little harder.

Page 7–9. There is a bite to the brief passage on the Prince of Wales.

Page 10–11. Watch repetition of "mimetic marvel" in first paragraph on tenth and fifth line from bottom on 11. The Le Gallienne episode is fine. Max's abstemious love for Cissi Loftus deserves more comment from you.

Page 13 et seq. We come to the problem of the Turner correspondence. It is essential to the book and we'll have to talk about ways and means of getting permission. Turner's pathetic attempts to write novels and Max's indulgence of them should give you a chance to extemporize in your own inimitable way about the folly of earnest but inept writers.

Can you make more of the courtship of Miss Conover? The reflections of fires come to an anticlimax on page 20.

---

[3]The closing years of the nineteenth century saw a breaking away from the rigidity of Victorian conventionality and an acceptance of a realism and a freedom in writing rarely expressed in English literature of that time. In 1894 there appeared a periodical called *The Yellow Book,* edited by Henry Harland, with Aubrey Beardsley as art editor. The yellow color of its cover was inspired by Whistler's frequent use of that color in his paintings.

While the first issue shocked the sensibilities of most of the English public, there were many who were delighted with its contents, especially with Max Beerbohm's essay "In Defense of Cosmetics."

What about the lifetime aversion for Rudyard Kipling? That's too good to miss.

Page 21. What *was* the solecism committed by Jefferson's hat? Merely that he kept it on his head?

The story of how Herbert almost missed out on acquiring *Trilby* through Max's good sense in considering it rubbish is the sort of anecdotal material that adds immeasurably to the impressionist portrait. What follows on John Lane and J. G. Riswald is suggestive and the disdain Max has for success is revealing, as are all the accounts of the caricatures.

Can we use a little diminuendo of our own on "the Jewish friends of Edward's" (page 33)?

Page 34. I wonder whether the allusion to FDR and Cal Coolidge belongs here. I'll talk to you about that.

Page 35. Whatever you write about Turner is interesting and revealing. But without the letters it would all lose point. We must get those letters in.

What follows on Oscar Wilde and the Leversons is also of great interest. In fact, whenever you are anecdotal the whole portrait becomes more vivid. Note the Constance Collier story at the end.

Perhaps this is what I want to stress most: that you use anecdote as only you can, to portray Max and the people he knew and caricatured and loved and endured.

From all the foregoing do I make myself clear in the matter of the need for expansion and elaboration? You can afford greater length because the material is so richly suggestive and I'm willing to bet that your asides will match Max's any day. Don't hesitate to make them!

As I said in the beginning, this longish letter is only a memo, the agenda that can be amplified when we get together. It is a quick improvisation on a typewriter that is giving me trouble. Many of the letters get stuck and don't fall back into place and nothing could be worse for making what I want to say less halting than what I've said. But you can read in and between the lines, can forgive this goddamned b b bbbb (that letter is the worst offender) and me too!

All love

Alas! Saxe was never to see the finished book; it came off the press after his death.

In the fall of 1947 Saxe had before him a new manuscript by Robinson Jeffers, consisting of a long narrative poem, The Double Axe, and twenty-seven short poems, all written during World War II. The collection was to be Jeffers's fourteenth book of verse. In it Jeffers advocated complete political isolation. He saw American participation in World War I as a grave mistake and our entry into World War II as even more disastrous. He maintained that we had not been forced into World War II but that our national leaders had misled us.

It is obvious from his memo to Bennett Cerf that Saxe found the manuscript upsetting.

13 October 1947

To: Bennett Cerf
From: Saxe Commins

Robinson Jeffers's new manuscript, *The Double Axe,* raises questions of policy that must be considered with the utmost care. That the tone and purport of the poems themselves indicate a bitter malevolence toward man in nature, a kind of dying howl of pessimism into a black sky in the presence of death, is the poet's view and can be argued endlessly for its validity. Agree or disagree with him in his central argument that mankind is not important in the universe and is the only blemish in nature, no one can deny that Jeffers has earned the right to deliver his last dicta on man, no matter how sophomoric some of them may be.

It is on other counts, however, that his pessimism must be examined (1) for the impression it will leave of his tight and narrow thinking as a Cassandra-like prophet, and (2) for our tolerating angry and irresponsible statements about America and more particularly about Roosevelt. The first makes him an out-and-out champion of isolationism, and the second a wildly prejudiced slanderer.

In a rather loosely thought-out preface, Jeffers's second sentence runs: "it had long been evident that our government was promoting war—not with threats, like the Germans, but with suggestion and pressure and personal promises—and would take part in it." This is the opening statement of the theme that torments him through the poems, long and short: America has been committed by its leaders—notably Roosevelt—to an insane power dream.

Hoult Gore, the dead soldier whose ghost returns to haunt and torture his mother, declares on page 26:

He [Roosevelt] had already duped us
Deep into war, he'd fooled us into doing everything
Except declare it and send armies abroad: but if we were blooded,
Then we'd be mad. Germany wouldn't attack
Although we sank her boats and supplied her enemies:
He needled the touchy Japs and they did his business for him.
And don't for God's sake,
Pretend that we had to fight while we still had friends
In Europe: what do we want of Europe?

(Bear in mind that Hoult is Jeffers's mouthpiece)
    Pages 28–29

Be sorry for the decent and loyal people of America
Caught by their own loyalty, fouled, gouged and bled
To feed the vanity of a paralytic and make trick fortunes
For swindlers and collaborators.

Again page 47

Destruction's bride. "Curious," he said, "the power-mad vanity
Of one paralytic politician—"

Roosevelt and Tojo are linked on page 51, and without preference.
Page 57

. . . beseech God
Forgive America, the brutal meddler and senseless destroyer;
    forgive the old seamed and stinking blood-guilt of England.

Page 91

                        . . . Human antics, human antics:
Or Roosevelt's if he really believed the enormous phrases
He buttered his bloody work with, while Churchill grinned

Among the shorter poems, there is "Fantasy" (page 122)

On that great day the boys will hang
Hitler and Roosevelt in one tree,
Painlessly, in effigy,

To take their rank in history;
Roosevelt, Hitler and Guy Fawkes
Hanged above the garden walks,
While the happy children cheer,
Without hate, without fear,
And now men plot a new war.

Page 125 (dated December 1941)

The war that we have carefully for years provoked

For his position on isolationism—Page 126

You knew also that your own country, though ocean-guarded,
   nothing to gain, by its destined fools
Would be lugged in.

Page 129 "Wilson in Hell" (dated 1942)

Wilson accuses Roosevelt of "having too much murder on your
   hands"
Calls him liar and conniver and by his presence [Roosevelt's]
   makes heaven a hell for Wilson.

Page 135 "Historical Choice." Here is the explicit statement for isolationism.

                     . . . we were misguided
By fear and fraud and a great tricky leader's orotund cajoleries
To meddle in the fever-dreams of decaying Europe. We could have
   forced peace, even when France fell; we chose
To take sides and feed war.

Page 136 "Teheran." (Teheran is seen as a plot by "attendants on a
world's agony")

                     . . . there will be Russia
And America; earth-power and air-power; earth is the breeder—
but what was poor hopeful ambitious Germany
Doing in this squeeze!

(Shocking to see Jeffers weep for the Fascists)

Page 137 "What Odd Expedients." (The repetition of phrase is most
damning to Jeffers)

> The crackpot dreams of Jeanne d'Arc and Hitler; the
>   cripple's-vanity of Roosevelt . . .

Page 139 "An Ordinary Newscaster." (Again the obstinate isolation-
ist speaks)

> We are not an ignoble people, but rather generous; but having been
>   tricked
> A step at a time, cajoled, scared, sneaked into war; a decent
>   inexpert people betrayed by men
> Whom it thought it could trust: our whole attitude
> Stinks of that ditch.

Page 142 "So Many Blood Lakes." (Again)

> But we were tricked

Page 143 "The Neutrals."

> I praise thee Ireland . . .
> And high Switzerland . . . and Sweden . . . these three hold all but
>   all
> That's left of the honor of Europe.
>   I would praise also
> Argentina, for being too proud to bay with the pack,
> But her case is a little clouded.

(Peron should be pleased!)

Page 150 "War-Guilt Trials." (Tribute to Ezra Pound and a slap at
us!)

Page 151 "Moments of Glory." (So that Truman should not feel
neglected, he comes in for a slap on the wrist)

Consider little Truman,
That innocent man sailing home from Potsdam—rejoicing, running
  about the ship, telling all and sundry
That the awful power that feeds the life of the stars has been
  tricked down
Into the common stews and shambles.

In all charity, I can only explain this melancholy book as proof of
early senility. What the provocation for all these maledictions in our
time and the insane hatred of Roosevelt, I can't guess. Well, we've
marveled at Jeffers's brooding hatreds before, but they were disguised
in horses and hawks and incestuous relationships. Now he personifies
his bitterness in Roosevelt and in the whole human race.

The human race is bound to defile . . . whatever they can reach or name;
they'd shit on the morning star if they could reach. Page 59

I don't see how we can do anything else but protest to Jeffers about
the Roosevelt and isolationism passages that are manifestly obnox-
ious. If we can't make him see reason, we'll have to take a strong
position on principle. If he does take out the objectionable passages,
we will then have a book obscurantist enough to please the dwindling
Jeffers following. This book has made me *dwindle!*

*Two days later, Saxe was writing to the poet himself, setting down
his misgivings about Jeffers's politics but not mentioning a word about
his poetry. In saying he was writing on his own responsibility, Saxe was
primarily trying to protect Random House from any accusation that it
was frightened of unpopular opinions; yet he was also motivated by a
desire to protect the poet.*

15 October 1947

Mr. Robinson Jeffers
Tor House
Carmel, California

Dear Robin:
    During all these years—and it is now over twenty—I have been
writing to Una, knowing, of course, that you would realize that my

letters were meant equally for you. Always I must have made it plain enough how meaningful and important every word you wrote has been to me. Ever since *Roan Stallion,* and in book after book in which I was so honored to have a hand, mine was a labor of love.

And now, before anyone else has had a chance to see the manuscript of *The Double Axe,* I made a lunge for it, as a matter of earned right. Once again I was made to feel your elemental force and could only wonder at your endless resources in creating images and symbols of overwhelming power. Hoult, as the spokesman of the young dead in war, is indeed a daring and frightening conception, and his brutality grows out of the brutality on which he was nurtured.

But I am disturbed and terribly worried, and that's why I can do no less than be completely candid about my misgivings. I want to put them down here without even mentioning the matter to Bennett, or anyone else, and I do so entirely on my own responsibility, counting on you to understand my motives. I refer, of course, to the frequent, damning references to President Roosevelt. Manifestly he cannot defend himself, and on that score there arises the question of fairness and good taste. But what is worse, in my opinion, is the conviction that these bitter charges will feed the prejudices of the wrong people, especially those, with the worst motives in the world, who have tried so hard and so vindictively to discredit him. It is startling indeed to find that time after time you lash out at his memory, as if the need to do so had become almost obsessive. On page 26 indirectly; on page 29—"to feed the vanity of a paralytic"—on pages 91, 122, 125, 126, 129, 135, 137 (and here for the second time you used the phrase "the cripple's-vanity of Roosevelt"). And so on, page after page, to the end.

Frankly, I cannot make myself understand it. This may be because I do not share your bitterness toward Roosevelt and his historic role; nor do I believe, as you reiterate so frequently, that this country was drawn into the carnage by fools and treacherous men or that a better destiny would await us if we had isolated ourselves from the rest of the world.

As I said, I am writing this letter on my own responsibility, and with the hope, for the sake of your book and the effect it will have, that you can temper these references before we think of beginning composition. Please understand that this is in no way, and I can't make this too emphatic, an attempt to intrude upon your rights as a free artist. It is meant to be the friendliest of suggestions, made with the hope that you can be persuaded to my strongly personal view. I would hate, above everything else, to have you, of all people, linked with the most reactionary elements in America. That would be unthinkable!

Please give this your most serious thought, and write me privately about your own feelings, as you would to an old friend.

Always,
Saxe Commins

4 December 1947

Mr. Robinson Jeffers
Tor House
Carmel, Calif.

Dear Robin:

I keep wondering why there has been no word from you on *The Double Axe.* Our Spring catalogue is being prepared now, but I cannot make an announcement in it until I hear from you. May I have word soon as to when the revised manuscript will be coming my way?

I can tell by the difficulties my wife and daughter have had in getting seats for *Medea* that it is a tremendous hit. On your account I am happy indeed. Who deserves such a success more than you?

Best,
Saxe Commins

12 February 1948

Mr. Robinson Jeffers
Tor House—Route 1, Box 36
Carmel, California

Dear Robin:

At long last I have been able to go over the script of *The Double Axe.* I noticed, of course, all the changes you have made and in almost every instance they are immense improvements. There are two, however, which give rise to misgivings on my part. I refer to page 25, where you changed the line

To feed the vanity of a paralytic and make trick fortunes

to

To feed the power-hunger of a paralyzed man and make trick
fortunes.

This is hardly a change at all. Would you consent to a further revision
to make it read

To feed the power-hungry and make trick fortunes.

I do wish I could persuade you to take out the word "little" describing Truman on page 136. To me it seems that the adjective, referring to size, is as gratuitous an insult as if you described a man by a physical defect, as "boneless hunchback Steinmetz." It would be hitting below the belt in that instance. As it is, your poem, without the adjective, is contemptuous enough.

Otherwise I can make no specific recommendations for changes, although in general I still disagree—and vehemently—with some of your interpretations of recent world and political events and the causes underlying them. But that is a matter of opinion and consequently open to debate. Certainly I can't subscribe to your apologia for Peron, when you say on page 132, "I would praise also Argentina, for being too proud to bay with the pack," nor your defense of isolationism in "Historical Choice" and in "Fourth Act."

I cannot subscribe to the mildness with which you chasten Hitler (cf. page 101) and with the scourging remark with which you flay England and America, and their war leaders. Because these are matters of opinion and you hold yours so firmly, there is a moral obligation to present them in your terms and on your responsibility.

Lest there be any misapprehension about the difference of views between us, it occurred to me to write a publisher's note to appear on the flap of the jacket and also in the front matter of the book as a statement of our position. Here it is as I have written it for that purpose. Tell me candidly how you feel about it. At best it is an honest statement of my viewpoint and at worst it will seem to underline certain passages which otherwise might even go unnoticed. Since both of us are responsible for our convictions and must stand by them, why not have them out in the open?

A Publisher's Note

The Double Axe and Other Poems is the fourteenth book of verse by Robinson Jeffers published under the Random House imprint. During an association of fifteen years, marked by mutual confidence and accord, the issuance of each new volume has added strength to the close relationship of author and publisher. In all fairness to that constantly interdependent relationship and in complete candor, Random House feels compelled to go on record with its disagreement over some of the political views pronounced by the poet in this volume. Acutely aware of the writer's freedom to express his convictions boldly and forthrightly and of the publisher's function to obtain for him the widest possible hearing, whether there is agreement in principle and detail or not, it is of the utmost importance that difference of views should be wide open on both sides. Time alone is the court of last resort in the case of ideas on trial.

Best to Una and you,
Saxe Commins

P.S. By the way, you did not provide a dedication. Did you want one? To whom?

Tor House Carmel, California
Route 1, Box 36

19 February 1948

DEAR SAXE:

(1) If you insist, let the verse read "To feed the power-hunger of a politician"—instead of "paralyzed man." And I hope you will always protest when Caesar's epilepsy is mentioned. Or Dostoevski's—though it influenced his genius, just as Roosevelt's paralysis influenced, and to some extent excuses, his character. This is my reason for speaking of it.

(2) As to "little Truman"—the adjective cannot possibly refer to physical size, since Truman is a bigger man than either Churchill (except the fat) or Hitler. But you will admit that he is "little" in a historical sense (and also "innocent") compared to either of them.

However—to show you what a good fellow I am—write "Harry," if it really matters to you, instead of "little."

(3) As to other things, I'm sorry we don't agree completely. And I do agree that Hitler deserves worse then he gets—but you know the whole world is full of people cursing Hitler.

(4) As to the suggested "Publisher's Note"—it will certainly make every reader think of politics rather than poetry, and is therefore deplorable. But put it in, by all means, if it is a matter of conscience. I shall probably in that case have to add a short paragraph to my own "Note," saying that any political judgments in the book are not primary but part of the background, the moral climate of the time as I see it; and perhaps ending with a sentence from Shaw's preface to *Heartbreak House*—I quote badly, from memory—"Only a man who has lived attentively through a general war, not as a member of the military but as a civilian, *and kept his head,* can understand the bitterness . . ."

(5) No—I didn't think of any dedication.

Thanks for your clear and fair letter. And for your not complaining about the dirty manuscript—I didn't have time or energy to type it over again. It was a joy to see you recently; and I hope to repeat the pleasure if we go to Ireland this spring, as appears likely.

Yours—
Robinson Jeffers

24 February 1948

Dear Robin:

First of all, let me tell you how much I appreciate the friendliness of your letter. It is heartening to know that mere differences of opinion need not affect a relationship tried by the years. If only the same tolerance could exist where other differences of view separate whole peoples. All moralizing aside, I can only say that I was made happy by your letter.

The changes have been incorporated; the Publisher's Note will appear and I await your addition of a short paragraph to your own "Note." If it comes before we get into galleys, you will see it in proof; otherwise it will be added to the galleys themselves. Please prepare it as soon as you can so that your statement will get as prominent a place in the Note as you want it to have.

I look forward to seeing you this spring. Best to you and Una.

Yours,
Saxe Commins

March 2, 1948

Dear Saxe,

Will you please substitute the enclosed page for the "Note" that I think is page 1 of the manuscript?—As you see, it is practically the same thing, except one paragraph added in response to your "Publisher's Note." And since there are now three paragraphs I call it "Preface"!

Best wishes,
Robin

Preface

The first part of *The Double Axe* was written during the war and finished a year before the war ended, and it bears the scars; but the poem is not primarily concerned with that grim folly. Its burden, as of some previous work of mine, is to present a certain philosophical attitude, which might be called Inhumanism, a shifting of emphasis and significance from man to not-man; the rejection of human solipsism and recognition of the transhuman magnificence. It seems it is time that our race began to think as an adult does, rather than like an egocentric baby or insane person. This matter of thought and feeling is neither misanthropic nor pessimistic, though two or three people have said so and may again. It involves no falsehoods, and is a means of maintaining sanity in slippery times; it has objective truth and human value. It offers a reasonable detachment as a rule of conduct, instead of love, hate, and envy. It neutralizes fanaticism and wild hopes; but it provides magnificence for the religious instinct, and satisfies our need to admire greatness and rejoice in beauty.

The shorter poems that tail the book are expressions, in their different ways, of the same attitude. A few of them have been printed previously;

three in *Poetry Magazine,* one in the *University of Kansas Review,* two in the *Saturday Review of Literature;* several in some recent anthologies.

As to the Publisher's Note that introduces this volume, let me say that it is here with my cheerful consent, and represents a quite normal difference of opinion. But I believe that history (though not popular history) will eventually take sides with me in these matters. Surely it is clear even now that the whole world would be better off if America had refrained from intervention in the European war of 1914; I think it will become equally clear that our intervention in the Second World War has been—even terribly—worse in effect. And this intervention was not forced but intentional; we were making war, in fact though not in name, long before Pearl Harbor. But it is futile at present to argue these matters. And they are not particularly important, so far as this book is concerned; they are only the background, or moral climate, of its thought and action.

R.J.

4 March 1948

Dear Robin:

Many thanks for sending me the new Preface. I am really happy that you have stated your position so clearly and precisely. Even though we differ, it is certainly reasonable that our opinions should be stated forthrightly. It will be interesting to watch the reaction of a jury of readers.

Best to you and Una.

Yours,
Saxe Commins

PASCAL COVICI

Born in 1885, Pascal Covici remained a prominent and distinguished editor until his death in 1964. For many years he was an editor at The Viking Press, where he edited many important writers. However, his career is most closely identified with that of John Steinbeck. Covici became Steinbeck's editor in 1935, when he published *Tortilla Flat* under the Covici-Friede imprint. When Pascal Covici went to Viking after the failure of Covici-Friede, he continued as Steinbeck's editor.

· · ·

"Between Author and Editor," by Thomas Fensch, appeared in *Discovery* magazine, published by the University of Texas, Austin, where Professor Fensch teaches at the School of Journalism. The essay offers an intimate and fascinating glimpse of the close editor–author relationship between Covici and Steinbeck—one equaled only by the relationship between Maxwell Perkins and Thomas Wolfe.

Following the essay there is a selection of correspondence and commentary concerning the genesis and writing of *East of Eden,* the great success of Steinbeck's later career, from Mr. Fensch's book *Steinbeck and Covici: The Story of a Friendship.* It makes clear how vital Pascal Covici was to John Steinbeck in personal and professional terms. Perhaps Steinbeck said it best when he wrote: "Pat Covici was much more than my friend. He was my editor. Only a writer can understand how a great editor is a father, mother, teacher, personal devil and personal god. For 30 years Pat was my collaborator and my conscience. He demanded more of me than I had and thereby caused me to be more than I should have been without him."

BETWEEN AUTHOR AND EDITOR

by Thomas C. Fensch

For an author, the act of writing a book-length manuscript and watching it progress through the publishing processes may be, to paraphrase Charles Dickens, the best of times and the worst of times. It is the best of times because a creative intellect brought forth the idea, the germ of individuality, the book. It may be the worst of times because any number of actual or imagined tragedies may befall the project during the editing and design and publishing stages.

Even if the manuscript is accepted for publication by a reputable company, the author may feel that he is at the whim of a merciless editor and a company of pirates and thieves. He may think that the design of the book itself, the printing, publication and distribution and attendant advertising and promotion may cause the book to fail rather than to succeed. He may seriously believe that the editor or publisher is conspiring to hinder rather than help his project.

One of the least studied and least understood aspects of successful publishing is the author-editor bond: an implied contract between every editor and every author. This bond—acceptance by the editor of the author's work and acceptance by the author of the editor's judgment—is an ethereal one at best.

Unpublished correspondence between John Steinbeck and his editor, Pascal Covici, reveals how well the author-editor relationship can develop and how that relationship can lead to "the best of times." More than 800 letters from their correspondence are located in the Humanities Research Center at University of Texas at Austin. The Steinbeck archives, as in the case of many such literary collections within the Humanities Research Center, still have not been plumbed to their full depths.

John Steinbeck's first book, *Cup of Gold,* was published by the firm of Robert M. McBride in 1929. His second book, *The Pastures of Heaven,* was published by Brewer, Warren and Putnam in 1932, and his third book, *To a God Unknown,* was issued the next year by the New York firm of Robert O. Ballou. All three firms went bankrupt during the latter stages of the Depression.

While Steinbeck's first three books were largely languishing on the bookstore shelves of mid-Depression America, Steinbeck was working on his fourth book, *Tortilla Flat.* As he was completing that manuscript, a chance meeting in Chicago between two old friends helped change Steinbeck's career. The meeting was between a bookstore owner, Ben Abramson, and Pascal Covici, who had previously owned a Chicago bookstore and later his own publishing company, Pascal Covici, Inc., Publisher. Covici, with a shock of white hair in his latter years, looked very much like Robert Frost, but had the build of a professional football player.

Abramson urged Covici to read copies of Steinbeck's books, which had been selling for a few cents each on remainder tables. Covici was delighted with what he had read and obtained Steinbeck's *Tortilla Flat* in manuscript. Covici published it in 1935. The relationship between Steinbeck as author and Covici as editor and publisher remained stable and grew stronger through the years, to be broken only by Covici's death in 1964. Covici saved all of Steinbeck's letters and copies of his own replies to Steinbeck, and this collection, covering the years 1935 to 1964, was obtained intact by the University after his death.

To analyze their relationship, one would ask why did their collaboration endure? What qualities did each bring to the other? Why did these two men spark such an enduring friendship?

Covici merged his firm into a partnership with Donald Friede, forming the company Covici-Friede, but it went bankrupt in 1937. Steinbeck, who had his books published by Covici-Friede, was then free to contract with any other major publishing house, but he chose to follow Covici. Covici accepted a position with The Viking Press. Steinbeck's first book published under The Viking Press imprint was *The Long Valley* in 1938. But as Covici joined The Viking Press, Steinbeck already had a partially completed manuscript, which would make them both famous: *The Grapes of Wrath,* published in 1939.

Because Steinbeck lived in California during the 1930s and was a war correspondent in the early 1940s, while Covici lived in Chicago and then in New York, their relationship was largely based on correspondence. Only after World War II—from 1945 until Covici's death in 1964—did they meet occasionally and confer personally. After 1945 their friendship became unusually deep, although the correspondence indicates a mutual trust and understanding before that time.

How are we to interpret their correspondence and, thus, their relationship? All good editors should be good copy editors; they should understand grammar, punctuation, and nuances of printing and publishing problems. But few good editors are simply copy editors. Someone else can get paid for that. Covici was a *manager,* a *manipulator* in the best sense of that word. He could offer guidance and encouragement:

I, too, see what you can give and I am jealous for it. In my little life, which is about three-fourths done, you are my rarest experience. Take that with all its implications, cynically as well if you want to.

Covici knew instinctively how Steinbeck should prepare himself to begin a novel. In the mid-1940s, when Steinbeck was contemplating his short novel *The Pearl,* Covici wrote:

I hope you will take a few days off and relax completely before you start working on Pearl. Quietly soak in some ocean breezes and let your mind dwell in the depths measureless to man, then cover yourself with the hills, and the dreams will come. The Pearl should be pure fantasy and imagination, grounded on reality.

Shortly afterwards, when Steinbeck was working in California (in a rented office above a bank) on *Cannery Row,* and with Covici in New York City, Covici wrote, offering encouragement. He spoke of an intimacy which he wished with his favorite author: separated by the entire continent, they could breakfast together only in Covici's imagination:

I should be there when you start out of your office, meet you casually and go for breakfast. What will you have? Yes, let's have coffee first, lots of it. Orange juice? No. Let's have some Persian melon this morning, ham and eggs, please, for two, rye toast, and please have it well done, almost burned. Do you think they will give it to us burned? Probably not. The coffee is good here, is it not? Very good.

Well, now that we have had breakfast you can start to work.

After *Cannery Row* had been published and the publication-date excitement had abated, Covici reread the book. He then wrote Steinbeck:

I read "Cannery Row" over again. It's a good book, John. You poured a great deal of poetry into it. You give a good many reasons for living and for dying. And I am glad you were born and happy that you are alive. Certainly life is an accident. Man is no more important to the Universe than an ant on the Sahara Desert. But we are important to each other— we are born in each other's image.

Covici always stood ready to aid Steinbeck in more mundane ways. For many years Covici supplied Steinbeck with pencils and yellow legal pads (Steinbeck wrote in longhand when working on a book manuscript). Religiously Covici sent the pencils, dozens and dozens, without ever questioning why Steinbeck couldn't keep himself in the tools of his own trade.

Covici also acted as surrogate father to Steinbeck's sons. As Steinbeck traveled, Covici remembered dates and occasions which Steinbeck forgot. With two boys in summer camp, Steinbeck forgot a birthday for one. Covici responded with presents for all:

For both the boys and their bunk-mates there will be 24 (tin) whistles, 24 balloons and 24 water guns. Enclosed . . . are two under-water masks for the boys and two boxes of cookies. It was impractical to send cakes. I think they will have a wonderful time, so you have nothing to worry about.

It is logical to assume that Covici happily ran errands for Steinbeck because "walking in Steinbeck's shoes" kept Covici close to understanding the day-to-day problems of Steinbeck's life. There is no indication that Covici ever passed these minor errands to a secretary or office worker at The Viking Press. He did everything for Steinbeck himself.

After Covici's death, Arthur Miller, the playwright, said that Covici

stood rather alone, superbly himself, eager to be moved by something true
. . . He was the slave of an appetite for excellence, and, while he could
set forth all the right reasons for his judgments, his real calculus was that
of the heart. He loved best whatever lifted up the human possibility; what
really made him slap the table and roar out his laugh was the outbreak
of light over passionate dark.

In late 1945, Covici wrote Steinbeck, who was in the middle of a
minor bout of personal depression, "Well, you didn't get the Nobel
Prize this year, but I am willing to make a bet that you will in the next
three years. It is inevitable . . ." Covici was wrong about the Nobel
Prize—but only about the year. Steinbeck was to win it seventeen
years later.

Thomas Guinzburg, [then] president of Viking-Penguin, successor
to The Viking Press, has said of Covici:

He was an extraordinary guy—he was some part psychiatrist, some
part lawyer, some part priest . . . Covici didn't work on books, he worked
on people. He fought for his people, inside and outside the publishing
house.

Covici was able to explain Steinbeck's problems, conflicts, and
psyche in ways Steinbeck appreciated. Steinbeck was better able to
write when Covici charted the course of Steinbeck's personality. A
letter to Steinbeck from Covici in late 1948 is indicative of Covici as
"some part psychiatrist, . . . some part priest":

You are best when you do the things you know best. You often stray in
alien places. You can't always help that because of your restless and
creative spirit. When done with one thing you must immediately tangle
up with something else, whether it's writing or other things. I only know
that when you paint your house or weed a garden . . . and you talk of
many things, something passes through you, something deep and human
is communicated to your soul and becomes part of your book and it is
great.

Covici's letter is a litany of personal characteristics.

Only a careful study of the correspondence between John Steinbeck
and Pascal Covici offers an understanding of the depths of their
relationship. Clearly such a relationship is not possible, nor even

likely, for all authors and all editors. Many authors do not need such close personal introspection as Covici gave Steinbeck. Some authors (Ernest Hemingway and Norman Mailer come to mind) might resent it and take their books to other publishing firms. Covici did not need to help others in his coterie as he needed to guide, illuminate, and help Steinbeck. Arthur Miller needed no such close help, nor did Saul Bellow, nor did Malcolm Cowley, the novelist and critic. All published successfully under Covici's aegis.

While Covici's methodology was often mysterious to Steinbeck during their relationship, Steinbeck ultimately recognized Covici's worth. When *East of Eden* was published (and Steinbeck considered it his best work), he dedicated it to Covici. After Covici's death, Steinbeck wrote:

Pat Covici was much more than my friend. He was my editor. Only a writer can understand how a great editor is a father, mother, teacher, personal devil and personal god. For 30 years Pat was my collaborator and my conscience. He demanded more of me than I had and thereby caused me to be more than I should have been without him.

Selected Correspondence Between Pascal Covici and John Steinbeck

Friday, July 13, 1951

Dear Pat:

The mss. which I am putting in the mail at the same time I post this will be one day short. I took Thursday off and went fishing. However, I am going to try to work tomorrow so that next week there should be an extra day. I know it doesn't really matter that I keep to ten pages a week but it is a kind of good feeling that I can do it.

The fishing trip got no fish and I got a painful sunburn, but out of it I got a whole new extension of the book. I guess I never really do stop working. I am not going to tell you that extension now but it will gradually be incorporated in the notes. It is not new, but simply a method for making this book well rounded.

I am sorry about Dorothy's headache. It could be a little like part of the litany—"the various parts of the body, curse thee." It is a new field of criticism—criticism by neck, by wrist, by line.

Yesterday, out on the water, I got a funny thought about you. I am going to tell you and if it doesn't amuse you, at least it will amuse Dorothy to whom I hope you will read it. You have been publishing things for many years and there must be a special feeling a publisher has for a book, a continuation of proprietary, creative, etc. but very especially a publisher's feeling. The failure, or denunciation or attack or praise of a book would arouse an emotion but it would be a publisher's emotion. Now, I think, for the first time, although I may be wrong, I think you will have to experience writer's emotions. I think you are so close to this, to the making of it, that an attack on the book, even a raised eye, will send you into a rage. See if this is not true. You are not used to writer's emotions as I am. I think you will be more deeply hurt by attack and more proud of praise than I will be, because it will be your first experience. See if I am not right. And I am sure you will tell me if I am.

In your last letter, you said you liked to do the errands I ask. Will you do one more very silly one for me? Again it concerns Abercrombie & Fitch. First I would like you to go there and ask whether they have a section or a personnel which takes care of queries by mail. In other words, if I want to ask about something, to whom do I write. Second—in either the boat department or the gun department, probably the latter, they used to have small cannons used for starting yacht races. They were pretty little things and they fired 10 gauge shotgun blanks. I would like you to go and inquire about them—whether they still have them. How much they cost, and how much the blanks cost. Then I would like you to put this information on a separate page in your next letter to me so that I may put it aside and not show it to Elaine. My reason is both absurd and good. On her birthday I would like to fire her a 21 gun salute and I don't want her to know about it. Her birthday is August 14 and she puts great stock in it. I shall have other things to request before then. If A & F do not have these little cannons, will you find out where I can get one. They will know. They used to have them. There it is— now back to work.

July 16, 1951

Dear John,

The five books of Moses, which I now have, with Hebrew on the right side and English translation by Isaac Leeser on the opposite, phrased the Cain passage as follows:*

If thou doest well, shall thou not be accepted? and if thou doest not well, sin lieth at the doer; and unto thee is its desire, but thou canst rule over it.

Last Saturday I was out in Cold Spring† and I found a Bible in an old home which interested me very much. It's a large octavo. Part of the title page reads as follows:

*Steinbeck had asked Covici to research *timshel,* a Hebrew word that the King James version renders as "thou shalt" but Steinbeck felt would be more truly translated as "thou mayest," thus giving man a responsible moral choice, the dignity of free will.

†Cold Spring, New York, the home of Robert Ballou. Ballou, one of Steinbeck's earlier publishers, had joined The Viking Press as a consulting editor.

The Holy Bible, translated from the Latin Vulgate diligently compared with the Hebrew, Greek and other editions in diverse languages. The old testament first published by the English College at Douay, A.D. 1609. This edition was published in Manchester, 1812.

The translation of the Cain passage in this edition runs as follows:

If thou do well, shall thou not receive? but if ill, shall not sin forthwith be present at the door? but the lust thereof shall be under thee, and thou shalt have dominion over it.

The phrase "over it" has the following note at the bottom of the page (which, of course, refers to the whole sentence):

This is a clear proof of free-will. To destroy its force, Protestants translate "over him" as if Cain should still retain his privilege of the first-born, notwithstanding all his wickedness, and should rule over Abel, who would willingly submit, "unto thee his desire," etc. But God had made no mention of Abel. The whole discourse is about doing well or ill, and Cain is encouraged to avoid the stings of conscience, by altering his conduct, as it was in his power, how strongly so ever his passion might solicit him to evil. The Hebrew is understood by Onkelos and the Targum of Jerusalem, in the sense of the Vulgate.

I am looking forward to seeing you soon.

                                                        Love,

                                                          July 18, 1951

Dear John,

What you say about my reaction to praise and criticism of your novel, E. of E., is not funny. It is too true for comfort. Not only do I know the inception of it, the hell you went through before the story took shape in your mind, but I have made myself a part of the book as you put it on paper. The father always believes he feels worse than the pregnant mother when she gives birth. And because of my nearness to it I so much dread the possible criticisms and am constantly searching in my mind, after each chapter I read, for literary generalizations and theories of art in general which could be used against you.

Something I have never done before. I am fully conscious that this is your greatest creative effort and the vaguest feeling of possible disaster fills me with horror.

Some smart aleck, for instance, may probably ask, has it the intense, moral preoccupation that any major work of art must have? thinking undoubtedly of Dante, Shakespeare and Tolstoy. Or somebody might ask of the novel whether it stands in some meaningful relation to recognizable life. A classicist might ask, does the author know that in art half is greater than one and hasn't he over-written and over-emphasized, etc., etc.? So you see, what you said wasn't funny. But your perspicacity is too damn keen.

The change in Adam when he is with Kate in the whore house is good and sound and Samuel's influence is evident and certainly felt. You almost hear Samuel talking through Adam.

The beginning of the third part must have been difficult to write, and yet you tell of the economic change with great simplicity and lucidity. It seems almost too easy.

Love,

P.S. At last Dr. Negrin has rendered me a bill. I am much relieved.

The person to write to and who takes care of all queries by mail at Abercrombie and Fitch is Mr. Edward Shade.

The small cannon for starting yacht races, I mean the one they have on hand, cost $74.65.

The blank cartridges cost $3 for a box of 25.

They can get you a blue steel cannon for $40.25, which may take 10 days to 5 weeks after you order it.

The man to write to about this is Mr. W. Schroeder.

On the 18th, as Covici was writing to Steinbeck, Steinbeck was writing in his daily log, to Covici, again about the collaboration between author and editor. He wrote:

Your notes on other versions of "thou canst" came yesterday and I can see that you, even as I am, are like a hound on the scent. And isn't it interesting that this word has been a matter of such concern for so long. You are having fun, aren't you? This is a time of great joy. It will never be so good again—never. A book finished, published, read—is always an anticlimax to me. The joy comes in the words going down and the rhythms crowding in the chest and pulsing to get out.

During August, Covici and his wife planned to spend some vacation time with the Steinbecks. On the 24th, Steinbeck mentioned the box he was carving for presentation to Covici, the box which would eventually contain the manuscript of the book:

I am going to work on the present I am making for you while you are here. I think you might like to watch the process of trial and error. You don't love tools and working with your hands as much as I do but I think you will like to watch it. So you shall and it will not interfere at all with conversation.

And again, on the 30th, Steinbeck repeated, in his daily journal, how much he wished Covici to understand the joys of woodworking and the hours of work he put in, on the box for the manuscript.

And I'm glad for you to see the carving of the box to hold this manuscript. Now you will know how much goes into it. If I had finished it alone you would not have known the hours and hours that went into it. It's a good thing to see. And maybe you will get some small tools to work with. I think it is good for both hands and brain, and when you finish, you have something and even if it isn't very good it is yours.

Steinbeck also felt compelled to write in his journal of August 2 that Covici might find him irritable and unpleasant during the creation of his novel. Covici undoubtedly knew that.

I feel a little mixed-up. Too many things happening I guess. I get confused. The single-track mind is overloaded. And the only danger is that I might turn mean. I almost always do when my pups of thought are endangered. You will probably regret that you came to the island because I am not very pleasant when I am working and sometimes I am downright nasty. I am not very large in that but I try.

Pascal and Dorothy Covici arrived on July 27 and returned to New York on August 6, but Steinbeck had been right in his prediction; his concentration on the novel did, in fact, ruin a dinner party during the Covici visit. Steinbeck mentioned his rude behavior in a journal entry dated August 6, and in an additional letter to Covici:

Dear Pat and Dorothy—

I want to say that I am sorry for my beastly disposition. I guess I threw a pall over your nice dinner last night and I didn't want to nor intend to. My nerve ends were spurting hot little flames and sounds crashed on me like waves. It had nothing to do with anyone but me. And I have not Elaine's strength to cover and dissemble such a feeling. I was in a nervous collapse. I'm sorry if I made you sad. Last night all night I had it and today it is better. Please believe that it had absolutely nothing to do with anything but my own insides. It is some inner confusion that comes on me sometimes with a frightening intensity. Forgive it please.

It has been good to have you here. I'm glad you have got to know the boys and they surely share our love for you both. I hope, in spite of my ugliness that you had some joy and rest here. It was a joy to have you.

A book is so long. It takes so much. It must be desperately hard to live with and I do not envy Elaine having to do it. And when it boils over, as it did last night, it must have been pure hell. I'm all right today. And I have no explanation.

Thank you both for everything, the lovely presents and Thom's birthday and all.

Love to you both and happy landing.

John

In his journal entry for August 9, Steinbeck again commented on the manuscript box and how he wished that East of Eden would never end:

Everyone who sees it falls in love with your box. And there is still lots of work to do on it. Lots. But if I get it done when the ms. is done, that will be time enough. It gives me lots of time. And I need lots of time.

Now the sun comes out. It is going to be a warm and lovely day.

And I'll have to stay in and work. I can see it is going to be slow today —very slow. And I don't much care. It's funny—I am reluctant to start on the last book because it will mean I must go through to the end and I guess I don't want to finish this book. I don't want it finished. It will be a sad day for me when it is done. I have never loved my work more, in fact never as much. And I don't mean the finished work but the working. But now I guess I really must get to it.

By the 16th of August, Steinbeck had completed the first three parts of East of Eden and was ready to begin Part Four. To sustain his own enthusiasm for the last segment of the novel, Steinbeck began to number the pages, from 1, to add newness to this section in his mind. He also summarized the remaining structure in his journal entry of August 19, to Covici:

All of this is of course a kind of evaluation before going into the final section. I feel able to go into it. And I am now ready to discuss it in notes. It amounts to a whole novel in subject matter. I think it will be in the neighborhood of 80,000 words. Maybe a few less. It has three preceding books to fulfill and resolve. It will continue and carry out the design of the earlier two books. I know most of its incidents. I think it will have power and development. . . . So—now we are about ready to go. We have a new kind of a world in the Salinas Valley and our timeless principles must face a new set of facts and react to them. Are you interested to see what happens? I am.

Two days later, Covici returned all of Part Three of the novel, which had been typed in the Viking offices from Steinbeck's handwritten manuscript. Covici still felt compelled, compounded perhaps by Steinbeck's moody behavior during the Covici visit, to encourage him to continue and successfully complete his project.

August 21, 1951

Dear John,

Here is the end of Book III; 636 typewritten pages or about 172,000 words. No untyped manuscript on hand. I am not complaining, I am just stating a fact because you have written a hell of a lot of words in comparatively so short a time. You have earned a holiday, and what better time to take it than the week of Elaine's birthday. What shooting there must have been. I celebrated the week by reading again the chapters I am mailing you. I found them good and the Dessie chapter best of all. It was a fine feeling I had reading them over again.

I am awaiting the beginning of Book IV. Right now I feel like a man sitting on a mountain top, deliberately majestic, knowing full well that I may be sitting on a volcano.

We enjoyed tremendously Elaine's lovely letter. It was thoughtful, considerate and affectionate. She's a great little girl.

Love to you all,

Steinbeck was able to sustain his own enthusiasm for the book; in his journal entry dated August 23, he wrote to Covici:

The typescript came and I glanced through it. Pretty good in places, quite good but needs lots of delicate cleaning-up work. Well I will do it.

You know after the summer and boys and play and the days being too short, I am glad that my last 30,000 words will be done in New York. There won't be any distractions there. And I'll want full concentration for my ending. But I seem to be able to concentrate pretty well even here.

From the number of pages I guess my estimate was pretty accurate —between 240,000 and 250,000 words.

I do hope you like the return of Lee. I think it is pretty good and short enough. I need Lee, not only as an interpreter but as an active figure. I have a feeling of goodness about the book now but there is so much more to come. I don't for the life of me know how I got in what I have already.

On an impulse I just went back and read the opening notes addressed to you. I wanted to see whether I had failed in any part to carry out my intention and I do not think I have. The direction has not changed a bit and this book which seems to sprawl actually does not at all. It is almost as tight as a short story. And I am pleased about that.

Now—I have a little over three weeks left here. Elaine has more ms. here than she can ever get done before we leave. Therefore, I think you should not send any more ms. here, either original or typescript. Of course, as always, I will send you the week's work as I finish it. And do you realize that after this week, there will be three more 10's—40,000 words nearly, counting this week's work. And about one more month in town will finish it.

On August 28, Steinbeck got a welcome surprise—first copies of The Log from the Sea of Cortez. *He wrote in his journal:*

The *Log* came and it is a very good-looking book. It would not seem to me that it would sell very well but these are curious times. I think it will in Europe. And it is barely possible that it might catch on a little here. When, I wonder, does it come out? It is a curious time for books. People do seem to like thoughtfulness—or do they? Maybe they only want reassurance.

The Log from the Sea of Cortez *was officially published September 17, 1951, with a relatively small first printing for a Steinbeck book: 7,500.*

On August 28, Covici commented for the first time about the last book of East of Eden:

August 28, 1951

Dear John,

You need not worry about the beginning of Book the Last. It is very well thought out together with the scheme of the whole book. The beginning is a refrain of Book I—slow and majestic as it should be. The Lee episode is delightful and heart-warming into tears. The Abra and Aron colloquy is an illuminating, moving and intricate piece of child psychology, perfectly convincing and frightening with its tragic undertones.

It was very lonesome last week without your week's work. What slaves habit makes of us and how I love that kind of slavery.

It will be good to have you back again. I feel fine.

Love,

Early in September, Covici received another portion of Part Four from Steinbeck, read it, had it retyped and sent the typescript back with his comments. That Steinbeck based the character of Kate on his worst-perceived faults of his first and second wives, Carol and Gwyn, is seen in this letter from Covici, in which he wrote, "All the ancient wounds were opened . . ."

September 6, 1951

Dear John,

After I read the conversation between Cal and Lee, upon Cal's return from the whorehouse, I knew what had happened to you the week of your writing this chapter. All the ancient wounds were opened; disappointments and fears, and a kind of pain of what may come gripped your mind and heart. A terrible darkness must have been yours. The writing of it has great tensity and sharply compressed feelings. And again you hint at greater tragedy to come.

It is too much for any human being to do so exacting a piece of work, draining as the work does so much energy out of you, and still have other worries, too. I hate to think what would have happened without Elaine.

It will be good for you to get back. I am counting the days.

Love,

By the middle of September, Steinbeck was beginning to show the strain of constant work on his novel.

September 11, 1951

Dear Pat;

I am so punchy that I forget whether I have written to you or not. I'm saturated with story and with many outside matters. The really deep tiredness is creeping up but I'm pretty sure I have two or three months more of this kind of energy. And it is a very curious kind of energy. I have never used so much of it for so long a period. I have worked more wordage for shorter periods. I have been much longer on this for instance even now than I was on the Grapes of Wrath. I am fascinated with this week's work. As you are becoming aware, I hope—Cal is my baby. He is the Everyman, the battle ground between good and evil, the most human of all, the worry man. In that battle the survivor is both. I have been trying to think how long it is since a book about morality has been written. That is not to say that all books are not about morality but I mean openly.

Now the summer closes. We will get up at four in the morning on Sunday and tool our way homeward. And we have had our triumphs this summer in addition to the work. Thom has taken great jumps. Elaine almost despaired a number of times but at the end of the summer Thom can read and do his arithmetic. He will start ahead of his class, and more important, he knows he can start. The block is gone. Catbird is the one who might have the trouble. He is so gifted in charm and cleverness and beauty that he will not have to go through the fire for a long time, if ever. Poor Thom has it early and will have it long. But he will be fired and there is no fire without heat. We have done well this summer if you were to make a score. I do not feel ashamed. Now if I can only get a good book too, it will be fine.

Your letter came, Pat, and we'll have to take a rain check on that dinner Monday night. The boys won't be with us and we'll be so tired after moving and unpacking that we will probably fall into bed. Besides, I am going to try to get back to work on Tuesday so that I will only lose one day. The book isn't done, remember. I wish the move were over. I kind of dread it.

Anyway—we'll probably talk to you when we get in.

John

The length of the novel-in-progress continued to make Steinbeck weary. In his journal entry for September 12, he noted that:

When I get home I am going to put new blotters on my writing table and sharpen absolutely new pencils and open a new case of paper and I'll be going into the last part of the book. And God knows how long that will take. I just really don't know in spite of my brave words about Oct. first. I just don't know. It stretches on and on. . . .

On October first, Steinbeck was stalled at his work, and needed to talk to Covici by telephone. Covici happened to be out of his office when Steinbeck needed his support and guidance:

I am stuck this morning because I don't know exactly where I am and what was in the work. You aren't in your office. Of course I know you are out for coffee. But I will have trouble starting until I can talk with you. But that's all right.

This may be one of the episodes Covici was referring to when he told Charles Madison, "I had to hold his hand . . . he seemed unable to do anything for himself."

Steinbeck continued on, with increasing weariness, and completed his first draft of East of Eden *November 1, 1951.*

For Christmas 1951, Steinbeck presented Covici with the original manuscript of East of Eden, *in the presentation box.*

December, 1951

Dear Pat—

Do you remember you came upon me carving some kind of little figure out of wood and you said—

"Why don't you make something for me?"

I asked you what you wanted and you said—

"A box."

"What for?"

"To put things in."

"What things?"

"Whatever you have," you said.

Well here's your box. Nearly everything I have is in it and it is not full. All pain and excitement is in it and feeling good or bad and evil thoughts and good thoughts—the pleasure of design and some despair and the indescribable joy of creation.

And on top of these are all the gratitude and love I bear for you. And still the box is not full.

John

This letter appears as the dedication to East of Eden.